American Public Opinion

Its Origins, Content, and Impact

Sixth Edition

Robert S. Erikson
Columbia University

Kent L. Tedin
University of Houston

Longman

New York   San Francisco   Boston
London   Toronto   Sydney   Tokyo   Singapore   Madrid
Mexico City   Munich   Paris   Cape Town   Hong Kong   Montreal

Publisher: Priscilla McGeehon
Senior Acquisitions Editor: Eric Stano
Marketing Manager: Megan Galvin-Fak
Senior Production Manager: Valerie Zaborski
Project Coordination, Text Design, and Electronic Page Makeup: Pre-Press Company, Inc.
Cover Designer/Manager: Wendy Ann Fredericks
Cover Illustration: © Jane Sterrett
Senior Manufacturing Manager: Dennis J. Para
Printer and Binder: Courier-Stoughton
Cover Printer: Coral Graphics Services, Inc.

Library of Congress Cataloging-in-Publication Data

Erikson, Robert S.
   American public opinion : its origins, content, and impact /
Robert S. Erikson, Kent L. Tedin.—6th ed.
     p. cm.
   Previously published: Boston: Allyn and Bacon, c1995.
   Includes bibliographical references and index.
   ISBN 0-205-29696-3
   1. Public opinion—United States. I. Tedin, Kent L. II. Title

HN90.P8 E74 2000
303.3'8'0973—dc21   00-063351

Please visit our website at http://www.ablongman.com

ISBN 0-205-29696-3

2 3 4 5 6 7 8 9 10—CRS—03 02 01

Contents

List of Figures and Tables

Figures

Tables

Preface

In this sixth edition of *American Public Opinion,* we present an accounting of the role of public opinion in the democratic politics of the United States. As in previous editions, we base our analysis on the most recent data available. Our discussion draws on public opinion data from 2000 and earlier, and our analysis of public opinion and elections draws on data from the 1996 and 1998 American National Election Studies.

The book provides an in-depth analysis of public opinion beginning with its origins in political socialization, the impact of the media, its relevance for democratic values, political trust and social capital, and the role of public opinion for elections, political parties and interest groups. The book provides the most recent data and analysis of opinion on such contemporary issues as abortion, gun control, race relations, and health care. *American Public Opinion* is unique in that it goes beyond a simple presentation of data, and includes a critical analysis of the role of public opinion in American democracy. As in previous editions, the sixth edition examines the relationship between public opinion and policy. The analysis is updated throughout to incorporate the most recent literature.

In the sixth edition, there is an expanded analysis of the history of public opinion, and an expanded chapter on the science of public opinion polling, including sampling, question wording, and response rate. New to the sixth edition is a comprehensive list of public opinion websites broken into three categories: websites for contemporary opinion data, websites to locate data archives, and websites for professional organizations in the field of public opinion.

Like previous editions, the sixth includes many examples from the National Election studies that pertain to presidential elections. For the sixth edition, these examples are updated from the 1992 presidential election to the 1996 presidential election.

As this book has evolved through six editions over 25 years, so too has the list of authors. The first edition (1973) was authored by Robert S. Erikson and Norman Luttbeg. With the second edition, Kent L. Tedin joined the team as the third author. That triumvirate held through three editions. When time came to produce the fifth edition, Luttbeg decided to pursue new scholarly challenges. The last two editions of *American Public Opinion* again had two authors, but Luttbeg's intellectual contribution to the book remains, most notably in the five linkage models of public opinion which he originated.

Because the data and literature are always changing, the chapters are often extensively rewritten and rearranged. In the fifth edition, we made major changes in the structure of the book and the organization of the chapters. In the sixth edition, the structure remains intact from the previous edition, with updates to the literature and data. The most important change since the publication of the fifth edition has been the Internet revolution and the availability of public opinion data online. In Chapter 1 we present a list of the useful web sites for finding information on and about public opinion. This information will be kept up-to-date at the APO web site at crystal.polsci.uh.edu\uhdps.

The preparation of this volume relies heavily on the survey data of the National Election Studies, conducted by the University of Michigan, supported by grants from the National Science Foundation, and made by the Inter-University Consortium for Political and Social Research. We also relied extensively on the General Social Survey (also funded by the National Science Foundation) and the data available online from the Roper Center Data Archive at the University of Connecticut. These organizations bear no responsibility for the analysis of interpretations presented here. We are greatly indebted to them for making their data available to us, and to other scholars upon whose research we depend. We also owe thanks to the following individuals whose review feedback guided this revision: John W. Books of the University of North Texas, Robert E. Botsch of the University of South Carolina, Aiken, and Terri Susan Fine of the University of Central Florida. Finally, we benefited from the assistance provided by colleagues, students and staff at Columbia University and the University of Houston, as well as by our editor, Eric Stano.

Robert S. Erikson
Kent L. Tedin

Credits for Figures and Tables

Table 4.1: From National Election Studies, 1996.

Figure 4.1: From National Election Studies, 1970–1996.

Figure 4.2: From National Opinion Research Center, Gallup, and General Social Survey.

Figure 4.3: From the US. Role in the World Poll, 1996: University of Maryland, Gallup, National Opinion Research Center, and General Social Survey.

Figure 4.4: From Roper and General Social Survey.

Figure 4.5: From Gallup and General Social Survey.

Table 4.2: From National Election Studies, 1996; General Social Survey, 1998; and CBS/*New York Times*, 1997.

Figure 4.6: From Niemi, Mueller, and Smith (1989), General Social Survey (1989–1998), Harold W. Stanley and Richard G. Niemi, *Vital Statistics of American Politics*. 7th ed. (Washington, D.C., 2000).

Table 4.3: From pooled surveys by CBS News/*New York Times*.

Figure 4.7: From James Stimson.

Figure 4.9: From Gallup Poll.

Table 5.1: From Roberta S. Sigel and Marilyn B. Hoskin, *The Political Involvement of Adolescents* (New Brunswick, NJ: Rutgers University Press, 1981), p. 73.

Table 5.2: From M. Kent Jennings and Richard G. Niemi, *The Political Character of Adolescence* (Princeton, NJ: Princeton University Press, 1974), p. 78. Reprinted by permission of Princeton University Press.

Table 5.3: From M. Kent Jennings and Richard G. Niemi, *The Political Character of Adolescence* (Princeton, NJ: Princeton University Press, 1974), p. 41. Reprinted by permission of Princeton University Press.

Table 5.4: From *The Gallup Opinion Index*, Sept. 1975, 19.

Table 5.5: For 1984 students and faculty, from Boyer and Whitelaw (1989); for 1999 faculty, from Denise E. Magner, "Faculty Attitudes and Characteristics: Results of a 1998–1999 Survey," *Chronicle of Higher Education*, September 3, 1999), A20–A21. (1999); the 1999 college seniors data are courtesy of Dr. Jerry Jacobs, Department of Sociology, University of Pennsylvania.

Figure 5.1: From the Institute for Higher Education, University of California, Los Angeles.

Table 5.6: From Gallup Poll reported in Robert Chandler, *Public Opinion* (New York: Bowker, 1972), pp. 6–13; 1996–1998 pooled General Social Survey (18–22-year-olds, whites only).

Figure 5.2: From *The Public Perspective* (December/January 1999): 65.

Table 6.1: From John L. Sullivan, James Pierson, and George E. Marcis, *Political Tolerance and American Democracy* (Chicago: University of Chicago Press, 1982), p. 203.

Table 6.2: From John L. Sullivan et al., *Political Tolerance and American Democracy* (Chicago: University of Chicago Press, 1982); General Social Survey (GSS), 1985; Robert Chandler, *Public Opinion* (New York: Bowker, 1972); Herbert McClosky, "Consensus and Ideology in American Politics," *American Political Science Review*, 58 (June 1964); CLS: Herbert McClosky and Alida Brill, *Dimensions of Tolerance* (New York: Russell Sage Foundation, 1983); Louis Harris and Alan F. Westin, *The Dimensions of Privacy* (Stevens Point, WI: Sentry Insurance, 1979); James L. Gibson, *Freedom and Tolerance in the United States* (NORC: unpublished codebook, 1987); *Washington Post* 1997; Pew Research Center 1997; the Freedom Forum 1997.

Table 6.3: 1954 data are from Samuel Stouffer, *Communism, Conformity, and Civil Liberties* (New York: Wiley, 1954); 1972 and 1998 data are from the General Social Survey; GSS, 1976.

Table 6.4: From James Gibson, *Freedom and Tolerance in the United States* (NORC: unpublished codebook, 1987).

Figure 6.1: From National Election Studies (1958–1996); Gallup (1999).

Table 7.1: From General Social Survey, 1998; National Election Studies, 1992.

Figure 7.1: From National Election Studies, 1996.

Table 7.2: From National Election Studies, 1976 and 1992.

Table 7.3: From National Election Studies, 1996 election data.

Table 7.4: From Survey Research Associates, 1996 and 1997; CBS News, 1996; General Social Survey, 1993.

Table 7.5: From National Election Studies; Gallup, 2 Feb. 1999.

Figure 7.2: From National Election Studies.

Figure 7.3: From Gallup Polls reported in Stanley and Niemi (2000, 105); National Election Studies, 1988, 1992, 1996.

Table 7.6: From National Election Studies, 1998, 1996, 1992; Gallup, 1998.

Figure 7.4: From Gallup Poll, 1952-1976; National Election Studies, 1980–1992, Voter News Service, 1996.

Table 7.7: From General Social Survey, 1996; National Election Studies, 1992, 1996, 1998; General Social Survey, 1998.

Table 7.8: From General Social Survey, 1989–1993; National Election Studies, 1992.

Figure 7.5: From National Election Studies.

Table 7.9: National Election Studies, 1992, 1996.

Table 7.10: 1956 data adapted from Howard Shumann, Charlotte Steeh, and Lawrence Bobo, *Racial Attitudes in America* (Cambridge, MA: Harvard University Press, 1985), p. 78; the 1985 data are from the General Social Survey.

Figure 7.6: From National Election Studies.

Table 7.11: From Gallup Polls, 6–7 Apr. 1999, 30–31 Jan. 1998, 16–18 Jan. 1998, 19–21 Feb. 1999, 5–7 June 1998; Roper Center Poll, 22–26 Aug. 1994; Princeton Research Associates, 31 July 1997–17 Aug. 1997; General Social Survey, 1998; National Election Studies, 1996, 1998.

Table 8.1: From William Schneider and I.A. Lewis, "Views on the News," *Public Opinion 8* (Aug./Sept. 1985): 7. Reprinted with permission of the American Enterprise Institute,

Table 8.2: From Norman R. Luttbeg, "News Consensus: Do U.S. Newspapers Mirror Society's Happening?" *Journalism Quarterly 60* (Autumn 1983): 486.

Table 8.3: From John P. Robinson and Mark R. Levy, *The Main Source: Learning from Television News*, (Beverly Hills, CA.: Sage, 1986), p. 91. Copyright © 1986 by Sage Publications, Inc. Reprinted by permission of Sage Publications, Inc.

Table 8.4: From National Election Studies, 1996 election data.

Table 8.5: From National Election Studies, 1996 election data.

Table 8.6: From National Election Studies, 1996 election data.

Figure 9.2: From National Election Studies election data.

Table 9.1: From National Election Studies, 1996 election data.

Table 9.2: From National Election Studies, 1996 election data.

Table 9.3: From National Election Studies, 1996 election data.

Table 9.4: From National Election Studies, 1996 election data.

Table 9.5: From National Election Studies, 1996.

Table 9.6: From National Election Studies, 1996 election data.

Figure 9.4: From Gallup polls reported in Harold W. Stanley, and Richard G. Niemi, *Vital Statistics of American Politics, 1999–2000* (Washington, DC: Congressional Quarterly Press, 2000), pp. 145–46.

CHAPTER 1

Public Opinion in Democratic Societies

Few Americans in the twenty-first century can remember a time when public opinion polls—like television, shopping malls, and eight-lane freeways—were not part of the popular landscape. Polls tell us which television shows are the most popular, how frequently people attend church, what person Americans most admire, plus a myriad of opinions on political topics currently in the news. We shall see, however, that the study of public opinion is much broader than simply gauging popular reaction to recent events. It is, for example, also concerned with how people learn about government, their trust in existing political institutions, their support for the political "rules of the game," the interrelationships among their opinions, or their beliefs about the effectiveness of political participation. The list could go on. But more than anything else, the study of public opinion is justified by the simple notion that democratic institutions should result in government decisions that reflect the views of everyday people. It is this presumption, and its implications, that guides the systematic analysis of mass opinion.

1-1 PUBLIC OPINION AND GOVERNMENT

Rousseau, in 1744, was among the first to use the term "public opinion" (*l'opinion publique*), meaning the customs and manners of all members of society (as opposed to some elite). By 1780 French writers were using the term interchangeably with "common will," "public spirit," and "public conscience" to refer to the political aspects of mass opinion (Price 1992, 8). "Public opinion" soon came into common usage among those writing about government.

However, long before scientific methods were developed to measure attitudes or the term "public opinion" gained currency, political theorists speculated about the "group mind" or "the general will" and how it might influence the political order. Writers beginning with Plato and Aristotle, through Locke and Hobbes as well as Rousseau, did not see "public opinion" as an aggregation of individual opinions, as is common today. Rather they saw the whole as greater than the sum of its parts, much in the way a mob with a united purpose behaves in a fashion that would be foreign to any individual member. To these predemocratic theorists, public opinion was a mass entity, which if brought to bear on public affairs had potential for enormous influence. It was like a force in nature, constrained perhaps by certain regularities, but a unified whole that changed continually, like the currents in the ocean (Palmer 1936; Spitz 1984).

It was not until the rise of popular sovereignty that thinking about public opinion began to consider individual or group characteristics. By the eighteenth century, no Western political regime could afford simply to ignore the views of the masses. This change was brought about by the construction of electoral institutions and parliamentary bodies for regular consultation with the public, and the gradual extension of the franchise to the lower classes. Henceforth, governments would find it necessary to take account of public opinion and its distribution throughout the polity. This "accounting" was not simply a question of government responsiveness to mass policy desires. Government also had to take account of popular support for the ongoing political order. A strong argument can be made that only when the political status quo was threatened did political elites, in an act of self-preservation, grudgingly extend the franchise to portions of the mass public (Ginsberg 1982). But in granting the franchise, there soon developed an ethical imperative that governments are morally obligated to heed public opinion in formulating policies.

In the early years of the American republic, to speak of "public opinion" was mostly to speak about a thin layer of the educated, affluent public in a position to communicate their views to government. While the Founding Fathers agreed on the principle of popular government, they greatly distrusted the wisdom and good judgment of the masses on matters political. To Alexander Hamilton:

> The voice of the people has been said to be the voice of God; and however generally this maxim has been quoted and believed, it is not true in fact. The people are turbulent and changing; they seldom judge or determine right (Farrand 1961, 299–300).

While not all took such an uncharitable position, it was generally thought that public opinion was easily swayed and subject to fits of passion. Thus institutions were developed, such as the electoral college and the indirect election of senators, to distance political leaders from the opinions of everyday citizens.

Nevertheless, by the mid-nineteenth century, many who followed the American political scene voiced concern about an excess of influence on political decision-making by public opinion. One reason was the integration of the working class into the electorate via the universal franchise. By the 1850s it became impossible to argue that the public's opinion could be ignored. Writing in 1848, Alexis de Tocqueville, perhaps the most astute observer of nineteenth-century America, thought "there was no country in which . . . there is less independence of mind and true freedom of discussion than in America" (Tocqueville 1966, 254). He felt the numerical majority intimidated the minority, so that only a narrow range of opinion could be expressed. In the end he feared that the views of the majority could result in either social or governmental tyranny (Spitz 1984, 70). History was, of course, to prove him wrong. But those writing later agreed with his assessment of the importance of public opinion. In 1888, the perceptive British journalist and author James Bryce would claim that "in no country is public opinion so powerful as in the United States" (Bryce 1900). He also noted, "the obvious weakness of government by opinion is the difficulty of ascertaining it."

Of those writing before the development of the modern opinion poll, perhaps the most influential critic of public opinion was Walter Lippmann. Like many of the Founding Fathers, he believed mass opinion was subject to passions that could be induced by elite propaganda. He was convinced that the manipulation of public opinion by those opposed to the League of Nations was responsible for the tragedy of America's failure to join. He perceptively observed that the images of politics received by the public are not direct pictures of events, immediate experiences of action, or provable economic and social theories. Rather, they are "pictures in people's heads" generated by political interests to benefit their cause. In a prescient analysis of major findings by modern survey research, Lippmann challenged traditional democratic theory and its notion of an informed and rational public basing opinions on a considered judgment of the facts. He argued that the average person had little time for affairs of state, and would rather read the comics than consider the pros and cons of weighty political issues. It should not be expected, therefore, that the mass public would be competent in matters of state. Lippmann's prescription for democracy was for the public to choose leaders, but for public policy to be developed and implemented by scientifically oriented experts (Lippmann 1922, 1925).

The debate over the role of public opinion in democracy was given a new focus by the appearance of scientific polling in 1936. Among the most outspoken proponents of polls as a guide to government decision-making was George Gallup, a pioneer of the new technology (Gallup and Rae 1940). Gallup was a "prairie populist" with a Ph.D. in psychology who believed in the collective wisdom of everyday citizens. He distrusted intellectuals and experts, and thought elite rule and democratic government were incompatible. The challenge for democracy, as he saw it, was "shall the common people be free to express their basic needs and purposes, or shall they be dominated by a small ruling clique?" In other words, how does one make those holding high public office responsive to the needs and wishes of the public?

Poll results, Gallup argued, could be considered a "mandate from the people," a concrete expression of the policies the public desires the government to enact. No longer would elected officials have to rely on the ambiguities of elections, self-serving claims by interest groups, or other non-representative channels of public sentiment. Rather, they could turn to the latest opinion poll. In the past, claims that elected officials should heed popular preferences directly when formulating policy could always be countered with arguments like those of sixteenth-century political theorist Michel de Montaigne (1967) who wrote that "public opinion is a powerful, bold, and unmeasurable party."

Gallup saw the modern opinion poll as the high-tech equivalent of the New England town meeting—an opportunity for all citizens (or at least a representative sample) to voice their opinions. The scientific poll gave crispness, clarity, and reliability to mass opinion. Gallup and his supporters argued that through polls the will of the people could accurately be determined. No longer could failure to take seriously popular preferences when enacting public policy be justified by claims that public opinion is unknowable. With the aid of the modern opinion poll, it was the moral responsibility of elected officials to convert the public will into public policy.

Not all were enthusiastic about the new technology and George Gallup's prescriptions for it. Sociologist Herbert Blumer and political scientist Lindsay Rogers soon launched frontal assaults on the opinion poll and its implications. Blumer (1948) asserted the "one person, one vote" definition of pubic opinion inherent in polls was precisely what public opinion *was* not. Public opinion could not be reduced to a nose count among citizens. Rather, it was the interactions and communications among functional groups that percolated through society and came to the attention of government. These interactions and communications were not aggregations of individual opinions, but "an organic whole of interacting, interrelated parts." To Blumer, not all opinions counted equally. They merited the label "public opinion" only to the extent opinions surfaced in a public forum and were taken seriously by those in government with power and influence.[1] This view, of course, clashed directly with the populist inclinations of Gallup and other early pollsters.[2]

Lindsay Rogers, on the other hand, was convinced that the public was not intellectually or emotionally fit to play the role Gallup's opinion-poll democracy required of it. But, in any case, polls were not technically able to ascertain the public's message. Rogers (1949) reformulated the position of the English philosopher Edmund Burke that it is the duty of elected representatives to follow their conscience and best judgment, and not be slaves to moments of popular passion.[3] Only in this fashion, argued Rogers, could the true public interest be served. Rogers was also one of the first to raise serious methodological questions about polls—that is, to challenge pollsters on their own turf. He addressed questions of measurement, opinion aggregation, intensity, and framing effects that occupy a great deal of attention among contemporary students of public opinion. In essence, he claimed that polls of public opinion did not really measure "public opinion." Rogers argued that "Dr. Gallup does not make the public more articulate. He only estimates how in replying to certain questions it would say 'yes,' 'no,' or 'don't know.' Instead of feeling the pulse of democracy, Dr. Gallup listens to its baby talk." (Rogers 1949, 17).

A somewhat related argument holds that public opinion changes in a capricious fashion—that over short periods of time policy preferences shift rapidly, frequently, and arbitrarily. This belief was used by the author of the Federalist Paper No. 63 for an indirectly elected senate, which would serve as "an anchor against popular fluctuations" and protect the people against their own "temporary errors and delusions." In 1950, this same sentiment was reflected by political scientist Gabriel Almond (1950, 53), when he noted that on matters of foreign policy the public reacts with "formless and plastic moods which undergo frequent alteration in response to changes in events."[4] This view of public opinion was used to buttress arguments about limiting the role of mass opinion in policy decisions, and is still a touchstone of the "realist" school of foreign policy (Russett and Graham 1989).[5]

On the other hand, the liberal democracy school of thought (Dahl 1989) holds that an essential element of democracy is the creation of institutions and practices that allow for meaningful public input into the governing process. Democratic government works best when elected office-holders and appointed officials respond to the popular will. Citizens are more likely to comply with government decisions when they are backed by the moral force of popular approval. In addition, advocates of liberal democracy argue that decisions based on popular will are most likely to be the correct decisions. This idea traces its heritage to Aristotle's view that the pooled judgments of the many are likely to contain more wisdom than the judgments of the few.[6] The liberal democratic model does not hold that public policy must be driven only by the engine of public opinion. Rather, public opinion must count for something of consequence in government decision-making.

The arguments we have just outlined are still occasionally elaborated upon today. However, most current research on public opinion does not address normative issues about the proper role of opinion in the governmental process. Rather, empirical questions dominate the field—that is, questions about "what really is" as opposed to "what ought to be." But empirical questions often have important normative implications. Clearly of consequence is, "How much does the public know about public affairs, and how is that knowledge organized?" Or, "How is public opinion articulated?" "Whose voices are heard?" Are some segments of society (presumably the more affluent) better able to communicate their opinions to political decision-makers than those with fewer economic resources? The answers to these questions are important for theories of how the just polity should be structured.

1-2 PUBLIC OPINION DEFINED

Public opinion is notoriously difficult to define.[7] There are scores if not hundreds of variations on a definition (see Childs 1965 for a sampling). A standard definition of "public" is a group that has something in common. Some argue that there is no such thing as a single public; rather, there are many publics (MacDougall 1966). Thus one can refer to the tennis-playing public, the snowmobiling public, or the television-watching public. Others, however, take a broader view. For political scientists, what members of the "public" in public opinion have in common with each other is a connection to government. At a minimum, all citizens 18 and older have the right to vote. That binds them together with a common interest, even if they choose not to exercise the right.[8] And, of course, everyone is impacted in some way by government. That creates a common interest as well. Students of government also regularly speak of several specialized publics. They talk of the "attentive public," those persons who generally pay close attention to politics; or "issue publics," those persons who focus on specific issues while paying less attention to others. It is perhaps helpful to think of these as "sub-publics" of the overall public (i.e., the adult population).

We may first describe an opinion as a verbal expression of an attitude.[9] There are, of course, other ways in which attitudes can be expressed, such as marches, demonstrations, or riots. But we reserve the term "opinion" as the manifestation of attitudes in words or writing.[10] Attitudes are "latent"; they cannot be directly observed. Social psychologists typically define an attitude as an enduring predisposition to respond. Normally, attitudes do not change on a weekly or monthly basis. Although change is clearly possible, attitudes are mostly stable over extended periods of time. Opinions are imperfect indicators of the underlying, unobserved attitude. Because opinions are imperfect measures, we sometimes find they are inconsistent or display contradictions. We shall deal with this problem at length in Chapter 3.

Second, opinions are disagreements about matters of preference, which cannot be resolved using the rules of science. Thus, when it comes to music, I may prefer opera. You may prefer hard rock. But there is no systematic way of demonstrating the virtue or goodness of one over the other. The same is true for opinions about welfare policy, foreign aid, or gays in the military. Disagreements about questions of fact are not opinions, but beliefs.[11] There was once disagreement as to whether the earth circled the sun. Some believed the reverse, that the sun revolved around the earth. That disagreement has been resolved by scientific methods. There is still disagreement over whether massive doses of vitamin C will prevent colds and other illness. Some believe this notion is nothing more than a hoax; others take large doses of the vitamin on a daily basis. But one's position on this issue is a belief, not an opinion, because in principle the question may someday be resolved with finality. Disagreements over classical versus rock music will not be resolved.

No one has yet advanced a definition of public opinion that satisfies a substantial number of students in the field. We prefer to keep our definition short and simple. We define public opinion as *the preferences of the adult population on matters of relevance to government.* The first implication is that not all opinions are "public opinion." Thus one's preference for computer operating systems—Windows, Linux, UNIX—is excluded from our definition because it has nothing to do with government. The second caveat is that while in the broadest sense we are talking about all adults, that does not exclude the possibility of referencing subgroups, such as the attentive public. A third point is that by the term "preferences" we mean more than simply the *affective* component of an opinion. "Affect" refers to feelings—like or dislike, approve or disapprove. But, we must also be concerned with the cognitive component of an opinion. "Cognition" refers to the process of knowing, to the intellectual sophistication one brings to the ordering of political opinions. Obviously, the amount of political information one has affects the ability to link one political concept with another, and is important for our understanding of public opinion. Finally, while we have defined "opinions" as verbal manifestations of attitudes, events such as riots, demonstrations, and marches are also indicators of "public opinion" for certain attentive publics.

In the recent era, the meaning of public opinion sometimes seems to have evolved into whatever opinion polls show public opinion to be. In many ways, the findings of public opinion polls (or survey research in general) should inspire trust. Counterintuitive though it may seem, mathematical statistics and decades of experience reveal that one can generalize from a random sample of one or two thousand individuals to the nation as a whole. And one rarely has reason to believe that survey respondents systematically lie to pollsters.

We must be careful, however, not to reify. Public opinion and the results of public opinion polls are not necessarily the same thing. As shown in later chapters, the results of opinion polls must be interpreted with great care. Findings can vary considerably with different question wordings or different shadings of how the issues are presented. Also, survey respondents sometimes tend to give socially desirable responses. For this reason, surveys often underreport attitudes and behaviors such as nonvoting, racist feelings, or tolerance for pornography because of a tendency for respondents to give socially desirable answers.

1-3 THE EVOLUTION OF THE PUBLIC OPINION POLL

Before the appearance of the modern public opinion poll in 1936, popular sentiment was assessed by newspapers and magazines through a variety of informal and haphazard soundings called "straw polls."[12] The *Harrisburg Pennsylvanian* is credited with conducting the first of these polls, in the summer of 1824. It showed Andrew Jackson, with 63 percent of the vote, an easy winner over John Quincy Adams and Henry Clay.[13]

But it was not until 1896 that straw polling became a serious business. In that year the *Chicago Record* conducted an elaborate and very expensive straw poll to tap voter preferences in the bitterly fought presidential contest between

William McKinley and William Jennings Bryan. It sent out postcard ballots to every eighth voter in 12 midwestern states, as well as ballots to every registered voter in Chicago.[14] The owner of the *Chicago Record* had clear Republican sympathies, and the Democratic party feared the poll was nothing more than a Republican trick. The party urged Democrats not to return the ballots. Nevertheless, with the aid of a team of eminent mathematicians, the *Record* predicted in October that McKinley would win Chicago with 57.95 percent of the vote. Amazingly, he received 57.91 percent on election day. Outside of Chicago, however, the *Record*'s predictive record was a failure (Jensen 1968).

With the dawn of the twentieth century, straw polls were becoming a regular feature in many magazines and newspapers. Like today, the poll results were "newsworthy." Approximately 84 straw polls were conducted during the 1928 presidential election, of which six were national. The straw polls occupied thousands of column inches in the print media. If anything, they were featured even more prominently than is currently the case.[15] The polls were of major importance to their sponsors as a promotional gimmick. They created interest in the publication. Also, those publishers using mail-out ballots usually included a special subscription offer along with the ballot. By all indications, the scheme worked remarkably well to boost circulation (Robinson 1932).

And like current opinion polls, the straw polls did not limit themselves simply to electoral contests. They polled on the issues as well, most notably the burning issue of the 1920s: Prohibition. The wet-dry controversy was as emotion-laden as any issue to surface in American politics. If popular sentiment on the issue was to be measured by a cutout ballot from a newspaper, one side would sometimes attempt to secure a monopoly on that issue and send in all the ballots. Or one side would urge its people not to participate in a straw poll when the sponsor's sentiments on the issue were known. Thus a poll in Delaware sponsored by Pierre du Pont, a well-known wet, was boycotted by drys. It wound up showing 97 percent of its respondents in favor of repeal. Mr. du Pont wisely decided against publishing the poll results as an indicator of public opinion. Rather, he submitted the returned ballots as a petition to the Delaware legislature urging the repeal of Prohibition (Robinson 1932).

The straw polls were a public relations disaster waiting to happen. By the 1930s, considerable advances had been made by market researchers in the field of applied sampling. However, the magazines and newspapers sponsoring the straw polls were oblivious. Their major concern with straw polls was how they contributed to profitability, not the technical quality of the poll itself. Methodologically, straw polls stayed in the rear guard, learning nothing from the advances in sampling methods, using the same outdated methods year after year.

Straw polls were, in fact, known to be notoriously unreliable. In 1932 Claude Robinson published an analysis of the state-by-state error margins of the major straw polls of the day.[16] The average error of the polls conducted by the Hearst newspapers was 12 percent in 1924. The poll by *The Pathfinder*, a weekly magazine, was off by an average of 14 percent in 1928. The *Farm-Journal* poll of 36 states in 1928 had an average error of 17 percent. Even the best-known and most professionally operated of the straw polls—the *Literary Digest* poll—was off the mark by an average of 12 percent in both 1924 and 1928.

It was the 1936 election and the notorious misprediction of its outcome by the *Literary Digest* that brought an end to the era of straw polls. The *Literary Digest* was the largest-circulation general magazine of its time, with over two million subscribers. Much of this success could be traced directly to its straw poll, a regular feature since 1916. While the *Digest* poll experienced more than its share of mispredictions, it had managed each time to get the winner of the presidential election right. And it was not modest. The *Digest* claimed "uncanny accuracy" for its poll, congratulating itself frequently on its amazing record. But in the 1936 presidential election, the *Digest* poll wildly mispredicted the outcome, giving Alf Landon 57 percent of the vote and Franklin Roosevelt 43 percent. Roosevelt won with 62.5 percent of the vote. The *Digest* was off the mark by almost 20 percentage points. Its credibility shattered, the *Literary Digest* went bankrupt a year later.

In that same year, three young pollsters with backgrounds in market research, using "scientific" methods of sampling, did correctly predict the win by Roosevelt. The three were Archibald Crossley, Elmo Roper, and George Gallup, each of whom went on to found his own poll. The best-known of these was, of course, George Gallup, founder of the Gallup Poll.

Gallup was a talented self-promoter. In the 1936 election, he taunted the *Literary Digest*, offering clients a money-back guarantee that his poll would be closer to the actual vote on election day than the *Digest*'s.[17] He urged newspapers and magazines to run the two polls side-by-side (J. Converse 1987, 116–20).

Gallup used in-person interviews as opposed to mail questionnaires, and employed "quotas" to insure that his samples looked demographically like the overall population. His poll forecast Roosevelt with 55.7 percent of the vote—6.8 percent off the mark. But he got the winner right, and he used that fact along with the *Digest*'s disaster to quickly become the nation's preeminent pollster.

But all was not right with the Gallup Poll. While Gallup continued to forecast the correct winner in the 1940 and 1944 presidential contests, his surveys consistently overestimated the Republican vote (Moore 1992b, 66–68). Then in 1948 the Gallup Poll incorrectly forecast that Republican Thomas Dewey would defeat Democrat Harry Truman by a margin of 49.5 to 44.5 percent. It is important to note that the Crossley Poll and the Roper Poll also predicted a win by Dewey. Roper had the margin at 52.2 percent Dewey and 37.1 percent Truman. Something was clearly wrong with the sampling methodology used by all three of these polls. That something was quota sampling. In a comprehensive study of the failure of the polls in 1948, the Social Science Research Council recommended the abandonment of quota samples and their replacement with probability samples (Bradburn and Sudman 1988). Probability sampling is the method used in today's public opinion polls (see Chapter 2).

Gallup, Crossley, and Roper were commercial pollsters. They did polls for clients, and by necessity were concerned with costs and profitability. They had little incentive for pure research, or for the lengthy surveys necessary to answer complex academic questions.[18] Those topics would be addressed by the major academic survey organizations, most notably the National Opinion Research Center (NORC) at the University of Chicago and the Survey Research Center (SRC)[19] at the University of Michigan. NORC was founded in 1941, and its associates produced several classics in the field of public opinion, including *The American Soldier* (Stouffer 1949) and *Communism, Conformity and Civil Liberties* (Stouffer 1955). The SRC, founded in 1946, has focused on studies of the American electorate. Perhaps the most influential book to date on public opinion and voting, *The American Voter* (A. Campbell et al. 1960), was published by a group associated with the SRC.

Both the NORC and the SRC devote considerable resources to technical issues involving sampling and question wording. The NORC pioneered the "split ballot technique," in which different forms of a question are asked of random halves of a sample to investigate the effects of question wording. Researchers associated with the SRC have also devoted extensive time and energy to problems of question wording (Schuman and Presser 1981). But most important are the periodic surveys conducted by each of these institutions. Since 1948, the SRC and the Center for Political Studies have been conducting, on a biennial basis, the National Election Studies (NES).[20] These are large, in-person national surveys of issues relevant to elections. Respondents are interviewed in the autumn before an election, then reinterviewed after the election is over. The total interview time is often three to five hours, and hundreds of questions are asked. Since 1971, NORC has sponsored the General Social Survey (GSS), usually conducted on an annual basis. The GSS has a general set of questions, often repeated from year to year, and a topical module that addresses a specific substantive concern at considerable length. Both the NES and GSS are publicly available, formatted and ready for analysis with common computer statistical packages. A great deal of the data presented in this book comes from these two sources.

Both the NES and GSS surveys interview people in their homes, a very expensive undertaking. By the early 1970s, techniques were being developed to scientifically sample telephone numbers using a random-digit-dialing methodology. This greatly reduced the cost of surveys, and encouraged the media to conduct their own public opinion polls, much as they did in the days of the straw polls. In 1976, CBS News and the *New York Times* went into partnership to conduct their own polls. They were soon followed by the NBC/*Wall Street Journal* and the ABC/*Washington Post* polls. Others, such as CNN, also poll on a regular basis.[21] The principal advantage to the media of in-house polls is that they can decide on the topics and timing of the surveys, rather than being confined to the topics and timing of independent pollsters like Gallup. In-house polls also free the media from having to rely on leaks from political campaigns about how candidates are faring with the voters. They can find out for themselves on an impartial, firsthand basis. Media polls are occasionally of interest to academic students of public opinion. But their value is limited by their interest in topical issues, and the abbreviated number of questions they ask.

The most recent polling innovation is the election day exit poll, developed by CBS News in the late 1960s (Moore 1992b, 255). It did not, however, gain prominence until the 1980 election, when it was first used to forecast the outcome of a presidential election. With an exit poll, one chooses a representative sample of precincts in a state and interviews voters as they leave the polling place. The networks usually know by 3 P.M. who has won the election, although they do not reveal this information for any one state until the polls have closed in that state. Beyond forecasting, exit polls have proved extremely valuable for understanding why people voted for specific candidates. Until recently, each network conducted its own exit polls. But in 1990, the major networks along with CNN and the Associated Press, formed a consortium, Voter News Service (VNS), to conduct common exit polls and share the information.

A final innovation in polling worth mentioning is the development of a code of standards for those in the field of public opinion. Unlike physicians, lawyers, or morticians, pollsters are not subject to government regulation. On occasion there have been calls by some in Congress for regulation. The first of these came in 1948, with many Democrats charging that the polls were biased in favor of Republicans. Another came in response to using exit polls to call the winner of the presidential election in 1980 before the voting booths had closed on the West Coast. It was argued that many Democrats failed to vote once they learned that President Carter had been defeated. However, most attempts by the government to regulate opinion polls would probably run afoul of the First Amendment's guarantee of the right of free speech.

In 1986 the American Association for Public Opinion Research (AAPOR) adopted a code of ethics and practices for the profession.[22] Among the major features of this code are full disclosure, confidentiality, and responsibility to those being interviewed. Pollsters must make available full information about who sponsored the survey and give details of relevant methodology, such as how the sample was selected. They must hold as confidential the responses to questions by specific individuals. They must avoid any practice that would harm or mislead a respondent. While the AAPOR has a standards committee, its only power of sanction is the glare of adverse publicity.

1-4 THE MODERN PUBLIC OPINION POLL AND ITS POLITICAL CONSEQUENCES

Prior to 1940, politicians judged public sentiment mainly from newspapers (Herbst 1993; Kernell 1993). For example, William McKinley kept tabs on "public opinion" by compiling a scrapbook of newspaper articles from every section of the country called "Current Comment" (Hilderbrand 1981). Contemporary political leaders clearly have much better information on the content of public opinion than they did prior to the advent of scientific polling. John Geer (1996) argues that politicians well-informed about public opinion use a qualitatively different leadership style than those without reliable opinion information. In particular, he argues certain skills historically associated with "leadership" are found less frequently in today's political leaders. They include the ability to craft good arguments and a willingness to remain committed to a stand.

According to Geer, before polling politicians were uncertain if the electorate was on their side, and a premium was placed on the ability to convince both citizens and other politicians of the merits of an argument. Today this skill is less essential as more certainty exists about the electorate's preferences. For example, staff disputes on issues are often resolved by reference to public opinion rather than nuanced argument. Modern politicians are also less likely to remain committed to issue positions if the polls show them to be electoral losers. William Jennings Bryan ran for president in 1896 on the platform of "free silver." Despite being soundly defeated, he showcased the same issue in his 1900 presidential bid. Bryan remained convinced that public opinion was on his side (Anderson 1981). Geer argues that in absence of reliable opinion data as a reality check, politicians' estimate of public opinion is driven by their own personal views and reinforced by those around them who often think as they do. On the other hand, Ronald Reagan in the 1960s and early 1970s was a strong proponent of a voluntary social security program. When polls showed a large proportion of public disagreed, it is probably no accident that Reagan dropped the issue when he ran for the presidency. Finally, the modern opinion poll has likely forever changed the standard by which political leadership is judged. Every decision is now evaluated in reference to public opinion. How, for example, would history treat Lincoln's Emancipation Proclamation if a Gallup Poll in June of 1862 showed 72 percent of Northerners wanted to abolish slavery? (Geer 1996).

Change is not neutral. New innovations benefit some at the expense of others. The modern public opinion poll is no exception. Benjamin Ginsberg (1986), however, makes the counterintuitive argument that replacement by the modern opinion poll of traditional methods for expressing public opinion has served to "domesticate" public opinion. In other words, public opinion is a less potent force in American politics now than it was prior to scientific polling.

By traditional methods of expressing public opinion, we are referring to letters to newspapers and public officials, personal contact, elections, advocacy group activity, marches, demonstrations, and riots—to list the more obvious. Such methods are still available, but when these indicators of public opinion differ from those reported in polls, it is universally assumed that polls are more representative. If one conceives of public opinion as an aggregation of equally weighted preferences, that assumption is almost certainly correct. However, polling by simply totaling individual opinions has, according to Ginsberg, changed some very important aspects of "public opinion" as expressed by methods commonly employed before the advent of the scientific survey.

For example, public opinion was once largely a group phenomenon. At election time, elected officials would consult closely with the leaders of various advocacy groups, such as farmers or organized labor, to be informed of membership opinion. Opinion polls have undermined the ability of group leaders to speak for their membership, as the members can now be polled directly. Any difference between the polls and the characterization of group opinion by leaders is usually resolved in favor of the polls. During the Nixon administration, wage and price controls were strongly opposed by organized labor. However, polls showed Nixon was popular with the rank and file, thus undercutting the ability of union leaders to threaten reprisals at the voting booth.

Where it had once been a behavior (letter writing, marches, etc.), public opinion is now mostly a summation of attitudes. In fact, the citizen is relieved of all initiative whatsoever. Pollsters contact respondents, determine worthwhile questions, analyze the results, and publicize them. If a citizen feels strongly about an issue, one mode of expression not available is to call a survey house and demand to be included in the next opinion poll.

Polls weaken the connection between opinion and intensity. It requires little effort to "strongly agree" with a statement proffered by an interviewer. Converse et al. (1965) have demonstrated that public opinion as measured in surveys is much less intense than that offered in voluntary modes of popular expression. Polls, in practice, submerge intense opinions with those held by the much larger, more apathetic population. This characteristic of opinion surveys can be employed by elected officials to promote their policy choices. Both Lyndon Johnson and Richard Nixon used evidence from polls to justify their policies in Vietnam as being in step with majority preferences, despite widespread public protests. Ginsberg claims a good argument could be made that if decision-makers had accepted the more intense behavioral indicators of sentiment about the Vietnam War, as opposed to the evidence from polls, the Vietnam War would have ended much sooner.

Finally, modern opinion polls have changed the character of public opinion from an assertion to a response. Before polling, citizens themselves chose the topics on which to express their opinions. Now, according to Ginsberg, these subjects are chosen mostly by polling technocrats. Most publicly expressed opinion is based less on the concerns of citizens than on the concerns of whomever is paying for the poll. Thus in 1970, a year of both racial strife and antiwar protest, the Gallup Poll devoted 5 percent of its questions to American policy in Vietnam, less than 1 percent to race relations, and had no questions on student protests. On the other hand, 26 percent of its questions (in a nonpresidential year) concerned the electoral horserace.

Whatever the merit of Ginsberg's arguments, they suffer from the same problem as those of Lippman, Blumer, and Rogers—a rejection of the normative view that all opinions ought to count equally. Whatever its faults, the modern scientific opinion survey best approximates just what democracy is supposed to produce—an equal voice for all citizens (for a dissent see Berinsky 1999). In the beginning of the twenty-first century, there are few who endorse less democratic input into the political system as opposed to more democratic input, whatever might be the imperfections of the latter. Polls may have shortcomings, but as measures of public opinion they are clearly more representative of all opinion than are the traditional measures. In fact, the traditional measures may be even more nonrepresentative today than they were in the past. In recent years, paid political consultants have become very sophisticated at marshaling local interest groups on issues of importance to their clients, raining letters, faxes, and phone calls on Congress and the White House, as well as newspapers and talk shows (Engelberg 1993; Mitchell 1998). It is often difficult to distinguish between these mobilized outbursts of public sentiment and those that are genuinely spontaneous.

Implicit in Ginsberg's analysis is an assumption that modern opinion polling has discouraged the communication of public opinion by other methods. But all the means available to express public opinion prior to 1936 are still available, and are often used effectively. One need only witness the controversy over lifting the ban on homosexuals in the military in the early months of the Clinton administration, or the failed attempt by the administration in 1993–1994 to reform the nation's health insurance system (Koch 1998).

Explicit in the analysis is a claim that the appearance of public opinion polls has domesticated public opinion—that it is not as powerful a force in political decision-making as it once was. There is, however, no systematic, hard evidence to support this assertion. The simple truth is that poll results are brought forcefully to the attention of government authorities at all levels (P. Converse 1987, 14). The relationship of public opinion to public policy in the modern era is an empirical question, about which we will have much to say in this book.

1-5 SOURCES OF INFORMATION ON PUBLIC OPINION

Since the 1930s, tens of thousands of surveys have been conducted, hundreds of thousands of questions have been asked, and millions of respondents have been interviewed (T. Smith 1990a). Much of this data has been housed in several "data libraries" or archives. In addition, a great deal of public opinion information can be accessed through the Internet. (A list of useful Internet addresses is presented in the section that follows.)

The most comprehensive and up-to-date method for finding particular public opinion items is a computerized database called POLL (Public Opinion Location Library), located at the Roper Center in Storrs, Connecticut. Members can access the Roper Center archives through the Internet. By simply entering one or more key words, such as "gun control," they can obtain question wording, item frequencies, and basic documentation for questions housed at the archive. They can also obtain cross-tabulations on key demographic items. The surveys themselves are available from the Roper Center, but at a cost. The Institute for Research in Social Science at the University of North Carolina houses the surveys conducted by Lou Harris and Associates plus more than 350 statewide-level polls. An excellent multipurpose site for public opinion data and other social data is Data on the Net maintained by the University of California at San Diego. It serves as a gateway to almost 100 data archives throughout the world. Finally, World Associates for Public Opinion Research is a source for public opinion data across a range of subjects. This site tends to focus on market research, but it also archives political surveys. In addition, there are often short feature stories about polling and research methods.

For academic students of public opinion, including undergraduate and graduate students, the most valuable data archive is the Inter-University Consortium for Political and Social Research (ICPSR) at the University of Michigan. Many colleges and universities are members of "the Consortium," while membership in other data archives is less frequent. The Consortium publishes annually a complete catalog of its holdings and distributes a newsletter informing members of new acquisitions. This information as well as the frequencies for some of its data sets can be accessed at its Website. The Consortium also disseminates the National Election Studies, the General Social Survey, and the World Values Survey. These are three of the most important nonproprietary academic surveys available for secondary analysis, and we rely on them extensively in this book. Each of these studies comes with a completely documented codebook. Both the codebooks and the data sets are routinely received by the universities who are Consortium members.[23]

In addition, there are a number of journals that publish opinion data on a regular basis. Each issue of the *Public Opinion Quarterly* has a section called "The Polls," in which survey data on a specific topic is reviewed. All articles published in this journal are indexed by subject, author, and title and can be found on its Website. General compilations for public opinion data are also published in *Public Opinion*,[24] *Public Perspective*, and *American Enterprise*. The best source for academic studies of public opinion is the *Public Opinion Quarterly*. The major journals in political science and sociology also serve as useful references.[25]

The major Websites through which information on public opinion can be accessed are listed below by topical category. Since these sites often change, we have created a Website that updates the information presented below. It can be accessed at http://crystal.polsci.uh.edu/apo. Two other useful sources for locating current public opinion Websites can be found at www.princeton.edu/~abelson, and at www.ukans.edu/cwis/units/coms2/po/index.html.

Current Polling Data These sites make available the latest public opinion polling data on a wide range of topics—from public reaction to an event recently in the news to the latest reading on presidential popularity or the current poll data on a high-profile election.

www.pollingreport.com A service of *The Polling Report*, a nonpartisan clearinghouse for public opinion data; provides free reports on current opinion on politics, the economy, and popular culture.

www.cloakroom.com Sponsored by the *National Journal*; provides the most complete up-to-date polling information on electoral contests, but requires a paid subscription to access the information.

www.epinet.org/pulse/pulse.html A consumer's guide to public opinion data sponsored by the Economic Policy Institution; provides links to the Websites of other major polling organizations.

www.gallup.com The site for the Gallup Poll.

www.cbsnews.com The site reporting the latest results from the CBS Television News/*New York Times* polling unit.

www.washingtonpost.com The site for polls conducted by the ABC Television News/*Washington Post* polling unit.

www.nyttimes.com The "PollWatch" site for the *New York Times;* provides a new story about polling every other Thursday; old stories are also archived and available.

www.wsj.com The site for polls conducted by the NBC Television News/*Wall Street Journal* polling unit.

www.usatoday.com The site for *USA Today* polls.

www.people-press.org The site for the *Pew Research Center for the People and the Press*, an independent research group that conducts surveys in some depth about current issues; regularly conducts polls on public attentiveness to news stories, and charts trends in fundamental social and political values.

www.vanishingvoter.org A site maintained by the Kennedy School at Harvard. Weekly polls of 1000 respondents were conducted during the 2000 presidential election, focusing on factors that encourage or discourage public engagement with politics.

www.zogby.com The site for Zogby International, the political polling agency for Reuters; mostly focuses on electoral choice.

Polling Data Archives Earlier in this chapter we discussed a number of "data libraries." The Websites for these archives are listed below.

www.icpsr.umich.edu The site for the University Consortium for Social and Political Research, home to the National Election Studies (NES) and archives the General Social Survey (GSS) and the World Values Survey, as well as others.

www.norc.uchicago.edu The site for the National Opinion Research Center, home to the General Social Survey and other NORC studies.

www.ropercenter.uconn.edu The site for the Roper Center, which houses the Gallup Poll, media polls, plus others.

www.irss.unc.edu/dataarchive The archive associated with the University of North Carolina, home to the Harris Poll and the National Association of State Polls, which houses more than 350 state-level studies.

odwin.ucsd.edu/data "Data on the Net" maintained by the University of California at San Diego; also provides links to other social data bases.

gort.ucsd.edu/calpol The archive for the Field Poll, devoted to political and social issues in the state of California.

Data Archives for Non-American Surveys Survey research now occurs all over the world on a regular basis. The best of the archives and their Websites are listed below.

www.za.uni-koeln.de/data/en/issp/index.htm The archive for the International Social Survey.

europa.eu.int/en/comm/dg10/infcom/epo/polls.html This site for archives for the Eurobarometer and the Central and Eastern Eurobarometer.

www.mori.com A British-based opinion research firm and archive. MORI holds mostly British opinion data, but also conducts and archives occasional cross-national studies.

Polling Organizations There are a number of professional polling organizations that offer useful and interesting information on survey research.

www.aapor.org The site for the American Association for Public Opinion Research, the oldest and most prestigious of the polling organizations; includes a complete index to articles published in the *Public Opinion Quarterly*.

www.worldopinion.com The site for the World Association for Public Opinion Research; often contains useful articles about opinion research.

www.casro.org The site for the Council of American Survey Research Organizations, the primary organization for those doing commercial survey research.

www.ncpp.org The site for the National Council of Public Polls; contains information on national standards, how to conduct and interpret polls.

1-6 LINKAGE MODELS BETWEEN PUBLIC OPINION AND PUBLIC POLICIES

In a democracy, public opinion is supposed to influence the decisions by the elected leaders. The mechanisms linking public opinion to government policies are more complicated than we might think. In this final section we outline five models, originally proposed by Luttbeg (1968), by which public opinion can be reflected in public policy.

The Rational-Activist Model

This model is the basis for the widely accepted concept of the ideal citizen's role in a democracy. Voting on the basis of issues is at the heart of the rational-activist model. By the standards of this model, individual citizens are expected to be informed politically, involved, rational, and, above all, active. On the basis of an informed and carefully reasoned set of personal preferences, and an accurate perception of the various candidates' positions, the voter is expected to cast a ballot for those candidates who best reflect the voter's issue preferences. The model suggests that elected officials who are not held accountable by an informed electorate will not responsibly enact public preferences into policy. Instead, such representatives may vote their own preferences or the preferences of limited segments of society, such as wealthy professional groups.

This model places great burdens on both elected officials and citizens, expecting both to be informed and to communicate with each other. In a complex and increasingly technical society, the task of the voter who seeks to be informed is indeed formidable. As we have noted, politics does not play a salient role in the lives of most Americans. Many people rarely or never vote. Those who do are often ill-informed, particularly when they participate in nonpresidential elections.

Certainly issue voting allows for some modest influence of public opinion on government policy. But in our search for methods by which political leaders can be held accountable, we must look beyond the rational-activist model.

The Political Parties Model

The political parties model greatly reduces the political demands placed on the citizen. The model depends on the desire of political parties to win elections as a mechanism for achieving popular control. According to the model, a party states its positions on the various issues of the day in its platform. Because of their interest in winning elections, parties can be counted on to take stands that appeal to large segments of the electorate. The voter then selects among platforms, giving support to the candidate of the party whose platform most conforms to his or her personal preference. Instead of facing multiple decisions for the numerous offices up for election, the voter need only make a single decision among the available choice of parties.

A number of questions are raised by a consideration of this model. For example, do people simply adopt the party identification of their parents and loyally support that party throughout their lives? Such loyalty violates the model's expectations that voters rationally chose the party most closely standing for issue positions they prefer. Does a party's electoral fortunes reflect the degree of public support for its policies, or is a party's vote largely independent of the policies it advocates?

The Interest Groups Model

In the preceding models we have emphasized the central importance of communication between elected officials and their constituents. For representatives to respond to public demands, they need to know what these demands are. For the public to achieve accountability from representatives, they need to know what the representatives have done, and what alternatives were available. Interest groups can perform this function. They can serve as a link between people and their representatives.

Numerous organized groups in society claim to speak for various segments of the electorate—the Sierra Club, the National Organization for Women, and the National Rifle Association, to mention a few. At one extreme, these groups could be so inclusive of individuals in our society and could so accurately represent their members' opinions that representatives could achieve accountability merely by recording the choice of each group, weighing them by the number of voters they represent, and voting with the most sizable group. This would be in accord with what might be called the interest groups model of popular control.

Under ideal circumstances interest groups might succeed in communicating public opinion to officials between elections and with greater clarity than can be communicated through election outcomes. Interest groups, like political parties, could simplify the choices for the individual voter, making it possible for an electorate that is largely disinterested in politics to nevertheless achieve accountability.

Several questions arise out of the interest groups model. Are the opinions of those citizens within an interest group similar, and do they differ from members of other groups? Does "group opinion," the somehow combined opinions of all those persons in all the relevant interest groups, coincide with public opinion? Or, do the opinions carried to government by interest groups reflect only the opinions of the wealthy or the business sector of our society? Who among everyday citizens belongs to interest groups? Are some segments of society over-represented, while others are mostly uninvolved in any type of group activity?

The Role-Playing Model

The role-playing model builds on the sociological concept of "role," or widely shared beliefs about how people in various social positions should act. The judge is supposed to be fair-minded, the doctor both expert and comforting, and the political representative willing to work to enact the preferences of his or her supporters. If elected officials believe they should learn constituency opinion and enact it into public policy, public policy may well reflect public opinion. Even if the public votes for candidates and parties with no concern for their positions on issues, public policy would still reflect public opinion because of the role orientation of the representative. He or she would attempt to learn public opinion and translate it into public policy regardless of the electorate's motives in casting the ballot. Of course, elected leaders will be more likely to heed public opinion if they perceive that the people are paying attention to what they do. Thus, representation of public opinion can be enhanced simply because elected leaders believe that they will be thrown out of office if they do not attend to voter opinion—whether or not the voters would actually do so.

Several questions are raised by the role-playing model: Can elected officials accurately learn public opinion, or do they receive a distorted view? To what extent do elected officials actually heed public opinion as they perceive it? What do elected leaders view as the consequences of ignoring public opinion? Finally, how often do elected officials see their role as representing constituency preferences, as opposed to their (possibly conflicting) personal views of the constituency's best interests?

The Sharing Model

Because as a society we do not designate leaders early in life and hold them as a class apart throughout their early lives, it is unlikely that the personal opinions held by elected officials on the issues of the day differ diametrically from those held by the rest of the electorate. This possibility is the final model of political linkage: the sharing model. This model simply states that since many attitudes are broadly held throughout the public, elected leaders cannot help but satisfy public opinion to some degree, even if the public is totally apathetic. Unilateral disarmament, total government takeover of the economy, a termination of public education, a complete disregard for the preservation of the environment—all are examples of actions so contrary to broadly held American attitudes that they would be rejected by any set of government leaders. Even on issues that provoke substantial disagreement, the distribution of opinion among political leaders may be similar to that among the public. If so, even when leaders act according to personal preference and are ignored by disinterested citizens, their actions would often correspond to citizen preferences. For this model, we need to consider how broadly opinions on national issues are shared, and how similar are views of elected officials to the public at large.

1-7 PLAN OF THIS BOOK

We have by necessity ordered facts into various chapters that strike us as convenient. Chapter 2 discusses the science of assessing public opinion. Chapter 3 is concerned with the psychology of opinion-holding, and focuses on the role of political ideology and party identification. Chapter 4 chronicles trends in public opinion over time. Chapter 5 discusses the formation of political attitudes. Chapter 6 evaluates data on broad public acceptance of certain attitudes that may be necessary for a stable democratic government, and Chapter 7 delves into the group basis of public opinion. Chapter 8 analyzes the effect of the media on those attitudes. Chapter 9 is an analysis of public opinion and elections, and Chapter 10 views the reverse aspect of political linkage—how elected officials respond to the views of their constituents. Chapter 11 considers the importance of political parties and interest groups in achieving correspondence between public opinion and public policy. In the final chapter, we assess the linkage models and draw conclusions about public opinion in the United States based on the data presented throughout this book.

NOTES

1. The Blumer view of public opinion is one still held by many in the field. For a more recent statement, see Zukin (1992).
2. The term "pollster" was coined by political scientist and pollster Lindsay Rogers to evoke in the minds of readers the word "huckster" (Hitchens 1992, 46).
3. Or as Winston Churchill put it, "Nothing is more dangerous than to live in the temperamental atmosphere of a Gallup Poll, always feelings one's pulse and taking one's temperature . . . There is only one duty, only one safe course, and that is to try to be right and not to fear to do or waver in what you believe to be right." (Quoted in Bogart 1972, 47.)
4. Almond moderated his opinion on this point in the reissue of his book in 1960.
5. For a detailed argument that the change in public opinion is not capricious but ordered and rational, see Page and Shapiro (1992).

6. The eighteenth-century French mathematician Marquis de Condorcet, using jury decisions as an example, was able to demonstrate mathematically a greater probability that the majority would come to the right decision than the probability the minority would come to the right decision.

7. For an analysis of the dimensions possible, see Herbst (1993).

8. Choosing not to vote may well be as much of a political statement as casting one's ballot. A nonvote can mean alienation from government, or may indicate acceptance of the status quo.

9. It also includes the functional equivalent of verbal expressions, such as filling out a written questionnaire.

10. One ambiguity with this conceptualization is that some people may never express orally or in writing some of their opinions. We could possibly conceptualize such opinions as internal, but that has the unhappy consequence of muddying the distinction between attitudes and opinions. Our simple solution for unexpressed opinions is to assert that if expressed they would have the same characteristics and qualities of expressed opinion.

11. It should be noted that our distinction between opinions and beliefs is not universal across all fields. In a court of law, for example, an expert witness is frequently asked to give an "expert opinion" on a matter of fact. In everyday conversation, it is quite frequently that someone asserts, "It is my opinion that ..." followed by some assertion of factual truth.

12. The name apparently comes from a practice in rural areas of throwing straw into the air to see which way the wind is blowing. Presumably, a "straw poll" is a method for determining the direction of the political winds. Pioneer pollster Claude Robinson (1932, 6) defined a straw poll as "an unofficial canvass of an electorate to determine the division of popular sentient on public issues or on candidates for public office." Today the term generally refers to any assessment of public opinion based on nonscientific sampling methods.

13. The sample consisted of 532 respondents from Wilmington, Delaware, selected "without Discrimination of Parties" (Gallup and Rae 1940, 35). Other straw polls were conducted in 1824 as well (see E. Smith 1990a).

14. Straw polls used three methods to gather data. One was the "ballot-in-the-paper" method, in which the reader filled out the ballot, cut it out of the paper, and mailed it to the sponsoring organization. The second was the personal canvass, in which solicitors would take ballots to crowded locations such as theaters, hotels, and trolleys, and get willing citizens to complete them. Sometimes ballots would simply be left in a crowded area in the morning, and those completed would be retrieved in the evening. The third method was to send out ballots by mail to a specified list of people, and ask that they send them back by return mail.

15. In publications such as the *Chicago Record*, there was a daily front-page feature from September 1896 through election day. The same was true of the *Literary Digest*.

16. The sample sizes for the straw polls were so large that they typically made projections on a state-by-state basis.

17. Gallup marketed a column to newspapers based on his polls, called "America Speaks."

18. Although early on, Gallup did do split-ballot question-wording experiments. These were not, however, publicly released.

19. Now a division of the Institute for Social Research.

20. Over the years, these University of Michigan–based surveys have undergone a number of name changes. In the early years, they were dubbed the "SRC" surveys,

after the Survey Research Center. Then the became the "CPS" surveys, named after the Center for Political Studies, a division of the Institute for Social Research. Currently they are referred to as the "National Election Studies" (NES).

21. However, only the CBS News/*New York Times* has its own in-house polling operation. ABC, NBC, and CNN contract with outside commercial polling houses for their opinion surveys.

22. For a copy of the code of ethics and a discussion, see Cantril (1991, ch. 4).

23. For more information on data archives, see Smith and Weil (1990) or Kiecolt and Nathan (1985).

24. *Public Opinion* ceased publication in 1991, but it is still a good source of opinion data from 1978 to 1991.

25. These would include the *American Political Science Review*, the *Journal of Politics*, the *American Journal of Political Science*, *Political Research Quarterly*, *Political Behavior*, the *American Sociology Review*, the *American Journal of Sociology*, *Social Forces*, *Sociological Quarterly*, and the *Social Science Quarterly*.

CHAPTER 2

Polling: The Scientific Assessment of Public Opinion

The analysis of public opinion and elections, using modern survey methods, has now been part of the public landscape for over 60 years. More and more people say they are paying attention to the polls. In 1944, only 19 percent of the public said that they regularly or occasionally followed poll results; by 1985 it was 41 percent, and in 1996 the figure had risen to 55 percent. Yet few among the mass public have even a rudimentary understanding of how a public opinion poll works. In a recent study, the Gallup organization asked a national sample whether interviews with 1,500 or 2,000 people (typical sample sizes for national polls) "can accurately reflect the views of the nation's population," or whether "it's not possible with so few people." Only 28 percent said a sample of that size could yield accurate results; 56 percent said it was not possible, and the remaining 15 percent had no opinion. While the public may not understand the technicalities of polling, a sizable majority, nevertheless, believes polls are always accurate or almost always accurate. In a 1996 survey 87 percent of respondents said polls are "a good thing" for the country—up from 76 percent in 1985 (Gallup and Moore, 1996).

In the popular press, however, polls have frequently been the subject of severe criticism. Following the 1980 election, the *Detroit Free Press* ran a headline story "Pollsters Kissed Off by Electorate: Have 1,001 Excuses." (Ladd and Ferree 1981, 13). Similar complaints were heard in other years. In 1986 an ABC polling analyst was quoted in the *New York Times* as saying, "I don't think it was a great year for pollsters" (Tolchin 1986, 17). In 1988, *Newsweek* reported that "polls are more accurate than in the past, but they are still wrong more often than their sponsors admit" (21 Nov. 1988, 26). In November 1992 the polls mostly performed well in estimating the division of the presidential vote. Only the Gallup Poll suffered a major embarrassment, overstating Clinton's share of the vote by 6 percent. In 1996, polls came in for particularly harsh criticism. Everett Carl Ladd, Director of the Roper Center, asserted that "Election polling had a terrible year in 1996. Indeed, its overall performance was so flawed that the entire enterprise should be reviewed" (Ladd 1996). In particular he singled out the *New York Times*/CBS poll that predicted a landslide 18 percentage-point win for Bill Clinton, who in fact won by a more modest 8 percent. Ladd's critique resulted in a detailed study by the National Council on Public Polls of 47 final preelection polls conducted between 1936 and 1996. The Council found the average error in 1996 was 1.7 percentage points; for polls conducted between 1936 and 1992, it was 2.5 percentage points. The study concluded that overall polling error in 1996 "was low relative to historical experience" and within sampling error (Mitofsky 1998).

Polling certainly deserves a critical look. Many surveys are badly conceived, poorly executed, and incorrectly interpreted. Nevertheless, much popular criticism of public opinion polls seems ill-informed. Few outside the professional survey community have an appreciation for why candidates who lead in the final preelection poll do not always win; why two surveys taken at the same time report different results; or even why Truman beat Dewey when the Gallup Poll predicted otherwise.

The news media is now saturated with polling reports. From September 1 to November 4 in 1996 more than 300 national and 400 state polls asked Americans who they preferred for president (Bogart 1998). This is more than twice as much polling as took place during the same period in 1992. Furthermore, polls are no longer confined predominantly to the analysis of elections. In the last several years abortion has been a major issue on the public agenda. Hardly a month goes by without a survey report on how Americans currently feel toward the abortion issue.

An understanding of what can and cannot be inferred from political polls has a practical importance that lies beyond the academic world. It is now agreed that a candidate's poor showing in preelection polls makes fund-raising difficult and dampens volunteer enthusiasm. To quote from Richard Nixon in 1968, "When the polls go good for me, the cash register really rings."[1] Polls that are going well also result in more media attention (Traugott 1992, 126). In addition, a strong showing in the polls can legitimize a candidate, insuring that he or she is taken seriously. A good example is the third-party candidacy of John Anderson in 1980. In June of that year, an ABC poll showed that 31 percent of the electorate would vote for Anderson, a clear asset for an unconventional candidate in attracting volunteers and raising money (Broh 1983, 32–33). The same could be said for Ross Perot in 1992, who at one point in June led both major party candidates in the polls. He did not, of course, need a strong showing in the polls to finance his campaign.

Polls also create expectations about who is the likely election winner. Larry Bartels has demonstrated that in presidential primaries with a number of more or less unknown candidates—such as 1988 for the Democrats—expectations about who will win are a major factor in determining candidate choice on election day (Bartels 1988, ch. 6). Thomas Patterson makes a compelling argument that the standing in the polls of a presidential candidate determines the way the candidate's personal qualities are described by the media. Candidates who are ahead in the polls are described in very flattering terms, while those behind are depicted as bumblers. In an analysis of reporting in *Newsweek*, Patterson shows that in 1988 when Michael Dukakis was doing well in the polls, he was described as "relentless in his attack" and "a credible candidate." As he later dropped in the polls, *Newsweek* described him as "reluctant to attack" and "trying to present himself as a credible candidate." Interestingly, the change in descriptors coincided quite closely with the point he fell behind George Bush in the polls (Patterson 1989, 104–6). Finally, standing in the polls can determine whether or not a candidate is invited to participate in the presidential debates. For example, when John Anderson's poll numbers fell below 10 percent in 1980, he was excluded from the final debate (Polsby and Wildavsky 1984).

Presidential popularity is now gauged at least every two weeks, and is watched with considerable interest by members of Congress as well as others in the political community. It is argued that one very important aspect of presidential power is the chief executive's personal standing with the public. The high level of job approval (about 70 percent) enjoyed by Bill Clinton in the months prior to the Senate vote to remove him from office on February 12, 1999, is credited by many as having saved his presidency.

A president may also use polls to gauge the popularity of his policies among certain segments of the population, or to try to identify those segments that are not supportive. Specific programs may then be targeted for the nonsupportive group. For example, in the spring of 1982, Ronald Reagan's advisors found his popularity was slumping badly with Roman Catholics. In an attempt to remedy the problem, President Reagan flew to Chicago, home of the largest Catholic school system in the nation, and announced a proposal to give tuition credits to allow families to send their children to private (e.g., Catholic) schools (Bradburn and Sudman 1988, 47–48). Survey results also directly affect who gets what from government. Formulas for allocations of federal grant money are based on surveys such as the monthly Current Population Surveys (CPS) done by the Bureau of the Census. Finally, democratic governments (as well as others) justify their existence by claiming to respond to "the will of the people." Public opinion polls have become the commonly accepted tool for uncovering the hopes, fears, wishes, preferences, and values of those whom government serves. In this chapter, we shall outline the major procedures used in conducting surveys of public opinion and how they can go awry.

2-1 SAMPLING

Most public opinion polls are based on samples. When the Gallup Poll reports that 50 percent of adult Americans approve of the way that the president is handling his job, it is obvious that the Gallup organization has not gone out and interviewed 210 million American adults. Instead it has taken a sample. The reasons for sampling are fairly straightforward. First, to interview everyone would be prohibitively expensive. The Census for the year 2000 is estimated to cost between $6 billion and $7 billion. Second, to interview the entire population would take a very long time. Months might pass between the first and last interviews. Public opinion might, in that period, undergo real change.

Sampling provides a practical alternative to interviewing the whole population—be it national, state, or local. Furthermore, when done correctly, sampling can provide very accurate estimates of the political opinions of a larger population. The theory of sampling is a branch of the mathematics of probability, and the error involved in going from the sample to the population can be known with precision. However, many surveys of public opinion do not meet the demanding requirements of sampling theory. The attendant result, of course, is a loss in accuracy.

Sampling Theory

The *population* is that unit about which we want information. In most political surveys three different populations are frequently polled: (1) those 18 and older, (2) those who are registered voters, and (3) those who will (or do) vote in the next election. These are three quite different groups. It is very important that the population be clearly specified. When one sees a poll addressing abortion, presidential popularity, or voter intent in an upcoming election, those reporting the poll should provide a clear description of the population about which they speak. It has been shown, for example, that Senator Edward Kennedy is more highly rated among all adults than among registered voters (Roper 1980, 48). Evaluations of Kennedy are, in part, determined by how one defines the population.

The *sample* is that part of the population selected for analysis. Usually, the sample is considerably smaller than the population. National political surveys conducted by reputable firms employ samples of 1,000 to 1,500 respondents, although smaller samples are sometimes used in state and local contests. But as samples get smaller, the probability of error increases. Sample size should always be reported along with the results of a survey. If that information is missing, the alleged findings should be treated with a great deal of caution.

When samples accurately mirror the population, they are said to be *representative*. The term "randomness" refers to the only method by which a representative sample can be scientifically drawn. In a simple random sample, each unit of the population has exactly the same chance of being drawn as any other unit. If the population is American attorneys, each attorney is required to have exactly the same probability of being selected in order for the sample to be random. Attorneys in big cities could not have a greater likelihood of getting into the sample than those from rural areas. This situation obviously requires a detailed knowledge of the population. In the case of attorneys, one could get a list from the American Bar Association and then sample from that list. But suppose the population was unemployed adults. To specify the population in a fashion to be able to draw a random sample would be very difficult. As a consequence, obtaining a representative sample of the unemployed is not easy.

A probability sample is a variant of the principle of random sampling. Instead of each unit having exactly the same probability of being drawn, some units would be more likely to be drawn than would others. But this would be a *known* probability. For example, if one were sampling voter precincts in a state, it is of consequence that some precincts contain more people than do others. To make the sample of people in those precincts representative, the larger precincts must have a greater likelihood of being selected than smaller ones.

We will use *simple random sampling* (SRS) to illustrate how the principle of probability works in selecting a representative sample. Let us assume our population is a large barrel containing 100,000 marbles, some of which are red and some of which are green. We do not know the percentage of each. Instead of counting them all (a long and tedious job), we will draw a random sample. The question is: How? We could just dip in our hand and take some out, but that would mean that those within our reach would be picked and those close to the bottom would have no chance of being selected. Or we could spin the barrel and take one out after every spin. That would probably work reasonably well, but it still would not be "scientific." Even with a spin, those marbles at the bottom might never get close enough to the surface to get picked. If we are insisting on a pure random sample, we would have to employ a table of random numbers, and give each marble a numeral between 1 and 100,000. Random number tables are computer-generated digits that are completely unrelated to one another (i.e., random). They can be found in the appendix of virtually any statistics book. Let us assume we sample 600 marbles. Our first random number might be 33,382. We would then find the marble with that number and note if it is red or green. Our next random number might be 12,343. We would again note its color. The process would continue until we drew 600 marbles and recorded the color of each.

Having completed that task, let us say our sample shows 65 percent red marbles. Given the sampling method, we now know some things about the population. Sampling theory (the *central limit theorem*) tells us that the most likely percentage of red marbles is 65 percent. Of course, it is very unlikely that the real percentage of red marbles is precisely 65 percent. It might be 65.5 or 64.3, for example. The same will not get the population value exactly correct for the same reason that flipping a coin 100 times will not likely yield exactly 50 heads and 50 tails—although it should be close if the coin is honestly flipped.

We need at this point to introduce the concepts of confidence level and sampling error. A sample will rarely hit the true population value right on the nose. The *confidence level* tells us the probability that the population value will fall within a specified range. The *sampling error* specifies that range. A commonly used confidence level is 95 percent (it is sometimes higher, but almost never lower). For a sample of 600, the sampling error is 4 percent. What all this means is that if we took 100 samples from our population, and each of these samples consisted of 600 marbles randomly drawn, then 95 out of 100 times we would be plus or minus 4 percent of the true population value. Our sample came up 65 percent red. While this figure may not be exactly correct, we at least know that 95 out of 100 times (our 95 percent confidence level) we are going to be within four points—one way or the other—of the true proportion of red marbles in the barrel. This much can be proved mathematically.

Let us turn to a political example. The Gallup Poll reported that President Clinton's approval rating shortly before the Senate voted to acquit him on impeachment charges of perjury and obstruction of justice was 69 percent (Gallup Poll, 1 Feb. 1998). Since the sample size in this survey was 1,000 adults, we know that if the poll were repeated 100 times, 95 of the 100 repetitions (the 95 percent confidence level) would produce results that are plus or minus 3 percent (the sampling error) of what we would find if we interviewed all American adults.[2] Thus Clinton's popularity on or about February 1, 1998, could have been as high as 72 percent or as low as 66 percent. The "best estimate" (according to the central limit theorem) is 69 percent. Sampling error decreases as we move away from a 50/50 split, and it increases as the population has more heterogeneous political attitudes. But by far the most important factor is the size of the sample.

The importance of sample size for sampling accuracy can be easily demonstrated by flipping a coin. In theory we know if a coin is flipped honestly a large number of times it should come up about equal proportions of heads and tails. Suppose we flipped a coin ten times. Given a large number of repetitions of ten flips we might frequently get seven heads, eight tails, etc. But if instead of flipping the coin ten times we flipped it 100 times, then our large number of repetitions would only occasionally yield 70 heads or 80 tails, and if we flipped it 1,000 times, our repetitions could tend to cluster around 500 heads and 500 tails, with 700 heads or 800 tails being rare events indeed. The larger the size of the sample (i.e., the number of times the coin is flipped), the closer we will come to the theoretical expectation of one-half heads and one-half tails.

Unlike the size of the *sample*, the size of the population is of little consequence for the accuracy of the survey. That is, it does not make much difference if we are surveying the city of Houston or the entire United States. With a sample size of 600, the sampling error would be identical for both the city and the nation—all other things being equal.[3] Table 2.1 presents the sampling errors associated with specific sample sizes.

Note that when the sample size drops to around 150, the sampling error gets very large. While one rarely sees a public opinion survey of 150 people, one often sees survey subgroups (men, college-educated, blacks, Republicans, etc.) analyzed where the number of respondents falls below 150. For example, a poll done in Texas following the 1996 election showed Bob Dole leading Bill Clinton among partisan Independents by a margin of 45 to 39 percent.[4] However, there were only 107 respondents in that subsample. With a sampling error of 10 percent, all we know is that for Independents, somewhere between 35 and 55 percent favored Dole, and somewhere between 29 and 49 percent favored Clinton. To say that Dole led Clinton among Independents is not supported by the data. Dole's lead was in fact statistically insignificant (i.e., it could

**TABLE 2.1   SAMPLING ERROR AND SAMPLE SIZE
EMPLOYING SIMPLE RANDOM SAMPLING★**

Sample Size	Sampling Error (plus or minus)★
2,430	2.0
1,536	2.5
1,067	3.0
784	3.5
600	4.0
474	4.5
384	5.0
267	6.0
196	7.0
150	8.0
119	9.0
96	10.0
42	15.0

★This computation is based on the assumptions of a simple random sampling (SRS) with a dichotomous opinion that splits 50/50.

have occurred by chance). When reading reports about the politics of those under 30, the gender gap, the politics of the religious right, and similar topics that involve the analysis of subgroups, one should pay special attention to sample size. A difference of 5 or 6 percent can be quite *meaningful* in a subsample of 300, and quite *meaningless* in a subsample of 50.[5]

Applied Sampling and Surveys of Public Opinion

Using a large barrel of marbles and a table of random numbers, we drew a "perfect" sample. That is, the sampling method fit perfectly with the mathematics of sampling theory. When we sample humans we cannot draw a perfect sample. Although a marble cannot refuse to tell us if it is red or green, a person may refuse to be interviewed. Sampling theory does not allow for refusals. Consequently, surveys of public opinion only approximate the underlying theory of sampling. If these deviations from theory are modest, opinion polls can and do work well. But there are many instances in which sampling theory is ignored (or those conducting the polls are ignorant). If the poll simply concerns political opinions (favor/oppose abortion, approve/disapprove of tax reform, favor/oppose the registration of handguns), there is no reality test. The survey may have been done badly and be considerably off the mark, but how would one know?[6] On the other hand, preelection day surveys have a reality test: election day. In these surveys, sampling mistakes have, in several dramatic cases, cast opinion pollsters in a highly unfavorable light.

In the previous chapter we discussed the prescientific straw polls that were used to gauge candidate fortunes prior to 1936. The best-known of the commercial publications conducting straw polls was the *Literary Digest*. The *Digest* accurately forecast the winner (if not the exact percentage points) of each presidential election between 1920 and 1932. In 1936, as in previous years, it sent out some 10 million postcard ballots "drawn from every telephone book in the United States, from the rosters of clubs and associations, from city directories, lists of registered voters, [and] classified mail order and occupational data" (*Literary Digest*, August 1936, 3). About 2.2 million returned their postal ballots. The result was 1,293,699 (57 percent) for Republican Alf Landon and 972,867 (43 percent) for President Franklin Roosevelt. On election day, Roosevelt not only won but won by a landslide, receiving 62.5 percent of the vote and carrying every state except Maine and Vermont. The *Literary Digest* was not only wrong; it was wrong by 19.5 percent. On November 14, 1936, the *Literary Digest* published the following commentary:

WHAT WENT WRONG WITH THE POLLS?

None of Straw Votes Got Exactly the Right Answer—Why?

In 1920, 1924, 1928 and 1932, the *Literary Digest* Polls were right. Not only right in the sense they showed the winner; they forecast the actual popular vote and with such a small percentage of error (less than 1 percent in 1932) that newspapers and individuals everywhere heaped such phrases as "uncannily accurate" and "amazingly right" upon us. . . . Well this year we used precisely the same method that had scored four bull's eyes in four previous tries. And we were far from correct. Why? We ask that question in all sincerity, because *we want to know.*

Why did the poll fare so badly? One reason that can be discounted is sample size. The *Digest* claims to have polled 10 million people (and received 2.2 million responses). Thus a large sample is no guarantee for accuracy. Rather, their sampling procedure had four fundamental defects. First, the sample was drawn in a *biased* fashion. The *Digest* clearly did not use random selection or anything approaching it. Even though questionnaires were sent out to 10 million people, a large part of the sample was drawn from telephone directories and lists of automobile owners—during the Depression, a decidedly upper-middle-class group, predominantly Republican in its political sentiments. In other words, the *Digest* did not correctly specify the population. A second factor contributing to the *Digest*'s mistake was time. The questionnaires were sent out in early September, making impossible the detection of any late trend favoring one candidate or the other. Third, 1936 was the year that marked the emergence of the "New Deal Coalition." The *Digest* had picked the winner correctly since 1920 using the same methods as in 1936, but in 1936 voting became polarized along class lines. The working class and the poor voted overwhelmingly Democratic, while the more affluent classes voted predominantly Republican. Since the *Literary Digest*'s sample was heavily biased in the direction of the more affluent, it is not surprising that their sample tended to favor

Landon. Finally, there was the problem of self-selection. The *Digest* sent out its questionnaires by mail. Of the 10 million they mailed, only a little over 2 million responded—about 22 percent. Those people who self-select to respond to mail surveys are often quite different in their political outlooks from those who do not respond. They tend to be better educated, to have higher incomes, and to feel more strongly about the topics dealt with in the questionnaire (Dillman 1978). So even if the sample of 10 million had been drawn in an unbiased fashion, the poll probably still would have been in error due to the self-selection factor (Squire 1988). One very fundamental principle of survey sampling is that *one cannot allow the respondents to select themselves into the sample.*

Despite the failure of the *Literary Digest*, several public opinion analysts did pick Franklin Roosevelt as the winner. Among them was George Gallup, who built his reputation on a correct forecast in 1936. In terms of percentage, Gallup did not get particularly close. He missed by almost 7 percent. But he got the winner right, and that is what most people remember. He was, in fact, closer in 1948 (off by 5 percent) when he made his infamous prediction that Dewey would beat Truman—that, too, is well remembered.[7]

The technique used by Gallup in 1936 and up until the Dewey-Truman disaster is called *quota sampling*. This technique employs the census to determine the percentage of certain relevant groups in the population. For example, what percentage is male, Catholic, white, and college-educated? Within these groups interviewers are then assigned quotas. They must interview a certain percentage of women, a certain percentage with less than high school education, a certain percentage of blacks, etc. But there are few, if any, constraints as to which specific individuals in these groups are to be interviewed. Once the interviews are completed, the sample is weighted so that it will be representative of the population on those variables. If 15 percent of the population is male, high school-educated, and making over $25,000 a year, the sample will be weighted to reflect those proportions. The principal problem with quota sampling is a variation on the problem of self-selection. The interviewer has too much opportunity to determine who is selected for the sample. An interviewer who must get a specified number of "female blacks" may avoid certain areas of town or may get the entire quota from a single block. There is a natural tendency to avoid shabby residences, long flights of stairs, and homes where there are dogs. Experience with quota samples demonstrates that they systematically tend to underrepresent the poor, the less educated, and racial minorities.[8]

Research on Gallup's misprediction in 1948 reveals he had too many middle- and high-income voters.[9] A second factor contributing to Gallup's mistake was that he quit polling two weeks before the election (Bradburn and Sudman 1988, 29).[10] When significant movement takes place, it often occurs just before the election. For example, in 1980 Jimmy Carter and Ronald Reagan were virtually tied even the weekend before the vote. A strong move toward Reagan over the weekend allowed him to pile up a substantial victory. To capture these changes, Gallup and other survey organizations now poll right up to the day of the election.

Contemporary Sampling Methods

We used simple random sampling (SRS) to illustrate the principles involved in drawing a scientific sample. However, SRS is seldom used in actual public opinion surveys. There is no master list of all Americans that could be sampled. Even if there were, the persons selected would be widely scattered throughout the country, making in-person interviews prohibitively expensive. For example, an interviewer might have to travel all the way to Kerrville, Texas, just to talk to one respondent. Rather, polls where respondents are personally interviewed use *multistage cluster samples*.

The first step in drawing a multistage cluster sample of the American electorate is to divide the country into four geographic regions. Within each region, a set of counties and standard metropolitan statistical areas (SMSAs) is randomly selected. To insure a representative selection of the national population, each county or SMSA is given a chance to be selected proportional to its population (probability sampling). National surveys typically include about 80 primary sampling units (PSUs). Once selected, the PSUs are often used several years before they are replaced. The reason is economic: Compact geographic areas save time and money. Interviewers are expensive to train, but once trained they can be used over and over.

About 20 respondents are chosen within each PSU. First, four or five city blocks (or their rural equivalents) are randomly selected. Then, four or five households are sampled within each block.[11] It is at the household level that the continued use of probability methods becomes most difficult. Ideally the interviewer obtains a list of all persons living in the household and samples from the list. And indeed, some academic polls (such as the General Social Survey and the National Election Studies) attempt to meet this ideal. Most survey organizations, however, abandon probability methods at the block level and rely on some type of systematic method for respondent selection. The problem is that specific individuals are hard to locate. Interviewers are given a randomly drawn starting point and then instructed to stop at every *n*th household. The interviewer first asks to speak to the youngest man of voting age; if no man is at home the interviewer asks to speak to the youngest woman.[12] If both refuse or no one is home, the interviewer goes to the next adjacent dwelling. Each interviewer has a male/female quota and an age quota, but this is not a *quota sample* because the interviewer cannot choose who gets into the sample.

Multistage cluster samples work well and are an efficient compromise given the expense involved in a simple random sample approach. The drawback is that cluster samples have a greater sampling error than SRS, as would be expected since the respondents are "clustered" into 75 to 100 small geographic areas. A simple random sample of 1,000 has a 3 percent sampling error. Gallup reports that its national samples (cluster samples) of 1,000 have a 4 percent sampling error.

In recent years, in-person surveys have mostly been replaced by telephone surveys. The principal advantage of the telephone is its low cost. It also frees one from having to use clusters, as the physical location of a respondent is irrelevant in a phone survey. However, there are disadvantages as well. Nationwide, it is estimated that 37 percent of all phone numbers are unlisted. In some areas, like Los Angeles, unlisted numbers are estimated as high as 62 percent. Those most likely to have unlisted numbers are younger, low income, renters, and nonwhite households with children.[13]

The solution to this problem is to use a random-digit-dialing scheme. A ten-digit phone number is composed of an area code (the first three numbers), an exchange (the next three), a cluster (the next two), and the two final digits. If one knows the geographic assignment of area codes, exchanges, and clusters by the phone company (which will usually provide this information for a fee), a population can be defined and sampled. In large cities (for example, Houston, Texas), there are approximately 10,000 of these seven-digit codes. The following is an example:

713-496-78__ __

The first eight digits would be randomly sampled from the population of 10,000. Then the last two digits would be chosen from a table of random numbers or with a computer program that generates random digits. These methods allow persons with unlisted numbers to get into the sample. On the negative side, calls are made to a large number of nonworking numbers. But the sample is quite representative. Once the household is selected, it is then necessary to sample residents within the household. Sophisticated methods to insure random selection have been developed by statisticians, but they require an enumeration of all household members by age and sex—information many respondents are unwilling to provide over the phone. A simple alternative is the "next (or last) birthday" method. Interviewers ask to speak to the person who has the next birthday. This technique gives a good approximation of random sampling within the household (Lavrakas 1993).

Another problem with telephone surveys, although it applies to in-person surveys as well, is refusal. The telephone, however, particularly lends itself to abuse, as persons selling aluminum siding, upholstery, or "can't miss" real estate deals will sometimes attempt to gain a respondent's confidence by posing as a pollster. The sales pitch comes later. A study by the Roper Organization showed that 27 percent of a national sample had experienced these sales tactics (Turner and Martin 1984, 73).

People, especially those in large cities, are becoming wary of those claiming to be taking polls. Nonresponse is an increasing problem in survey research. It is currently estimated that the refusal rate for telephone surveys is 34 percent (Rothenberg 1990). Nonresponse, however, involves more than refusals. It includes any reason why the designated respondent is not interviewed, such as ring-no answer or contacting an answering machine. It is an essential part of good survey practice that all efforts be made to contact designated respondents. But unless one is willing to make a large number of call-backs, or attempt to convert refusals, nonresponse rates are typically quite high. For example, in 1996 the average response rate for the Harris Poll was 40 percent (Bogart, 1998), and for some polls the response rate may be as low as 20 percent (Taylor 1997; Van Natta 1999). Nonresponse is of consequence only if those sampled, but not interviewed, differ on *questions of interest* from those sampled and interviewed.

In an analysis of the NES and GSS, Brehm (1993) found nonresponse led to an overrepresentation of the elderly, blacks, women, the poor, and the less educated. For simple frequencies, this bias in response can be corrected by weighting the sample. For example, we know from research by the Bureau of the Census that African-Americans are 12 percent of the U.S. adult population. If our sample contained only 9 percent blacks, we can easily use weights to raise the percentage. But weights are not an entirely satisfactory solution, as those reluctant to participate may not share the same opinions as the more willing. A study by the Pew Research Center (Flemming and Parker 1997) showed few opinion differences between those readily willing to be interviewed versus those who were reluctant (who initially refused, but were recalled one or more times and convinced to participate). The two groups did, however, differ significantly on race-related questions. The reluctant respondents held views a good deal less sympathetic to the political and economic aspirations of African-Americans than did the willing respondents.[14]

Finally, the exact percentage of households with telephones is a question open to debate. It is certainly high, but how high? The 1990 Census reports that 95 percent of all households have phone service, although in five states the percentage falls below 90 percent, with Mississippi being the lowest at 87 percent. The Census also reports that 43 percent of homes without telephones are found in tracts where the median income is less than $20,000.[15] Thus, those without phones are found among the least affluent segments of society. This "lumpen proletariat" is one population subgroup that rarely finds its way into any survey, regardless of methodology.

Reputable studies of public opinion will provide an account of their sampling procedures. The better journals will usually have an insert labeled "How the Poll Was Conducted," which includes a discussion of sample size, dates of the interviews, sampling methods, weighting methods, sampling error for the entire sample, sampling error for key subgroups, and notice that beyond sampling error other types of errors can occur due to the practical difficulties of polling.[16]

2-2 QUESTION WORDING

It should surprise no one that in survey research, as in everyday life, the answers received are often dependent on the questions asked. This reality has both an upside and a downside for opinion polling. The upside is that people are sensitive to the way survey questions are phrased. That means they are paying reasonably close attention to what they are being asked, and their answers can be taken seriously. If changes in question wording had no impact, the opinion poll would likely be too blunt an instrument to be of much use. The downside is that since the distribution of public opinion can be a function of question wording, incorrect or inappropriate inferences about its true nature are easily possible. Not all variations in question phrasing affect the distribution of responses. But in some cases they clearly do. In this section we will review some of the aspects of question wording that can affect the distribution of opinion.

Multiple Stimuli Many questions have more than one stimulus to which respondents may react. Such questions are not faulty, but rather are often a necessary requirement for measuring opinions on complex topics. Examples of commonly used single-stimulus questions are: "Generally speaking, do you consider yourself a Democrat, an Independent, a Republican, or what?" or "Do you approve or disapprove of the way the president is handling his job?" But suppose we were interested in public support for the First Amendment right of free speech. We could ask people to agree or disagree with the statement, "I believe in free speech for all, no matter what their views might be." In 1978, 89 percent of opinion-holders agreed (Sullivan et al. 1982). But that tells us little other than in the abstract there is a near consensus on a fundamental principle of the American Creed. However, real controversies over free speech do not occur in the abstract, but in concrete circumstances. Thus we might ask, "Suppose an admitted Communist wanted to make a speech in your community. Should he be allowed to speak or not?" In 1991, only 68 percent of opinion-holders said the person should be allowed to speak. If the admitted Communist was teaching in a college, 43 percent said he should be fired. It is quite clear that in specific circumstances, people are responding to both the "free speech" stimulus and "Communist" stimulus. As we shall see, the level of support for free speech is a matter of considerable controversy (see Chapter 6).

There are many less obvious instances of multiple stimuli that can affect the distribution of opinion. One way is to preface the question with the name of an authoritative or admired person or institution. Consider the responses of white Americans to different phrasings of a question about the controversial policy of minority set-asides (Sniderman and Piazza 1993, 113).

Form A	Form B
Sometimes you hear it said there should be a law to ensure that a certain number of federal contracts go to minority contractors. Do you favor or oppose such a law?	The Congress of the United States—both the House of Representatives and the Senate—have passed a law to ensure that a certain number of federal contracts go to minority contractors. Do you favor or oppose such a law?

Form A		Form B	
Favor law	43%	Favor law	57%
Oppose law	57	Oppose law	43
	100%		100%

Invoking the symbol of the "law" in this question transforms the policy of set-asides from one backed by a minority of white respondents to one backed by a clear majority—a change that may not be trivial in the politics of affirmative action. The use of authoritative symbols will also provide a cue for the uncertain, decrease the "don't knows," and raise the percentage of those favorable and unfavorable among those who know little or nothing about the issue in question (Smith and Squire 1990).

Framing Effects By framing effects we mean the effect the previous content of the interview might have on a specific question. For example, respondents usually desire to be consistent in their answers. When asked in 1980 if "the United States should let Communist newspaper reporters from other countries come here and send back to their papers the news as they see it," 55 percent said yes. But if the question is preceded by one that asks whether "a Communist country like Russia should allow American newspaper reporters to come in and send back the news as they see it," then 75 percent favor letting Communist reporters into the United States (Schuman and Presser 1996, 27). Since most answered "yes" to allowing American reporters in (Communist) Russia, it is obviously inconsistent to bar Communist reporters in the United States. Returning to the abortion issue, general support for abortion will increase if a specific item with a high level of support is asked first. Thus if respondents are asked if abortion should be permitted "if there is a strong chance of serious defect in the baby" (84 percent say yes), general support for abortion is 13 percent greater than if the specific abortion item is not asked first (Schuman and Presser 1996, 37).

Other examples of framing effects include the questionnaire placement of presidential popularity or presidential vote items. Incumbent presidents do worse on both if the question comes late in a survey as opposed to early. The reason is that content of the interview reminds respondents of troublesome aspects of the incumbent's presidency (Sigelman 1981). Pocketbook voting (voting on the basis of changes in one's personal finances) can be induced by asking questions about finances immediately before ascertaining vote choice (Sears and Lau 1983). Finally, pollsters sometimes provide information on somewhat obscure topics before asking opinions about the topic. Suffice it to say, the content of the information provided in the stem of the question can easily affect the answer given.

Balanced Arguments If a question mentions only one side of a controversy, that side will often get a disproportionate number of responses. An example is: "Do you favor the death penalty?" Since only one option ("favor") is given, we might expect that option would be more frequently chosen than if the question is balanced—i.e., "Do you *favor* or *oppose* the death penalty?" The same is true for questions that use an "agree/disagree" format (called *Likert scales*). The common practice is to inform the respondent of both options.[17]

At best, however, agree/disagree questions never really present clues about the consequences of agreement or disagreement or the reasons one might choose a particular option. In the example below, providing balanced alternatives on a question about unemployment yields quite different results compared to an agree/disagree alternative (Cantril 1991, 126).

Form A		Form B	
Do you agree or disagree with this statement: Any able-bodied person can find a job and make ends meet?		Some people feel that any able-bodied person can find a job and make ends meet. Others feel there are times when it is hard to get along and some able-bodied people may not be able to find work. Whom do you agree with most?	
Agree	65%	Can make ends meet	43%
No opinion	10	No opinion	18
Disagree	25	Sometimes hard to get along	39
	100%		100%

If one wishes to describe the level of opinion, questions that present two polar alternatives are clearly superior to Likert-type questions (see the Appendix for examples used in the 1996 NES). Likert items are most useful for building scales or perhaps comparing subgroup differences. A single agree-disagree question is usually of little value for gauging the level of public opinion, although several taken in concert can often be quite useful (see Chapter 4 on abortion).

The Middle Position The public seldom splits into polar camps on any issue, and even when a middle position is not offered, many will volunteer an intermediate alternative. When a middle position is offered in a question, it is usually taken by many more people than when not offered. Schuman and Presser (1996, 166) demonstrate that when respondents are asked on political issues if they "are on the liberal side or the conservative side," 16 percent volunteer that they are "middle of the road." But if the "middle of the road" option is offered, it is taken by 54 percent. While there is little doubt about the consequence of offering a middle position (or an "unsure" or "undecided" option for issue questions), there is no consensus about the desirability of doing so. Some argue that most respondents do have a preference, albeit in some cases a weak one. Offering the middle alternative encourages certain respondents not to express their opinion.

Response Acquiescence Often when people are asked whether they agree or disagree with an abstract statement, or one about which they know little, they tend to agree rather than disagree. This tendency is called "response acquiescence." It arises mostly because the public is ill-informed and may not have genuine opinions on many issues (see Chapter 3). We can illustrate this by using a 1986 study of attitudes toward pornography. Respondents were asked whether they agreed or disagreed that "people should have the right to purchase a sexually explicit book, magazine, or movie, if that's what they want to do." Evidently, people saw this statement as a referendum on individual rights, since an overwhelming 80 percent agreed with the statement. However, in the same poll respondents were also asked whether they agreed or disagreed with the opposite statement, that "community authorities should be able to prohibit the selling of magazines or moves they consider to be pornographic." Sixty-five percent agreed with this opposite view as well.[18] Overall, a large number of respondents agreed that the public had a right to purchase pornographic materials, and also agreed that the community has the right to stop people from purchasing the same material. The most likely explanation of this contradiction is response acquiescence. These examples indicate the danger of using single Likert-type items to measure the level of public opinion. The best strategy for dealing with response acquiescence is to use two or more items where half are worded positively and half negatively. That is, to support free speech the respondent must agree with one statement and disagree with one another.

Filter Questions Most people believe that good citizens should have opinions on current political topics. Thus, when interviewed by polling organizations, they have a tendency to offer opinions on subjects about which they know little or nothing. In an otherwise conventional survey of the Cincinnati area, Bishop et al. (1980) included a question asking respondents whether the nonexistent "Public Affairs Act" should be kept or repealed. Eighteen percent thought it should be kept; 16 percent favored its repeal. Given these findings on a fictitious issue, it should not be surprising that on real but somewhat obscure issues many will offer opinions on matters about which they have no true attitude.

One way to reduce this problem is through the use of filter questions. Respondents are read a question and response alternatives and then asked, "Where would you place yourself on this scale, or haven't you thought much about this?" Using the 1996 NES question that asks people to indicate on a 1-to-7 scale if they feel more or less money should be spent on defense, 13 percent of the sample indicated they had not thought enough about the issue to have an opinion. But that does not mean that all the remaining 87 percent have a "true" attitude. Another 29 percent took the middle position on the scale. It seems likely some taking this position have either no attitude or one that is poorly developed.

One danger in using screening questions is that some people with real attitudes, but hesitant to express them, may be filtered out of surveys (Berinsky 1999). An alternative is to use branching questions, where those who say they are undecided or unsure are encouraged in follow-up probes to make a choice (T. Smith 1984; Krosnick and Kerent 1993). But, of course, this strategy runs the risk of eliciting opinions where no true underlying attitude exists.

Conclusion Variations in question wording can clearly influence the distribution of public opinion. That fact should be recognized and considered when using opinion data. Some questions are obviously biased (see next section). Read carefully the questions. What are the stimuli? Are authorities being invoked? Are inferences being made about the level of opinion from single Likert items? Are "no opinion" screens used on obscure issues? Are balanced questions truly presenting both options in a fair manner? All of these possibilities are cause for concern. Some types of inferences are more reliable than others. Multiple questions on the same issue can give insight into the range of opinion. But the most reliable strategy is to compare responses to the same question. Thus subgroup differences on the same question are usually quite meaningful. Even better is to compare change over time in response to the same question. Since the stimulus is identical, variation is likely due to a change in the public's view.

2-3 THE MISUSE OF SURVEYS

Back before the advent of probability sampling, the media attempted to measure public sentiment by using "straw polls." The principal defect of straw polls, like those conducted by the *Literary Digest*, is the ability of respondents to "select themselves" to be counted in the poll. As a consequence, there is no way of assessing the sampling error. The factors by which a person gets into the sample are unknown. One might think that with the advent of modern survey methodology, straw polls would have disappeared. Not so. They are in fact alive and well—and most are as unreliable now as they were in the 1930s.

Modern Straw Polls

A natural poll that receives a fair amount of media play consists of letters to the president (the media also sometimes pick up on letters to Congress). When a national crisis occurs that is generally perceived as presenting the president in a poor light, the White House will frequently report that "the mail" is running 10 to 1, 5 to 1, etc. in favor of the president. When Special Prosecutor Archibald Cox was fired during the Watergate scandal, the Nixon White House reported that the mail was running more than 2 to 1 in favor of the president's actions. Many in the Senate and House of Representatives, on the other hand, reported that their mail was running overwhelmingly in opposition to the president's action. A lesser crisis early in the Clinton administration provides a somewhat different example. In response to the revelation that President Clinton's first nominee for attorney general, Zoe Baird, had employed illegal aliens for child care, mail to U.S. senators was running more than 400 to 1 in opposition. On the other hand, an ABC/*Washington Post* poll done at the same time showed a more modest 58 percent opposed to her confirmation (Clymer 1993). Letters of this sort are basically meaningless as an indication of public sentiment. We know that those who "self-select" to write to public officials overwhelmingly tend to write to those whom they feel are sympathetic. If people like the president and support him in a controversy, they will write to the White House. If they are hostile, they will write to someone else, such as their senator or representative, or not at all.

Another common straw poll involves surveys sent out by public officials or various partisan organizations. These are sometimes published by the media, heralded in bold headlines as if they constituted a reasonable assessment of public opinion. For example, a story in the *Houston Chronicle* carried the following headline: "Survey Here Shows Opposition to President's Energy Program." The "survey" turned out to be responses to 200,000 questionnaires mailed out by Houston area Republican Congressman Bill Archer. There were a total of 43,010 responses to this mailout, or about 22 percent (about the same response to the *Literary Digest* poll). The poll also reported that respondents favored production of the B-1 Bomber and retention of "right to work laws."[19] Suffice it to say, a survey of this sort measures virtually nothing. It is severely contaminated by self-selection. There is no way to compute sampling error, given the bias in the way respondents got into the sample. While the information might be valuable to Congressman Archer as an indication of what his attentive constituents think, it has little or no value as a measure of public opinion.

A variety of partisan organizations sometimes claim they are assessing "public opinion" by using mail surveys, often in combination with highly biased questions. For example, a questionnaire from the Democratic National Committee with a return date of October 16, 1995 (in time for the presidential campaign), included the following items:

- Do you favor or oppose Republican proposals to dismantle Head Start and programs that provide health care and nutrition to young mothers in poverty?
- Republican leaders are advocating a welfare reform plan that would end welfare benefits to single parents who cannot find work and spend the money on orphanages to house their children. Do you support or oppose this approach?

Even more biased is a question in a newsletter poll sent by then–Democratic Congressman John Dowdy of Texas which asked the following question (Morin 1997):

A drive has recently been announced to destroy the independence of Congress by purging Congressmen who refuse to be rubber stamps for the executive arm of government. Would you want your representative in Congress to surrender to the purge threat and become a rubber-stamped Congressman?

In April 1993, Ross Perot paid $190,000 to *TV Guide* to have a 17-question survey inserted in the magazine (Kolbert 1993). The questions were clearly slanted in a fashion to reflect his personal views on American politics. For example:

- Should we eliminate foreign lobbyists completely—no loopholes—and make it a criminal offense?
- Should laws be passed to eliminate all possibilities of special interests giving huge sums of money to candidates?

Given the highly loaded questions, it should come as no surprise that Perot supporters would be more likely to detect the "correct" answer and then return the questionnaire than those who preferred other candidates.[20] These polls have many of the same defects as the mail surveys that are periodically conducted by *Playboy* and *Penthouse* about sexual habits.[21] There is a great like-lihood that those willing to divulge information about their sex lives will dif-fer in important ways from those who are unwilling. Mail surveys are not always meaningless, but they must be conducted with great care by people with specialized training. Most that are done correctly are published in aca-demic journals and their findings rarely show up in the popular media.

Regrettably, television, including highly regarded network news programs, has gotten into the straw poll business. Television journalism is a combination of news and entertainment, and often in the competition for ratings, enter-tainment takes precedence over hard news. That was certainly the case in 1992 when CBS News ran a program immediately following President Bush's State of the Union address, called "America On Line." The idea was to provide pro-gram viewers with a toll-free number that they could call and respond to a short survey (mostly about the state of the economy). More than 24 million citizens attempted to call, of which about 315,000 got through. Simultane-ously another "scientific" poll was being conducted, also for use on the pro-gram.[22] However, the anchors frequently referred to the call-in poll as though it was a representative survey. The poll was introduced by Dan Rather as "tak-ing the public pulse." Based on call-in results, Connie Chung reported that "53 percent were worse off [financially] than four years ago. It's important here to note that this is quite dramatic." She explained to Dan Rather that only a month ago a periodic CBS News poll had found only 30 percent claiming to be "worse off." According to Chung, "This does not bode well for President Bush on his night of the State of the Union." Of course, the 53 percent to which Chung referred was meaningless as a measure of public opinion. Al-though not mentioned on the show, it was later revealed that the companion "scientific" survey showed only 32 percent "worse off" than four years ago (Tierney 1992).

Following harsh criticism from the professional polling community, the executive director of ABC News vowed that call-in polls would not be used in the future due to their nonrepresentative nature (*New York Times*, 6 July 1987, 15). That promise, however, was not kept. Call-in polls are now a regular fea-ture on television news programs, including ABC's *Nightline* (Brady and Orren 1992).[23] The program host usually introduces these polls with a disclaimer that "we don't pretend the results are scientific, but here's what we found." Viewers should treat that statement as the equivalent of "certain bored people with strong feelings on some subjects are willing to pay a long-distance charge to register their views in a poll that means nothing. Here are the results."

A highly unethical polling innovation called "push polls" began to appear in the mid-1990s. The "interviewers" for these pseudopolls are actually paid workers for political candidates posing as if they were doing legitimate public opinion research. In fact, their job is to damage the electorate prospects of opposing candidates. Thus, if a respondent supports candidate Smith, she is told, "would you still support him if you knew he voted to raise your income tax?" The purpose of this question is not to gain information for analysis but to weaken the respondent's support for Smith under the guise of a legitimate public opinion poll. Push polls have mostly been used in congressional races, but 1996 Republican presidential candidate Bob Dole used them during the primary elections. Push polls have been declared "an unethical campaign practice" by the American Association for Public Opinion Research.

2-4 INTERPRETING SCIENTIFIC SURVEYS

Polls that are correctly executed do not always "predict" the actual election-day winner. Polls taken at the same time will sometimes show conflicting numbers. Occasionally the numbers will swing wildly over a short period of time. These characteristics do not necessarily mean the polls are defective, but they do require explanation.

Preelection Surveys

The media tend to attribute more accuracy to preelection polls as "predictors" of the election-day outcome than even the best-designed polls can possibly deliver. First, an obvious point. Preelection polls refer to sentiment at the time they are conducted, not on election day. The "horse race" analogy commonly used to discuss elections is, in this case, appropriate. The horse that is ahead going into the stretch is not always the horse (or the candidate) that wins. But even given the overall trend, there are still "house effects"[24]—variations in survey results due to idiosyncratic ways in which different survey organizations conduct their polling. For example, there is surprisingly great variation in the way the candidate choice question is asked in presidential elections.[25] Thus we frequently find the polls at some variance with one another during the campaign due to question-wording effects. In fact, in an analysis of preelection polls in 1996, Erikson and Wlezien (1999) show most of the movement in these polls, a subject of much interpretation by the popular media, is nothing more than survey error—due to house effects and routine sampling error.

We see examples of these house effects in Figure 2.1, which presents the final polls between 1980 and 1996, as reported by the major survey houses. Note in the last two elections all the major survey firms (save Zogby in 1996) overestimated the Clinton vote. This overestimate has led some to claim there is a "Democratic bias" in the presidential preelection polls. One observer calculates that the odds of seven out of eight polls being as much in error as they were in 1996 on a chance basis is 9,800 to 1. Others have argued that what we see in 1996 is pro-incumbent bias rather than a pro-Democratic bias, a pattern that has appeared in six of the last eight elections (Morin 1996). A more plausible explanation is that Dole supporters, being better educated with higher incomes, were more likely to turn out on election day than Clinton supporters.

Nevertheless, the reason why the polls can differ so much over the course of the campaign, up to and including the weekend before the election, merits explanation. Typically 15 percent or more of the electorate is undecided during

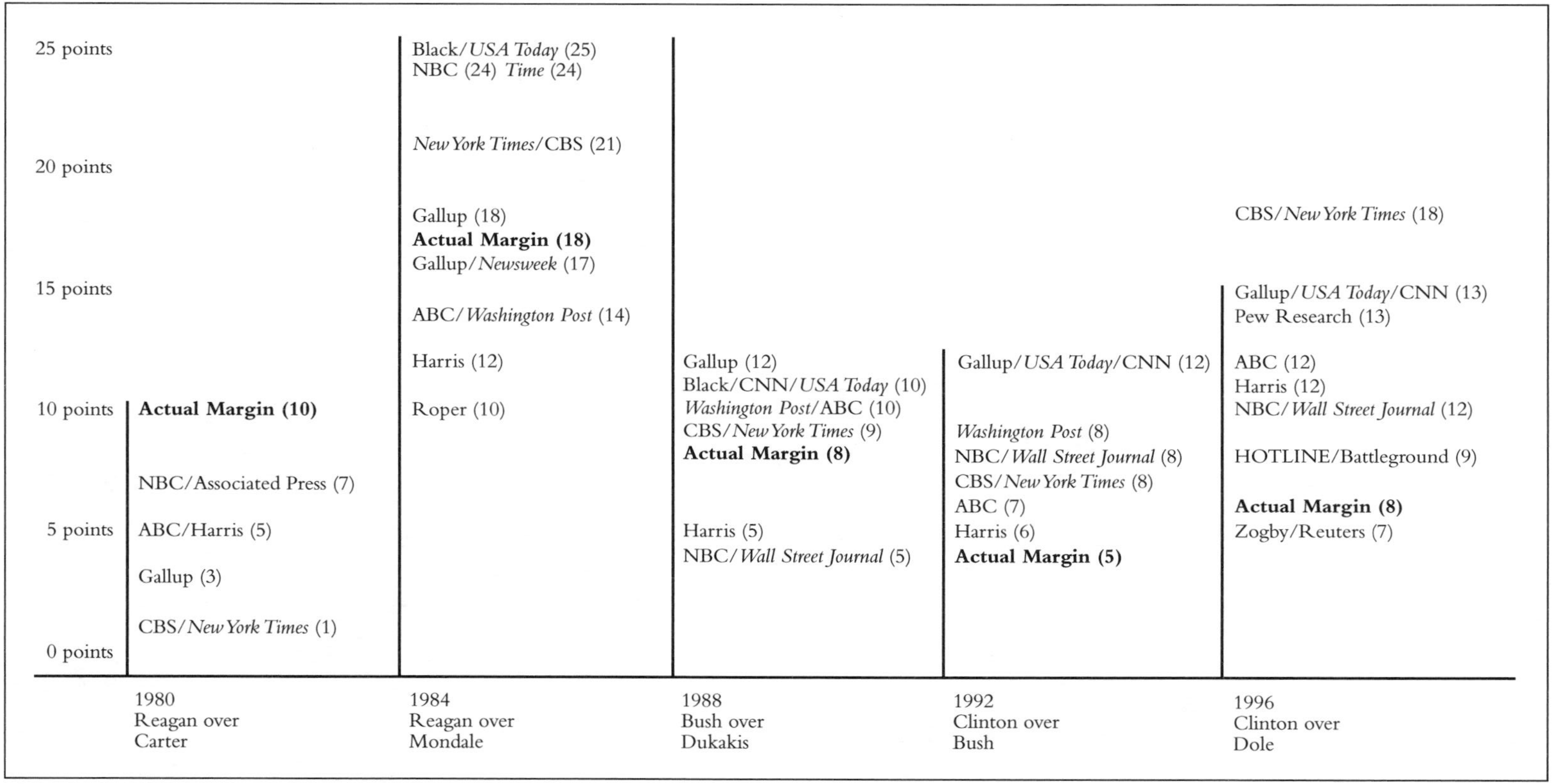

Figure 2.1 Two-party candidate margins in final preelection polls by survey house.

Points	1980 Reagan over Carter	1984 Reagan over Mondale	1988 Bush over Dukakis	1992 Clinton over Bush	1996 Clinton over Dole
25 points		Black/USA Today (25) NBC (24) Time (24)			
20 points		New York Times/CBS (21)			
18 points		Gallup (18) **Actual Margin (18)** Gallup/Newsweek (17)			CBS/New York Times (18)
14 points		ABC/Washington Post (14)			
13 points					Gallup/USA Today/CNN (13) Pew Research (13)
12 points		Harris (12)	Gallup (12)	Gallup/USA Today/CNN (12)	ABC (12) Harris (12) NBC/Wall Street Journal (12)
10 points	**Actual Margin (10)**	Roper (10)	Black/CNN/USA Today (10) Washington Post/ABC (10) CBS/New York Times (9) **Actual Margin (8)**		HOTLINE/Battleground (9)
8 points				Washington Post (8) NBC/Wall Street Journal (8) CBS/New York Times (8)	**Actual Margin (8)**
7 points	NBC/Associated Press (7)			ABC (7) Harris (6) **Actual Margin (5)**	Zogby/Reuters (7)
5 points	ABC/Harris (5)		Harris (5) NBC/Wall Street Journal (5)		
3 points	Gallup (3)				
1 point	CBS/New York Times (1)				

Sources: Michael R. Kagay, "Why Even Well-Designed Polls Can Disagree," in Thomas Mann and Gary Orren, eds., *Media Polls in American Politics* (Washington, D.C.: Brookings, 1992); Robert M. Worcester, "A View from Britain: You Can Do Better," *The Public Perspective* 4 (Nov./Dec. 1992); *The Public Perspective*, 8 (Dec./Jan. 1997: 52 (corrected table).

a presidential campaign (the figure is much higher for lower-level races), winding down to 5 to 8 percent a few days before the balloting. Survey houses differ in the way they handle these undecideds.[26] While common sense might dictate a simple reporting of candidate preferences plus undecideds, most media polls do not follow that strategy. If voters claim to be "unsure," they are pressed in a follow-up question to indicate which candidate they "lean to." Voters who maintain they are in fact really "undecided" must be quite firm in their conviction in the face of pressure to make a choice. The inevitable result of this strategy is a sizable swing in candidate preferences, mostly accounted for by those forced to make a choice when their initial reaction was "undecided" (Crespi 1988; Moore 1992b).

Another practice common to media polls is allocating the "undecideds" to one candidate or the other. If the undecideds *are not* split, there is an implicit assumption that either they will not vote, or will vote in proportion to those who have decided. As one approaches the election, there is often a momentum that favors one of the candidates—the undecideds do not split 50/50. This flow of the undecideds was one reason Truman beat Dewey (the last Gallup Poll showed that 19 percent of the electorate was undecided). It is also the reason that Richard Nixon squeaked out a win of less than 1 percent over Hubert Humphrey in 1968, when the polls had shown Nixon with a 15-point lead in the final weeks of the campaign. And it is the reason Ronald Reagan soundly defeated Jimmy Carter in 1980, when polls showed the contest to be very close, and why Ross Perot performed better in 1992 and 1996 than almost all preelection polls indicated.

If undecideds in preelection polls do not split evenly on election day, how then is one to allocate them before the election? There is no one correct answer for all circumstances. Sometimes the undecideds are reported as just that— "undecided." However, the poll will then underestimate the percentage of the vote going to a candidate who has momentum. Sometimes undecided respondents are asked to rate candidates on a 0 to 10 scale. The undecideds will be allocated to the candidate they like best. If there is a tie on that question, party identification is used to assign the undecideds to a candidate.[27] Other polls exclude the undecideds altogether and base their preelection forecasts only on those voters willing to make a choice.[28] In 1992, the Gallup Poll, in particular, engaged in some very dubious practices in assigning the undecideds. On the weekend before the election, it assigned all the undecideds in its tracking poll to Clinton, causing Clinton's lead to grow from 2 points on Friday to 12 points on Monday. Gallup made this decision based on electoral history, which suggested that most undecideds in a presidential election vote for the challenger. But in 1992, rather than moving to Clinton, the undecideds moved to another challenger, Ross Perot (Morin 1992).

Allocating undecideds in a contest that pits a black candidate against a white candidate causes particular problems, and polls in a number of races have greatly overestimated the proportion of the vote going to the black candidate. Studies of a number of such races now suggest the best strategy is simply to assign all the undecided voters (who normally are almost entirely white) to the white candidate. What seems to be operating is a cross-pressure in which some white Democrats are reluctant to vote for a black candidate and declare to pollsters that they are undecided. On election day, however, they vote Republican (Morin 1991; Davis 1997).

Perhaps the most fundamental problem with pre–election-day polls as predictors is an inability to define the population properly. Recall that a random sample must be drawn from a finite population. But it is impossible to define the election-day population. Only about one-half of adult Americans vote in presidential elections. No one has yet determined a method that, with any degree of accuracy, predicts who will vote. Yet it is those election-day voters who constitute the population, not adult Americans or even registered voters. In a preelection survey in 1996, the Pew Research Center asked a national sample of those over 18 if they were "absolutely certain," "fairly certain," or "not certain" to vote in the upcoming election for president.[29] Here are the results:

Absolutely certain	69%
Fairly certain	18
Not certain/unsure	13
	100%

Actual turnout in 1996 was about 49 percent. But specific issues can boost election turnout in a fashion not anticipated by pollsters. For example, in 1997 an initiative to ban affirmative action in Houston, on the ballot along with the contest for mayor, increased the total proportion of the black electorate from a typical 25 percent to 35 percent. This 10 percent increase in the African-American vote over the historical pattern caused preelection polls and exit polls to substantially underestimate the vote totals for African-American mayoral candidate (and ultimate winner) Lee Brown.

Screens are of consequence for poll results. The tougher the screen in terms of weeding out potential nonvoters, the greater the support for Republican candidates. For example, in surveys taken in 1992 between August 26 and 31, a *Washington Post*/ABC News Poll had Clinton leading Bush by 19 percent, while a Harris Poll had Clinton ahead by only two percentage points. The *Washington Post* Poll used an easy "registered voter" screen—that is, the interviewer simply asked the respondent if he or she was registered. The Harris Poll used a battery of "tough" screens to identify "likely voters" and weed out nonvoters. Surveys with the tougher screen not unexpectedly showed a higher proportion favoring George Bush in 1992 and Bob Dole in 1996 than favored Bill Clinton (Lipset 1992; Taylor 1997). In 1992, one week before the election the Gallup Poll changed its screen from the "easy" registered voter question to a much tougher "likely voter" screen. This change in the definition of the population cut about 4 points from Bill Clinton's margin over George Bush in the CNN/*USA Today* tracking poll conducted by Gallup. One can debate whether this surge by Bush was an illusion due to the change in the screen (and thus a change in the definition of the population), a real gain by the president, or both (Hugick and Molyneux 1993; Erikson 1993; Ferree 1993). But

the important point is that the type of screen can have an important consequence for a poll result.[30]

It is, by the way, the use of screens to define likely voters (plus weighting
factors) that allows a pollster working for Democratic candidate Smith to say
his client is ahead while the pollster working for Republican candidate Jones
says her client is ahead. Neither has "faked" the numbers; rather they disagree
on the probable composition of election-day voters. The Republican pollster
sees a big turnout among affluent whites; the Democratic pollster sees an atyp-
ically high minority turnout. As one prominent pollster observes:

> I think there is a little bit of Julia Child in every pollster. There is an impulse
> to cook things in a way most favorable to [your] candidate. People do not
> want to carry bad news. So there is a tendency, if you're a Democratic poll-
> ster, to weight black respondents at their proportion of registered voters even
> though there is a lot of historic data that the black turnout is disproportion-
> ately lower.[31]

Election-Day Exit Polls

An important innovation in opinion polling is use of the exit poll. Representative precincts are selected within an electoral district, and voters are
interviewed immediately after leaving the voting booth. These polls are com-
missioned by the news media so they can "project" the winner of a contest
early on election day, and understand the demographic and issue correlates of
the vote choice. Prior to 1990, all three networks conducted their own exit
polls. There was often a lively competition among them to see which could be
the first to "call" the election-day winner. The expense of this operation led
the networks, along with CNN and the Associated Press, to pool resources
and create a single polling unit, Voter News Service (VNS), which now does
all the election-day exit polling. Consequently, all networks now rely on a single source for exit poll information, which has somewhat diminished the
"news value" of an immediate presentation of the results.

Exit polls could usually project the winner of a statewide election by 3:00
P.M., even though the polls do not normally close until 7:00 P.M. The media
have, however, agreed not to release the results of exit polling in a specific state
until the polls in that state have closed. But when the winner is forecast in the
East Coast and Midwestern states in a presidential election, the polls will re-
main open for several hours on the West Coast (due to different time zones).
The polls were still open in 11 states when CBS News first projected that Vice-
President Bush had won the 1988 presidential election (*New York Times,* 10
Nov. 1989, 17). In 1980, Jimmy Carter actually conceded the election to
Ronald Reagan based on network projections while voting was still in progress
in the West. The effect on West Coast voters of learning these election results
has been the subject of lively controversy.

The claim is that voters in the West, having heard the election winner projected by the networks, will be less likely to go to the polls. While it is true

these voters cannot affect the outcome of the presidential contest, there are many other contests on the ballot that could be affected by a drop-off in voter participation. Research on this question is mixed. Based on a study of the 1980 election, John Jackson concluded that the exit polls and Carter's early concession resulted in a turnout decline of 6 to 12 percent—to the detriment of down-the-ticket Democrats—in those states where the polls were still open.[32] The data show conclusively that those who had heard the early projections were more likely to abstain from voting than were those who had not heard these projections. However, this simple relationship begs the question of cause and effect. Was the turnout differential due to those hearing the projection not voting? Or is the explanation for the fact those who *did not* hear the projection voted in greater numbers than those did hear explained by the fact that they were occupied at the voting booth when the projections were made?

There have been many calls for the media to voluntarily restrain from projecting the winner until voting is finished in all states. Congress has held hearings on the subject, and there are numerous calls for legislation requiring the polls to stay open for the same hours in the contiguous 48 states. Some states have tried to make it difficult for exit pollsters to do their work by restricting how close they can get to the voting booth. Such laws have been invalidated by federal courts. The networks argue that any government-imposed limitations on exit polls would constitute censorship and violate the First Amendment.

2-5 CONCLUSION

During the 1930s, 1940s, and 1950s, public opinion polls received little attention from the mass media. Reporters saw pollsters as potential competitors—given the technical nature of their subject, they might want a byline of their own. Those fears have now largely subsided, although, as we noted in the chapter's introduction, poll-bashing is still a frequent phenomenon in the media. Polls are ubiquitous, and commentary on public opinion is fair game for all. Attempts to mislead deliberately occur, but they are not frequent. Rather, the key to understanding polls is a realization that the numbers do not speak for themselves; they require interpretation. Among the keys to that interpretation are how the sample was selected, how the questions were phrased, an appreciation for the context in which the survey was conducted, and a comparison to other surveys taken at the same time or an analysis of trends over time.

NOTES

1. The quote from Nixon comes from *Time* magazine, reported in Crespi (1989, 27).
2. Strictly speaking in terms of statistical theory, if the poll were repeated an infinite number of times, in 95 percent of the trials, the result would be between 66 and 72 percentage points.
3. National samples are usually larger than state or local samples because one other factor that affects sampling error is variation, and there is likely to be more variation

in attributes measured nationally, as opposed to those in a geographically smaller area. Also, those conducting national samples are often interested in looking at subgroups (e.g., blacks or women). The larger the sample, the lower the sampling error when doing a subgroup analysis.

4. The data are from a 1996 postelection survey in Texas done by the Public Affairs Research Center at the University of Houston.

5. From a technical standpoint, the real question is whether or not the differences are statistically significant. A subsample of 50 showing a larger difference than for our example may surpass commonly accepted levels of statistical significance.

6. One's suspicions are aroused, however, if polls on the same topic at about the same time with similarly worded questions show quite different results.

7. Lest we complacently assume the polls inevitably get more accurate, it should be noted that with the wealth of polls in 1996, some of the final predictions were in the range of accuracy of the infamous Gallup misprediction of Dewey over Truman in 1948. Gallup had Dewey at 49.5 percent and Truman at 44.5 percent (with 6 percent going to minor party candidates). The vote in fact was Truman 49.5 percent and Dewey 45.1 percent, with others getting 5.4 percent. But Gallup in 1948 got the winner wrong, while the *New York Times*/CBS got the winner right in 1996, so its wide-of-the-mark forecast will likely be forgotten. The Roper Poll in 1948 was even further off the mark than Gallup. Roper had Dewey at 52.2 percent and Truman at 37.1 percent (with 10.7 percent going to minor party candidates).

8. While quota samples have been abandoned by major survey houses in the United States, virtually all surveys done in Britain and many other European countries rely only on quota samples. In fact, all 56 preelection polls done prior to the 1992 British general election were based on quota samples. That election was, of course, a major embarrassment to British polling—on the order of Gallup's famous 1948 misprediction that Dewey would beat Truman. And, like Gallup in 1948, the misprediction of a close election by British pollsters (the Conservatives won easily by a margin of 7.6 percent over Labour) can be attributed to the inherent shortcomings of quota samples (Jowell et al. 1993).

9. In his book *The Superpollsters* (1992a), David Moore interviewed a number of those who worked as field staff for Gallup during the days he used quota samples, and provides an interesting firsthand account of the hazards and biases of allowing the interviewers leeway in selecting respondents.

10. It should be noted that Gallup was not the only national pollster to mispredict the 1948 election. The other well-known national polls, the Crossley Poll and the Roper Poll, both had Dewey ahead of Truman. One suspects that the same sort of sampling errors that afflicted Gallup afflicted these other polls as well, since they used essentially the same methodology (Bradburn and Sudman 1988, 29).

11. For a more detailed discussion of sampling by the NES or GSS, see the sampling appendix that is usually included with each codebook.

12. Interviewers usually ask for the youngest male or female because they are the least likely to be home. However, if a sufficient number meeting specified age and sex distributions are met, interviewers will then ask for the oldest male or the oldest female.

13. Among some groups, the proportion of unlisted phone numbers is quite high. For those under 34 years of age, it is 51 percent; for blacks, it is 55 percent; for Hispanics, it is 58 percent; and for renters, it is 54 percent. This information comes from *Genesys News* (spring 1996), published by Genesys Sampling Systems of Fort

Washington, Pennsylvania, and *The Frame* (March 1933), published by Survey Sampling of Westport, Connecticut. Both are commercial sampling firms.

14. The Pew Research Center conducted two surveys of 1,000 adults, one rigorous and the other less rigorous. The rigorous survey spanned an eight-week period. In addition, respondents were sent advance letters announcing the survey, offered a small monetary gift for participating, and those refusing were recontacted to persuade them to participate. The response rate was 79 percent. The less rigorous survey was conducted over five days and had a response rate of 65 percent. The response rate of 65 percent for the less rigorous survey is still, however, a good deal higher than many critics contend is currently the case for atypical media surveys. Almost all major polling organizations refuse to disclose their response rates, so the exact response rates are difficult to know.

15. *The Frame,* March 1993. The other states falling below 90 percent are New Mexico, Arkansas, West Virginia, and Kentucky.

16. For a good review of the methods used by the major polling organizations, see Voss, Gelman, and King (1995).

17. The evidence is that using only "agree" or "favor" in a question as opposed to a balanced form of the question often makes no difference. Nevertheless, it sometimes makes a difference, and it is easy to write balanced questions using these types of formats (Schuman and Presser 1996, 181–82).

18. A 1986 *Time*/Yankelovich Survey, cited in "Opinion Roundup," *Public Opinion,* Sept./Oct. 1986:32.

19. Reported in the *Houston Chronicle,* 8 Oct. 1977:3. More recently, in another mail survey by Congressman Archer, the *Houston Chronicle* ran a front-page story asserting "Bush's Popularity Falls in Own Houston District." The story reported that only 43 percent of the residents in his old highly Republican district approved of his job performance when national approval rates were around 50 percent Archer mailed out 250,000 questionnaires and received 18,000 in return (stamps were not provided) (Bernstein 1992). Most likely the low ratings were due to those in the hard-pressed oil industry self-selecting to vent their frustration. In the 1992 election, Bush carried the district by a wide margin.

20. In the case of the Perot poll, CNN conducted a poll in which half the sample was asked the Perot version of the question (80 percent said "yes") and the other half was asked a more neutral version, which read "Should laws be passed to prohibit interest groups from contributing to campaigns, or do groups have the right to contribute to candidates they support?" In this latter version, only 40 percent said laws preventing contributions should be passed (Kolbert 1993).

21. Another example of this type of survey are those done by pop psychologist Shere Hite. Hite has published a number of books on the sexual and romantic relationships between men and women. For *Women and Love, a Cultural Revolution in Progress* (Hite, 1987), she mailed out 100,000 questionnaires to women selected from the mailing lists of a variety of women's organizations. She received 4,500 responses (4.5 percent). Given the self-selection problem (women most likely to respond were those who had unsatisfactory romantic relationships), some of the "findings" were quite surprising. For example, Hite reported that 75 percent of the women in her study married more than five years had extramarital affairs. A survey by ABC News/*Washington Post,* using conventional sampling methods, found 7 percent of women reported extramarital affairs. The ABC poll was reported in the *Houston Chronicle* (27 Oct. 1987, p. 2, sec. 1).

22. This "scientific" poll was a panel back from a survey of 2,800 respondents that CBS/*New York Times* had conducted two weeks previously. These respondents were also provided with a (different) toll-free number and asked to call back immediately after the State of the Union address. The response rate from the original panel was only 43 percent, casting considerable doubt on the validity of the "scientific" survey used in the program (Frankovic 1992).

23. For a discussion of the continued use of call-in polls by *Nightline* and other news organizations, see Cantril (1991, 144–46). Call-in polls have even found their way to PBS, where in February 1992, MacNeil/Lehrer Productions produced a three-part series, "America on Trial." Proponents of varying agendas made their case in a courtroom-style setting. After the program, viewers were asked to respond as "jurors" on the question of the evening and dial one toll-free number to record a "yes" or another toll-free number to record a "no" (Cantril 1992).

24. For a good analysis of house effects on other errors in preelection polling, see Crespi (1988).

25. For a list of the way the major polling firms ask this question, see Crespi (1988, ch. 5).

26. The option of "unsure" is usually not offered to respondents. Rather, they are asked to choose between or among the candidates (Moore 1992b).

27. This practice of pushing undecideds to make a choice is defended by Frank Newport, editor-in-chief of the Gallup Poll, in the following words: "[I]f pollsters allow voters the explicit option to call themselves 'unsure' about their vote, the number of reported undecideds would jump. All major polling organizations, however, eschew this structure because it would make polling less valuable and less interesting. Most voters, when asked in which direction they lean, have a preference and are willing to express it. It would not be very instructive . . . to allow large numbers of voters to claim they are undecided through the election season. We would miss the dynamics of change, we would be unable to tell how well the candidates were doing in response to events, and publicly released polls would be out of synchronization with private, campaign polls" (Letter to the editor, *New York Times,* 6 Nov. 1992, sec. A).

28. Irving Crespi, "Letter to the Editor," *New York Times* (7 Sept. 1988, sec. A).

29. The Pew Research Center for the People and the Public. News Release (2 Aug. 1996).

30. The same is true for the number of callbacks. If a respondent cannot be located on the first call, it is standard practice to make another two or three attempts to contact the person before replacement. Research by Gallup has shown that the more callbacks used by a survey house, the more Republican the sample. In other words, substitution of the appropriate respondent by a new respondent biases the sample in a Democratic direction. This finding means that "overnight" surveys, in which only one call is made to a specific person, may have some serious biases (Cantril 1992, 102).

31. The quote is from Harrison Hickman, of Hickman and McWheter, a polling firm that works predominantly for Democrats. See Edward Walsh, "Polls Are Telling Us More, But Are They Telling It Like It Is?" (*Washington Post,* 13 Apr. 1987, natl. ed., p. 37).

32. For arguments that exit polls do affect turnout, see Jackson (1983) and Delli Carpini (1984). For a study arguing there is no effect on early projections, see Epstein and Strom (1984).

CHAPTER 3

Microlevel Opinion: The Psychology of Opinion-Holding

In theory, democracy works best when the people actively attend to public affairs—ideally, when they direct policymakers toward the problems most deserving of attention and actively monitor their deliberations. In this best of all worlds, people might disagree among themselves, but their opinions would be soundly reasoned and logically consistent. Their preferences would transcend conflict among self-interested parties, to reflect a concern for the general welfare.

In actuality, public opinion falls considerably short of this ideal. As early survey researchers explored the nature of public opinion, they found several reasons for pessimism. For instance, respondents often express preferences so thoughtless as to arguably be too shallow for consideration as meaningful opinions. The opinions that people do hold sometimes seem like unconnected preferences in no logical relationship to one another. Where predictability exists, opinions often flow from disturbing prejudices rather than thoughtful consideration. Often it appears that political leaders find it all too easy to manipulate political symbols in such a way as to fool a politically gullible mass public.

Although recent discussions of the capabilities of mass opinion vary in theoretical perspectives, they find some significant reason for optimism. (Compare Page and Shapiro 1992; Zaller 1992; Miller and Shanks 1996; Delli Carpini and Keeter 1996; Fishkin 1996; and Alvarez 1997.) Many ordinary people do stay politically informed and can be considered to be politically sophisticated. Actually, it may seem remarkable that people hold political opinions at all. Why, we might ask, do people bother to develop and maintain political opinions when the time spent on politics might be better devoted to dealing with matters that affect their private lives? Since most of our political involvement is as passive spectators watching helplessly on the sidelines, why do we not only pay attention but invest time and effort developing opinions? Indeed, a strong argument can be made that if the main purpose of following politics is to affect policy outcomes, staying informed and thinking about politics is, from a cost/benefit perspective, an irrational investment (Downs 1958).

Since many people are sufficiently political to have ignored such advice, political opinions must be of some benefit to the people who hold them. It has long been recognized that holding political opinions serves several positive psychological functions (Smith et al. 1956). Opinions can serve a social function—for instance, when people learn to agree with the prevailing views within their preferred social groups. Opinions can serve a direct psychological function—when political opinions follow as an extension of personality. An often cited example is the person who seeks an ordered and disciplined personal environment being more susceptible to authoritarian political ideologies (Altmeyer 1997). Opinions can also promote economic self-interest—when people develop political opinions consistent with their economic standing as rich or poor. Sometimes people develop elaborate ideologies to rationalize their economic status—when rich people adopt a conservative economic ideology to justify the wealth they have accumulated.

As one would expect, opinions often reflect self-interest—for example, when the rich adopt more conservative economic positions than the poor (see Chapter 7). But the pull of self-interest is far from universal. People often derive opinions from values that have little if anything to do with obvious self-interest (Sears and Funk 1990). Examples of attitudes that do not reflect self-interest include concerns for the plight of others, but they can also include nationalism or racial resentment (Kinder and Sanders 1996). Even economic interests are not always subject to obvious self-interest calculations. In a study of school districts affected differently by court-ordered financial equalization, property-rich districts had to pay more school taxes and property-poor districts had to pay less. While attitudes toward this decision generally reflected how one's district was affected, many liberals who had to pay more taxes favored the equalization and many conservatives who had to pay less opposed the measure—contrary to their economic self-interest (Tedin 1994b).

While sometimes it may seem that people generate opinions in arbitrary fashion, opinions usually have reasons behind them. Consider opinions about the issue of whether the government should spend more on welfare for the disadvantaged. People who favor less spending will argue the principles of limited government and self-reliance, or they will possibly voice concern about people falling into a welfare "trap." People who favor more spending will cite egalitarian arguments and express sympathy for the immediate needs of the poor (Feldman and Zaller 1992).[1] Abstract values such as egalitarianism or liberal-conservative ideology are important to politics because they cause people to have opinions when they have no direct stake in a particular issue (Bawn 1999). For example, many Americans living in small, homogeneous, midwestern farming communities have opinions about bilingual education.

These opinions have political consequences, even though their lives are almost certainly not touched by the issue.

This chapter examines public opinion at the microlevel of the individual citizen, usually when observed as a survey respondent. We will first examine the extent of political knowledge and the depth of opinion holding. We will then explore the core values and beliefs that sometimes hold opinions together. For politically sophisticated respondents, it is possible to summarize core political values in terms of position on the liberal-conservative ideological spectrum. Finally, we explore a source of political orientation that is adhered to by sophisticates and nonsophisticates alike. That is, the respondent's party identification, or relative allegiance to the Democratic or Republican party.

3-1 POLITICAL ATTENTION AND OPINION-HOLDING

When public opinion is reported on some issue, underlying the division of opinion is a considerable diversity in terms of attention and caring about the matter at hand. At one extreme we find highly attentive citizens who follow public affairs closely and hold informed (if diverse) opinions regarding even complicated questions of public policy. These citizens vote regularly, and their vote is based on issue preferences that have been well thought out. Moreover, they make their views known to elected leaders, even during the time intervals between political campaigns.

At the other extreme we find citizens who can be best described as "apolitical." Virtually disengaged from politics, they ordinarily pay no attention to the political happenings reported in newspapers and on television, and they do not vote. Their interests in politics is perked up only by unusual events, such as the threat of war or a political sex scandal. But by being passive, they collectively forfeit their influence on policy outcomes.

Most people fall between these two extremes, and their attention to the world of government and politics varies considerably. Cognitive ability or general intelligence is certainly an important factor for understanding politics and holding political opinions (Delli Carpini and Keeter 1996). But we should not assume that when people are politically inattentive they lack the mental capacity to follow public affairs, or the politics is too complicated for ordinary folks to figure out. Whether one follows politics closely is largely a matter of personal taste, similar to the choice of whether to follow certain sports, like football and baseball. And just as sporting events are more fascinating and comprehensible to regular followers of the sport, so too is following politics easiest for those who have invested time and effort learning about the political world. For those who choose not to invest in an understanding of politics, following political events and holding informed opinions is a considerably more difficult task (Zaller 1992).

Just as it is misleading to describe public opinion by focusing on the typical citizen, it can be misleading to assume that a citizen's attention level regarding one aspect of politics extends to all others. People vary not only in their taste for public affairs but also in regard to which aspects of public affairs

engage their interest most. For instance, some people focus on national politics but ignore their local political environment, while some do the reverse.
Some people are "issue serialists" who become members of the attentive public only when issues dear to their interests enter the public agenda. For some
issues, they hold strong opinions and make their views known. On others,
they react with indifference.

Political Knowledge

In March 1999, NATO armed forces conducted an intensive bombing raid on
the nation of Serbia in an attempt to halt "ethnic cleansing" by Serbs in the predominantly Albanian province of Kosovo. Suffice it to say, prior to the bombing
most Americans had never heard of Kosovo. However, within a few days of the
bombing, a Pew Research Center Poll (29 Mar. 1999) found that 43 percent of
Americans were able to identify Kosovo as a province of Yugoslavia located in
central Europe. This was a remarkable amount of learning for a nation often
scolded for its lack of geographical knowledge. But of course this event was unusual. Other political events can attract near universal attention, but only if they
contain the necessary elements of drama—the United States going to war, a
hostage drama, or a sex scandal. Complicated political matters are often ignored
by much of the general public. For example, when a controversial presidential
appointment consumes the attention of Washingtonians "inside the Beltway,"
polls suggest that most Americans tune out. With rare exceptions, even the best-
known Cabinet members, Supreme Court justices, senators, and congressional
representatives will be anonymous to most Americans.[2]

A common assumption in American political discourse is that democracy
functions best when its citizens are politically informed. Since the 1930s, more
that 2,000 factual "pop quiz" political knowledge questions were asked of the
American public. An analysis of these queries by Delli Carpini and Keeter
(1996) documents that only 13 percent of the adult public could correctly answer 75 percent or more of the questions, and only 41 percent of the public
could correctly answer 50 percent or more of the items. To many, the results
of these knowledge surveys show levels of ignorance that often appear shock-
ing when observed for the first time. Table 3.1 presents a sampling of factual
questions across a variety of issue domains. For the most part, the public seems
woefully uninformed.

Although the items presented in Table 3.1 are taken from a variety of years,
there has been little change over time in the level of political knowledge.
Americans are no better informed about political matters than they were 50
years ago (Delli Carpini and Keeter 1996, 105). For example, the table shows
that 50 percent could recall the name of their congressional representative in
1942 compared to 40 percent in 1997. Given the rise in levels of education
and the greater availability of political media, many find this lack of improvement puzzling. Perhaps there are countertrends of a negative sort that cancel
out improvements in education and technology. Or there may be inherent limits to how much political information the public can absorb.

TABLE 3.1 LEVEL OF INFORMATION AMONG THE ADULT U.S. POPULATION

Percentage		Year	Source
96	Know United States is a member of the United Nations	1985	D&K
96	Know president's term is four years	1989	D&K
89	Know Republicans have a House majority	1996	NES
88	Know Cuba is communist	1988	D&K
74	Know governor of home state	1989	D&K
72	Know states cannot prohibit abortion	1989	D&K
70	Know there are 50 stars on the American flag	1998	Marist
63	Know party of congressional representative	1995	IRC
58	Know *Roe v. Wade* is about abortion rights	1989	D&K
57	Know how congressional representative voted on Gulf War	1991	D&K
54	Can identify Newt Gingrich as Speaker of the House	1995	IRC
50	Can name president of Russia (Yeltsin)	1994	T-M
47	Know congressman's vote on Clinton impeachment	1999	WP
40	Know name of congressional representative	1997	Luntz
37	Know job of Yasser Arafat	1988	NES
36	Know how many senators needed to convict president	1999	Gallup
34	Can name the secretary of state	1990	GSS
32	Can locate Vietnam on a map	1988	D&K
31	Know what affirmative action is	1985	D&K
27	Know that more is spent on Medicare than foreign aid	1995	IRC
22	Know Senate passed Balanced Budget Act	1995	IRC
12	Know who presided over Clinton impeachment trial	1999	Pew
08	Can name chief justice of U.S. Supreme Court	1987	CBS/NYT

Sources: NES (National Election Studies), D&K (Delli Carpini and Keeter 1996), Luntz (Luntz Research), IRC (IRC Survey Research Group), WP (*Washington Post*), Pew (Pew Center for People and the Press), T-M (Times-Mirror), CBS/NYT (CBS News/*New York Times*), GSS (General Social Survey).

Public knowledge does improve when an issue is consistently in the news. The U.S. involvement in Nicaragua's civil war in the 1980s provides a case in point. Back in 1983, only 29 percent knew that the United States backed the rebels and not the government in Nicaragua. By mid-1986, after years of headlines about the controversial funding of the Contra rebels, this figure had increased to 46 percent. Following the publicity of the "Iran-Contra" scandal, the figure "soared" all the way to 54 percent in mid-1987 and 66 percent in early 1989 (Sobel 1989). After many years of publicity, a majority of Americans had finally absorbed the most rudimentary facts about American involvement in Nicaragua. On the other hand, years of controversy about whether the United States should support the Contras evidently went over the heads of almost half of all Americans.

One concern about the public's low attention to politics is that policy preferences of the "informed public" may differ substantially from the uninformed majority. There are two ways of looking at this problem. On one hand, those who believe that informed opinion should carry greater weight can argue that poll results are contaminated by the counting of passive, uninformed opinions. On the other hand, those who believe that people should have equal influence can argue that poll results are a useful corrective to the perhaps one-sided views of the assertive minority who make their views known. The differences between informed and uninformed opinion that are known to exist are generally attributed to the greater education and income of those who are more knowledgeable.

We present below some examples from the 1996 National Election Studies (NES) survey. For this task, we introduce a summary index of political information. We score respondents on the basis of their knowledge of candidate policy differences, which studies show to be a good measure of relevant political information (Luskin 1987; Zaller 1992). Details of this index are presented in the Appendix to this book. When we use this index, we compare voters at two information extremes. High-information respondents are the 29 percent (32 percent of voters) who correctly saw Dole to the right of Clinton on six separate issues. Low-information respondents are the bottom 39 percent (33 percent of voters) whose knowledge of candidate differences on issues appears to be so impoverished that their evaluation of candidate positions approached the "guess" range.

Table 3.2 shows some differences in opinion-holding by knowledge level in the NES survey. Generally we would expect the largest differences to be on issues where opinions are in flux. The more knowledgeable will be quicker to learn the new conventional wisdom, and adjust their opinions accordingly. Thus back in 1992 high-information respondents were more likely to favor increased aid to Russia, and in both 1992 and 1996 they were more likely to favor a reduction in defense spending than were low-information respondents. Evidently, the more knowledgeable were the first to learn that the cold war had ended, and Russia was now more of a friend than a foe. Some other issues showed modest tendencies for liberal opinion to increase with knowledge, perhaps an indication of greater acceptance of liberal social policies among the most politically sophisticated. High-information respondents tend to be more liberal on social issues such as abortion, the environment, and the status of women. But there are exceptions. Low-information respondents are more likely to favor gun control, and they are decidedly more liberal on issues like national health insurance and increased government services.

Converting Information into Opinions

Information is the basis for (most) opinions about politics. But what is the process by which information becomes converted into opinions? One interpretation popularized by Anthony Downs (1957) in *An Economic Theory of Democracy* holds that citizens translate information into opinions using the rules

TABLE 3.2   OPINION BY LEVEL OF
POLITICAL INFORMATION, 1996

Opinion	High Information (%)	Low Information (%)	Difference (%)
Increase U.S. aid to Russia★	46	19	+27
Believe government should help minorities	30	22	+08
Oppose death penalty	24	22	+02
Increase domestic spending	41	56	–15
Reduce defense spending	50	43	+07
Support national health insurance	43	58	–15
Legalize abortions	66	49	+15
Protect environment, even if it costs jobs	69	56	+13
Support equal role for women	79	72	+07
Favor isolationism in foreign affairs	14	34	–20
Liberal (of ideological identifiers)	43	28	+15
Democratic (of party identifiers)	51	69	–18

Source: National Election Studies, 1996. Coefficients represent percentages among opinion-holders. For measure of high- and low-income respondents, see the Appendix.

★NES, 1992.

of instrumental rationality—that is, for the issue at hand citizens form opinions based on the personal costs and benefits that accrue to them. For example, farmers favor free trade because it opens more markets for their products.

Another approach is based on psychology, and it stresses the consequences for opinions in the way information is processed. There are two popular variations on this approach. The *on-line perspective* starts with the messages sent out by candidates, interest groups, the media, and others. Some of these messages are noted by citizens and, based on the information conveyed, opinions are formed or existing opinions are updated immediately on-line. The process is seen as a "running tally," with opinions constantly being updated in response to new information. Updated opinions are then stored in long-term memory and recalled when needed (Lodge et al. 1995). The second approach is *memory based* (Zaller and Feldman 1992; Zaller 1992). But rather than retrieving a formed opinion from memory, what is retrieved from memory are a series of considerations that favor one side of an issue or the other. A weighted average is mentally computed of the considerations that come to mind, and based on that weighted average an opinion is expressed (a more detailed explanation of this approach is presented below). Both approaches cannot be correct, at least as stated in their pure form. On-line processing is particularly applicable to political campaigns, where information is relatively abundant and attitudes are accessed with some frequency. The memory-based approach helps us understand opinions where information is less plentiful, and it may be more appropriate for attitudes not accessed as regularly.

Depth of Opinion-Holding

Chapter 2 presented some examples of how seemingly minor variations in the framing and wording of survey questions can provoke major variations in survey results. Such phenomena could not occur if people were not often ambivalent about their political convictions. On a given political issue, some survey respondents can call from memory long-term convictions that they have held on the particular subject. Many, however, can offer no more than the top-of-the-head casual opinions of the kind sometimes known as "doorstep" opinions. One consequence is a disturbing degree of response instability when people are interviewed more than once, in what is called a "panel" survey. Many panelists who offer opinions in successive interviews change their position from one side to the other—seemingly inconsistent with the traditional notion of an attitude as an enduring predisposition. The implications are important for understanding public opinion.

Table 3.3 shows some examples of response turnover, from a special (pilot) National Election Studies survey in 1989. The issues shown varied from the hotly debated (abortion, death penalty) to the technical and obscure (funding the Stealth bomber, building a new Alaska pipeline). Respondent views were measured in the summer and again in the fall of 1989. The questions were part of framing experiments, in which different subjects were randomly assigned different ways in which the questions were framed. Different subjects received different framing conditions, which sometimes also varied for the same respondent over time. Still, the exact question asking for an opinion was the same for all respondents for all issues. Respondents received no filter to encourage nonresponses, and over 90 percent offered opinions to each question.[3]

The table shows from 13 to 22 percent switching sides between interviews just a few months apart. As discussed below, analysts agree that almost all of such switching represents not true opinion change but rather some sort of response "error." As one would expect, more response error appears for obscure issues such as Alaska pipelines and Stealth bombers which people typically do not think much about than for salient moral issues like abortion and the death penalty.

The setup of Table 3.3 enhances the observed stability because multiple respondent choices are collapsed into two alternatives. Responses appear less stable when a middle ground is included. Table 3.4 presents the abortion example again, this time with three alternatives.

Whereas in Table 3.3 the various choices for restrictions on abortion were combined as one, for Table 3.4, we separate out the extreme "right to life" position that abortions should never be permitted or permitted only under exceptional circumstances from the more moderate or middle position that abortions "should be permitted...but only after the need has been clearly established." The turnover table now shows 25 percent changing their position from one survey to the next, with many respondents finding the middle position attractive. Notably, however, virtually no respondent switched from pro-choice to pro-life or vice versa.[4]

If the amount of turnover of responses to the abortion question seems high, consider that abortion positions are probably the most stable of political atti-

TABLE 3.3   TURNOVER OF OPINION RESPONSE ON SELECTED ISSUES, 1989 NES PILOT STUDY

Death penalty

		Summer 1989	
		Oppose	*Favor*
Fall 1989	*Oppose*	19%	5%
	Favor	5%	73%

Stealth bomber

		Summer 1989	
		Oppose	*Favor*
Fall 1989	*Oppose*	41%	8%
	Favor	9%	42%

Abortion

		Summer 1989	
		Legal	*Restrictaed*
Fall 1989	*Legal*	34%	5%
	Restricted	6%	53%

More welfare spending

		Summer 1989	
		Favor	*Opposed*
Fall 1989	*Favor*	35%	11%
	Opposed	11%	43%

Affirmative action

		Summer 1989	
		Favor	*Oppose*
Fall 1989	*Favor*	13%	8%
	Oppose	5%	74%

New Alaska oil pipeline

		Summer 1989	
		Oppose	*Favor*
Fall 1989	*Oppose*	36%	10%
	Favor	12%	42%

More gun control

		Summer 1989	
		Favor	*Oppose*
Fall 1989	*Favor*	59%	7%
	Oppose	13%	21%

More cooperation with Russia

		Summer 1989	
		Favor	*Oppose*
Fall 1989	*Favor*	38%	10%
	Oppose	13%	39%

More spending to fight AIDS

		Summer 1989	
		Favor	*Oppose*
Fall 1989	*Favor*	48%	8%
	Oppose	15%	29%

More aid to Nicaraguan Contras

		Summer 1989	
		Oppose	*Favor*
Fall 1989	*Oppose*	49%	11%
	Favor	10%	30%

Source: National Election Studies, 1989 pilot study data. In some instances, framing of question varied with respondent and with wave.

tude responses, rivaled perhaps only by party identification (Converse and Markus 1979; Wetstein 1993). Less morally charged issues show considerably less response stability. Typical is the turnover of responses to the NES's "guaranteed living standard" question between the preelection and postelection surveys in 1984, shown in Table 3.5.

Only a minority of the respondents (40 percent) had a sufficiently firm attitude to take the same side consistently (pro/pro or con/con) in both interviews. A few (10 percent) changed sides completely from one interview to the next, and others (14 percent) took no position in either interview. The remainder (35 percent) took sides in one interview but not in the other.

TABLE 3.4   OPINION CONSISTENCY ON ABORTION, 1989

	Summer 1989		
Fall 1989	Never permitted, or only if rape, incest, or woman's life in danger	Other than if rape, incest, or woman's life in danger, after need established	Always permitted as matter of personal choice
Never permitted, or only if rape, incest, or woman's life in danger	31%	6%	1%
Other than if rape, incest, or woman's life in danger, after need established	6%	12%	4%
Always permitted as matter of personal choice	2%	5%	34%

Source: National Election Studies, 1989 pilot study.

The most studied patterns of response instability are from two four-year three-wave panels as part of the National Election Studies (Converse 1964; Converse and Markus 1979). In a "1950s" panel, the same respondents were interviewed at two-year intervals, in 1956, 1958, and 1960. The NES "1970s" panel interviewed the same respondents in 1972, 1974, and 1976.

One important fact from the NES panel studies is that the time interval between panel waves has little bearing on the observed amount of response stability. For instance, the degrees of response turnover to questions on abortion and guaranteed living standards asked four years apart in the NES 1970s panel are only slightly larger than the amount of response turnover shown in Tables 3.3 and 3.4 for the same issues when the same question was asked only a few months apart.

This evidence suggests that response change does not represent true change in underlying attitudes. If people were really changing their minds frequently, long time intervals would produce greater decay of initial positions. While scholars agree that response instability generally does not indicate true attitude conversion, they disagree in what the unstable responses mean. One position, developed by Philip E. Converse, holds that people who change positions usually have no position but instead respond randomly. This "nonattitude" explanation has been challenged by other scholars, who prefer a "measurement error" explanation. While the details of the opposing interpretations are too complicated to receive full treatment here, we can present brief sketches of the competing points of view.

TABLE 3.5   OPINION CONSISTENCY ON GOVERNMENT
GUARANTEE OF A JOB AND GOOD STANDARD OF LIVING*

Postelection Response, 1984	Preelection Response, 1984		
	Government should guarantee job and good standard of living	In between, no opinion	Government should let each person get ahead on own
Government should guarantee job and good standard of living	14%	9%	4%
In between, no opinion	8%	14%	7%
Government should let each person get ahead on own	6%	12%	26%

Source: National Election Studies, 1984 election data.

*Cell entries represent percentage of the entire sample.

The "Nonattitudes" Explanation

After analyzing turnover patterns from the 1950s panel, Philip Converse (1964) proposed that virtually all respondents who change their position over time hold no true convictions, but instead express random responses or "nonattitudes." The strong evidence for infrequent true change is that response instability varies little with the time between surveys. Surveys four months or four years apart yield about the same amount of response turnover. If people were actually changing their minds, observed opinions would be more stable over the briefer time interval.

If the nonattitude thesis is correct, most observed response change is random error, as if changers are simply flipping coins. Just as coins can be flipped heads one time and tails the next, they can also be flipped consistently heads or tails both times. Thus a further implication of the nonattitudes thesis is that many consistent responses are random responses that appear stable only by chance. On one notorious issue from the 1950s panel, the abstract "power and housing" question (whether "the government should leave things like electric power and housing for private businessmen to handle"), Converse reached a startling conclusion (1964, 293). He estimated that less than 20 percent of the adult public held meaningful attitudes on this issue even though about two-thirds would venture a viewpoint on the matter when asked in a survey.

Many have found the implications of the "nonattitudes" explanation to be quite disturbing. In a democracy, public officials presumably respond to the policy preferences of the public, enacting these preferences into law. But if large segments of the public do not really have coherent preferences or preferences at all, why should elected officials heed their views? How, in fact, could they?

The "Measurement Error" Explanation

If the "nonattitudes" explanation is correct, the reason why many people give unstable responses to opinion questions is that these individuals lack the political sophistication necessary to form crystallized opinions. But contrary to this prediction, response instability varies little if at all with measures of political sophistication or political knowledge (Achen 1975; Erikson 1979; Feldman 1989). The disturbing level of instability found for surveys of the general public is also found for subsamples representing the sophisticated and informed. If even politically sophisticated individuals respond with a seeming random component, what is to blame? It probably is not a lack of capability on the part of those being interviewed.

For this reason, a "measurement error" explanation has been proposed to account for response error (Achen 1975; Erikson 1979). This explanation does not challenge the evidence that most response instability represents error rather than true change. But by the measurement error explanation, the "blame" for the response instability is placed not so much on the capabilities of the respondents as on the survey questions themselves. Even the best survey questions will produce some instability from respondents who hold weak or ambivalent attitudes about policy issues. Some inherent limitations in the survey enterprise make measuring attitudes an imprecise task. These include ambiguities in question wording, the problem of investigator-defined responses to close-ended questions that may not be congruent with the way respondents think about issues, and the problems of respondents having to give immediate answers to perhaps 100 or more questions with virtually no opportunity for reflection or considered judgment. Thus it is the inherent limitations of the survey method that mostly explain response instability, not the inherent limitations of the respondent.

An Explanation Based on Response Probability

In 1992, John Zaller and Stanley Feldman offered a "theory of the survey response" that provides a more general explanation for response instability, and incorporates the findings of both the nonattitudes and measurement approaches (see also Zaller 1992). From this perspective, respondents do not have fixed, stable attitudes on many issues but they do have propensities to respond one way or another. The answer they give, however, depends on the *considerations* that come to mind when a question is asked. A consideration is simply anything that affects how someone decides on a political issue, one way or another. For example, when one is asked for an opinion on universal health insurance, considerations may include higher taxes, sick people unable to get medical care, and big government. The actual survey response depends on the considerations that are accessible when the question is asked. Assuming the considerations listed above were of equal importance, the respondent would oppose universal health insurance as two considerations point in that direction versus one that points to support.

But the considerations that come to mind at one point in time may not be the same as at another point in time. Usually, for our hypothetical respondent, the considerations that come to mind will induce opposition to universal health care. But perhaps she recently saw a TV news story about a hard-working man paid poverty-level wages who could not afford medical treatment for his bedridden wife. When asked the universal health care question, that consideration may be "at the top of the head" and induce support for universal health care. But the news story will eventually be forgotten, and considerations that induce opposition will again predominate. Thus, for many issues, responses are probabilistic. There will be a propensity to come down on one side of an issue, but the probability is something less than 1.0.

The measurement approach can also be treated in terms of response probabilities. Considerations relevant to the survey response can be brought to mind by the way a question is phrased, or where it is placed in the questionnaire. For example, question location may affect the probability of a response. As we noted in Chapter 2, a respondent is more likely to "disapprove" of presidential job performance when the item is asked late in the questionnaire than when it is asked early. The content of the questionnaire brings to mind considerations (mostly negative), which increases the probability of a "disapprove" response. If the question had been asked early in the questionnaire, the probability of a "disapprove" response is reduced as negative considerations brought to "the top of the head" by the content of the questionnaire come after the "approve/disapprove" item has been answered. Like the TV news program discussed above, the survey instrument itself can be a source of considerations that affect responses to questions.

Even though there may be variation in the opinions expressed on an issue, the underlying attitudes that give rise to these opinions may be quite stable. Suppose our hypothetical individual has a 70 percent probability of choosing the conservative response on national health insurance, and further assume that this places her at the eightieth percentile of conservatism on the issue (the respondent is more conservative than 80 percent of citizens). Within a period of two to four years, our respondent should still be near the same eightieth percentile. Stimuli in the environment might cause minor variations in probabilistic responses—for example, a liberal national mood swing might lower everybody's probability of a conservative response. But our hypothetical respondent would still be more conservative than 80 percent of citizens.

Of course, if people's attitudes are as stable as just described at the *micro*level, could we expect opinion trends at the *macro*level? We will see in the next chapter that net public opinion on an issue is often very stable over time. We will see interesting exceptions, however, and these occur when the electorate responds in a uniform way to one-sided environmental stimuli.

3-2 LIBERAL-CONSERVATIVE IDEOLOGY AND THE ORGANIZATION OF OPINIONS

When a person expresses viewpoints on a number of political subjects, we might expect that these opinions would be connected to each other in some pattern. One expectation is that opinions would be connected by logical consistency with core political values. For instance, a person who believes strongly in individual responsibility would be inclined to respond negatively toward government help for the inner cities or toward the government guaranteeing a job and a good standard of living. A person with strong egalitarian values would be expected to respond in an opposite fashion. To take another example, a person committed to traditional social values probably would oppose abortion rights and oppose gays serving in the military. A person with a strong belief in individual choice would take the opposite view.

We could try to account for opinions in terms of how people weight political values such as individual responsibility, equality, tradition, and individual freedom. When we describe peoples' core political values in this way, we begin to describe the person's political ideology. In the broadest sense, a person's ideology refers to any set of beliefs about the proper order of society and how it can be achieved. People with strong ideologies use their personal ideology as a guide for understanding the political world.

As a convenient shorthand, observers often prefer to reduce ideology to the single dimension of the left–right ideological continuum, classifying peoples' political values simply according to their relative liberalism versus conservatism. The left–right ideological distinction between liberals and conservatives has considerable meaning when describing the opinions of political elites, or politically active people. For instance, delegates to national political conventions clearly understand ideological labels and tend to polarize as consistent liberals or conservatives (Herrera 1992; Jennings 1992). Because the ideological liberal-conservative continuum holds lesser meaning to those near the bottom of the sophistication ladder, the importance of liberal-conservative ideology within the mass public has been a matter of uncertainty and controversy.[5]

A standard poll question is to ask respondents their ideological identification, usually with the three choices of liberal, moderate, or conservative. As discussed in Chapter 2, one-fourth or more will decline to classify themselves ideologically given the choice of "not interested." Of those who choose, almost half will choose the "moderate" or "middle-of-the-road" alternative when offered.

Ideally, ideological classification would be a convenient way to measure peoples' core political values and to summarize their political views over a variety of issues. In practice, the result is mixed. The most politically sophisticated segment of the public approximates the ideal. For them, ideological identification goes a long way toward describing their political convictions. But when less sophisticated people respond to the ideological identification question with a response of liberal, moderate, or conservative, we can be less sure of what the response means. At worst, the response can represent some idiosyncratic meaning known only to the respondent or perhaps a doorstep opinion made up on the spot.

Liberal and Conservative Terminology

What do the terms "liberal" and "conservative" actually mean? At the philosophical level, political thinkers with reputations as liberals and conservatives differ in several ways. Conservatives view society as a control for humanity's worst impulses; liberals view the human condition as relative to the quality of society. Conservatives consider people to be inherently unequal and due unequal rewards; liberals are egalitarian. Conservatives venerate tradition, order, and authority; liberals believe planned change brings the possibility of improvement.[6]

Of course people who are liberal or conservative in their practical politics need not strictly adhere to the particular philosophy associated with their ideological label. Nevertheless, we can see the implications of these philosophic distinctions at work in the common applications of the ideological labels to particular political points of view. Conservatives are more afraid than liberals of "big government," except on matters of law-and-order and national security; during the cold war era, conservatives were the more anti-Communist in their rhetoric. Conservatives are more likely to see harmful consequences of government help for the disadvantaged, while liberals see the benefits. Conservatives tend to be moralistic; liberals are more permissive.

These kinds of relative distinctions are familiar to people who follow politics closely. But the language of ideology holds lesser meaning for the mass public as a whole. One test is whether the individual can both identify the Republicans as the more conservative party and offer a plausible definition of the term "conservative." Roughly half the public passes this test of understanding of ideological labels (Converse 1964; Luttbeg and Gant 1985).

What do people think of when they hear the terms "liberal" and "conservative"? Table 3.6 summarizes the responses from a 1994 NES study of how people describe liberals and conservatives. Respondents were asked, "What sorts of things do you have in mind when you say that someone's political views are liberal?" and similarly, "What sorts of things do you have in mind when you say that someone's political views are conservative?" They were allowed up to three responses to each question, six overall. Seventy-eight percent of the sample gave at least one response.

As typical for other years, the economic distinctions were used most often to explain the difference between liberals and conservatives. Liberals spend; conservatives save. Liberals are seen as favoring the welfare state and giving away programs; conservatives are seen as favoring free enterprise and opposing big spending social programs. Liberals were also seen as being more change-oriented and innovative while conservatives were viewed as more status quo-oriented and rigid. All these are reasonably broad distinctions. But the public also sees differences between liberals and conservatives on more narrow issues. Conservatives are seen as moralistic and religious, while liberals

TABLE 3.6 PERCEIVED MEANING OF IDEOLOGICAL LABELS, 1994

Question: *What sorts of things do you have in mind when you say someone's political views are liberal?*

What sorts of things do you have in mind when you say someone's political views are conservative?

Type of Mention	Example	Percentage Mentioning
Change	L's accept change/new ideas/innovative. C's resist change/protect status quo/rigid.	23
Fiscal	L's for socialism/welfare state/give-away programs. C's for free enterprise/capitalism/oppose social programs.	24
Personality	L's are open-minded/not concerned with consequences. C's are moralists/concerned with consequences.	14
Morality	L's not interested in setting moral standards/not religious. C's have definite moral standards/religious.	13
Spend/save	L's free spenders/favor government spending. C's thrifty/economize on government spending.	24
Civil liberties	L's support upholding of Bill of Rights/human rights. C's want to limit Bill of Rights/human rights.	5
Class	L's for little people/working people/unions. C's for big business/the rich.	12
Abortion	L's are pro-choice. C's are pro-life.	15
Gay rights	L's favor gay rights. C's oppose gay rights.	9
Defense	L's weak on defense/national security. C's strong on defense/national security.	4
People	L's identify label with prominent national figures. C's identify label with prominent national figures.	5

n = *595*

Source: Adapted from National Election Studies, 1994. The questions allow for multiple responses.

are seen as having more flexible moral standards and not as religious. The contemporary issues of abortion and gay rights show up in the expected fashion. However, with the end of the cold war fewer respondents mention defense and national security issues than in the past. In addition, a number of responses dealt with peripheral matters such as liberal and conservative positions on narrow policy issues.

When survey respondents are asked to classify themselves on the liberal-conservative spectrum, their answers tend to correspond to their policy positions. Some examples of the relationships and positions on specific issues are show in Table 3.7. Self-declared liberals, in fact, take positions considerably more liberal than do self-declared conservatives.

This tendency is even clearer when issue positions are summed over several issues. Table 3.8 shows that, as measured by their composite stands over ten

TABLE 3.7   IDEOLOGICAL PREFERENCES AND OPINIONS ON SELECTED POLICY ISSUES, 1996*

Belief	Support Among Self-Declared Liberals	Support Among Self-Declared Conservatives
The government should provide "more services even if it means an increase in spending"	88	47
The government should guarantee "that every person has a job and good standard of living"	47	14
Favor "government insurance plan which would cover all medical and hospital expenses for everyone"	65	35
Government "should reduce differences between rich and poor"	59	25
The government "should make every effort to improve the social and economic position of blacks"	55	17
Always permit abortion "as a matter of choice"	94	68
"Tougher regulations are needed to protect the environment"	88	50
Favor "stricter government control of handguns"	60	36
"Homosexuals should be allowed to serve in U.S. armed forces"	83	49
Oppose "death penalty for persons convicted of murder"	86	64
The United States "should spend less on defense"	40	33

Source: National Election Studies, 1996.

*Reported figures are percentage of opinion-holders only.

separate issues, people who are very liberal identify as liberals and people who are very conservative overwhelmingly identify themselves as conservatives. It may also be noted that people who cannot identify themselves as liberal, moderate, or conservative tend to cluster in the center of the political spectrum as measured by their stands on specific issues.

Use of Ideological Language

Although the ideological terms are within the vocabularies of a large share of the American public, few actually employ them to defend their choices of party or candidate. For each National Election Study, respondents are asked what they like and dislike about each major party and presidential candidate. The profile of responses to these questions in 1956 is reported in the classic study of American voting behavior, *The American Voter* (Campbell et al. 1960, 216–49). The researchers were interested not only in the individuals' image of the parties and candidates but also in the conceptual sophistication of the responses. Respondents who spontaneously and knowledgeably evaluated the

TABLE 3.8 CORRESPONDENCE OF IDEOLOGICAL SELF-RATINGS AND SUMMARY OF POSITIONS ON TEN ISSUES, 1996

Summary Position on Ten Issues*

Ideological Self-Rating	Very Liberal	Liberal	Center	Conservative	Very Conservative
Liberal	66%	25%	12%	6%	2%
Moderate	15	27	33	19	10
Conservative	5	24	29	53	81
Don't know	11	24	26	22	7
	100%	100%	100%	100%	100%
(Percentage of total sample)	(12)	(20)	(25)	(25)	(8)

Source: National Election Studies, 1996 election data.

*See the Appendix for construction of ten-item summary scores. The full distribution of scores is shown in Figure 3.1. The categories here are as follows: Very liberal −10 to −6, Liberal −5 to −2, Center, −1 to +1, Conservative +2 to +5, and Very Conservative +6 to +10.

parties and candidates in terms of their placement on the liberal–conservative spectrum were labeled as "ideologues."

Thus began a search for "ideologues" within the electorate that continues to hold a central place on the research agenda of public opinion analysts. In some respects, *The American Voter*'s label "ideologue" was unfortunate, because in popular usage it holds a negative connotation: the ideologue as ideology-driven fanatic. As used in the sense of *The American Voter,* however, the ideologue is a political sophisticate whose central view of political actors is in terms of their place on the ideological spectrum. The ideologue's own political perspective could be moderate, extremist, or anywhere in between.

Even with a generous definition of what the ideologue response would demand (to include what *The American Voter* calls "near ideologues"), only 12 percent of the 1956 respondents fit the ideologue category. A typical ideologue response was that of an Ohio woman who, when asked what she liked about the Democratic party, answered, "Nothing, except it being a more liberal party, and I think the Republicans as being more conservative and interested in big business." A weaker ideologue response was given by a Texas man: "I think the Democrats are more concerned with all the people . . . they put out more liberal legislation" (Campbell et al. 1960, 232).

An added 42 percent of the 1956 sample expressed their likes and dislikes about the candidates (Eisenhower and Stevenson) and parties in terms of the groups they represented. Farmers often expressed their political likes and dislikes in terms of "group-benefits" (e.g., "I think [the Democrats] have always helped the farmers"; Campbell et al. 1960, 236). Most group-benefit responses were class-related, evoking the notion that Republicans favor big business while the Democrats favor the "little person."

Still another 24 percent of the 1956 respondents referred to the "nature of the times" the different parties are associated with when in power. Nature-of-the-times voters were guided by perceptions of past performance, such as which party brought economic prosperity or which party kept their promises. Finally, 23 percent were found to offer no issue content whatsoever when asked to describe their partisan likes and dislikes. Typical was the North Carolina man who answered as follows (with interviewer questions abbreviated):

(Like about the Democrats?)	"No, Ma'am, not that I know of."
(Dislike?)	"No, Ma'am, but I've always been a Democrat, just like my daddy."
(Like about the Republicans?)	"No."
(Dislike?)	"No." (Campbell et al. 1960, 246)

This distribution of how people conceptualize partisan politics may be interpreted to mean that Americans are not very ideological, and in one sense this would be correct. The authors of *The American Voter* account for the scarcity of ideologues in terms of the public's "cognitive limitations," particularly a lack of intellectual ability to think in terms of ideological abstractions (Campbell et al. 1960, 253). But our knowledge that many citizens use the liberal-conservative terms and can apply them to issues positions suggests the alternative interpretation that the American public does not always find the ideological terms particularly useful to describe their partisan likes and dislikes. Now many political scientists see *The American Voter* judgment as overly harsh. Although the authors did not realize it at the time, the 1956 presidential election was probably the least ideological of all modern campaigns, conducted essentially as a referendum on President Eisenhower's first term. Because the 1956 campaign was not conducted at an ideological level, 1956 respondents were not apt to explain their likes and dislikes about parties and candidates in terms of ideological nuances. They chose the easier criteria of group representation and the nature of the times.

In later elections, ideology and policy issues played greater roles. The 1964 (Johnson vs. Goldwater) and 1972 (McGovern vs. Nixon) campaigns were particularly ideological. As ideological cues became more visible, the proportion of the public who could be labeled ideologues increased considerably.[7]

Table 3.9 enumerates the electorate by "level of conceptualization" for each presidential year, 1956 to 1988, based on NES surveys. In recent presidential elections, the electorate has divided roughly equally into the four levels of conceptualization. To summarize: At the top level, "ideologues" view parties and candidates in terms of their ideological and policy differences. At the second level, "group-benefits" people see party and candidate differences in terms of the differences in the groups they represent rather than the policies they offer. At the third level, "nature-of-the-times" people evaluate parties and candidates only by past judgments of party and candidate performance. At the bottom, "no-issue-content" types seem unresponsive to political cues.

TABLE 3.9   LEVELS OF POLITICAL CONCEPTUALIZATION, 1956–1988

	1956	1960	1964	1968	1972	1976	1980	1984	1988
Ideologues	12%	19%	27%	26%	22%	21%	21%	19%	18%
Group benefits	42	31	27	24	27	26	31	26	36
Nature of the times	24	26	20	29	34	30	30	35	25
No issue content	22	23	26	21	17	24	19	19	21
	100%	99%	100%	100%	100%	101%	101%	99%	99%
Number of cases	1,749	1,701	1,431	1,319	1,372	2,870	1,612	2,257	2,040

Source: Paul R. Hagner and John C. Pierce, "Correlative Characteristics of Levels of Conceptualization in the American Public: 1956–1976," *Journal of Politics,* 44 (Aug. 1982): 779–809; updates compiled by Paul Hagner and Kathleen Knight.

As we have seen, a greater proportion of the electorate can utilize the ideological language than are classifiable as ideologues. One explanation is that many individuals can use ideological labels without pursuing much ideology. For instance, many at the "group-interest" level identify with liberals or conservatives as a group with which they share a common interest, much as some may feel about teachers or labor unions (Tedin 1987).

Some people learn to associate terms like "liberal" and "conservative" with groups and symbols rather than specific policies (Conover and Feldman 1981). A person might associate the term "liberal" with "black" or "feminist" or the term "conservative" with "the middle class" or "business" (Miller et al. 1991). These cues may serve to simplify politics and provide an informational shortcut (much like party identification), even if in most instances they are unaccompanied by a high degree of ideological sophistication. If one knows a candidate for public office is a liberal, or a policy is characterized as liberal, one need seek no further information to make a judgment. The labels can be used to minimize the costs of gathering information.

Ideology as Liberal-Conservative Consistency

One might suspect that many people are actually quite liberal or quite conservative in the views they express, even when they do not choose these terms to describe their political orientation. Figure 3.1 shows one distribution of the American public's liberal-conservatism "scores" as measured by their cumulative responses to ten opinion questions in the 1996 NES survey. A person with all liberal opinions would score at −10, whereas a person who expresses conservative outlooks on all ten issues would score at +10. Most respondents were near the midpoint of the scale (0), indicating that their liberal and conservative viewpoints balanced each other out.

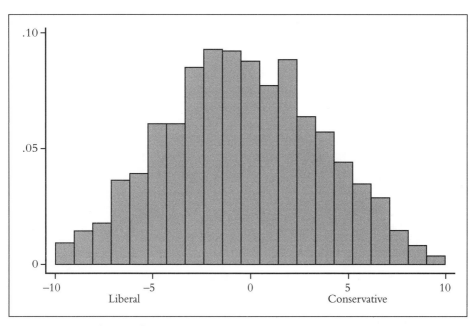

Figure 3.1 Distribution of ten-issue composite opinion scores, 1996. *Source:* National Election Studies, 1996.

Since over a series of issues most people give some liberal and some conservative positions, there is a temptation to label the public as political moderates. But these voters in the center cannot be grouped together as sharing the same moderate ideology, because they differ greatly in their pattern of responses on individual issues. For instance, one voter with balanced liberal and conservative views may be liberal on social welfare issues and civil rights but conservative on foreign policy and law and order, while another with equally balanced views professes exactly the opposite opinions. Still a third person may have an overall score that is neither very conservative nor very liberal for the reason that he or she expresses few opinions at all.

It is sometimes argued that if ideology influences people's opinions, opinions on two separate issues should be predictable from one another since both are "constrained" by the opinion-holder's ideological perspective. Table 3.10 shows some 1996 examples of the search for ideological constraint.

For a pair of issues, an individual is more likely to offer consistently liberal or conservative positions if the issues are logically related or share some common content. The top row of Table 3.10 presents several examples: In Table 3.10(a), people's opinions regarding government involvement in health care are predictable from their general views on domestic government spending. In Table 3.10(b), people's opinions regarding government help to provide jobs and a good standard of living show consistency with their views on government aid for minorities. In Table 3.10(c), people's opinions on abortion appear consistent with their views on whether women deserve an equal role with men in business

TABLE 3.10   CORRELATIONS BETWEEN OPINIONS
ON SELECTED ISSUES, 1996

(a) Increase domestic spending			(b) Guaranteed job, living standard			(c) Legalize all abortions		
	Pro	Con		Pro	Con		Pro	Con
National Pro	30%	16%	**Federal** Pro	19%	5%	**Equal** Pro	51%	26%
health			**aid to**			**role for**		
insurance Con	16	38	**minor.** Con	10	65	**women** Con	8	14
Gamma = .63			Gamma = .92			Gamma = .53		

(d) Legal abortions			(e) Gays in military			(f) More domestic spending		
	Pro	Con		Pro	Con		Pro	Con
National Pro	31%	18%	**Guar.** Pro	25%	7%	**Cut** Pro	24%	24%
health			**living**			**military**		
insurance Con	27	24	**stand.** Con	43	25	**spending** Con	23	29
Gamma = .23			Gamma = .35			Gamma = .15		

Source: National Election Studies, 1996 data. See the Appendix for the full text of opinion questions.

and government. Each example shows many exceptions, however, of individuals holding a liberal position on one issue but a conservative position on the other.

When issues are not closely related in terms of content, liberal–conservative consistency tends to fade. Table 3.10(d) shows that one cannot predict an individual's position on abortion from the individual's position on national health insurance. Table 3.10(e) shows a similar lack of predictability for the issue pair of a guaranteed living standard and gays in the military. Of course, for neither of these pairs is there a requirement of logical consistency. But consider also the relationship between domestic spending and less military spending, shown in Table 3.10(f). Seemingly people should gravitate to ideologically consistent choices of either more domestic spending and less military spending (liberal) or less domestic spending and more military spending (conservative). Table 3.10(f) shows instead a slightly negative correlation. Many people favor either more spending for both domestic and military purposes or less spending for both.[8]

The low levels of ideological constraint within the general public reflect very real variations in ideological sophistication. Liberal–conservative opinion consistency is quite high among those most knowledgeable about politics, such as people identified as "ideologues" (Stimson 1975; Knight 1985). We can illustrate this point by comparing the respondents classified as least knowledgeable and most knowledgeable in the 1996 NES survey. Among the select "high information" group, opinions on different issues are very highly correlated, while for the "low information" group, there is essentially no correlation at all. Our illustration is for the relationship between opinion on a national health insurance program and opinion on abortion.

		Low Information Legal Abortions		High Information Legal Abortions	
		Pro	*Con*	*Pro*	*Con*
National Health	*Pro*	28%	30%	36%	07%
Insurance	*Con*	21%	21%	30%	27%
		Gamma = .07		Gamma = .66	

We see that with the accumulation of a high level of political information, people tend toward consistently liberal or consistently conservative positions, while we see no relationship at all for those with low levels of information. A broader illustration compares the high-information group and the low-information group in terms of their distributions on the composite ten-item liberal-conservative scale. Figure 3.2 shows the results. The informed show some gravitation toward the liberal and conservative poles. The uninformed are very highly clustered in the center of the spectrum.

Despite the fact that the most knowledgeable are the most responsive to liberal versus conservative distinctions, we should not insist that use of the liberal-conservative dimension is a requirement for political thinking. Liberal-conservative consistency is not the only possible ordering principle for political opinions. On foreign policy, for example, core values regarding the morality of warfare and ethnocentrism appear to be important (Hurwitz and Peffley 1987). More generally, people can make their opinions consistent with their own personal ideologies and need not apply the notion of liberal versus conservative ways of thinking. Consider abortion attitudes, which until recently did not correlate much with conventional liberal-conservative orderings as measured by other policy opinions. According to Kristen Luker, attitudes concerning

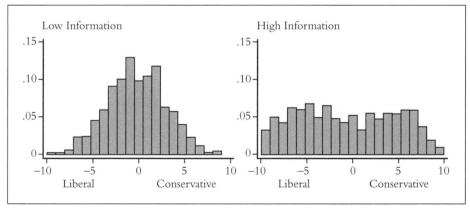

Figure 3.2 Composite opinion by information level. *Source:* National Election Studies, 1996.

abortion result from "beliefs and attitudes about motherhood; about sexuality; about men and women; about the role of children; and more broadly, about such global things as morality and the role of rational planning in human affairs" (Luker 1984, 31).

Ideological Thinking: A Summary

The public is mixed in its understanding and usage of ideological language and thinking. Most citizens do not engage in the ideological thinking of the sort found among political elites. But ordinary citizens often use ideological labels in at least a limited way as part of their politcal vocabulary. Many, however, do not even do this. Perhaps for as much as half the electorate, the liberal versus conservative component of political discourse is nothing more than a confusion of background noise. The fact that there is little idealogical consistency to people's issue positions demonstrates that few people use their idealogical position as a cuing devise to arrange their responses to the political world. The kind of attitudinal constraint that motivates people toward consistently liberal, conservative, or moderate political viewpoints is reserved for a relatively small, politically active segment of the public.

In our effort to understand public opinion, we should not ignore this politically sophisticated segment of the American public, which does follow government and politics in terms of the liberal-conservative continuum. Thinking about politics in liberal versus conservative terms is sophisticated not because it is preferable to hold ideologically extreme convictions or to view the political world through a distorted lens. Rather, to have the liberal-conservative spectrum as a political frame of reference is necessary to understand the language of politics as it is practiced by political elites. Many ordinary Americans do follow this ideological discussion.

3-3 PARTY IDENTIFICATION AND THE ORGANIZATION OF POLITICAL OPINIONS

So far, we have ignored partisanship as a way of organizing political opinions. More than on the basis of ideology, Americans divide on the basis of their party identifications. Whereas ideological identification may be of particular relevance only for a select segment of the public, people at all levels of sophistication appear to hold meaningful party identifications. Whereas the pollster's ideological identification question is intended to summarize the person's political values, party identification represents the person's net evaluation of the Republican and Democratic parties. It is relatively easy to prefer one party over the other without considering nuances of ideological placement.

For most people, party identification is a central aspect of political identity. Compared to ordinary political opinions, people's party identifications are quite stable over time, both before and after adjustment for measurement error (Green and Palmquist 1990). For instance, when interviewed during two successive presidential campaigns four years apart, most respondents persist with their original basic identification as a Democrat, Independent, or Republican. Only a small percentage of respondents switch party identification from Democratic to Republican or vice versa. Those who switch generally move in and out of the Independent category rather than "convert" from one side to the other.

As discussed in Chapter 5, the source of one's party identification is often the political values that were transmitted in the family during childhood. At the other end of the causal chain, party identification is the best predictor of how people vote. Following the sequence through, we find that people vote for the party with which their parents had identified.

Survey researchers normally ascertain party identification by asking respondents whether they consider themselves Democrats, Independents, or Republicans. Republican partisans may then be asked whether they consider themselves "strong" or "not so strong" (often translated as "weak") Republicans (or Democrats). Classifying on strength plus partisan direction makes four categories of partisans. Meanwhile, Independents are sometimes asked whether they "lean" toward one of the parties. The Independents can be classified as Republican leaners, Democratic leaners, and pure Independents. Pure Independents typically make up no more than about 10 percent of a national sample, suggesting that few citizens are purely neutral when it comes to partisanship. Altogether, there are seven potential categories of party identification, on a scale from "strong Democrat" to "strong Republican." Usually, however, the three-category classification is sufficient. Except where otherwise indicated, this book will employ the simple three-category division of party identification as Republicans (strong plus weak), Democrats (strong plus weak), and Independents (pure plus partisan leaners).

Party identification can be a handy cue by which to orient the remainder of one's political beliefs. An alert Republican, for example, would learn that a good Republican is supposed to subscribe to conservative positions on certain issues and would respond accordingly. At the same time, we might expect that the rare event of a partisan conversion results when the convert becomes aware that his or her ideological views are out of alignment with his or her partisan heritage. These causal processes could not occur, however, unless people were aware of the Democratic versus Republican differences on the issues of the day.

Perceptions of Party Differences

As we will see in Chapter 11, Democratic and Republican leaders are ideologically different, with the Republicans generally conservative and Democrats generally liberal. In other words, at the leadership level the usual party stereotypes are true. Here, we can ask: To what extent does the public perceive these party differences?

National election studies regularly ask their respondents to place the major parties' positions on selected issues of the day. Respondents can rate the Democrats to the left of the Republicans (correct), the Republicans to the left of the Democrats, rate them tied at the identical position, or declare no interest in the issue. Table 3.11 presents the perceptions of the parties' relative positions

TABLE 3.11   PUBLIC PERCEPTIONS OF PARTY DIFFERENCES ON ISSUES, 1988–1996

Perceptions of Which Party Is More in Favor of . . .	Democrats	Republicans	No Difference, Don't Know, No Interest
More domestic spending (1996)	67%	15%	18%
National health insurance (1988)	43	8	50
Guaranteed living standard (1992)	42	8	50
Aid to minorities (1988)	44	8	44
Abortion rights (1996)	57	9	34
Regulating the environment (1996)	48	9	44
Cutting defense spending (1996)	62	10	27

Source: National Election Studies data.

in recent NES surveys. Typically, about half rate the Democrats as the more liberal (left) party. Very few guess incorrectly and identify the Republican party with the more liberal position.

Interestingly, the public's perceptions of party differences on issues have been growing over the years. As recently as the early 1960s, the public saw party differences only in terms of social welfare issues. The public image of the parties as distinct on social welfare issues goes back to the New Deal era of the 1930s, when the parties began to develop opposite philosophies toward the role of the federal government in the economy. Until about 1964, party differences on issues outside the social welfare sphere were not sharply focused at the leadership level, such as congressional and presidential politics. It is no surprise, therefore, that before the 1960s people generally did not see either party as more liberal or conservative on civil rights or foreign policy issues.

Nowadays, Americans generally perceive the Democrats as the more liberal party, not only on social welfare issues but on civil rights, foreign policy, and even social issues like gay rights. This happened largely because the parties became more polarized at the elite level. Public perceptions simply followed the behavior and the rhetoric of party leaders. The biggest change occurred with the idealogical Goldwater election of 1964 (Carmines and Stimson 1989). Senator Goldwater, the 1964 Republican candidate, campaigned as a forthright conservative. By opposing the Civil Rights Act of 1964, he altered the Republican image on civil rights. By his tough posturing about the Soviet Union, he made the Republicans appear to be the most belligerent on foreign policy. His Democratic opponent, President Lyndon Johnson, was able to exploit Goldwater's image as an extreme conservative. Goldwater lost the election in a landslide, but he and his supporters moved the Republican party sharply to the right in a manner that has lasted into the twenty-first century.

Events after 1964 added to the growing perceptions of party differences. In 1972, it was the Democrats' turn to run a candidate targeted as an ideological extremist. President Richard Nixon successfully tagged his opponent, South Dakota Senator George McGovern, as the candidate of "amnesty, abortion, and acid." This unfair label helped to generate the impression that the Republicans were the party of conservative reasonableness on social issues and that the Democrats were the party of liberal permissiveness. These themes continued through the Reagan, Bush, and Clinton presidencies, with sharp divisions between congressional Democrats and Republicans maintaining the liberal-conservative party polarization that began in 1964.

Party Identification and Party Preferences

On most issues, the views of Democratic and Republican identifiers diverge in predictable liberal versus conservative ways. Some examples from 1992 NES data are shown in Table 3.12. Although the differences among "weak Democrats," "Independents," and "weak Republicans" are slight, the policy differences between "strong Democrats" and "strong Republicans" generally are rather sharp. Following historical tradition, party differences are greatest on social welfare issues.

TABLE 3.12   PARTY IDENTIFICATION AND POLICY OPINIONS, 1996

	Percentage of Liberal Opinion-Holders					
Issue	Strong Dem.	Weak Dem.	Ind.	Weak Repub.	Strong Repub.	Gamma
More domestic spending	79	58	47	26	08	.63
Job guarantee	61	37	33	17	06	.53
Less defense spending	60	58	50	34	23	.35
Aid to minorities	51	26	24	09	06	.53
National health ins.	71	61	52	33	08	.54
Protect environment	69	81	71	56	42	.30
Gays in military	83	77	72	64	41	.38
Oppose death penalty	37	25	19	11	11	.37
Favor gun control	56	50	46	44	28	.21
Favor abortion rights	66	64	62	55	36	.19
Favor affirmative action	56	33	34	21	17	.30
Oppose tax cut	70	54	39	32	13	.40
Mean	63	52	46	34	20	
Liberal identifiers	74	62	38	10	02	.76

Source: National Election Studies, 1996.

On one issue, aid to Russia, Republicans are slightly more liberal, perhaps because friendship with Russia was an idea associated with Republican presidents.

Figure 3.3 displays the difference between Democratic and Republican identifiers in terms of scores on the composite ten-item index of liberalism-conservatism. In terms of their net ideological direction, most Democrats are left of center and most Republicans are right of center, but there are many exceptions. In fact, the reader might be surprised by the proportions of the public who appear as conservative Democrats and liberal Republicans. Clearly, ideology and partisanship are not the same thing.

The correlation between partisanship and ideological direction sharpens if we isolate informed citizens. Figure 3.4 repeats the ideological comparison of Democrats and Republicans, this time separately, for voters at the low and high end of the information scale.

Among low-information voters, there exists almost no correlation between partisanship and ideology; among this set, Democrats are only barely to the left of Republicans on average, with considerable overlap. But among high-information voters, virtually all Democrats are to the left of center and virtually all Republicans to the right. In other words, find an informed voter and partisanship follows ideology, or perhaps it is the other way around.

Issue differences between Republican and Democratic identifiers have grown in response to the perception of widening party differences. While Democratic identifiers have been somewhat more liberal than Republicans on social welfare issues since the 1930s, only recently have Democratic identifiers become more liberal than Republican identifiers on other issues. As with perceptions, differences in Democratic and Republican views showed their greatest increase around the time of the ideological 1964 election. Before that time, Democrats in the electorate were not identifiably more liberal on civil rights, foreign policy, or social issues. Of course, they had no reason to be, since people saw the two parties as differing only on the social welfare dimension.

What causes the consistency between political opinions and party identification? Do people learn their political opinions from their party identifica-

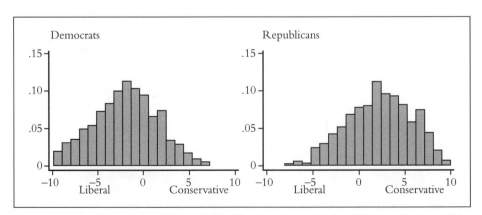

Figure 3.3   Composite opinion by party identification. *Source:* National Election Studies, 1996.

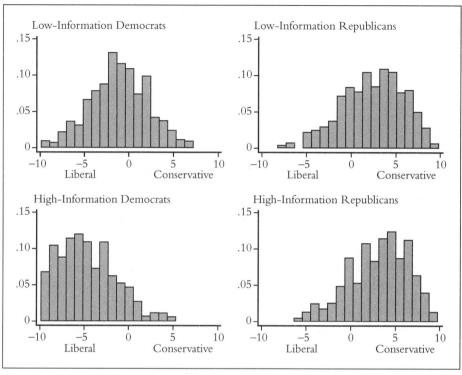

Figure 3.4 Democratic and Republican composite opinion, by information level. *Source:* National Election Studies, 1996.

tions, or do political opinions shape party identifications? Undoubtedly both causal processes are at work, but their relative contributions can only be roughly estimated.

Because party identification can be such a strong and stable attitude, some have argued that partisanship drives policy opinions more than the reverse (Campbell et al. 1960, ch. 6; Luttbeg 1981). Often, when parties realign their positions on an issue, their supporters will follow. Consider, for example, the opinions of partisans after Republican President Nixon initiated the thaw in U.S. relations with the People's Rebublic of China in the early 1970s. Republicans abandoned their hostility to "Red China" faster than Democrats.[9] Similarly, when President Reagan initiated a new friendship with the Soviet Union, Republicans were quicker to think the cold war was over.[10] When in early 1991 many congressional Democrats balked at supporting President Bush's intervention in the Persian Gulf, the Democratic rank and file became more dovish and Republican rank and file became more hawkish (Zaller 1992, 104–5). Finally, just the reverse occurred in the spring of 1999 when congressional Republicans balked at supporting President Clinton's policy of halting ethnic cleansing in Kosovo by bombing Serbia.[11]

While partisanship influences people's perceptions of the world and shapes their opinions, often it is party identification that changes when initial partisanship and issue positions get out of alignment (Markus and Converse 1979; Page and Jones 1979; Franklin and Jackson 1983; Jacoby 1989). Some who become ideologically disaffected from their home party become Independents (Luskin et al. 1989). Those who go all the way and shift from one party to the other often display the ideological zeal of true converts.

Party Identification: Psychological Identification or Running Tally?

Political scientists still do not fully understand party identification. *The American Voter* (Campbell et al. 1960, ch. 6) presented one influential interpretation: that one's party identification is essentially a psychological attachment or "affective orientation" to one's favorite party. By this view, party identification can approach blind loyalty, as when people find reason to support their party's position and vote for its candidates long after they have rational reasons for doing so.

Some scholars, however, emphasize the more rational aspects of party identification. By this view, people learn a party identification based on what Morris Fiorina (1977) calls a "running tally" of their partisan decisions. For example, voters who find repeated reason to vote Republican will begin to call themselves Republican—not so much out of psychological attachment as by way of learning a convenient shorthand rule for deciding how to vote. If reasons develop for such voters to vote Democratic instead, they will not blindly continue down the Republican path in the face of contrary evidence. Instead, they will vote Democratic or even change partisanship in response to the new running tally.

Both interpretations of partisanship carry some validity. For example, many partisans persist in voting loyally for their party even when their party no longer represents their views on issues. But many partisans casually change their allegiance when circumstances seem to warrant it. Perhaps our question should be whether by forming a standing decision to vote Democratic or Republican, people enhance or detract from their ability to vote rationally. We will address this question in later chapters.

NOTES

1. Analysts must be sensitive to the accuracy of the reasons people give for their opinions. For instance, people can recall their position on some matter but not the original reasons, and then rationalize their choice with new reasons that may not have had any bearing on their choice. There now exists a lengthy literature on how people store and retrieve political information when making or remembering political judgments. For some recent examples, see Lodge and Stroh (1993) and Wyer and Ottati (1993).
2. Two examples show the relative anonymity of Washington personalities among the public at large. When Edwin Meese was appointed attorney general by Reagan in 1991, one-quarter admitted to having heard the name. Of the remainder, one-quarter could not remember anything about him. Overall, most did not identify Meese as the new attorney general (Robinson and Clancey 1984). As a second example, a 1993 Times-Mirror survey asked respondents to evaluate several supposedly well-known newspeople.

   While the national sample had little difficulty rating television celebrities such as network anchors, many respondents had difficulty with the one person on the list whose primary role was in print rather than broadcast journalism. This person was George Will, the well-known conservative columnist. Slightly more than half failed to rate Will, including 41 who said they did not know who he was.

3. Sample sizes represent 500+ respondents. The fact that the responses shown in Table 3.3 are part of a framing experiment is not a source of serious distortion. In some instances, different framing in the two waves enhances response turnover. Yet this contamination appears slight. For issues in which some respondents were given variable framings and others the same framing, the effect of this difference in stimulus appears to have been but a few percentage points. Where some respondents repeatedly received an elaborate framing of the underlying arguments for the two points of view while a control group got none, responses were more stable when respondents received framing.

4. The abortion question was actually asked three times in the 1989 NES pilot study. The pilot respondents were first asked their abortion views in late 1988, as part of the regular NES 1988 election survey. Over three waves, only 26 percent took a consistent pro-life position and only 27 percent took a consistent pro-choice position. An even smaller 5 percent were consistently in the middle, but 42 percent took a middle position in at least one wave.

5. As a practical matter, the single dimension of liberal-conservative ideology is a better measure of underlying political values than specific values measured individually. Zaller (1992, 26) states the case nicely: "There is . . . a tendency for people to be fairly consistently 'left,' 'right,' or 'centrist' on such disparate value dimensions as economic individualism, opinions toward Communists, tolerance of nonconformists, racial issues, sexual freedom, and religious authority. The correlations among these different value dimensions are never so strong as to suggest that there is one and only one basic value dimension, but they are always at least moderately strong, and among highly aware persons, the correlations are sometimes quite strong. And, of course, there are also moderately strong correlations between people's self-descriptions as liberal or conservative and their scores on the various value measures.

6. For discussions of the origins of liberal-conservative terminology, see Kerlinger (1984) and Rotunda (1986).

7. On the increase in ideologues in 1964, see Field and Anderson (1970); Pierce (1970); Nie et al. (1976); and T. Smith (1990). Some studies (Nie et al., Smith) define ideologues far more generously than we do here, to include any mention of the liberal-conservative language.

8. Correlations between opinions appear to have increased since the early readings in the 1950s. The greatest jump occurred at the time of the ideological 1964 election (Nie and Anderson 1974; Nie et al. 1976). Some scholars believe this increase is largely illusory, the result of better questions asked by survey researchers (Sullivan et al. 1978; Bishop et al. 1978).

9. For instance, between 1966 and 1971, the percentage of Democratic opinion-holders who told Gallup they favored UN admission for China rose from one-third to nearly half. Meanwhile Republican support rose from 1 in 4 to a clear plurality in favor of admission.

10. For instance, in 1984 (pre-Gorbachev) and 1988, "strong Democrats" (with opinions) increased their support for cooperation with Russia by four percentage points. "Strong Republicans" (with opinions) increased their support by 24 points (1984 and 1988 NES data).

11. Pew Research Center Poll, June 9–13, 1999.

CHAPTER 4

Macrolevel Opinion: The Flow of Political Sentiment

Public opinion specialists begin their investigations of survey data by analyzing the "frequencies," or the percentaged divisions of opinion for the sample. The frequency distributions reflect the content of public opinion at the moment of the poll. When a particular survey question has been repeatedly asked in the past, the latest frequencies also provide information about the opinion trends.

Frequency distributions must be interpreted with caution because, as we saw in Chapter 2, responses are often influenced by question wording. When the polls show a certain percentage favoring a particular response to a question, we need some anchor, some reference point, by which to measure the significance of the finding. One way is to compare the frequencies for one question with those for slightly different but related questions. This comparison allows us to see what distinctions the mass public makes in the kinds of policies it is willing to support. A particularly useful anchor is to compare answers to the same question over time. If the public displays a different level of support for some policy today than one year ago or five years ago, then we may have located a potentially important change in public opinion.

Unfortunately, the data that would allow for the accurate assessment of trends in public opinion are often not as available as one might expect. Commercial pollsters naturally ask questions that are of current interest to their media clients. As popular interest fades, those questions are often not repeated. Academic polling units are more concerned with the continuity and comparability of questions over time, but even they are not immune to the wax and wane of topical issues. Thus questions dealing with civil liberties were frequently asked in the "McCarthy era" of the early 1950s, when many people thought our basic personal liberties were threatened. Such questions were not asked again until the early 1970s. Questions about race relations were seldom asked prior to the 1960s, when the aspirations of the black minority were given little thought by white politicians, press, and public. Even when the polls monitor opinions on the same issue over time, they often vary question wording so it is difficult to separate real change from question-wording effects.

In the following sections we present an overview of macrolevel public opinion, or what polls tell us about the content of public opinion both today and in the past. Poll trends are often described in ideological or partisan terms, as if the public's frame of reference is shifting on the liberal-conservative or Democratic-Republican continuums. We begin by first examining opinion on specific policy issues that have been polled over the years, searching for liberal or conservative trends that might be specific to the issue at hand. Second, we consider the possibility of general ideological movement. Third, we examine changes in the distribution of party identification over the years. And fourth, we consider one important partisan question well-known for its volatility: the president's approval rating.

4-1 TRENDS IN POLICY OPINIONS

For convenience, most policy questions can be divided into four general domains: (1) social welfare, (2) civil rights, (3) foreign policy, and (4) social issues. Social welfare controversies pertain to the distribution of wealth and government efforts to help the disadvantaged; civil rights refer to the quest for equality under the law; foreign policy obviously refers to views about the U.S. role abroad, and social issues usually involve differences over lifestyles or "moral values," such as abortion, prayer in the public schools, or capital punishment.

Social Welfare Issues

From the New Deal to the present, the American public has been receptive to government programs to accomplish economic welfare objectives. In fact, on social welfare legislation, mass opinion has often been well ahead of congressional action. For example, the earliest polls revealed an overwhelming majority (89 percent) in favor of "old age pensions" prior to the adoption of the Social Security Act in 1936 (Cantril 1951, 521). A majority also supported the right of workers to organize and bargain collectively before the 1941 Wagner Act enacted these principles into law (Page and Shapiro 1992, 136). Majority approval has continually been found prior to each increase in the federal minimum wage (Erskine 1962b, 26; Gallup Poll Index, Sept. 1985, 17).

It has long been noted that the American public is ideologically conservative, but operationally liberal (Free and Cantril 1968; Cantril and Cantril 1999). Polls persistently show self-identified conservatives outnumbering self-identified liberals. When it comes to specific social welfare programs, however, most people generally are supportive of liberal spending. For example, when NES asked in 1996 if the government should "provide fewer services, even in areas such as health and education in order to reduce spending" or should the government "provide more services and spending" 39 percent chose more services and spending, 32 percent chose fewer services and less spending, with the remainder taking the middle position.[1]

Table 4.1 shows that very few Americans want reductions in federal spending for a wide variety of social programs. The most frequent preference, in fact, is not to reduce spending or even to keep spending the same, but to increase spending across a wide variety of social programs such as social security, job training, medical research, grants to college students, and consumer product safety, as well as other programs. Despite occasional rhetoric to the contrary, the services provided by government to its citizens are very popular.

Of course, there are limits to the public's enthusiasm for social welfare programs. Most notably, Americans clearly make the classic distinction between the "deserving poor" (those who have fallen on hard times through no fault of their own) and the "shiftless poor," who would rather receive a government handout than hold a job.[2] Thus, in the mid-1980s one poll showed that 88 percent of those with opinions agreed that the government ought to help those "who are unable to support themselves," while at the same time 91 percent agreed that "too many people on welfare could be working" and 94 percent said "too many people on welfare get money to which they are not entitled" (Page and Shapiro 1992, 125). This distinction can be seen most graphically by large changes in poll numbers when slight changes are made in the way questions are phrased.

TABLE 4.1   OPINIONS ON SELECTED FEDERAL WELFARE PROGRAM, 1996–1998

Should spending increase, decrease, or stay the same for:	Increase	Stay the Same	Decrease
Social Security[†]	60%	33%	7%
Improving and protecting health[†]	69	25	6
Improving educational system[†]	71	22	7
Welfare[†]	16	38	46
Assistance to the poor[†]	63	24	11
Protecting the environment[†]	63	29	8
Food stamps★	10	42	46
Aid to college students★	55	38	8
Aid to homeless★	57	31	12
Research on AIDS★	56	33	11

★National Election Studies, 1996.

[†]General Social Survey, 1998.

For example, in a question-wording experiment, one-half of the 1998 GSS sample was asked their view on spending "for assistance to the poor." Sixty-three percent said the government should increase spending.[3] The other half of the sample was asked for their views on spending "for welfare." Only 16 percent said the government should increase spending. More than a mere illustration of question-wording effects, this experiment reflects a belief among Americans that the government should help those who cannot help themselves, but that those who can work and do not merit little sympathy. There is a widespread belief among the American public that people who receive financial assistance ought to work for their money, even if the work they do is of little use.

Health Care As we noted earlier, the public has frequently been out in front of elected officials on many innovations in social welfare policy. This has certainly been the case with regard to health care. Since the 1930s, opinion polls have consistently shown the public favors some form of government intervention. In 1937, a Gallup Poll showed that over 70 percent favored the notion that "the federal government should provide free medical and dental care for those who cannot pay." During the 1950s and 1960s, 60 to 65 percent supported the principle of the government paying the medical bills of the elderly, which was enacted into law in 1965 with Medicare (Erskine 1975). In 1975 and 1985 Roper Polls, 76 percent and 73 percent respectively, thought adequate medical care was a "right" to which citizens were entitled. But these sentiments do not necessarily mean the public wants socialized medicine or the government directly running health care. Most Americans seem to prefer a mixed system, with private insurance available, perhaps subsided by the government or employers, with the state acting only as the provider of last resort (Page and Shapiro 1992, 131).

Using the NES seven-point Medicare question—where point 1 represents a "government health insurance plan which would cover all medical and hospital expenses," and point 7 indicates that expenses would be "paid to individuals through private insurance"—we can see that preferences for the two approaches are about equal as shown in Figure 4.1. The only exception occured in 1992 when Clinton's reform package—the Health Security Act—was a prominent campaign theme.[4] Preference for a government plan rose to an all-time high of 45 percent, and preference for a private plan dropped to 24 percent. As congress was poised to act on the Clinton plan, the health care industry mounted a major counterattack and two years later, in 1994, only 37 percent preferred a government plan and 35 percent favored a private plan. By 1996, fortunes had reversed and a slightly larger percentage of the public (38 percent) preferred a private health plan over a government health plan.[5] The failure of the Clinton health care initiative demonstrates the difficulty of achieving fundamental change on a complex issue. It is easy to point out certain negative aspects of a proposal, even if taken in whole the proposal has considerable merit. There seems little doubt that the reversal in public opinion was a major factor leading to the defeat of Clinton's proposed Health Security Act (Koch 1998, Jacobs and Shapiro 2000).

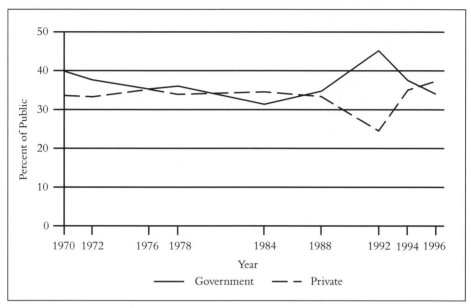

Figure 4.1   Private versus government health insurance. *Source:* National Election Studies, 1970–1996.

Taxes Regardless of how the question is phrased, a majority of the public invariably respond that taxes are too high. When asked in 1998 how to spend the projected federal budget surplus, 66 percent said a tax cut should be the top or a high priority. When asked in 1997 if federal taxes were too high, about right, or too low, 65 percent respond "too high." Only 1 percent said "too low." In 1991, 77 percent said taxes in this country were "unreasonable," and 66 percent claimed that high taxes had pushed their family to the breaking point.

Antitax sentiment has fluctuated over time. Gallup has asked its sample question about "too high" federal income taxes regularly since 1947. For this question, the least antitax sentiment was in March 1949, when only 49 percent said taxes were too high. With new taxes to pay for the Korean War, the number quickly shot up to 73 percent in March 1952. It then declined gradually, dropping to 49 percent in 1961. The costs of the Vietnam War helped push the figure upward again, to 73 percent in 1969. After the war, antitax sentiment declined through the mid-1970s, only to rise again in the late 1970s as part of an overall antigovernment right turn. With the Reagan tax cuts of 1981, sentiment that taxes were too high declined to 55 percent in 1988 (Page and Shapiro 1992, 162–63). But with the Democrats recapturing the White House and memories of the Reagan tax cuts fading, sentiment that taxes are too high had risen to 68 percent by 1999.

Some cynical observers point to the seemingly inconsistent poll data on spending and taxes as a demonstration that the public irrationally expects to have its cake and eat it too. Citizens want a plethora of public services (as shown earlier in Table 4.1), but they do not want to pay for them (Free and Cantril 1967; Sears and Citrin 1985). But when the views of the public are assessed with realistic questions designed to measure the trade-offs between taxes and services, the public appears quite rational on the subject. An example of a question assessing trade-offs is "Do you favor cuts in national defense spending in order to cut the taxes paid by ordinary Americans?" Using this strategy, Hansen (1998) probed trade-offs among domestic spending, military spending, taxes, and deficits. Majorities in 1994 rejected all trade-offs that would cut services to reduce taxes but accepted every trade-off that would cut military spending. The public mostly endorsed the status quo, but in a fashion that lends strong evidence to the "rational public" argument. That is, the respondents clearly recognized they cannot have it both ways—more spending and lower taxes.[6]

Civil Rights

Discerning the true attitudes held by white Americans on civil rights issues has proved to be a difficult and controversial task. Taking easy issues first, polls clearly show at a minimum that Americans have rejected the prevalent "white supremacist" ideology that pervaded mass attitudes as recently as a few decades ago. Poll data from the 1930s and 1940s suggest that perhaps a majority of white Americans once believed blacks to be intellectually inferior and undeserving of equal status with whites. In 1939, a Roper Poll found 76 percent of white respondents agreeing that "Negroes" had generally "lower" intelligence than white people (Page and Shapiro 1992). As late as 1944, just 44 percent believed that "Negroes are as intelligent as white people" (Erskine 1962a). But only 12 percent of whites, in a March 1994 Harris survey agreed with the stereotype that blacks have less native intelligence than other races. Nevertheless, even as we begin a new century some argue that much of the white population still holds blatantly prejudicial attitudes (Kuklinski et al. 1997).

In an analysis of public opinion on racial issues, it is common to distinguish between questions concerning the goals or ideals of the civil rights movement, and government action to actually implement those goals into public policy. The public is more supportive of the abstract goals of the civil rights movement than their implementation. For example, when asked in 1985 if black and white children should go to the same or separate schools, 93 percent of whites preferred the ideal of both races "going to the same schools" (GSS). But when asked if the government in Washington "should see to it" that black and white children attend the same schools, or if this is "not the government's business," just 41 percent of whites supported implementation of the ideal by government action (NES 1994).

We see a somewhat similar pattern in the trends over time. Whites have become much more liberal on questions concerning the ideals of the civil rights movement, but not on the implementation of these ideals. In terms of ideals, endorsement of fair employment practices for blacks rose from 42 percent in 1944 to 96 percent by 1972 (Smith and Sheatsley 1984, 15–16). In 1958, only 37 percent of white respondents indicated they would vote for a well-qualified black candidate for president, but by 1996, 93 percent would do so (Niemi et al. 1989; GSS 1996). In 1944, 45 percent said Negroes should have as good a chance as whites to get a job; by 1972, a near-consensus of 97 percent shared that belief (Page and Shapiro 1992, 69).

Figure 4.2 presents trends in white support for integrated schools, both in terms of principle and implementation. First, consider the question of whether white and black children should attend the same or separate schools. In 1942, just 30 percent said "same school" and 66 percent said "separate schools." Figure 4.2 picks up the series in 1956, when the trend had moved 19 points in a liberal direction to 49 percent for "same school." By 1985 (the last year the question was asked), 93 percent of the white public favored the ideal of black and white children attending the same school. Thus from 1942 to 1985, there was a 62 percent increase in white support for integrated schools, perhaps the largest change in public opinion for which we have data.

Figure 4.2 shows a different trend, however, on the question of whether the "government in Washington should see to it" that black and white children go to the same schools. When framed in terms of possible federal action, there is less support for the integration positions, with white Americans more in favor of government action in the 1960s than in the 1970s and later. While opposition to racial discrimination is almost universal, attitudes about government intervention are anything but consensual.

Still, not all implementation trends are conservative. Figure 4.2 shows that in the case of busing, whites have become more supportive. While busing re-

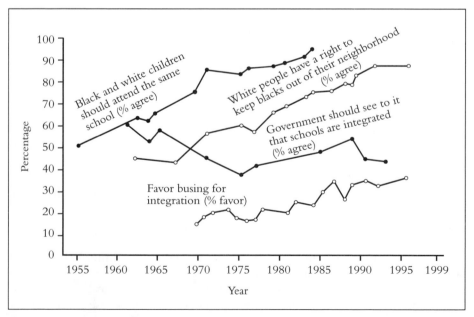

Figure 4.2   Support for school integration, open housing, and busing to integrate public schools. *Source:* National Opinion Research Center, Gallup, and General Social Survey.

mains generally unpopular, there is nevertheless a steady liberal trend amounting to a 19 percentage point increase in support over a 20-year period. Perhaps busing is not as threatening now as it was in the past. Few white children are actually bused out of their neighborhoods, and the magnet school approach, which often requires busing, has generally met with approval.

Finally, Figure 4.2 shows that whites have increasingly rejected the right to keep blacks from their neighborhoods. Note, however, that it was not until 1972 that a majority of whites settled on that view. By 1996, the number disagreeing that white people "had a right" to keep blacks out of their neighborhood had grown to 87 percent. This change in attitude is mirrored by a change in behavior. In 1966 only 20 percent of whites said there were blacks living in their neighborhood. In 1996, 62 percent said blacks lived there (GSS).

Affirmative Action Certainly the most controversial issue in the implementation of civil rights is "affirmative action." Whites are overwhelmingly nonsupportive, as seen from responses to the following NES questions:[7]

Some people say that because of past discrimination it is sometimes necessary for colleges and universities to reserve openings for black students. Others oppose quotas because they say quotas give blacks advantages they haven't earned. What about your opinion—are you for or against quotas to admit black students?

	For	Against	Unsure
1988:	33%	58%	9%
1994:	20%	74%	6%

Some people say that because of past discrimination, blacks should be given preference in hiring and promotion. Others say that such preference in hiring and promotion is wrong because it discriminates against whites. What about your opinion—are you for or against preferential hiring for blacks?

	For	Against	Unsure
1988:	19%	75%	6%
1996:	17%	78%	5%

White attitudes on affirmative action are very firmly held. In a series of experiments designed to see if respondents could be "talked out" of various positions on race-related issues, Sniderman and Piazza (1993) had considerable success on a variety of social welfare issues, but little success on affirmative action. They also found a correlation between negative stereotypes about blacks and attitudes about affirmative action. One might infer that such negative stereotypes lead to an opposition to affirmative action. But Sniderman and Piazza (1993, 97–104) present evidence for the reverse effect as well—that opposition to affirmative action leads to a negative stereotyping of blacks. One-half of a sample was selected randomly and asked if they agreed or disagreed with a variety of stereotypes about African-Americans—they are irresponsible, they are lazy, they are arrogant. These questions were then immediately *followed* by a single question about affirmative action in employment. The other half of the sample was asked the same questions about blacks, but they were immediately *preceded* by the question about affirmative action in employment. The data show significantly higher percentages of negative stereotypes about blacks for the sample getting the affirmative action question preceding as opposed to following the racial stereotype questions. Sniderman and Piazza (1993, 109) concluded that "affirmative action is so intensely disliked that it has led some whites to dislike blacks—an ironic example of a policy meant to put the divide of race behind us in fact further widening it."

How does one explain the lack of support among whites for specific remedies to solve the problem of racial discrimination in the face of their overwhelming support for the ideals of racial integration? Two explanations are commonly debated: race per se and the politics of race. The first of these, the "symbolic racism" argument (Sears and Kinder 1971; Kinder and Sanders 1996), holds there has been very little change in whites' attitudes about African-Americans which remain mostly hostile. When asked opinions about policy questions with racial implications, whites are more likely to respond to the racial symbol (e.g., "black") rather than the policy content of the question. However, over the years public expression of racist sentiment became increasingly unfashionable. Outright racial discrimination also became illegal. Consequently, people learned it was socially unacceptable to express overtly racist opinions. Instead, racial hostility is expressed indirectly by a glorification of traditional values such as "the work ethic" and "individualism," in which blacks and some other minorities are seen as deficient (Sears et al. 1997). Thus some of the apparent liberal trend in racial attitudes is not real change but simply reflects the need to express "socially desirable" opinions. Opposition to implementation, usually on grounds other than race, is simply disingenuous.[8]

A rival explanation is simple, straightforward politics. Sniderman and Piazza (1993, 107) argue that "the central problem of racial politics is *not* the problem of prejudice" (italics in the original). The agenda of the civil rights movement has changed from one of equal opportunity to equal outcomes. No fair-minded person could find consistency between the American Creed and denial of voting rights, segregated universities, workplaces, and lunch counters, and confinement to the back of the bus. But in the eyes of many, the new civil rights agenda of racial quotas and affirmative action very much clashes with the principle of equal treatment for all. Its implementation also requires an activist, expansionist government. Antistatism, manifested as hostility to federal power, is a long-standing tradition in American politics. The political explanation holds that inconsistencies with the American Creed, and concerns about the power and trustworthiness of the federal government, prevent many whites (particularly conservative whites) from translating an abstract commitment to racial equality into support for specific federal policies (Sniderman and Carmines, 1997).

Foreign Policy

Scholars often depict public opinion on questions of foreign policy as being particularly shallow and without meaningful content. Typical is the observation by Light and Lake (1985, 94) that "public opinion polls show that people do not follow foreign affairs closely and often do not know enough about the specifics of a particular issue to form opinions." As applied to most citizens on most foreign policy issues, one cannot easily object to this statement. However, an important foreign policy matter can easily grab the public's attention and profoundly affect the popularity of the president or the outcome of the next election.

Foreign policy opinions are subject to more abrupt changes than are domestic policy opinions. If "abrupt" change is defined as ten or more percentage points over a single year, abrupt changes are twice as likely on foreign policy as on domestic issues (Page and Shapiro 1989). The explanation is straightforward: There are simply more dramatic events on the international scene than on the domestic scene. Few domestic occurrences have the impact of the Cuban missile crisis, the Iran hostage crisis, the invasions of Grenada and Panama, and the war in the Persian Gulf.

Internationalism versus Isolationism One volatile indicator of foreign policy sentiment is mass preferences for an internationalist versus an isolationist posture in foreign policy. Prior to World War II, American opinion was strongly isolationist. In 1937, 70 percent of opinion-holders said U.S. entry into World War I had been a mistake (Free and Cantril 1968, 62). That same year, 94 percent of opinion-holders said the United States should "do everything possible to keep out of foreign wars" rather than "do everything possible to prevent war. . . ." Between 1939 and late 1941, the percentage who said they would vote in favor of entering the war against Germany rose only from 13 to 32 percent. Support for war with Japan a month before Pearl Harbor was even lower, with just 19 percent endorsing the view that "the United States should take steps to keep Japan from becoming too powerful, even if this means risking a war with Japan" (Hero n.d.).

But once the United States was involved in World War II, internationalist sentiment increased sharply. By June 1943, 83 percent said the United States would have to play a larger part in world affairs than before the war (Page and Shapiro 1992, 176). Figure 4.3 tracks post–World War II internationalist versus isolationist sentiment as monitored by the question of whether the United States should "take an active part" or "stay out" of world affairs.

The high point of internationalist sentiment occurred in the mid-1960s, just before full American involvement in the Vietnam conflict. Poll results such as these helped to convince the makers of American foreign policy that the American public would put up with a long and protracted war in Vietnam. Of course, they were tragically mistaken. The public turned against the war, and internationalist sentiment took a sharp decline. In August 1965, 24 percent thought it was a mistake sending troops to Vietnam; by December 1967, this

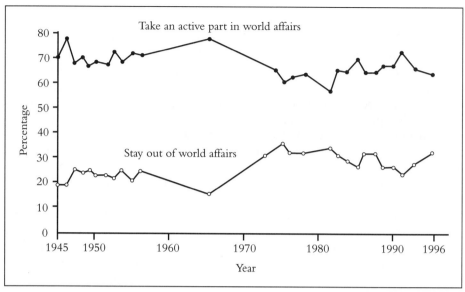

Figure 4.3   "Do you think it would be best for the future of this country if we take an active part in world affairs, or if we stayed out of world affairs?" *Source:* The U.S. Role in the World Poll, 1996: University of Maryland, Gallup, National Opinion Research Center, and General Social Survey.

number had risen to 45 percent, and as American involvement faded, it increased to 61 percent in May 1971 (Niemi et al. 1989, 71). By 1975, the proportion who wanted the United States to "stay out of world affairs" surged to 36 percent. The proportion has changed little since then (see Figure 4.3).

Just as Figure 4.3 shows most Americans have favored an internationalist position in foreign affairs, most Americans have historically also favored U.S. participation in the United Nations—despite a minority of vocal critics. In 1997, only 9 percent of the population said we "should give up" our membership in the UN (versus 88 percent who said we should not), 70 percent had a "mostly favorable" view of the UN (21 percent said "mostly unfavorable") and in 1998 73 percent favored paying the $1.6 billion in back dues owed the UN by the United States.[9]

Defense Spending   One source of frequently shifting opinion is public perception of the adequacy of defense spending. Figure 4.4 shows a roller coaster of changing beliefs regarding whether the United States is spending "too little on the military, armaments, and defense."

Beginning in 1978, large segments of the public began to believe that U.S. defenses were underfunded. This conservative trend resulted in part from the Soviet Union's invasion of Afghanistan in 1979, which President Carter denounced as "the worst threat to world peace since World War II." In protest, he withdrew American participation in the 1980 Moscow Olympics. Also in 1979,

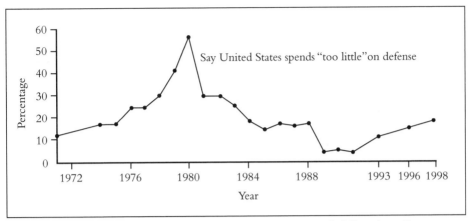

Figure 4.4 Percentage who say the United States is spending "too little" on the military, armaments, and defense. *Source:* Roper and General Social Survey.

American hostages were held in Iran, and the United States seemed powerless to get them back. Following a renewed military buildup under both Carter and Reagan, the citizenry became reassured that America's defenses were again strong. As the 1980s progressed, support for increased defense spending retreated to the level of the early 1970s. Finally, with the collapse of the Soviet Union in the early 1990s, support for increases in defense spending fell to record lows, but were followed by an uptick as the century drew to a close.

Russia and China Since the end of World War II, the most relevant foreign policy question has been how the United States conducts its foreign policy in relationship to the former Soviet Union and to China. Mass attitudes toward these nations have generally followed the lead of American foreign policy. During World War II, when the Soviet Union and the United States were allies, favorable attitudes toward the USSR grew until, at war's end, 55 percent said, "Russia can be counted on to cooperate with us once the war is over." This trust, born of wartime camaraderie, soon evaporated, and by October 1946, the percentage who thought Russia could "be trusted to cooperate with us during the next few years" dropped to 28 percent. By the late 1940s, most Americans thought it was more important "to stop Soviet expansion in Europe and Asia than avoid a major war." During the Korean War and in the early 1950s, a majority said they expected war with Russia during their lifetime (Hero n.d.).

The chill of the cold war reached its nadir in the early 1950s. As can be seen from Figure 4.5, in 1953 and 1954 only 2 percent of the public said they "like" the Soviet Union.[10]

But beginning in the 1950s, Americans gradually began to warm to the world's other superpower. By 1973, with the Vietnam War winding down, liking of Russia surged to 45 percent. Then following the 1979 Soviet invasion of Afghanistan and, later, President Reagan's rhetoric about the Soviet Union

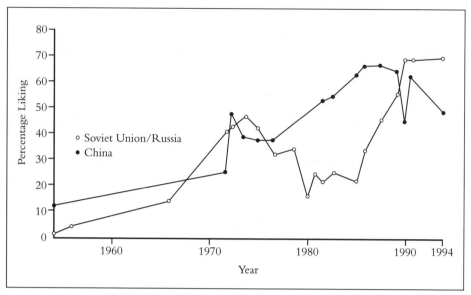

Figure 4.5   Percentage who "like" Russia/Soviet Union and China. *Source:* Gallup and General Social Survey.

as the "evil empire," a new chill in attitudes set in. Then a major warming of attitudes toward Russia occurred after the demise of the Soviet Union in 1991, the implementation of democratic elections, and the end of the cold war.

Americans' attitudes toward China have also responded to events. Back in the 1960s and earlier, the United States did not even recognize the Chinese government and vigorously opposed "Red China's" membership in the United Nations. As late as 1964, only 14 percent of the public favored UN membership for China (even in 1971, the year it was admitted, a majority of Americans still opposed membership). Public sentiment toward China gradually warmed (see Figure 4.5), except for a temporary plunge in 1990 following the crackdown on student protesters in Tiananmen Square. By 1993, favorable sentiment toward China, while on the increase, fell for the first time behind favorable sentiment toward Russia. By that index, Russia forged slightly into the lead.

Social Issues

In recent years, a new set of concerns called "social issues" have appeared on the American political agenda. In their broadest context, these issues involve conflicts between the forces committed to maintaining "traditional moral values." Examples of social issues include prayer in the public schools, decriminalization of marijuana use, government restrictions on pornography, and tolerance for gay lifestyles. Recent opinion on these issues is shown in Table 4.2.

TABLE 4.2 OPINION DISTRIBUTIONS ON SOCIAL ISSUES (PERCENTAGE OF OPINION-HOLDERS)

		Liberal	Conservative
Marijuana	Do you think marijuana should be made legal or not?†	29 (yes)	73 (no)
Gay rights	Should there be laws to protect homosexuals against job discrimination?★	64 (yes)	36 (no)
Pornography	Should there be laws against the distribution of pornography whatever the age?★	62 (no)	38 (yes)
Sex education	Do you favor sex education in the public schools?†	87 (yes)	13 (no)
Prayer in schools	Should prayer be permitted in public schools?‡	30 (no)	70 (yes)

★National Election Studies, 1996.
†General Social Survey, 1998.
‡CBS/*New York Times*, 1997.

On social issues, the public is generally thought to be rather conservative. Many but not all the divisions shown in Table 4.2 support this perception. One obvious limitation on the public's social conservatism is a willingness to support sex education in public schools.

Even on school prayer the public's conservatism should not be exaggerated, though when offered only the choice between prayer and no prayer a substantial majority will choose prayer (see Table 4.2). But consider responses to a 1997 CBS/*New York Times* survey in which respondents were offered three choices instead of two: (1) the Lord's Prayer or Bible verse said daily, (2) a silent prayer or meditation daily, or (3) no prayer or religious observation. Most (55 percent) preferred the "mild" solution that schools offer a moment of silence. The remainder split 22 percent in favor of a daily prayer or Bible verse and 21 percent favoring no religious observance.

Because most of the social issues presented in Table 4.2 are relatively new on the public agenda, it is difficult to establish trend lines of any length. Nevertheless, there are some trend data available. In the case of the legalization of marijuana, support peaked at 30 percent in 1978, declined to 16 percent in 1987, but by 1996 had risen to 27 percent. For pornography laws, the trend has been stable at least since 1973, with those favoring laws against its distribution ranging between 57 and 63 percent. The same stability occurs for sex education and prayer in the public schools, Opinion in these two areas has been more or less constant for the last 20 years (Niemi et al. 1989; NES 1996; CBS/*New York Times* 1997). Support for gay rights has increased in recent decades, support for laws protecting homosexuals against job discrimination went up by 10 percent between 1988 and 1996. Other surveys also show an increasing tolerance among the public for gay lifestyles.

Law and Order One set of issue opinions that show a decidedly conservative trend are those dealing with law and order (Flanagan and Longmire 1996). Opinion on the death penalty (which had trended liberal from the 1930s to the 1960s) provides the clearest example. As can be seen from Figure 4.6, support for the death penalty for convicted murderers rose from around 50 percent in the 1950s and 1960s to over 70 percent in the 1980s and 1990s, with 71 percent favoring the death penalty in 1999. However, if respondents are offered an option of "life imprisonment with no possibility of parole" in addition to the death penalty, support for the death penalty drops to 56 percent (Gallup 1999). Figure 4.6 also shows considerable public sentiment for the view that the courts do not deal harshly enough with criminals. By 1998, 80 percent endorsed that position, up 35 percentage points from 1965.

Figure 4.6 also shows that increases in support for the death penalty and beliefs that the courts do not deal harshly enough with criminals roughly tracked the rate of violent crime up to 1990. Some (Mayer 1992) have claimed that the increase in support for the death penalty was a reaction to the increase in violent crime. But as Figure 4.6 demonstrates, beginning about 1990 the rate of violent crime fell dramatically. There has, however, been only a slight decline in support for the death penalty or a preference for the harsh treatment of criminals. This trend suggests that political rhetoric and media attention are more proximate causes for opinion about crime than the level of crime itself.

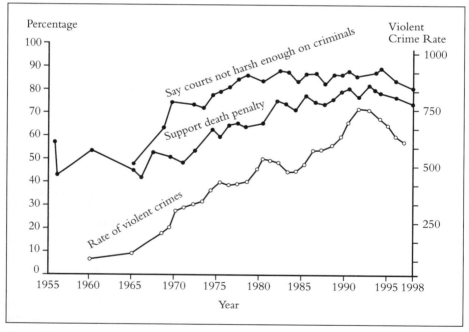

Figure 4.6 Law and order opinion and the rate of violent crime. *Source:* Richard G. Niemi, John Mueller, and Tom W. Smith, *Trends in Public Opinion* (New York: Greenwood, 1989), General Social Survey (1989–1998), Harold W. Stanley and Richard G. Niemi, *Vital Statistics of American Politics, 1999–2000* (Washington, D.C.: *Congressional Quarterly,* 2000).

In the 1980s elected officials clearly reacted to changing opinion on crime with policy innovations such as mandatory sentences and life terms for those convicted of three felonies. Although violent crime is decreasing, there is no discernible move to modify these harsher policies, which suggests there is no simple connection between the crime rate, public opinion, and the penal code.

Women and Politics If law and order questions have shown a strong conservative trend, opinion about the appropriate role of women in politics shows an equally strong liberal trend. From Gallup and GSS, we have data spanning 50 years on the question of whether the public would vote for a qualified woman for president—the ultimate nontraditional role. As shown below, we see a strong leftward flow of opinion on this issue, beginning with the advent of the women's movement in the late 1960s. The trend then abated somewhat in the late 1970s with the defeat of the Equal Rights Amendment and the organization of opposition to legal abortion, and then began another leftward move in the late 1980s.

Percentage Who Would Vote for a Qualified Woman for President

1937	33	1958	54	1972	70	1991	87
1945	38	1963	55	1975	78	1993	91
1949	50	1967	57	1978	79	1996	94
1955	52	1969	59	1983	83		

Over the decades, the public shifted from general opposition to the idea of a woman president to a general consensus accepting the idea in principle. Other opinion indicators on the role of women show a similar pattern. Since 1972, the NES has been asking respondents if women should have "an equal role with men in running business, industry, and government" or whether a "woman's place is in the home."[11] In 1972, 47 percent chose the "equal role" opinion. By 1980 it was 60 percent, and by 1996 it was 85 percent.

Abortion The most salient of the social issues from the 1980s on into the twenty-first century has been abortion. Americans tend to oppose abortion on moral grounds, while supporting the right to abortion as a matter of public policy. For example, in 1998 57 percent of respondents said that they "personally believe that abortion is wrong." But in the very next question, 69 percent said that regardless of their own personal view, they favor the right of a woman to choose an abortion (Gallup-*Newsweek* Poll, 30 Oct. 1998).

The public debate on abortion tends to stress the extremes, with the "pro-life" advocates demanding an end to all abortions, and the "pro-choice" advocates demanding abortion upon request. But most Americans favor neither polar position. In a 1999 Gallup survey, 27 percent said that "abortion should be legal in any circumstances," and 16 percent said that "abortion should be illegal under all circumstances." The majority, 54 percent, said that abortion should be legal, but only under certain circumstances (3 percent were undecided).

Fortunately, we can discover the circumstances under which the public feels abortion should be allowed. Since 1965, the General Social Survey has been asking respondents if "you think it should be possible for a pregnant woman to obtain a legal abortion …" and then six different circumstances are specified. We can group these circumstances into "traumatic" and "elective," with traumatic being external circumstances beyond the woman's control (Cook et al. 1992), including danger to her health, damage to the fetus, and rape or incest. Elective reasons include personal and economic considerations—for example, if a married woman wants no more children, the family cannot afford more children, or if an unmarried pregnant woman does not wish to marry the father. Opinion on these items has been remarkably stable since the *Roe v. Wade* decision in 1973. Public support for abortion rights in traumatic and elective circumstances in the 1998 General Social Survey was:

Traumatic Abortion		Elective Abortion	
Defective fetus	78%	Married, does not want children	41%
Health danger	88	Cannot afford children	43
Rape/Incest	80	Does not want to marry	41

Obviously, circumstances are crucial for the public's willingness to support abortion. Less than an absolute majority favor abortion for any of the elective reasons, while support is overwhelming in traumatic circumstances.[12] However, only about 7 percent of all abortions are done for traumatic reasons (Torres and Forrest 1988).

Given these mixed feelings, it is therefore not surprising to find that only a minority of the public favors reversing *Roe v. Wade* (which in some states would effectively outlaw abortions). When the public was asked in 1998 if the Roe decision should be overturned, 64 percent said "let it stand" compared with 36 percent who wanted the ruling overturned (USODFOX). On the other hand, Americans favor some restrictions on abortion rights. In 1998 a CBS/*New York Times* poll showed that 78 percent favored a law requiring parental notification before a pregnant teenager under 18 could get an abortion, and in July 1996, Gallup reported that over 70 percent of the public favored a law requiring physicians to inform patients about alternatives to abortion, notification of husbands if a married woman wants an abortion, and a 24-hour waiting period before the procedure. It seems clear that the public wants abortion kept legal, but with regulations and restrictions.

Despite the long-term stability of the six-item GSS abortion series, there was a decided uptick in support of abortion in the early 1990s. A Gallup question on abortion asked every year since 1975 showed that in 1994 an all-time high of 33 percent of the public said that "abortion should be legal under any circumstances." However, that proved to be the high-water mark in this series. Recent data show a decline in the view that abortion should be available under any circumstance, probably as a result of the highly charged debate over "partial birth abortions." Twenty-three percent supported abortion for any reason in January 1998, moving to 27 percent in April 1999.

Many politicians who once took hard-line stands against abortion moderated their positions in the late 1980s, apparently believing that the tide of public opinion had turned in favor of abortion rights. Pro-choice advocates became much more active as they responded to the Supreme Court restrictions on abortion in cases like *Webster v. Reproductive Health Services.* But the mild trend in opinion away from "abortion on demand" has not much altered the balance of power between the two opposing groups. Pro-choice partisans still hold a numerical advantage in public opinion, but antiabortion partisans are more likely to communicate their opinions to elected leaders. Verba, Scholzman, and Brady (1995) show that politically active citizens who hold pro-life preferences on abortion are about five times more likely to focus that activity on the abortion issue than are politically active citizens who are pro-choice. Politicians are known to pay greater attention to those who actively voice their convictions.[13]

4-2 GENERAL IDEOLOGICAL MOVEMENT

The preceding section has shown various trends on specific survey items. For a particular issue, opinion might become more conservative over time, or more liberal, or, as is often the case, it may just stay the same from one survey reading to the next. If there is a general ideological trend from the data we have examined, it would seem to be lost in the details. A challenging question is whether the public regularly undergoes changes in its "ideological mood." Conceivably, one could detect general currents of opinion that sometimes flow in the liberal direction and sometimes in the conservative direction. We do know that any general ideological movement cannot be large. From one year to the next, net opinion on any issue will rarely change more than a few percentage points. And large movements generally are responses to events unique to the issue, such as when defense spending preferences once fluctuated in response to the monetary intensity of the cold war.

This emphasis on the electorate's ideological stability may seem contradicted by the fluctuation in presidential election results. One might think, for example, that Clinton's victories in 1992 and 1996 represent a surge of support for liberalism, or that the earlier victories for Reagan and Bush represented an earlier surge for conservatism. Such claims, however, are greatly overstated. While candidate ideologies matter in elections (see Chapter 9), the electorate's ideological movement from one election to the next is slight.

One way to locate trends in liberalism or conservatism on the part of the public would be simply to record changes in the degree to which people call themselves liberals or conservatives. As shown in the previous chapter, self-rankings as liberals or conservatives are sometimes questionable for the reason that many people lack adequate understanding of these terms. At a minimum, however, changes in how people describe themselves ideologically should reveal shifts in how fashionable are the terms "liberal" and "conservative."

In polls taken between the late 1930s and the mid-1960s, respondents remained about evenly divided between self-declared liberals and self-declared conservatives. But then a conservative shift began, so that by 1970, conservatives clearly outnumbered liberals, typically by a ratio of about 3 to 2. This change is puzzling, since the public's stands on issues did not in obvious fashion become more conservative at the same time. Why did the liberal label go into disfavor so suddenly in the late 1960s?

To some extent, the sudden shift toward "conservatism" reflected an increased public concern about issues on which people saw themselves as conservative (e.g., law and order issues) and less public concern about issues on which people saw themselves as liberal (e.g., New Deal social welfare issues). Also, in the changing 1960s, opponents of civil rights legislation frequently justified their position in terms of conservative ideology rather than opposition to the equal-opportunity goals of the civil rights movement. Finally, the mid-1960s were a time when much liberal legislation (Medicare, federal aid to education, major civil rights protection) was enacted. As policy became more liberal, people's ideological frame of reference changed: To be a liberal was to seek even more liberal policies rather than simply supporting the new status quo.

In any case, the growth of conservative self-identification in the late 1960s was a one-time event. Table 4.3 shows the distribution of the electorate's ideological self-identification since 1976. Compiled from CBS/*New York Times* surveys, the table is notable for the absence of any trend. In terms of ideological identification, the electorate showed the same distribution in the Carter years of the late 1970s as the Reagan-Bush 1980s and the Clinton years of the 1990s. Most people choose the "moderate" option, with conservatives outnumbering liberals about 34 to 22 percent.[14]

A second way to monitor changes in general liberalism/conservatism is to carefully estimate movement by combining responses to multiple survey items containing left-right political content. Two ambitious sets of estimates have been reported which somewhat contradict both each other and the trend (or, recently, lack of it) in ideological identification. After assessing a variety of political and social issues, Tom Smith (1990) argues that opinions became gradually more liberal between World War II and the mid-1970s, and then leveled off in a "liberal plateau."

James Stimson (1999) made a similar investigation, restricted to a narrower set of strictly policy opinions. Stimson's updated findings, shown in Figure 4.7, indicate a more oscillating movement of what he calls the electorate's ideological "mood." His mood index shows an increase in liberalism in the 1950s and early 1960s, followed by a decline in the late 1960s and 1970s, followed again by a liberal surge in the 1980s, leveling off again in the 1990s. The scale shown represents movement on the scale of the percentage of liberal (among opinion-holders). Thus, the maximum difference in "mood" is a 17 point range from the liberal "high" of the early 1960s to a conservative "low" around 1979.

4-3 GENERAL PARTISAN MOVEMENT

From an electoral standpoint, one of the most important indicators is the distribution of party identification among the categories of Democrats, Republicans, and Independents. The conventional view among political scientists

**TABLE 4.3   IDEOLOGICAL IDENTIFICATION
OF THE U.S. PUBLIC, 1976–1999**

Question: *"How would you describe your views on most political matters? Generally do you think
of yourself as liberal, moderate, or conservative?" Don't know/no answer responses are
excluded.*

Year	Liberal	Moderate	Conservative
1976	25%	39%	36%
1977	23	45	32
1978	25	40	35
1979	23	41	36
1980	20	47	33
1981	20	44	36
1982	20	45	34
1983	21	45	34
1984	21	47	33
1985	21	45	33
1986	21	45	35
1987	23	43	34
1988	20	45	34
1989	22	42	36
1990	23	43	34
1991	23	43	34
1992	22	45	34
1993	22	44	35
1994	21	44	36
1995	20	44	37
1996	18	47	34
1997	21	45	34
1998	22	43	35
1999	22	43	34

Source: Pooled surveys by CBS News/*New York Times*. Yearly readings are composites of
multiple surveys.

regarding trends in party identification is that macrolevel partisanship is quite
stable except for the rare shock of a "partisan realignment." Partisan realignments are precipitated by political parties making major changes in their policy
orientations. As parties' policy images change in fundamental ways, the electorate can respond with surprisingly large shifts in party identification.

Two crucial realignment periods have occurred: the first around the time
of the 1896 election and the second in the early 1930s. The 1896 realignment
is evident from the fact that geographic voting patterns that had been stable for

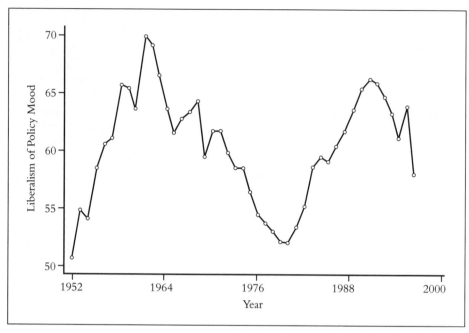

Figure 4.7   The public's policy "mood," 1952–1999. *Source:* James Stimson.

decades suddenly became disrupted and never returned to normal. In its 1896 convention, the Democratic Party accepted much of the platform of the Populists, a rising third party of economic protest, and nominated William Jennings Bryan, whose campaign for president featured the inflationary policy of "free silver." This new issue division attracted fresh adherents to the Democratic cause but panicked a great number into leaving. Consequently, the Republicans became the dominant political party until the 1930s (Burnham 1970, 119–20; Sundquist 1973, 183–217).

The New Deal realignment of the 1930s came in response to Franklin Roosevelt's early social welfare policies. Roosevelt was first elected in 1932, as the electorate demanded change at the top with the onset of the Great Depression. Once in office, Roosevelt's policies, known as the "New Deal," greatly expanded the role of the federal government to deal with the natonal emergency. People tended to align their partisanship anew based on their preferences for or against Roosevelt's economic liberalism. Although no polls were available until 1936, trends in election outcomes and voter registration clearly showed a major electoral shift in favor of the Democratic Party (Ladd 1970; Sundquist 1973, 183–217). To some extent, the electorate's division into Democrats and Republicans even today can be traced back to the New Deal realignment.

If there were polls in the 1920s, they would have shown a Republican dominance in partisanship. By 1937, when a national poll asked the party identification question for the first time, the Democrats predominated. In 99 percent of national polls conducted between 1937 and the present, Democrats outnumbered Republicans. On paper at least, the Democratic Party has had a decisive edge in identification.

As discussed in Chapter 3, individual-level party identifications are quite stable over time, as individuals rarely change their party preference. Still, when people do change partisanship (even if momentarily), they move in one-sided fashion in response to events. Figure 4.8 shows the annual reading of party identification in the Gallup Poll since 1945. Measured as the percentage of Democrats among Democrat and Republican identifiers, this macrolevel index has been dubbed "macropartisanship" (MacKuen et al. 1989). The graph shows palpable movement, with a Democratic edge that is sometimes quite narrow but at other times a hefty two-to-one advantage in the count of partisan identifiers.[15] The partisan landscape changes via gradual evolution as well as realignment shocks.

There were several changes in the nation's party identification over the last half of the twentieth century. The Democrats generally gained from World War II to a peak in Democratic support around 1964. Then, the Republicans rebounded, only to show precipitous losses following the Watergate revelations of 1973 and 1974. The Democratic gain was followed by a strong Republican trend in the 1980s. As we enter the twenty-first century, the electorate has been much more evenly divided between Democrats and Republicans than it was even 20 years earlier.

Close investigation of these trends shows that macropartisanship tracks both presidential approval (or more accurately the causes of approval) and economic

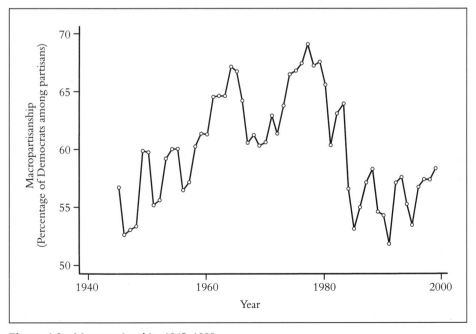

Figure 4.8 Macropartisanship, 1945–1999.

conditions (MacKuen et al. 1989; Erikson et al. 1998; but see Green et al., 1998 for another view). For instance, the combination of economic recovery and the positive appeal of President Reagan helped the Republicans gain in the 1980s. Some observers at the time even foresaw the emergence of a permanent Republican realignment. Republican gains following Bush's successful prosecution of the Gulf War only solidified such expectations. But it was not to be as the economy skidded under Bush. Then, with the prosperity of the Clinton years, the Democrats began to slowly regain some of their earlier partisan edge.

Interestingly, movement of party identification bears no resemblance to the movement of ideological mood or ideological identification previously discussed. The electorate's relative favor for Republicans or Democrats is totally unrelated to the electorate's swings between conservatism and liberalism. Although many people choose their partisanship based on ideology, the macrolevel movement of partisanship responds more to perceptions of party performance in office than to ideological preference.

One further trend of note in party identification is the growth in the proportion of the electorate who reject each major party, preferring to call themselves Independents. From World War II to about 1966, only between 22 and 25 percent of the public would typically call themselves Independents. Then, as the nation faced the Vietnam War, youth unrest, and the peak of the civil rights revolution, a major rejection of the parties began. Since the late 1960s, about one-third of the electorate has called itself Independents.

Some observers call this trend beginning in the mid-1960s a general "dealignment" as people seemingly disengaged from formerly strong partisan ties. But the growth of Independents is often exaggerated in discussions of the topic. Although the proportion who say they are Independents clearly grew in the late 1960s, it has not appreciably grown since then. And there is considerable contrary evidence that people became increasingly more rather than less partisan during the Reagan-Bush-Clinton years (Bartels 2000).

4-4 PRESIDENTIAL APPROVAL

Without a doubt, the most closely watched political indicator in the United States is the president's approval rating. Unlike the other macrolevel attitudinal indicators we have discussed, presidential approval shows fluctuations so large as to attract general attention from both politicians and the general public. The president's approval rating takes on importance because it is widely believed to measure the president's degree of political support at the moment, and it is also thought to be an important component of "presidential power." It may also provide a general guide regarding the president's prospects for reelection (Lewis-Beck and Rice 1982; Brody and Sigelman 1983).

While many polling organizations ask some variant of the "presidential approval" question, the standard measure is Gallup's question, asked regularly for over 50 years. When the Gallup Organization polls the American public, it regularly asks its respondents whether they "approve" of the president's performance, "disapprove" of the president's performance, or have no opinion. Attention generally focuses on the percentage (of all respondents) who "approve" of the president's current performance.

Gallup's sampling of presidential approval began with some sporadic monitoring of Franklin Roosevelt back in the late 1930s, when public opinion polling was in its infancy. However, regular readings of Roosevelt's approval rating were interrupted by World War II. But beginning with Harry Truman, presidents have been monitored in terms of their public approval on virtually a continuous monthly basis. This database provides enough information that, in general terms at least, we now know which kinds of circumstances increase a president's popularity and which lead to its decline. Figure 4.9 depicts the history of presidential approval polling, from Truman to Clinton.

All presidents enjoy some time above 50 percent approval; and most have unhappily spent some time below the 50 percent baseline. Presidents Truman, Nixon, and Carter all spent time below the critical 30 percent approval level. Three sources account for most variation in a president's approval rating: (1) the "honeymoon" effect, (2) the "rally-round-the-flag" effect, and (3) the effect of the economy.

The Honeymoon Every president starts the term with a rather high level of political support, with approval ratings in the 70 percent range not unusual at the beginning of the term. Then, as the president's term unfolds, the approval rating undergoes a gradual but inevitable decline. It is not surprising to find

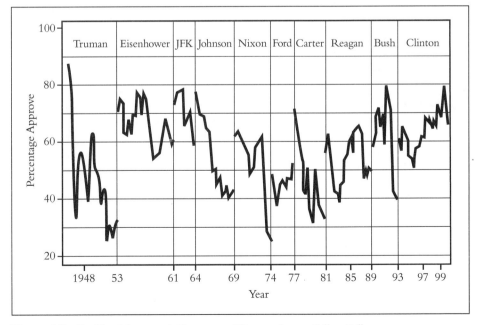

Figure 4.9   Presidential approval, Truman to Clinton. *Source:* Gallup Poll.

that presidents start out with an aura of goodwill, with even supporters of the defeated opponent offering their approval. The more interesting question is why does this honeymoon eventually fade? Some say the reason why presidents lose support over time is that they cannot please all segments of society all the time. Eventually, so this theory goes, the president must upset the expectations of some supporters, and this disillusionment creates a spiral of declining approval (Mueller 1973). Indeed, one might imagine a general rule that political support decays over time, with leaders inevitably becoming less popular the longer they govern. The implication is that no matter what presidents do to solve national problems, their political support will continue to erode.

A second interpretation is more optimistic. A president's early loss of popularity is best considered as a retreat from a starting point that was artificially high at the outset, rather than erosion of a natural base (Kernell 1978). About a year into a presidency, the president's popularity reaches its natural, lower equilibrium level. By this second year, a president's popularity level will converge toward the middle range of about 50 percent. From this point on, approval is as likely to rise as it is to fall. The approval rating will continue to vary around the usual average of about 50 percent, as a function of actual events that reflect sometimes positively and sometimes negatively on the president's stewardship.

The basic reason why presidents begin with an artificially high approval rating is that newly elected presidents start out free of criticism—either from other politicians or from the media. This hiatus from criticism arises in part because the president has just proved his popularity at the ballot box. It also arises because the new president is a blank slate; the new president has conducted few official acts to be second-guessed. Instead of criticizing a new president, politicians and the media respond with words of support. Ordinary citizens take their cue from these expressions of goodwill—they, too, express approval (Brody 1990).

As a presidential term evolves, however, the president must take actions that are subject to second-guessing and criticism from the media and from political opponents. The result is a natural decline in support. But after the first year, a new president's popularity generally stabilizes at a more natural level. Still, popularity will continue to move in response to how the president is perceived to cope with events and the task of national leadership. We examine next some sources in this variation.

Rally-Round-the-Flag Effect   From time to time, public attention is focused on some foreign policy event—perhaps an unexpected crisis or a major treaty or U.S. intervention in some foreign land. In the past, most of these were related to the cold war. Early examples include the Soviet shooting down of a U.S. spy plane (the Francis Gary Powers U-2 incident) in 1960; the Cuban missile crisis in 1962; and seizures of U.S. ships by communist foreign governments in 1968 (the *U.S.S. Pueblo* by the North Koreans) and in 1975 (the *Mayaguez* by the Cambodians). However, not all salient foreign policy events are anxiety-provoking. Examples would include events such as major treaties (e.g., Nixon's Moscow Treaty of 1972), "summits" (starting with Eisenhower's Geneva summit conference with Soviet leaders in 1955), and peace efforts such as Johnson's bombing halt (1968) or Carter's Camp David accords (1978) establishing the foundation for peaceful relations between Israel and Egypt.

What these events have in common is a focus on foreign policy. Generally, major foreign policy events are followed by a short-term surge in support for the president—what is called the "rally-round-the-flag" effect. These are "special moments" when eyes turn to the president, and the media and national politicians are seen to unite behind the chief executive.

Going to war is a special case. In the short term, wars traditionally result in the showering of approval on the president. One example comes from the early days of polling. While Roosevelt's approval ratings in the late 1930s were no more than respectable (typically in the mid-fifties), entry into World War II saw his numbers rise into the seventies. More recent wars show similar patterns. Truman gained 9 points following the start of the Korean War in 1950. Johnson gained 8 points following a major escalation of the Vietnam War in 1966. Lesser conflicts, such as Johnson's 1965 invasion of the Dominican Republic and Reagan's invasion of Grenada, also were followed by surges in presidential popularity. The biggest gain from a war certainly was George Bush's popularity surge to Gallup's record high of 87 percent in March 1991 following the brief Gulf War against Iraq.

But the political rewards from wars and invasions can be short-lived. The Johnson administration, for example, certainly miscalculated regarding the American public's taste for a prolonged war in Vietnam. Johnson fell in a few short years from the seventies to the low thirties in approval. During Korea, Truman declined even further—into the twenties, as did Carter during the Iran-hostage crisis. Both Truman and Johnson declined to seek reelection, and Carter was defeated in 1980. Bush's unique popularity after the Gulf War shows what a short successful war can do to presidential popularity. But Bush's approval decline in the war's aftermath (from 67 percent in August 1991 to 46 percent by January 1992) provides still a new lesson. The political benefit from any presidential success may be short-lived.

The Economy   It is common knowledge that the president's approval rating rises and falls with the state of the economy. When unemployment or inflation rise, the president is blamed. When these indicators of economic gloom decline, the president is praised. Naturally, the approval numbers reflect these tendencies. It is as if the electorate reads the state of the economy as a sign of the president's competence.

The exact mechanism by which the electorate converts economic perceptions into presidential approval has been the subject of considerable scholarly investigation. The simplest mechanism would be the straight-forward response of personal "pocketbook" considerations—that when people face good economic times they support the president, and when they face hard times they do not. By this interpretation, presidential approval would track the economy in direct response to the electorate's collective personal economic experience.

Consider, however, that most people, most of the time, know that they do not owe their current economic fortune to the president. If the economy is thriving, a person who just got fired or laid off is not likely to blame the president for his or her personal misfortune. Similarly, if the economy is clearly troubled, a person who earns a big raise and promotion is not likely to attribute this good fortune to the president.

But people do recognize the state of the general economy as having some relevance to their personal economic well-being. Consequently, citizens reward or punish the president not on the basis of their particular personal circumstances, but from their perceptions of the national economy. Such responses are called *sociotropic*, since people respond to how society is faring rather than how they personally are doing economically (Kinder and Kiewiet 1979). But the motive is still largely personal. People care about the national economy because they personally can be affected.

Sociotropic evaluations of presidential performance tend to be "prospective" rather than "retrospective." That is, people update their evaluations based on prospects for the economy's future rather than evaluating the economy's recent performance. We know this because statistically presidential approval tracks consumer expectations about the nation's economic future rather than consumer evaluations of current conditions (MacKuen et al. 1992).

The basis for these prospective economic evaluations by the public is mostly the current state of the economy. Everything else being equal, the electorate's forecast is predictable from current or recent conditions. But the electorate is also sensitive to signs of the future that are independent of the past, such as what economists call "leading economic indicators." It works this way. When economists look into their crystal balls, they are reading leading indicators. The trend of these indicators gets reported in the newspapers and on the evening news. In this way, knowledgeable people learn how the economy will behave before it happens. They do so not because they have special economic intuition; they learn about the economic future because they learn what economists say will happen before it happens.

Figure 4.10 shows how consumer expectations coincide with presidential approval. This graph shows quarterly approval from Eisenhower to Clinton, overlaid with one of the best economic predictors of presidential approval: the response (positive versus negative, with 100 = neutral) to the following question:

> Now turning to business expectations in the country as a whole—do you think that during the next 12 months we'll have good times, bad times, or what?

This item measures economic expectations as part of a battery of the "Index of Consumer Sentiment" produced by the Survey Research Center at the University of Michigan. As Figure 4.10 clearly shows, trends in presidential ap-

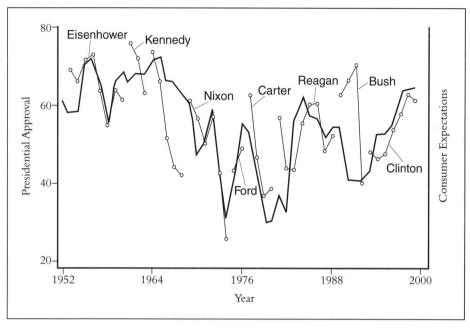

Figure 4.10   Presidential approval by consumer expectations, Eisenhower to Clinton.

proval track consumer expectations, although with important and obvious exceptions to be noted below.

4-5 ACCOUNTING FOR PRESIDENTIAL APPROVAL: SUMMARY

We have accounted for variation in presidential popularity in terms of three factors: the early-term "honeymoon," international "rally points," and the economy, especially in terms of expectations about the economic future. Referring again to Figure 4.10, we can see a distinct honeymoon effect as most presidents begin with more popularity than the overlaid trend line of consumer expectations would suggest. While Figure 4.10 generally shows a president's approval as tracking economic expectations, there are notable exceptions. With salient foreign policy crises in his administration, Kennedy's approval rode exceptionally high until his assassination. Johnson's popularity sagged noticeably as the Vietnam War became prolonged. Bush started his administration riding high from the end of the cold war, and then the successful Gulf War. Only as his term ended did Bush's approval approximate the low numbers predicted by the economic hard times. The best examples of presidents tracking the economy from start to finish are Eisenhower, Reagan, and Clinton, who each served eight years in office.

4-6 CONCLUSION: WHAT MOVES PUBLIC OPINION?

We have seen that public opinion has changed dramatically on many issues since reliable public opinion data have become available. Large shifts have sometimes occurred over short periods of time, or moves have been incremental over the years but have aggregated to a fundamental reversal in American political sentiment.

The most important reason for abrupt change in public opinion is response to political events of the time. In this chapter we reviewed many such instances, like the demand in the late 1970s for greater defense spending in response to foreign policy setbacks and elite rhetoric about a weakened military capacity, or the conservative trend on law and order in response to rhetoric about the increasing crime rate. Incremental change, however, is more complex to explain. Cohort replacement is certainly one factor. Almost 50 percent of the American electorate is replaced every 20 years (Abramson 1983, 54). When we see dramatic change in support for the ideals of the civil rights movement between 1960 and 1980, it is important to understand that only about one-half of those comprising the adult population in 1960 were still part of that population in 1980. The new 50 percent enter the electorate often socialized to a different set of political values. Thus the change that appears in support for the ideas of the civil rights movement does not necessarily mean that people have changed their minds, although that may have happened as well. Finally, the effects of modernization have certainly impacted upon the political opinions of the American public. Included here are demographic trends such as rising levels of education, the decline of the rural population, and the growth of large cities, as well as the increasing penetration of the national mass media to all sectors of society. Students of comparative politics argue that these trends have a long-term liberalizing effect on the populations that experience them (Dahl 1989).

NOTES

1. Responses to the services and spending question are based on a 7-point scale (see Appendix), where 1–3 are combined at one end, 4 is the midpoint, and 5–7 are combined at the other end.
2. See Charles Murray, *Losing Ground* (1985, ch. 1), for a discussion of the deserving and nondeserving poor. One survey showed that 37 percent believed people were poor because of "lack of effort," 29 percent said circumstances beyond his or her control, with the remainder saying both played a role (Mayer 1992, 90).
3. See Smith (1987) for a report on this experiment using earlier data.
4. On the seven-point scale, points 1, 2, and 3 are collapsed to indicate preference for a government health plan, and points 5, 6, and 7 are collapsed to indicate preference for a private plan.
5. Time/CNN/Yankelovich Partners Poll (29 Jan. 1998); Time/CNN/Yankelovich Partners Poll (11–12 Mar. 1997); Mayer (1992, 444–45).

6. For an additional attempt to salvage rationality in public opinion given seeming inconsistencies on taxing and spending, see Page and Shapiro (1992, 161–62).
7. For more data on trends in affirmative action attitudes, see Steeh and Krysan (1996).
8. According to this view, the racially prejudiced find a respectable outlet to express their views on symbolic issues such as the busing of school children for racial balance. It has been demonstrated, for example, that the most vocal opponents of busing often are nonparents with little direct stake in the matter (Sears et al. 1979).
9. Gallup (23 Oct. 1997); Wirthlin Worldwide (25 Aug. 1998).
10. The question reads: "You will notice that the boxes on this card go from the highest position of 'plus 5' for a country which you like very much, to the lowest position of 'minus 5' for a country you dislike very much. How far up the scale and how far down the scale would you rate the following countries?" The plus scores are combined for the positive rating and the minus scores are combined for the negative rating. In October 1953, 72 percent of the public gave Russia a "minus 5"; by 1991 that figure had dropped to 10.
11. Respondents place themselves on a 7-point scale in answering this question. Responses 1–3 were combined to indicate preference for an equal role of men and women in government and society.
12. Additional information can be gained though various combinations of six abortion items. Thus 76 percent of the public favors abortion for all three of the traumatic reasons, while only 7 percent oppose abortion in all three of these instances. For elective abortion, 37 percent of the public say they favor abortion for all three reasons, while 47 percent say they oppose abortion for all three of these circumstances.
13. For example, in a Harris Poll conducted between July 7 and 11 in 1989, voters who favored and opposed *Roe v. Wade* were asked, "If a candidate for political office stood for most of the things you believe in, took a stand on abortion that you disagreed with, you would certainly not vote for that candidate . . ." Of those who favored *Roe v. Wade,* 12 percent said they would certainly not vote for the candidate; of those who opposed *Roe v. Wade,* 23 percent would certainly not vote for that candidate.
14. For a thorough discussion of trends in ideological identification and whether they can be explained, see Box-Steffensmeir, Knight, and Sigelman, 1998.
15. The percentages shown in Figure 4.7 are adjusted for "telephone-survey bias"—a well-known but little understood fact that Gallup's phone surveys record more Republicans than Gallup's in-person surveys. Results from telephone surveys are adjusted to estimate the partisan distribution for in-home surveys.

CHAPTER 5

Political Socialization and Political Learning

Just as one learns to read and write, and what is fashionable in clothing, one learns about politics. A considerable portion of this learning occurs before the individual is old enough to enter the voting booth. Children, for example, tend to share the same partisan preference as their parents. A central premise of political socialization holds that what one learns as a preadult affects one's later political life. This assumption is crucial, for there is little reason for interest in the reaction of preadults to their political environment, except insofar as it affects their adult attitudes and behaviors.

To "socialize" someone means "to make social, make fit for life in companionship with others" (Random House Dictionary). Thus one perspective on political socialization focuses on the learning of attitudes, values, and acceptable forms of behavior necessary to fit into the political order. It is the learning or failure to learn the lessons of being a good citizen, as defined by the political status quo (Easton and Dennis 1969). Another perspective treats the field more akin to generic political learning. The emphasis is on individual political development rather than on molding the person to fit with the political community (Jennings and Niemi 1974). In this chapter we shall discuss both these perspectives on the socialization of citizens to political life.

5-1 THE PREADULT YEARS: SOCIALIZATION TO CITIZENSHIP

Every political system attempts to indoctrinate its children to accept and support the ongoing political order. From the perspective of systems theory, Easton and Dennis (1969, 5) advance the hypothesis "that the persistence of some kind of [political] system may in part be dependent upon the success of a society in producing children most of whom acquire positive feelings about it." But socialization is more encompassing than just encouraging the young to identify with the regime, and inculcating a benevolent view of the authorities. It is the transmission of the political culture from one generation to the next. From a systems perspective, the purpose of socialization is to maintain a stable political order. According to Easton and Dennis (1969, 31):

> If the socialization process raises children who upon reaching adulthood have among themselves conflicting aspirations, conceptions of the rules of the system, attitudes toward compliance, and feelings about authority, it is assumed that this will probably build social and political cleavages into the system and that instability will result.

Of course, if political training results in a total commitment to socially acceptable beliefs, the forces for change and improvement in society would be greatly diminished. For instance, if socialization were a complete success, the change we have seen in the status of women and minorities could not have occurred.

To analyze the development of preadult political orientations, we shall divide the early years into four periods: preschool (ages 3 to 5), early childhood (ages 6 to 9), late childhood (ages 10 to 12), and adolescence (ages 13 to 18). These are approximate categories, for just as children differ in their physical development, they differ in their political development. In conclusion, we shall discuss the consequences of socialization for citizenship.

Preschool

The dawning of political recognition begins before children ever commence their formal education. Political impressions are often vague and inaccurate, but early awareness may lay the foundations for later political development.

Preschoolers frequently confuse political authority with religious authority. In a study of kindergarten children in California, Moore et al. (1985) report that when asked, "Who does the most to run the country," 30 percent responded "God" or "Jesus." Perhaps the most important public figures for the young child are the president and the police officer. One school of thought contends that both officials play a major role in shaping the child's attachment to the political order. Schwartz (1975) found that 90 percent of her preschool sample were able to recognize the "man in the picture" as being "the policeman," and 75 percent were able to answer correctly when asked, "What does the policeman do?" The responses most frequently given concerned regulating traffic, helping lost children, and "catching bad people." The children, for the most part, saw the police officer as a benevolent authority figure. Less visible was the police officer's punitive and prohibitive role. Fewer than 10 percent of the preschool sample recognized a picture of the incumbent president. When asked, "What does the president do?" only a few could give an accurate or specifically political characterization. The president is not viewed by these young children as being particularly benevolent, especially when compared to the policeman (Schwartz 1975, 236–37). This may be due simply to the president's lower visibility—a situation that, along with perceived benevolence, changes dramatically at the next stage of political development.

Public servants are not the only political symbols visible to the preschool child. Even at this early age, children manifest a sense of political community. When presented with a picture showing nine different flags, the vast majority were able to identify the American flag. When asked, "Which flag is your favorite?" 60 percent chose the American flag and another 19 percent identified the Liberian flag, which closely resembles the American flag (Schwartz 1975, 242–43). Thus preschool children both know and identify with the symbol of the American political community.

Early Childhood

With the onset of early childhood, the content of the young person's political world begins to expand rapidly. However, the increase in content is almost entirely in terms of feelings and affect. Political understanding and critical thought have yet to emerge. The young child now becomes very aware of the existence of the president. Government is personalized; that is, the child becomes aware of political authority by becoming aware of certain individuals—notably the president and the police officer. The child sees these figures as possessing great power and is aware that they stand above the family in the obedience hierarchy. Unlike adults, who often tend to be quite cynical about politics, the young child sees the president and the police officer (and political authority) as trustworthy, helpful, and benevolent. This outlook is illustrated by the following excerpt from an interview with a third-grade boy (Hess and Torney 1967, 42).

Q. What does the President do?

A. He runs the government, he decides the decisions we should try to get out of, and he goes to meetings and tries to make peace and things like that.

Q. When you say he runs the country, what do you mean?

A. Well, he's just about the boss of everything....

Q. And what kind of a person do you think he is?

A. Well, he's an honest one.

Q. Anything else?

A. Well, loyal and usually pretty smart.

Q. Who pays him?

A. Well, gee, I don't know if anybody pays him; he probably doesn't get too much money for the job—I don't know if he gets any money.

Q. Why would he take the job?

A. Well, he loves his country and he wants his country to live in peace.

To a surprising extent, young children believe that the policeman and especially the president "would always want to help me if I needed it," that "they almost never make mistakes," and that "they know more than anyone." Reasoning from the "primary principle" and the "benevolent leader hypothesis," students of political socialization attach considerable importance to the idealization of authority by young children. According to the primary principle, "what is learned early in life tends to be retained and to shape later attitudes and behavior" (Easton and Dennis 1969, 9). According to the benevolent leader hypothesis, the image of the president (the most visible symbol of political authority) that is formed in early childhood has a direct effect on the formation of attitudes and beliefs about other political figures and institutions. There is a hypothesized "spillover effect" from this early view of the president to later perceptions of other political authorities. Because the president is favorably viewed, they too tend to be viewed favorably. It is believed, therefore, to be very significant that the child's introduction to politics is a very positive one. Later in life, when the individual is able to make critical judgments about politics, this early idealization builds what David Easton (1965) refers to as "diffuse support." It is a reservoir of goodwill toward the political system that is independent of any benefit the individual might receive. It helps legitimize the political order, and in times of political stress, the residue of this early idealization helps maintain a positive attitude toward government.

Late Childhood

Beginning about the age of 10 or 11, children start moving away from a personalized view of government to one based on a more sophisticated understanding. During this period the child learns the "civics book" norm of not always voting for the same political party, but for the best person. In a national sample, 49 percent of fourth-graders say a good citizen would join a political party and vote for its candidates instead of voting for the best person. But by the eighth grade, only 26 percent endorse this strategy (Hess and Torney 1967, 96). Views of what constitutes "good citizenship" also undergo change. Young children tend to see the good citizen as someone who is "helpful to others" and "always obeys the laws." But by late childhood, good citizenship is defined more in terms of adult conceptions: political interest, voting, and getting others to vote (Hess and Torney 1967, 37). Sigel and Brookes (1974, 110) investigated conceptions of democracy among fourth-graders. They found only 17 percent answered "yes" to the question, "Is a democracy where the people rule?" ("I don't know" was the most frequent answer.) They interviewed the same students two years later (then in the sixth grade) and found that 44 percent could respond correctly. However, definitions of democracy in late childhood and even through adolescence seldom include the right to criticize government. Only 54 percent of the eighth-graders in Hess and Torney's sample checked the option "you can say things against the government" as one possible definition of democracy. And fully 84 percent of eighth-graders agree that "the government usually knows what is best for the people." Such open acceptance of government and intolerance for dissent are generally regarded as unhealthy for democracy (see Chapter 6). But from a systems theory stand-point, one can ask, "Do not such attitudes indicate successful socialization?" Acceptance of government and intolerance for dissent surely promotes "system stability." It is implications such as these that have led to trenchant criticism of the systems perspective on political socialization (Connell 1987).

It is in late childhood that young people begin to separate individual from institutional roles. They begin to understand the difference between the office and the man or woman who holds the office. The presidency and the presi-dent are no longer seen as the same. Children also display the beginnings of critical judgment; they are sensitive to partisan and policy considerations. For example, those raised in Democratic households are more critical of a Repub-lican president than children raised in Republican households. The president also becomes associated with certain policy positions (Weissberg 1974, 54). Still, political understanding is basically immature. Children will revert back to personalization if asked about something they cannot comprehend.

Adolescence

The major spurt in a child's political learning usually comes during adolescence. An important aspect of this growth is the ability to comprehend the abstraction of community interest apart from self-interest. Ideals such as community and society are usually beyond the grasp of 11-year-olds, but not beyond those who are 15 (Adelson and O'Neil 1966). By mid-adolescence the individual is in many ways politically beginning to resemble an adult. By the ninth grade, chil-dren have some ability to think along a liberal-conservative continuum. Adult levels of political efficacy are also reached by the ninth grade (Merelman 1971; Hess and Torney 1967). One orientation that shows surprisingly little growth is support for democratic values (free speech, minority rights, rules of the game, etc.). Merelman (1971, 79) finds no increase in support for democratic values between the ninth and twelfth grades. As we shall note shortly, many blame the failure of this development on the shortcomings of the public schools.

An orientation that begins in early childhood and, for the most part, con-tinues unchanged through adolescence is the positive view most preadults have of the political system. Despite a "de-idealization" of the authorities brought about by exposure to the seamier side of politics, such as the impeachment of President Clinton amid accusations of lying under oath about a sexual affair with a White House intern, American adolescents retain a positive perspective on the political order. But they can be quite negative about government offi-cials. Table 5.1 presents the views of high school seniors in 1974 (shortly after the Watergate scandal resulting in the resignation of President Nixon) toward the political community, the constitutional system, and the current govern-ment (Sigel and Hoskin 1981, 73–5).

Note that 59 percent were very positive about "the flag," and 57 percent were very positive about "the U.S.," with the negatives for both items being minuscule. The "constitutional system" does not fare as well, with 32 percent

TABLE 5.1 THE VIEWS OF HIGH SCHOOL SENIORS TOWARD
POLITICAL OBJECTS

	The U.S.	The Flag	Constitut'l System	Congress	The Courts	Current Govern't
Very negative	1%	3%	3%	6%	8%	24%
Negative	4	3	10	16	17	35
Neutral	8	13	20	32	27	19
Positive	31	22	36	31	31	17
Very positive	57	59	32	16	17	5
	100%	100%	100%	100%	100%	100%

Source: Roberta S. Sigel and Marilyn B. Hoskin, *The Political Involvement of Adolescents* (New Brunswick, NJ: Rutgers University Press, 1981), p. 73.

very positive (although 68 percent are either positive or very positive), but still the negatives are small. On the other hand, just 16 percent felt very positive about Congress and only 5 percent felt very positive about the "current government," while 24 percent felt very negative. During one of the darkest political periods in the twentieth century the data show, among adolescents, a substantial erosion in positive views of those running the government, but a strong fundamental commitment to the ongoing political order.

Fast forward to the first week in February 1999, after President Clinton was impeached by the House and just before he was acquitted by the Senate on February 12, 1999. Based on a Gallup Poll of adults and of adolescents between 11 and 18 years of age, we see a pattern that is in many ways similar, but with some unique twists.[1] Like the Watergate adolescents, the Monicagate youth cohort is very critical of those running the government—more so than a representative sample of adults. While 36 percent of the adult sample would have convicted the president, 47 percent of the youth sample would have done so; 55 percent of the adult sample had a favorable view of President Clinton, but only 43 percent of the youth cohort shared that opinion.

But once the questions moved away from the president to more abstract opinions about government, the younger sample was more positive than their elders. While 34 percent of the adult sample said they could "trust government to do what is right" all or most of the time, 55 percent of the youth sample said they trusted government. Beyond personalities, Monicagate adolescents are a good deal less cynical about government than are adults, as can be seen below.

	Do you personally think most public officials today are liars . . . ?		Do you think George Washington ever lied to the public . . . ?		Do you think Abraham Lincoln ever lied to the public . . . ?	
	Adults	*Youth*	*Adults*	*Youth*	*Adults*	*Youth*
Yes	55%	34%	72%	49%	65%	53%

Like the Watergate findings, these data cast doubt on the notion that idealization of the president is necessary to build diffuse support of the political system. When compared with adults, adolescents were very critical of the incumbent president, but more positive once we move past current officeholders. However, the socialization theory of diffuse support stresses the consequences of idealizing authority among younger children, usually between kindergarten and the eighth grade (Easton and Dennis 1969).

Socialization to Citizenship and Its Consequences

The most dramatic findings in the citizenship literature are the extent to which *young* children (kindergarten through eighth grade) "personalize" government and the remarkable degree to which they idealize authority, notably the president. But do these findings really mean anything for adult behavior? The theory of diffuse support, born of childhood idealization, is an appealing one, but difficult to verify empirically. The theory seems not to be general, since not all children idealize authority. African-American (Greenberg 1970), Mexican-American (Garcia 1973), and poor, isolated, rural white Appalachian children (Jaros et al. 1968) tend to see political authority as much less benevolent than do middle-class white children.

Children clearly learn about politics by exposure to political events. Even regular political occurrences, such as presidential elections, lead to substantial gains in preadult political socializations (Sears and Valentino 1997). It is therefore not unexpected that a traumatic event like Watergate would have a deep impact on those under 18, whose political identities for the most part are not yet fully formed. Several studies show that during the Watergate era, even middle-class white children came to see the president as almost sinister. Several studies done during the Watergate scandal (1972–1974) showed a "dramatic decline" in the positive image of the president (Arterton 1974; Dennis and Webster 1975; Hawkins et al. 1975; Rodgers and Lewis 1975). Christopher Arterton reports that, based on a Boston area sample, attitudes toward the president in fall 1973 "could only be described as wholly negative." The benevolent leader was transformed by Watergate into a "malevolent" leader. In the early 1960s, anywhere from 50 to 66 percent (depending on grade) reported the president was their "favorite of all" or "of almost all." By 1973, the range was 5 to 23 percent, with the older children (fifth-graders) being the least positive. Children in 1962 and 1973 were asked to "compare politicians" with "most people" in terms of power, selfishness, intelligence, honesty, and trustworthiness. The "spillover effect" of the president's image to other political authorities, which was positive in 1962, was negative in 1973. Particularly large differences between 1962 and 1973 exist on selfishness and trustworthiness. Fifty-four percent of the fifth-graders in 1962 thought politicians were less selfish than other people; only 19 percent thought so in 1973.

If the systems theory of childhood socialization is correct, we would expect to see substantial differences between those age groups that were in the fourth through the eighth grades between 1973 and 1975 and those that are both older and younger. Using a somewhat broader sweep, Delli Carpini (1986) reports that those socialized during the antiwar period of the late 1960s were somewhat more cynical as they entered the electorate than those socialized earlier. However, using the 1996 NES, we find those between 32 and 38 (who would have been in grade school during Watergate) are no more or less trusting of government than other age cohorts.[2] However, we should not make too much of a weak test. As we shall see later, in some issue domains there is convincing evidence to support the persistence hypothesis—that is, what is learned about politics early in life persists into late adulthood.

5-2 THE AGENTS OF PREADULT SOCIALIZATION

Having traced the development of political attitudes through the preadult years, we shall now attempt to sort out the agents most responsible for this development. The family seems to be the most influential source of preadult attitudes, but it certainly is not the only source. Schools make an effort to indoctrinate children, and it seems unlikely that the effort is totally unsuccessful. Other possible agents of early political socialization include childhood friends and the mass media. (See Chapter 8 for a discussion of the mass media.) Finally, when important historical events occur, it seems likely that they leave an imprint on the young.

The Family

Political influence is a function of two factors: communication and receptivity (Williams and Minns 1986). Parents score high on both these dimensions. Children, particularly young children, spend a large amount of time with their parents. The opportunities for children to learn parental attitudes and for parents to exert influence on children is considerable. Also, in terms of receptivity, few bonds are as strong as the affective ties between parents and children. The stronger this tie and the more personal the relationship, the greater the ability to exert influence.

A common assumption is that the political attitudes of family members are highly similar. Since most family members appear to share the same party preference, it seemed logical to many investigators that the same pattern would hold for other political orientations. Evidence to support this belief came from a number of early studies (pre-1960) in which parents and children were not independently interviewed.[3] Children (normally students) would be interviewed and then asked to report the political attitudes of their parents. The parents themselves were not actually interviewed. We now know that this methodology grossly overestimates the amount of parent-child similarity on most political issues. In reporting parent attitudes, children tend to "project" their own attitudes onto parents, artificially inflating attitude correspondence. In actuality, the similarity in political attitudes between parents and their offspring since World War II could at best be described as moderate. Table 5.2,

TABLE 5.2   RELATIONSHIP BETWEEN STUDENT AND PARENT OPINIONS ON FOUR POLICY ISSUES

Students	Federal Role in School Integration* (Parents)			Prayers In Public Schools* (Parents)			Elected Communists Can Hold Office (Parents)			Allow Speeches Against Churches (Parents)		
	Pro	Depends	Con	Pro	Depends	Con	Pro	Depends[†]	Con	Pro	Depends[†]	Con
Pro	83%	64%	45%	74%	62%	34%	45%	—	32%	88%	—	82%
Depends	7	17	14	3	8	7	1	—	0	0	—	0
Con	10	18	41	23	30	59	53	—	67	12	—	18
Total	100%	99%	100%	100%	100%	100%	99%		99%	100%		100%
	(961)	(202)	(453)	(1253)	(68)	(238)	(1337)		(1337)	(1376)		(523)
	$Tau_b = .34$			$Tau_b = .29$			$Tau_b = .08$			$Tau_b = .08$		

Source: M. Kent Jennings and Richard G. Niemi, The Political Character of Adolescence (Princeton, NJ: Princeton University Press, 1974), p. 78. Reprinted by permission of Princeton University Press.

*Based on pairs in which both parents were "interested enough" to give a pro or con response.
[†]Ten or fewer cases.

taken from a study by Kent Jennings and Richard Niemi, displays the relationships between a national sample of high school seniors and their parents on four policy issues.

Reading across the rows in the table we can see that the students are much more likely to be pro-school integration and pro-school prayer when their parents favor these positions. For example, of the pro–integration parents, 83 percent have children that also favor integration, but when parents oppose integration the percentage of children favoring integration drops to 45—a difference of 38 percent. This relationship weakens considerably for the question of an elected Communist being allowed to hold office and virtually disappears on the question of allowing speeches against churches. In the case of the latter, knowing the parent's attitude is of no use in predicting the student's attitude. Most students favor allowing speeches against churches regardless of what their parents think. One can infer that parents have little influence on these latter two issues. Similar low relationships exist for attitudes about a "legally elected Communist" and a "speech against churches." Also, parents seem to have little influence on more diffuse orientations like political efficacy and political trust.[4] However, Altemeyer (1997) and Peterson, Smirles, and Wentworth (1997) report strong links between the authoritarianism personality syndrome in parents and the same syndrome in their children.

The most thoroughly documented successful transmission of an attitude from parent to child involves partisanship. Table 5.3 documents the widespread agreement between parents and children on the question of party preference. Again, reading across the rows of the table, when we move from parents who are Democratic to those who are Independent to those who are Republican,

TABLE 5.3   STUDENT PARTY IDENTIFICATION BY PARENT PARTY IDENTIFICATION

| Student | Parents | | | |
	Democrat	Independent	Republican	Marginals*
Democrat	66%	29%	13%	(43%)
Independent	27	55	36	(36%)
Republican	7	17	51	(21%)
Total	100%	100%	100%	
Marginals*	(49%)	(24%)	(27%)	100%

Source: M. Kent Jennings and Richard G. Niemi, *The Political Character of Adolescence* (Princeton NJ: Princeton University Press, 1974), p. 41. Reprinted by permission of Princeton University Press.

*The marginal totals present the proportion of parents and students holding a particular party preference. For example, looking at the column marginals we can see that 49 percent of the parents call themselves Democrats. Looking at the row marginals we can see that 43 percent of the students in the sample call themselves Democrats.

the percentage of Democratic children drops dramatically. The reverse holds for the case of Republican parents. When parents agree between themselves on partisanship (74 percent do agree), 76 percent of the adolescents follow the preferences of their parents. Interestingly, when parents disagree on partisanship (one is a Democrat, the other a Republican), the child is more likely to adopt the mother's partisanship than the father's (although the number of Independent children rises substantially, as one would expect given the cross-pressures).[5] This generational continuity is important because it helps maintain the ascendancy of the dominant political party. Since the New Deal, the Democratic Party has been preferred by a majority of Americans. As long as parents continue to socialize children successfully to their own party preference, the Democratic Party seems well placed to continue its favored position with the electorate.

However, there is clear evidence that parents are not currently as successful in transmitting partisanship as they were in the 1940s, 1950s, and into the early 1960s. In 1958, 79 percent of children with Democratic parents and 72 percent with Republican parents adopted parental partisanship. By 1976 these figures had dropped to 62 percent and 56 percent, respectively. In 1992 it was 57 and 56 percent (NES). This failure of socialization is one of the causes of the current "partisan dealignment." The decrease in successful transmission is a function of an increasing conflict between parental partisanship and the issue preferences of the offspring. When these predispositions complement each other, transmission is successful. But when cross-pressures exist (e.g., parents are liberal Democrats but the offspring is antiabortion, antiaffirmative action, opposed to gay rights), the response on the part of the younger generation is political independence (Carmines et al. 1987; Luskin et al. 1989).

Even with current declines, party identification is still passed on from parent to child with much more success than other political orientations. The best explanation seems to be that most political questions are remote from the day-to-day concerns of the family. Few parents hold their political opinions strongly, and few children have an accurate perception of those opinions. In this regard, party identification is unique. It is one attitude that is normally of some consequence to parents and highly visible to children. At election time, young children will often ask if "we" are Democrats or Republicans. Tedin (1974) demonstrated that while 72 percent of a sample of high school seniors were aware of parental party identification, no more than 36 percent were aware of parent attitudes on any one issue. But when issue attitudes were about as salient and well perceived as partisanship, parent–child correspondence approached that for partisanship. Anders Westholm (2000) finds a similar pattern in socialization study in Sweden. If children accurately perceive the political attitudes of their parents, socialization is quite successful. But misperception is frequent. A variation in this point is illustrated by Beck and Jennings (1991). They found that high school seniors first interviewed in 1965 who came from politicized homes were much more likely to share their parents' 1965 partisanship 17 years later, in 1982, than were students from nonpoliticized homes. Thus parents seem to have the potential to exert more influence on issue attitudes than they often do. Perhaps in an era like the Depression of the 1930s, when politics were polarized and certain issues were seen by many as being highly important, parents would use considerably more of their available resources to politically socialize the young.

The Peer Group

Like parents, the peer group enjoys considerable opportunity to influence attitudes and behavior. There are strong affective ties involved, and young people normally spend a substantial part of their time with friends. Parents and peers differ, however, at the point in the preadult's life when influence is greatest. Parents dominate the lives of their offspring until adolescence, then peers become increasingly important (Beck 1977). Despite the considerable attention paid to peer groups in the United States, there is relatively little research and (perhaps as a logical consequence) little agreement on the role of peers as an agent of political socialization. Some scholars argue that peer groups are the most important of all adolescent socialization agencies, while others assert that the influence of peers is largely redundant.[6] Peers are seen as simply reinforcing the lessons learned in the family and school. It is clear, however, that adolescent peers can be influential in areas involving the individual's status in the group. But these areas usually involve matters of taste in music, clothing, and hairstyles, rather than politics. In the Jennings-Niemi national study of parents and students, a subset of the students were asked to indicate their best friend of the same sex, who was then included in the sample. As expected, for party identification the correlation between students and parents greatly exceeded that between students and peers. On the other hand, in the case of changing the voting age from 21 to 18 (one had to be 21 to vote at the time of the survey), the student-peer correlation exceeded the student-parent correlation.[7] This is the pattern one would expect. Partisanship is learned during early childhood and is not a particularly "youth-oriented" issue. On the other hand, preadults were more likely to become aware of the 18-year-old vote issue during adolescence, and the issue is particularly relevant to high school seniors. We would therefore expect more peer influence in the latter instance. In situations in which parents and peers disagree on partisanship, the student is more likely to follow the parent. But when parent and peer disagree on the 18-year-old vote, the student is more likely to follow his or her best friend (Sebert et al. 1974). Thus peer-versus-parent influence seems to be issue-specific.

It is difficult to make any absolute assessment of peer influence, but it seems certain that even in adolescence, peers are not as important as parents. When politics are remote from one's day-to-day concerns, and when family social harmony as well as one's status in the peer group are only slightly affected by politics, parents probably have an advantage over peers in the socialization process. We have noted that one important precondition for influence is communication. Politics are more important to the 35-to-50-year-old group (the common age of parents with adolescent children) than to those 18 years old and under (Eskey 1995). If one assumes all other things are equal, adolescents are more likely to be aware of and receptive to parent attitudes simply because most contemporary political issues are more important to parents (Tedin 1980). But when a matter is important to the esteem with which an adolescent is held by the peer group, parents usually cannot compete with peer influence. But for most American youth, everyday political issues are rarely of consequence for their standing in the peer group.

The Primary and Secondary School

Many political theorists, practical politicians, political reformers, and political revolutionaries believe or have believed that the school is an instrumental agent in the political training of the young. Examples abound. After the 1917 Russian revolution, children were removed from the family (presumably still attached to the old order and unsympathetic to Communist values) and required to spend long periods of time in school for political retraining. The Allied Powers followed a similar policy after the defeat of the Nazis in World War II. The schools were "de-Nazified," and German youths were instructed in the principles of democratic government as defined by the West. The same beliefs are reflected in the fierce debate over a multicultural curriculum in American schools. The school is seen as the appropriate vehicle for instructing students in the values necessary for life in a multiethnic society.

A popular assumption is that some nations spend an inordinate amount of time politically "indoctrinating" their young. Communist nations are usually singled out in this regard, most notably the Soviet Union during the cold war. One study showed, however, that during the cold war period of the 1950s, American schools expended more time on "political education" than did the schools in the USSR (Bereday and Stretch 1963). Regardless, it is important to understand that virtually all nations charge the public schools with the responsibility of teaching obedience to political authority. The practice is nearly universal, and from the standpoint of maintaining political stability and continuity, it is a necessity. One need only observe the difficulties encountered by nations in which primary loyalties do not reside with the national government. For example, in some nations ethnic or tribal loyalty comes before national loyalty. Political stability is highly dependent upon the ability of the agents of socialization to produce in children feelings as to the rightness, the oughtness, the legitimacy of the political order. In virtually all nations, this task is assigned to the schools. They are the one agent of political socialization over which the government has considerable control.

There can be little doubt, as we noted in the section on childhood political development, that preadults in the United States generally learn the lessons of patriotism and obedience. What is not clear is the relative role of the family and school in teaching these orientations. In one major study of the public schools, Robert Hess and Judith Torney concluded that "compliance to roles and authority is the major focus of education in elementary schools" (1967, 126). Most readers are undoubtedly aware of the patriotic rituals that characterize most classrooms—pictures of American heroes, the display of the American flag and proclaiming one's allegiance to it, singing of patriotic songs, "young citizens leagues," and the emphasis on obedience to authority. Teaching methods change periodically in response to changes in thinking about what is and is not effective for student learning. But the goal of socializing the young to be loyal citizens is never divorced from changes in the curriculum. This goal, for example, is evident in *America 2000: An Educational Strategy,* a national civics curriculum for grades K–12 endorsed by both the Bush and Clinton administrations.[8] Richard Merelman (1997, 56) concludes that "the proposed national civics standards are mainly a symbolic ritual masked as educational policy for reinforcing cultural hegemony." In other words, the curriculum is focused on teaching a common American culture and values as opposed to teaching individual and group differences.

However, students of political education agree that teaching loyalty and obedience is only one aspect of political education. There are other goals as well, such as teaching political knowledge, political participation skills, tolerance of competing political views, and acceptance and support for democratic values. On these goals there is consensus that education in the public schools is less effective than most would like. For example, a Gallup survey showed that 61 percent of high school seniors said they were "not very" or "not at all" interested in politics.[9] Niemi and Junn (1998) report that fewer than two-thirds of twelfth-graders were aware that it is legal to participate in a boycott, organize a recall election, and impeach legislators. According to the National Assessment of Educational Progress, often called "the nation's report card," only 26 percent of high school seniors in 1999 had a "proficient" knowledge of how the government worked, and fully 35 percent failed the national civics test (Hedges 1999). In terms of sophisticated thinking, 50 percent of a sample of high school juniors thought the assertion, "The American form of government may not be perfect, but it is the best type of government yet devised by man" was a factual statement (as opposed to being a value statement). Levels of factual knowledge tend to be quite low. Anderson et al. (1990) report that only 61 percent of high school seniors recognized (in 1988) that having more than one political party was a fundamental difference between the United States and the Soviet Union; only 58 percent knew the United States has a two-party system, and just 50 percent knew the governor is a member of the executive branch.

Finally, surveys of high school youth suggest that support for democratic values may be weak. One study of seniors found that 60 percent favored allowing the police and other groups to censor books and movies (Remmers and Franklin 1963, 62), and another reported that only 36 percent were in favor of allowing a legally elected Communist to assume office (Jennings and Niemi 1974). Niemi and Junn (1998) report that only 52 percent of high school seniors knew the right to religious freedom is part of the Bill of Rights, and only 47 percent knew there is a constitutional ban on double jeopardy. While these data are taken over a variety of years, the evidence seems to indicate that young Americans are becoming less interested, not more interested, in politics (Bennett 1997; 1998; Mann 1999).

The thrust of the early empirical research indicated that the high school civics curriculum had little if any effect on the learning of political knowledge or political values. The most influential of these studies (Langton and Jennings 1968; Jennings, Ehrman, and Niemi 1974; Anderson et al. 1990), showed that whether or not students had taken any civics courses was largely irrelevant to their levels of political knowledge, political interest, political discussion, political efficacy, political trust, and participatory orientation. However, a detailed analysis of the data from the National Assessment of Educational Progress (NAEP) civics assessment by Richard Niemi and Jane Junn (1998) turned up significant effects for the civics curriculum on trust in government—the more courses taken, the most trusting the respondents (high school seniors)[10]—and substantial effects for political knowledge. In a multivariate equation with controls for factors strongly related to knowledge, such as parents' education and plans for college, the difference between little or no civics education and at least some increases political knowledge by 4 percent. While at first blush this increase may seem modest, almost all students have at least been exposed to the civics curriculum, which certainly dampens the effect. In addition, if one looks at all factors relevant to civics instruction—amount and recency of course work, variety of topics studied, and discussion of current events—there is a combined effect of nearly 11 percentage points in amount of political knowledge (Niemi and June 1998, 122–23). Although the analysis of the NAEP data is mostly limited to gains in political knowledge, it serves to rehabilitate the civics curriculum as a significant contributor to political learning.[11]

However, it is not entirely clear how the curriculum in high school leads to higher levels of political knowledge or support for democratic values. There is, for example, no doubt that the better educated are more politically tolerant. The 1998 GSS shows that while only 51 percent of those with a grade school education support free speech for an atheist, 70 percent of those with a high school degree are supportive. Forty-five percent of those with a grade school education would allow a homosexual to teach in college, but 69 percent of those with a high school degree would be willing. Numerous other examples can be offered. It may be that a high school education simply "slots" people into social, economic, and political positions in which they have a greater opportunity to learn democratic norms. Or it could be that high school does have an impact, but we simply have not come up with the appropriate research designs to definitively identify effects and unravel the causal connections.

College: Higher Education and Its Impact

Although most students are legally adults when they enter college, the college experience is for many a transition period between life with the family and being truly on one's own. Today almost one of every two high school graduates goes to college. At the turn of the century, most young people did not even graduate from high school, let alone contemplate attaining a college degree.[12] Consequently, the proportion of the adult population with college experience has been rising steadily. For example, between 1950 and 1990, the proportion of adults with at least some college rose from 16 percent to 45 percent. In the short period between 1972 and 1998, the proportion of adults over 25 with college degrees rose from 13 percent to 27 percent (GSS). It is, however, important to understand that most of this recent increase is due to the departure of older, lesser educated citizens rather than an increase in the number of citizens receiving college degrees. In fact, there is currently little growth in the educational attainment of the youngest age cohort. Thus in future years we will likely see little gain in the overall percentage of the population that is college educated (Nie et al. 1998, 112–18).

What are the political implications of the growth in the college-educated public? As we shall discuss at greater length in the following chapter, education is strongly correlated with political tolerance and support for democratic values. As the population has become better educated, its expression of support for these values has also increased. In addition, college generally has a liberalizing effect on noneconomic political opinions. Evidence in support of this view can be found going back to the 1920s. College seniors are consistently found to be less conservative than entering freshmen.[13] An example taken from the mid-1970s is presented in Table 5.4. The obvious inference is that students track to the left as they move through the years in college.

Three explanations are commonly advanced for these gains in liberalism: increased awareness, enlightenment, and indoctrination. None of these standing alone is entirely convincing. The *awareness* explanation is predicated on the fact that two of the stronger correlates of education are political knowledge and use of the media. Being informed about innovations and current events is directly related to education. One scholar advances the hypothesis that "thanks largely to wider personal contacts and greater exposure to the media of opinion, the better educated are the first to sense changes in the climate of opinion and quickly respond to new fashions in social thought" (Stembler 1961, 172). For example, in a study of support for the civil rights of women and blacks, one investigator found a large increase in support for women's rights occurring among the educated shortly after the media began devoting considerable attention to the issue. However, no parallel increase was found in support for black civil rights (which received no attention out of the ordinary), indicating that increased liberalism on women's issues was due to an awareness factor (Schreiber 1978). Early in the

---

TABLE 5.4   IDEOLOGICAL SELF-PLACEMENT OF COLLEGE STUDENTS BY YEAR IN SCHOOL

	Liberal	Moderate	Conservative	Don't Know
Freshman	30%	44%	24%	2%
Sophomores	40	38	20	2
Juniors	41	29	22	2
Seniors	40	24	20	3
All students	35	36	22	2

Source: The Gallup Opinion Index, Sept. 1975, 19.

1990s this same pattern appeared for "black" as opposed to "African-American" in terms of the preferred identifier for members of this racial group. Among blacks in the mass public, the college educated were the most likely to prefer "African-American."[14] And the media (much influenced by the college educated) moved steadily to favor the newer label (Smith 1992). Since conservatism has an important status quo component and liberalism an important change component, a critic might argue that the *awareness* explanation is confusing becoming liberal with simply being trendy. The explanation is also time-bound. What is trendy at one point in time may be quite different at another time.

A second argument asserts that education leads to "enlightenment," which in turn leads to liberalism. According to William C. Stephens and C. Stephen Long (1970, 17):

> Students learn in school. They become more sophisticated, knowledgeable, broadened, and attuned to the world outside, and this is why they become more liberal and politically aware. . . . Education promotes enlightenment; enlightenment promotes liberalism, political interest, and participation.

This somewhat gratuitous statement presumes that with education the scales fall from one's eyes, enlightenment occurs, and the virtues of the more liberal political options become apparent. However, as we shall demonstrate in Chapter 7, education is not always a correlate of liberalism. On economic issues, the better educated tend to be more conservative. But as education increases, so does one's ability to think analytically and critically. The consequence is likely to be the rejection of stereotypes and prejudice, an increased tolerance of diverse lifestyles, and an increased liberalism across a variety of social issues.

A third explanation holds that the "liberal" college faculty *indoctrinates* students in the direction of their own political views. As Table 5.5 shows, college

TABLE 5.5   POLITICAL ORIENTATIONS OF COLLEGE FACULTY AND COLLEGE SENIORS, 1984 AND 1999

Year	Liberal	Middle of the Road	Conservative	
Faculty				
1984	42%	27%	31%	100%
1999	45	37	18	100%
Students				
1984	35%	39%	26%	100%
1999	36	31	33	100%

Sources: For 1984 students and faculty, Ernest Boyer and Mary Jean Whitelaw, *The Condition of the Professoriate: Attitudes and Trends, 1989* (New York: Harper, 1989); for 1999 faculty, Denise E. Magner, "Faculty Attitudes and Characteristics: Results of a 1998–1999 Survey," *Chronicle of Higher Education* (September 3, 1999) pp. A20–A21; the 1999 college seniors data are courtesy of Dr. Jerry Jacobs, Department of Sociology, University of Pennsylvania.

faculty members are decidedly more liberal than college seniors. Moreover, this table underestimates the liberalism of the relevant American professorate. Those disciplines that directly deal with government, society, and the human condition have the most liberal faculty. For example, one study showed that 70 percent of the social science faculty considered themselves liberal, compared to 41 percent among engineers (Boyer and Whitelaw 1989). When asked, students report that the college experience has a considerable influence on their political values, and certainly the faculty makes an important contribution to the college experience.[15]

But the indoctrination explanation probably underestimates the ability of students to make independent judgments. As students become better educated, they become more adept at critical thought and consequently more resistant to indoctrination. When asked about changes in their political opinions, the most frequent reason students give is an "increased thinking about political questions."[16] Further, the degree of leftward movement among students varies across historical eras. Kesler (1979) demonstrates that students reported moving significantly to the left in 1969 and 1970 (the height of the Vietnam antiwar movement), but much less so in surveys done between 1961 and 1963 and in 1977 and 1978. These historical effects cannot be explained by changed attitudes among faculty.

There is some evidence that the current crop of college students is more conservative then students 20 years ago. We see evidence of this in the UCLA survey of college freshmen, reported in Figure 5.1. College freshmen are seen

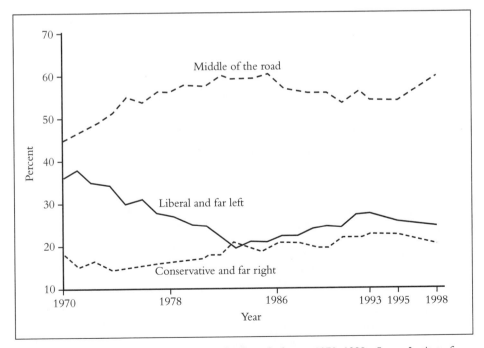

Figure 5.1   Ideological self-identification of college freshman, 1970–1998. *Source:* Institute for Higher Education, University of California, Los Angeles.

to be a good deal more conservative at the end of the twentieth century than in 1970. Among freshmen in 1970, liberals outnumbered conservatives by about a two-to-one margin. By 1985, perhaps due to the "Reagan Revolution," the ratio was about even. Since then liberals have slightly outnumbered conservatives, but not by much. In 1998, 24 percent of freshman said they were liberal (down from a high of 38 percent in 1970), and 20 percent said they were conservative. The big surge in student preferences was for "middle-of-the-road" (up from 46 percent in 1970 to 50 percent in 1993 to 57 percent in 1998). The move to the middle coincides with a dramatic drop in political interest among college freshmen. In 1966, 58 percent of freshmen said that "keeping up to date with political affairs" is very important; this number declined to 38 percent in 1979 and fell to an all-time low of 26 percent in 1998 (Sax et al. 1998).

Most observers would agree that college has an impact on student political views. There are substantial differences between young people in college and young people who do not attend college, as can be seen from data in two different periods presented in Table 5.6. However, not all these differences can be attributed to the college experience. We know from panel studies (where respondents are reinterviewed over time) that many of the differences we see between those who choose to go to college and those who do not *already* exist before the individual ever sets foot on campus. In 1965, a national sample of high school seniors were interviewed and then reinterviewed in 1973. With this panel design, it is possible to compare those who went to college with those who did not, and to analyze the differences between these two groups in 1965, when they were still in high school. The data show both an effect for

TABLE 5.6   OPINIONS OF YOUTH ATTENDING AND NOT ATTENDING COLLEGE

Opinion	College	Noncollege
There is too much concern with equality and too little with law and order★	17%	42%
Patriotism is very important★	35	60
There should be more respect for authority★	59	86
Religion is very important★	38	64
Handgun permits should be allowed†	84	72
Abortion should be allowed if pregnant woman does not want to marry father†	57	40
A communist should be allowed to speak in local community†	89	72
Identify ideologically as liberals†	36	24

★Gallup Poll reported in Robert Chandler, *Public Opinion* (New York: Bowker, 1972), pp. 6-13.
†1996–1998 pooled General Social Survey (18–22-year-olds, whites only).

preadult socialization and an effect for education. In some instances the opinion differences between those college-bound and those not were already apparent when the respondents were seniors in high school. On questions of civic tolerance, the college-bound were already more liberal than their non-college age cohorts. But by 1973 these differences had increased even further. Thus, there seems to be both a self-selection factor at work as well as an impact of higher education. On the other hand, there was little difference in 1965 on questions of prayer in the public schools and support for racial integration. By 1973, however, there were substantial differences between those with a college degree and those who had not been to college, leading to an inference that college had caused opinion change in a liberal direction (Jennings and Niemi 1982, 257–60).

5-3 POLITICAL GENERATIONS

When we speak of "political generations," we are talking about a group of people who have been socialized by the same historical events during their formative years. Of course, "the sixties generation" is the best-known recent incarnation of the idea that certain age groups hold opinions that sharply distinguish them from others. Another frequently discussed age group is "the Depression generation," those persons who were in their impressionable years during the Great Depression of the 1930s. Currently there is much commentary on the politics of "the baby boom generation," those people born between the end of World War II and 1964 and "generation X," those born in 1965 and later. When one speaks of a "generation gap," the common understanding is that the young and old differ in their political outlooks. There are, in fact, many nontrivial differences of opinion between persons of varying ages (see Table 7.7 in Chapter 7 for examples). Two explanations receive the bulk of the attention: life-cycle effects and generational effects. The unit of analysis for these discussions is the "age cohort," which is persons who fall into the same age group at a particular point in time.

A *life-cycle effect* exists when people's political views are influenced by maturation. As a reference point, assume each new political generation enters political life with identical political attitudes. Then, any difference across generations would be due to aging. When we find, as we often do, that the young are more liberal than their elders, these age differences would be explained by life-cycle effects. The implication is that the young, having few responsibilities, can afford to be idealistic. As they age, however, they take on the responsibility of raising a family, paying a mortgage, and holding down a full-time job. The effect is nicely captured in a comment about partisan politics by Winston Churchill: "Those at 18 who are not socialist have no heart; those at 40 who are still socialist have no head." In addition, it is often noted that learning continues throughout life, but reevaluation seems more frequent early in life than later (Dawson et al. 1977, 73–92). Certain predispositions become reinforced over time, as people are more likely to expose themselves selectively to political stimuli with which they agree than to those with which they disagree. The life-cycle concept assumes a process that is similar for all age groups over time. It has been asserted, for example, that as one gets older, political parties of the right become more attractive. This assertion (which we shall investigate shortly) posits an independent effect of aging on partisan predispositions.

A *generational effect* exists when a specific age cohort is uniquely socialized by a set of historical events. The logic of generational analysis dictates an interaction between age and experience. The usual assumption is that certain events in history make an indelible imprint upon the young (defined approximately as the 17-to-26-year-old cohort). It is argued that a generation's singular personality is shaped when its members leave the family and step out into the world on their own. Those that are younger remain shielded to a certain extent from the trauma of external events by the family. Those who are older are better equipped to resist its influence by their previous life experiences. For a distinct political generation to exist, something of historical consequence must have happened during their "impressionable years" (about ages 17 to 26).[17] It is difficult to imagine anything occurring in the 1950s that would have distinctively stamped a generational cohort. On the other hand, one can easily conceive of the Vietnam War era (1965–1972) or the Great Depression of the 1930s as defining unique generations.

To complicate matters further, strong political shocks can affect young and old alike—for example, when the cold war ended, all age groups relaxed their interest in further defense spending. Such general shocks are usually called "period effects."

Generations and Party Identification

Much of the research on generational politics has concerned change in party identification. Generational effects are most important in the *direction* of party identification (Republican, Independent, Democrat), but variation in the *strength* of partisanship (strong partisan, weak partisan, Independent) responds more to life-cycle effects.

Partisanship can often be imprinted on a political generation by historical events. We can see examples in Figure 5.2, which displays the relationship between age and the direction of party identification for an accumulation of Gallup Polls. The data are presented for 1990, which reveal very clear generational effects, and the more recent data for 1998.[18]

Let us look first at the data collected in 1990. We see those citizens who were in their impressionable years during the 1930s Depression (those between 66 and 77) were the most Democratic age cohort in the electorate. But note also the partisanship of those in their impressionable years during the boom times of the 1920s, when Republicans were ascendant. These citizens, in their eighties in 1990, were the most Republican age cohort. The difference in partisanship between those 74 to 77 in 1990, and those 82 and over, illustrates the profound effect of being socialized in the "Roaring Twenties" versus the "Great Depression" of the 1930s. The gap in partisan preference between these groups

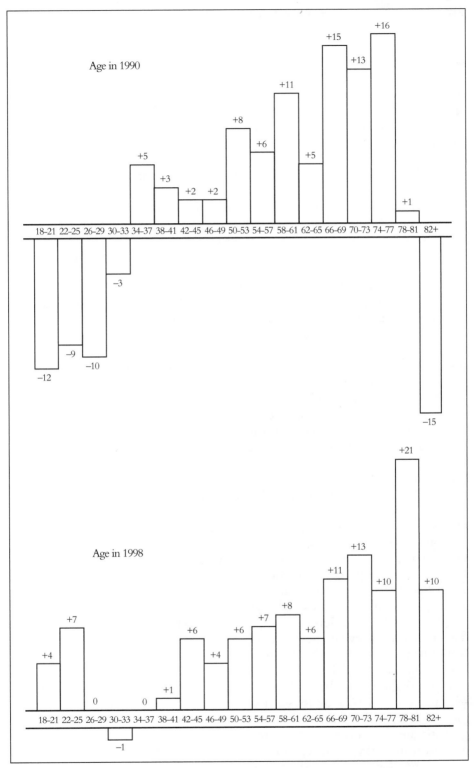

Figure 5.2 Party identification by age in 1990 and 1998 (percentage Democratic minus percentage Republican. *Source:* "America's Views and Mood 1998," *The Public Perspective* (December/January 1999): 65.

who differ only modestly in chronological age is quite startling. Finally, the youngest cohorts in 1990 were more Republican than their elders (save those over 80), having been socialized under the beleaguered President Carter or the optimistic years of the early Reagan administration. For those under 30, the Republicans averaged about a 10 percent edge over the Democrats in partisan attachment.

Moving forward to 1998, the youthful Republicans in 1990 are now between 26 and 37 years old. They are still the most Republican cohort in the electorate as of 1998, but the fact they experienced the good times of the 1990s while still in their impressionable years has probably undercut their earlier more Republican leanings. Unlike 1990, the new entrants into the electorate now lean decidedly Democratic. They were socialized at a time the bloom had worn off the "Reagan Revolution" and during the economic prosperity of the Clinton administration.

The most Republican cohort in 1990—those 82 years old and over socialized under Presidents Harding, Coolidge, and Hoover—have now exited the electorate. The New Deal generation is also getting older. The most Democratic age group—those between 78 and 81 years old—would have been in their teens and early twenties during the Great Depression. Early in the twenty-first century, this group too will mostly exit the electorate, and the age differences we currently see in Figure 5.2 will likely smooth out.

Although not depicted in Figure 5.2, the 1960s generation (socialized between 1965 and 1973) also uniquely responded to the events of the time. If we look at a very special subcohort, those college graduates who protested the Vietnam War, and compare them to college graduates who did not protest, we find a strong, persistent generational impact. Jennings (1987) has made this analysis using a subset of the parent-child socialization panel. The panel contained 129 college graduates who had protested the war and a matching sample of college graduates (about twice as many) who had not been war protesters. These two groups differed little when they were in high school. Protesters "to be" were 39 percent Democratic; nonprotesters were 38 percent Democratic. By 1973, the two groups had shifted in opposite directions, with the protesters 48 percent Democratic and the nonprotesters 27 percent. By 1982 these percentages had changed little. The antiwar movement had clearly left its partisan mark on those who were actively involved.

But not all age differences in partisan direction are generational. Some scholars see a life-cycle effect: a tendency for the electorate to become more Republican as it ages (Abramson 1983, 124; Delli Carpini 1986, 208–11; Knoke and Hout 1974, 700–13). For example, the parents in the socialization panel showed a slight Republican increase (39.5 percent in 1965 to 43.3 percent in 1973), although no Republican increase was evident among their children, who were then entering adulthood. Thus there is some support for the contention made by the authors of *The American Voter* that Republicanism, because of its "air of respectability, conservatism, and social status," may have an increasing appeal to people as they mature (Campbell et al. 1960).

Life-cycle effects are particularly operative for the *strength* of partisanship. Any survey will show that young adults have weaker partisan attachments than their elders. For example, the 1996 NES data showed 38 percent of those over 55 claiming to be "strong" partisans, compared to only 22 percent under 30. Similarly, only 23 percent of those over 55 were Independents, compared to 38 percent of those under 30. With figures such as these, one might forecast a general decline in partisanship as older cohorts with firm partisanship exit the electorate and get replaced by younger cohorts with weaker partisan attachments. But this does not happen—at least under equilibrium conditions—since each new generation acquires stronger partisan attachments as it ages. Under equilibrium conditions, the electorate's net partisan strength is stable, with each age cohort showing the same strength of partisanship as previous cohorts at the same point in the life cycle.

However, the development of partisan intensity is strongly susceptible to the shock of historical events that defines political generations. Earlier we saw the directional change in party identification among war protesters. For most youth of the late sixties, the partisan impact of the Vietnam years was a profound drop in the strength of partisanship. Those cohorts in their impressionable years after 1965 have been much more likely to call themselves Independents and much less likely to show increases in the strength of their partisan attachments over time. Thirty-six percent of the younger generation in the parent-child socialization study were Independent in 1965, rising to 48 percent in 1973 and then declining to 43 percent in 1982. Even with the decline, this generation stands out in its unwillingness to adopt a party preference (Jennings and Markus 1984, table 2).

In the case of the socialization panel (with the same persons being interviewed in 1965, 1973, and 1982), the number of Independents among the 1965 high school seniors had actually increased by 1973. But between 1973 and 1982 there was a fairly substantial move away from independence toward partisanship. The increase in partisanship was found mainly among those who voted. Those who did not vote tended to remain Independents. Thus one aspect of age that may lead to the acquisition of partisanship is simple learning based on experience. Even though the 1965 seniors seem to have increased their partisanship, they also seem, due to generational effects, unlikely to reach the level of partisan intensity of their parents (Jennings and Markus 1984).

Generations and Issues

Is there evidence of a generational effect on issue positions? Delli Carpini made an intensive study of the 1960s generation and isolated a number of instances in which this generation differed from surrounding age cohorts. What we would expect among this generation, of course, is a leftist bent to their political ideology. For the most part, Delli Carpini finds that the generation of the 1960s was more supportive than other cohorts of government involvement in the issues of race, civil liberties, economics, and social concerns. But the differences were not large, and as the generation has aged, its distinctiveness has begun to erode. There is a pull toward the political center that is exerted by society as one moves through the life cycle (Delli Carpini 1986, 120–38).

If lasting effects of the sixties generation are to be located, they would most likely be found among the subcohort of sixties antiwar activists. A failure to find generational effects would be a severe setback for the generational thesis. An analysis was performed by Jennings (1987) using the sample of college graduates who protested the war and the matching sample of college graduates who were not protesters. An advantage of the panel approach is one can look back to high school and see if the differences are explained by self-selection. On many issues there were substantial generational effects. In 1965, while in high school, the protesters (to be) were 8 percent less favorable to prayer in the public schools than the nonprotesters, but 17 years later they were 30 percent less favorable than the nonprotesters. The protesters were 13 percent more supportive of a federal role in school integration in 1965, but 43 percent more supportive in 1982. But on many other issue orientations, the once very liberal protesters began to move in a conservative direction. While 83 percent of the protesters considered themselves "liberals" in 1973, only 63 percent did so in 1982. Declines of at least 20 percent also occurred on questions of government responsibility for providing jobs, legalization of marijuana, rights of accused, helping minorities, and equality for women. The protesters were still considerably more liberal than the nonprotesters in 1982, but they had lost at least some of their distinctiveness.

By 1982, the protesters' attitudes had been shaped by both generational and life-cycle effects. Their experience as antiwar protesters stamped them with an indelible liberal print, while life-cycle effects pushed them back in a conservative direction. Furthermore, their liberalism had been eroded by exposure to the conservative ethos of the 1980s. Opinion change resulting from this exposure is an example of a "period effect," a concept we will explore directly.

Period Effects on Political Attitudes

The events that shape those in their impressionable years can also affect older citizens as well. When historical events influence all age groups, the result is known as a "period" effect. To some extent, all citizens are influenced by the periods of time through which they live. One specific example of a period effect was the impact of Vietnam and Watergate on political trust, as trust in government decreased among all age groups.

While the magnitude of an event's impact may be diminished for citizens beyond the formative years of young adulthood, these older citizens add the force of numbers to their response. The notion of period effects also serves as a reminder that political socialization through adulthood is more than a gradually increasing conservatism of outlook or a hardening of political partisanship

Generations and Political Realignment

The responses of new generations of young voters are particularly relevant to the understanding of partisan realignments. The United States has periodically undergone a partisan realignment. During realignments, the pace of partisan change quickens, with unusual numbers of voters changing their partisanship in response to new issues and events. The most recent realignment occurred during the 1930s, in response to the Depression and New Deal, and featured dramatic gains for the Democratic Party. Since the 1960s, pundits have occasionally forecast the next realignment to be around the corner. Such forecasts became quite frequent in the early 1980s, when observers commonly expected that a Republican realignment was imminent.

There is reason to believe that when a new realignment arrives, the vanguard will be young voters. Young voters lack strong partisan attachments, so they are particularly susceptible to political trends. (Note in Figure 5.2 the quite different outcomes in 1990 and 1998 of the youngest cohorts, as they reacted to the political events that occurred during their childhood and adolescence.) Moreover, young voters who have come of political age since the mid-1960s have shown an unusual degree of partisan independence. Many of these "young" Independents now face middle age. Perhaps they are still waiting for the right political movement to represent them.

The idea that young voters lead realignments is labeled the "mobilization" theory of realignment, because it involves the mobilization of new voters. However, period effects could also create realignments, with both new voters and old voters showing equal rates of partisan conversion. If events are strong enough to cause a realignment, they may be strong enough to convert both old and young from one party to another. This view is known as the "conversion" theory.[19]

Will young voters lead the next realignment? Predictions based on the 1930s realignment are difficult, because that realignment happened just as public opinion polling began. We saw, however, that the Depression cohort, which began voting in the 1930s, even today leads other age groups in allegiance to the Democratic Party. But young voters in the 1930s were not numerous enough to account for a massive realignment by themselves. Examining early Gallup Polls and *Literary Digest* Polls (see Chapter 2), Erikson and Tedin (1981) found evidence of considerable voter conversion during the realignment era. Realignments, it seems, are events of such force that even older generations of voters find the pressures difficult to resist.

5-4 THE PERSISTENCE OF POLITICAL ORIENTATIONS

At the outset of this chapter, we noted that a key assumption justifying the study of political socialization is that orientations formed early persist over time. There is a good deal of evidence that many important political predispositions do endure over a considerable time span. There is also a good deal of evidence that people continue to learn and adjust their political perspective in response to their adult environment and the events in their lives.

It is important to understand that when we speak of persistence, what mostly persists are core values and predispositions rather than specific opinions on issues of the day. Thus overarching values, such as partisanship, liberal-conservative orientation, or racial attitudes, tend to persist, while trust in government or attitudes about defense spending tend to be more fleeting.

Regarding persistence, two major points merit elaboration. First, political attitudes are very malleable through "the impressionable years." The basics of political socialization are not completed by the end of grade school, as some argue (Hess and Torney 1967). Second, after the impressionable years, political orientations harden considerably. Change still occurs, but stability markedly increases.

It is the persistence of early childhood orientations that are most questionable. One can ask if children below the eighth grade really have meaningful political attitudes at all. Vaillancourt (1973) found the responses of these children to questions about the idealization of government authority were highly unstable, suggesting attitudes were weak or nonexistent. Kolson and Green (1970) demonstrated that young children were very prone to response acquiescence. In addition, the grade-school children that so idealized government in the late 1950s and early 1960s became cynical and disillusioned in the 1970s as a result of the Vietnam War and Watergate, indicating that early childhood socialization may have little staying power. While Greenstein (1965) found that 60 percent of his fourth-grade sample identified as Republicans or Democrats, Jennings and Niemi (1982) demonstrated that partisanship was highly malleable into early adulthood.

There is considerable evidence that much—perhaps a majority—of basic political learning takes place during the impressionable years. Once those years have passed, the stability of core political values increases greatly. There now exist three long-term panel surveys all demonstrating this same point. The longest of these, and the most dramatic example of persistence, is the Bennington study originated by Theodore Newcomb. Young women (16 to 20 years old), mostly from conservative homes, matriculated at Bennington College, which in the 1930s had an avowedly liberal faculty. Students were first interviewed between 1935 and 1938, then reinterviewed in 1960, and again in 1984. The data thus stretch over almost 50 years. Using a number of items to create a scale of "liberal-conservative" political orientations, Alwin et al. (1991) found a high level of persistence over a 50-year period. The authors concluded that 60 percent of the variance in the 1984 political predispositions could be predicted from the predispositions in the 1930s when the students were attending Bennington, whereas the remaining 40 percent reflected attitude change (Alwin et al. 1991, 265). A second long-term panel survey (spanning 37 years) is the Terman study of gifted children (Terman and Oden 1959). Respondents were interviewed four times, beginning in 1940 and ending in 1977 (when they were about 30 and 67 years old). A reanalysis of these data by Sears and Funk (1999) showed that 65 percent held the same party preference and 54 percent held the same political ideology in 1977 that they did in 1940.[20] One conclusion is that socialization to core values for many people is largely complete by the late twenties.

Both the Newcomb and the Terman studies suffer from using highly unusual and nonrepresentative samples. The parent-child socialization study begun by M. Kent Jennings in 1965 (when respondents were 18) has a much stronger claim to overall generalizability.[21] The fourth wave of this study was completed in 1997 (when respondents were 50), so it now spans 32 years. These data clearly support the impressionable years—later persistence hypothesis. Attitudes were subject to considerable change between 18 and 26 years of age, but became considerably more stable in the following years. The correlation between partisanship in 1965 (at age 18) and partisanship in 1973 (at age 26) is .50. However, between ages 26 to 35 it rises to .65, and remains at .65 from ages 35 to 50. For civic tolerance, the correlations for the three time points are .41 (ages 18–26), .60 (ages 26–35), and .65 (ages 35–50) (Jennings and Stoker 1999).[22] Once the respondents had passed through their impressionable years, their attitudes stabilized. The cohort data presented in Figure 5.2 make the same point using a different methodology. Those respondents in adolescence and early adulthood during the "Roaring Twenties" (before the Great Depression) are markedly different from those who spent their impressionable years during the Great Depression—despite the fact that more than 50 years had passed since they were adolescents and young adults. This evidence as well as other data (see Sears 1991 for a review) support the general proposition of openness and change during the impressionable years, followed by a stabilizing and persistence of core political attitudes.

5-5 CONCLUSION

In this chapter we focused mainly on the preadult sources of political learning. Some political learning takes place in childhood, although the impressionable years (17–26) seem to be the most important. While attitudes crystallize in later adulthood, political learning still takes place as individuals respond to their environment and life events. Even partisanship, the most stable of political predispositions, responds in adulthood to issues and political personalities (Markus 1979; Fiorina 1981; MacKuen et al. 1989). But generally speaking, political change in adulthood is incremental. It is the impressionable years that offer the greatest potential for a radical break from the past.

NOTES

1. Gallup conducted a survey between February 4 and 8 of 1,022 adults and 305 young people between the ages of 11 and 18 for CNN/USA Today. For an additional discussion of the poll results, see Owen and Dennis (1999).
2. To make this a fair test so there would not be possible overlap, we compared the levels of trust in government among those between 32 and 38, those between 18 and 28, and those between 46 and 54. A one-way analysis of variance revealed no difference. The trust items used are those reported in Chapter 6, Figure 6.1.
3. Many of these studies are reviewed in Hyman (1959).
4. Another explanation for low relationships is measurement error. Dalton (1980) corrects for measurement error and finds a substantial increase in parent-adolescent relationships using the Jennings-Niemi data.
5. Following the conventional wisdom, the evidence indicates that when husbands and wives disagree on party preference, wives are more likely to change in the direction of the party preference of their husband. However, most data on this issue are taken from the 1960s and 1970s and may not reflect gender relationships in the twenty-first century (Weiner 1978).

6. The former point is made by Harvey (1972, 601); the latter point is made by Silbiger (1977, 174).

7. For party identification, the student-parent correlation was .66; the student-peer correlation was .26. For the 18-year-old vote, the student-parent correlation was .08; the student-peer correlation was .29.

8. The U.S. Department of Education and the Pew Charitable Trusts awarded grants to the Center for Civics Education to develop a comprehensive, standardized curriculum for teaching civics education in grades K–12. For a discussion of the proposal, see Mann (1996) and Dry (1996).

9. "Gallup Survey: Six of Ten Teenagers Show Little Interest in Politics, Politicians," *Houston Post* 19 Oct, 1977. For similar findings for college freshmen, see Mann (1999).

10. The principal difference is between little or no civics education to any degree. Students having more than a small amount of civics education were about 10 to 15 percent more trusting of government (Niemi and June 1998, 72).

11. In a seven-nation study (including the United States) of 12- to 18-year-olds, Flanagan et al. (1998) found democratic school climates had a weak but significant effect on the civic commitment of their respondents.

12. It is important to appreciate that the meaning of a college education in the twenty-first century is quite different from the 1930s or earlier. Prior to World War II, someone with a college education was a rarity. Now it is an everyday part of the social landscape. Thus, the impact of a college degree today may be quite different than 50 years ago, particularly when it comes to slotting people in social and economic networks. For an extended discussion of this point, see Nie, Junn, and Stehlik-Barry (1998, ch. 6).

13. For a summary of the extensive literature on this point, see Feldman and Newcomb (1969). A research project sponsored by William F. Buckley's journal, *The National Review,* came to the conclusion that "attending college still makes it more likely that a student's thinking will be deflected leftward"; see Kesler (1979). For a view challenging the notion that education leads to liberalism, see Jacob (1956). The most recent statement on the matter can be found in Nie, Junn, and Stehlik-Barry (1998).

14. In a reading of preferences for this term in March 1997, 30 percent of the racial group preferred "Black," 30 percent preferred "African-American," 8 percent preferred some other term, and 32 percent said either term was acceptable (Hart and Teeter for *The Wall Street Journal*).

15. A 1969 poll for CBS News asked students: "Which of the following events, if any, have had a great effect on your life and values, which have had a moderate effect, and which have had no effect?" Sixty-six percent of the college students said the "college experience" had a "great effect." This was the highest percentage of the nine possible options (Kesler 1969).

16. On the question of the influence of college on political attitudes, 42 percent attributed their change in attitudes to either "lectures or course readings" or "personal contact with faculty" (Kesler 1979, 1488).

17. There is no agreement about exactly what ages constitute the impressionable years, other than that they extend from adolescence through to early adulthood.

18. The "1990 data" is a compilation of Gallup Polls from 1989–1991, and contains 12,600 cases. The 1998 data is based on a single year. The exact number of cases was not reported in the original source.

19. The best statement of the mobilization theory is found in Andersen (1979); an argument for the conversion hypothesis is found in Erikson and Tedin (1981); for a critique, see Campbell (1985); see Erikson and Tedin (1986) for a response. For a somewhat different approach to generations and changes in party identification, see Beck (1974).

20. For party identification, 59 percent were perfectly stable over the four waves between 1940 and 1977 and another 6 percent moved around between waves but would end up in 1977 at the same place they started in 1940. For ideology, 42 percent were perfectly stable and 12 percent moved around but returned to their 1940 position by 1977.

21. But the panel is still not representative, as the sample of 18-year-olds in 1965 was limited to high school seniors. Those who dropped out of high school were not included. And, like all panels, those who fail to be reinterviewed usually differ in some ways from those who remain in the panel.

22. It is important to distinguish between absolute and relative continuity. By absolute continuity, we mean those who were strong liberals at Time 1 remain strong liberals at Time 2. By relative continuity, we mean those who were most liberal at Time 1 are the most liberal at Time 2, but they may not have maintained their exact position on the scale. Correlation coefficients measure relative continuity, so what we are referring to in this section is the tendency, over time, for the most liberal respondents at Time 1 to be the most liberal at Time 2, not that they maintain the exact position on issues between time points. It would be unreasonable, for example, to think that in the Bennington study respondents would maintain the same issue position over a 50-year period.

CHAPTER 6

Public Opinion and Democratic Stability

In a democracy, public opinion is important because it can influence the decisions that political leaders make. In previous chapters we have discussed the level of public opinion on questions of public policy. Certain other types of political orientations are particularly important because the extent of their existence may influence the functioning of democratic government. In this chapter we shall analyze attitudes and predispositions considered by many as necessary to maintain a democracy, as well as examine the degrees to which Americans appear to hold these attitudes.

Ideas about what is vital for the functioning of democratic government can be divided into four groups. First, there should be widespread support for the rules of democracy. An apt analogy here is the rules of the road for driving an automobile. If most people did not accept the rule that one must stop when the light is red, chaos would ensue. The rules of democracy involve guarantees that the civil liberties of all shall be protected—that majorities rule, but minorities have rights.

Second, democracy's stability may rest on a social consensus regarding values and goals. Disagreements must not be so fundamental that neither resolution nor compromise can be gained by institutionalized procedures. Too great a division may overtax even the best procedures for resolving conflict. Contemporary examples include the Protestant-Catholic division in Northern Ireland, the Christian-Muslim division in Lebanon, the Tamil (Hindu)-Sinhalese (Buddhist) conflict in Sri Lanka, and the Serb-Croat-Muslim division in Bosnia.

Third, if people are to accept government decisions, they must believe that their political actions can be effective and that they can trust the government to respond to their interests. If political alienation becomes sufficiently intense and widespread, it may pose a threat to democratic stability.

Fourth, in coping with personal anxieties and needs, certain personality types find comfort in blaming others. Alternatively (or simultaneously), some seek a solution to their problems in a strong leader. When such personalities are common, minority rights become very fragile, and the stability of democracy can be threatened.

6-1   SUPPORT FOR DEMOCRATIC VALUES

One of the great threats to any political system, democracies included, is the desire on the part of those who hold political power to maintain it, and to work their will free from constraints imposed by others. Ambition in political leaders is not, in and of itself, an undesirable trait. But history is strewn with examples of those in government warding off competition by the expeditious route of eliminating it. Consequently, democracies must anticipate that leaders may not suffer criticism gladly, and may not want to share or give up political power if there is a way to avoid it. One solution to this problem, developed by the framers of the American Constitution, was to build in a series of mechanisms designed to protect the rights of those outside government who aspire to political influence from those on the inside who hold political power. But constitutions can only go so far in making good on these protections. One need only witness the ineffectiveness of "constitutionalism" in a country like Lebanon. As Judge Learned Hand (1959, 144) once observed, "Liberty lies in the hearts and minds of men and women; when it dies there, no constitution, no laws, no court can save it." Some commitment to democratic values on the part of both political leaders and the public seems essential.

In using the term "democratic values," we are referring to procedural norms. These norms do not refer to the substance of legitimate political conflict, such as the desirable tradeoff between inflation and unemployment, but to the "rules of the game" in which that conflict takes place. One important set of procedural norms is found in the Bill of Rights. Here Americans are guaranteed the right to freedom of expression, freedom from unreasonable search and seizure, protection from self-incrimination, a speedy and public trial, free exercise of religion, and so on. Two related democratic values of great importance are majority rule and minority rights. At regular intervals the population is mobilized into opposing camps. Each camp proclaims its own virtue and criticizes the opposition. An election is then held, and the winners take control of the government. The losers remain free to rouse popular hostility toward the new leaders, in the hope of embarrassing them and ultimately replacing them in office. This procedure is normally the way decision-makers are chosen in the United States. One therefore hopes to find an understanding among the electorate that these are the methods that should be employed to select public officials.

As shown in Table 6.1, survey evidence does in fact demonstrate that when democratic values are stated in the abstract (e.g., "public officials should be chosen by majority vote"), there is an overwhelming positive consensus of support for them. But note that these assertions are very general, with no reference to any specific person or group. These statements basically constitute an official American political ideology—the sort of lessons that are taught in a variety of both political and nonpolitical contexts by the family and the school, and reinforced by the mass media.

However, when statements about the rules of the game have a double stimulus, with references both to democratic principles and to unpopular groups, support for these rules declines.

Relevant evidence is presented in Table 6.2, in which the statements are two-pronged. Each refers to a democratic norm plus some specific group or activity. For example, in the statement "Members of the Ku Klux Klan should be banned from running for public office," individuals are asked to respond to both the norm of free elections and feelings about the Klan.

One interpretation of these data is that public support for procedural rights is less than ideal. In the cases of elections and the Ku Klux Klan, 70 percent would ban a Klan member from running for public office. The pattern in Table 6.2 is clearly one of a lack of enthusiasm for the values of democracy when items refer to protests, demonstrations, or unpopular groups such as American communists. Critics can, of course, argue that this evidence is not drawn from actual behavior and simply represents ill-considered survey responses to hypothetical situations. However, Barbara Gamble (1997) demonstrates that when ordinary citizens are given the power to directly legislate

**TABLE 6.1   SUPPORT FOR DEMOCRATIC VALUES
STATED IN THE ABSTRACT**

Statement	Democratic Response	Uncertain Response	Undemocratic Response
People in the minority should be free to try to win majority support for their opinions.	89%	9%	2%
Public officials should be chosen by majority vote.	95	3	2
I believe in free speech for all, no matter what their views might be.	85	7	9
No mater what a person's political views are, he is entitled to the same legal protections as anyone else.	93	4	3

Source: John L. Sullivan, James Piereson, and George E. Marcus, *Political Tolerance and American Democracy* (Chicago: University of Chicago Press, 1982), p. 203.

TABLE 6.2 SUPPORT FOR DEMOCRATIC VALUES, BY SPECIFIC APPLICATION

	Democratic Response	Undecided	Undemocratic Response
[Should] people who want to overthrow the government by revolution [be] allowed to hold public meetings to express their views? (GSS 1996)	66%	05%	29%
[Should] books that contain dangerous ideas be banned from public libraries? (PEW 1997)	47	4	49
Should x-rated movies be totally banned for sale to adults? (Gallup 1985)	54	3	43
Freedom of the press should be protected under all circumstances. (WP 1997)	34	1	65
If the police suspect that drugs, guns, or other criminal evidence are hidden in someone's house, should they be allowed to enter a house without first obtaining a search warrant? (CBS 1970)	66	2	32
If a man is found innocent of a serious crime but new evidence is uncovered, do you think he should be tried for the same crime again? (CBS 1970)	38	4	58
Forcing people to testify against themselves [prohibited by the Fifth Amendment] may be necessary. (CLS 1978–79)	40	26	35
If a person is suspected of a serious crime, do you think the police should be allowed to hold him in jail until they can get enough evidence to charge him? (CBS 1970)	38	3	58
[Should] someone who believes blacks are inferior be allowed to speak in your community? (WP 1998)	63	1	34
Judges should be able to censor the press in criminal cases so jurors are not biased. (FF 1997)	42	7	51
If someone is suspected of treason or other serious crimes, he should not be entitled to be released on bail. (Gibson 1987)	21	14	65
Members of the Ku Klux Klan should be banned from running for public office. (Gibson 1987)	23	7	70
People ought to be allowed to vote even if they cannot do so intelligently. (McClosky 1958)	48	N/A	52
[It is] . . . a good idea for the government to keep a list of people who take part in demonstrations. (Harris and Weston 1979)	25	26	50

Sources: John Sullivan et al., *Political Tolerance and American Democracy* (Chicago: University of Chicago Press, 1982); General Social Survey (GSS), 1985; CBS: Robert Chandler, *Public Opinion* (New York: Bowker, 1972); Herbert McClosky, 1958; Herbert McClosky, "Consensus and Ideology in American Politics," *American Political Science Review*, 58 (June 1964); CLS: Herbert McClosky and Alida Brill, *Dimensions of Tolerance* (New York: Russell Sage Foundation, 1983); Louis Harris and Alan F. Westin, *The Dimensions of Privacy* (Stevens Point, WI: Sentry Insurance, 1979); James L. Gibson, *Freedom and Tolerance in the United States* (NORC: unpublished codebook, 1987; *Washington Post* 1997; Pew Research Center 1997; the Freedom Forum 1997.

using the ballot box, they have consistently used that power to deprive unpopular minorities of their civil liberties and rights. She looked at 74 ballot initiatives on public accommodations for minorities, school desegregation, gay rights, English language laws and AIDS policies. More than three-quarters of these elections resulted in the defeat of policies designed to protect minority rights.

A Growth in Democratic Tolerance

Table 6.3 shows the change over time in Americans' tolerance of some selected unpopular groups.

One point attracts immediate attention. There has been a substantial increase in political tolerance between 1954 and 1998. Or at least that is one possible interpretation of Table 6.3. For example, note that tolerance for someone speaking out against churches and religion has risen from 38 percent in 1954 to 75 percent in 1998. A simple conclusion is that the American public has become more tolerant. A common explanation for this change is based on social learning theory. The assumption is that increases in exposure to social and cultural diversity lead to increases in support for democratic norms. Two changes of consequence for this explanation are rising levels of education and the move from rural to urban areas. The proportion of people who have been to college has more than doubled since the 1950s (NES 1952–1996). Educated people are more likely to understand the importance of protecting democratic liberties, if only in their own self-interest. Also, social and cultural diversity, such as that found in the city, brings individuals into contact with people who are not like them. They learn that those who are different are not always dangerous (Williams et al. 1976).

A less obvious explanation for the rise in support for democratic values holds that there has been little "real" change between 1954 and 1998; rather, what we see is nothing more than an artifact of the question. That is, the groups used in 1954 to elicit tolerant or intolerant responses are not currently as threatening as they were in 1954. At the time of the 1954 survey, the climate of opinion in the United States was strongly influenced by the scare tactics of the ultra-right-wing junior senator from Wisconsin, Joseph McCarthy. He claimed to have proof that communists had infiltrated the American government, and more than a few people believed him (Goldstein 1978). The groups identified in the 1954 survey are those usually associated with the left—communists, atheists, and socialists. Tolerance may appear to have gone up simply because these groups no longer pose the danger than many once thought.[1]

In an ambitious project, Sullivan, Pierson, and Marcus (1982) devised a test to determine if the increased tolerance one sees in Table 6.3 is real or simply an illusion. They suspected that support for the civil liberties of a specific group was largely driven by emotion rather than considered judgment. If someone liked atheists, that person would have no problem allowing them the right of free speech. It takes no tolerance to "put up with" someone with whom one agrees, who is promoting a political agenda with which one concurs. On the

TABLE 6.3   PUBLIC TOLERANCE FOR ADVOCATES OF UNPOPULAR IDEAS, 1954–1998

	Person Should Be Allowed to Make a Speech			Person Should Be Allowed to Teach in College			Person's Book Should Remain in the Library		
	1954	*1972*	*1998*	*1954*	*1972*	*1998*	*1954*	*1972*	*1998*
An admitted communist	28%	52%	67%	6%	39%	57%	29%	53%	67%
Someone against churches and religion	38	65	75	12	40	58	37	60	70
Someone who favors government ownership of all railroads and large industries	65	77	*	38	56	*	60	67	*
Someone who believes that blacks are genetically inferior	*	61†	62	*	41	46	*	62	63

Sources: 1954 data are from Samuel Stouffer, *Communism, Conformity, and Civil Liberties* (New York: Wiley, 1954); 1972 and 1998 data are from the General Social Survey.

*Question not asked.

†General Social Survey, 1976.

other hand, the same person might heartily dislike members of the Ku Klux Klan and be quite willing to deny them free expression. The acid test for tolerance, according to Sullivan and his colleagues, is putting up with those whose ideas one finds repugnant. In other words, they suspected that support for procedural rights depended on whose ox was being gored.

Sullivan et al. (1982, 60–63) devised a "content-controlled" question in which respondents were given a list of groups and asked which one they liked least (with an option to supply a group not on the list). Respondents were then queried as to whether they would "put up with" (i.e., be tolerant of the procedural rights of) their least-liked group.

As Table 6.4 demonstrates, tolerance using a least-liked approach does not seem to have improved much since 1954.[2] For example, only 18 percent would allow a member of their least-liked group to teach in the public schools. These levels of tolerance are not much different from the 1950s. If true, this finding has disturbing implications. It calls into question the inherent willingness of Americans to embrace one of the pillars of democratic thought: tolerance. It also seems to offer little hope for improvement. The early studies showed a strong relationship between education and support for democratic values. One might suppose, then, as aggregate levels of education increased, so would political tolerance. However, the revisionist thesis holds this is not the case, since Americans are no more tolerant now than they were during the McCarthy era of the 1950s. Thus improvements in the general level of education, according to this viewpoint, are not the answer to what is seen as a dangerously low level of support for democratic values.

Not surprisingly, this general line of research has been subject to substantial criticism. Among the most telling is a claim that the questions used are inherently incapable of determining the "true" level of support for democratic values. The questions are flawed because by their very nature they have double

TABLE 6.4   LEVELS OF TOLERANCE USING CONTENT-CONTROLLED ITEMS

Item	Percentage Tolerant of Least-Liked Group
Members of the [least-liked group] should be allowed to teach in public schools.	19
The [least-liked group] should not be outlawed.	31
Members of the [least-liked group] should be allowed to make a speech in this city.	50
The [least-liked group] should not have their phones tapped by our government.	63
The [least-liked group] should be allowed to hold public rallies in our city.	32

Source: James Gibson, *Freedom and Tolerance in the United States* (National Opinion Research Center: unpublished codebook, 1987).

stimuli—support for a general principle and reactions to an unpopular group or political act. Further, these stimuli are not balanced. A very strong stimulus (one's *single most* disliked group) is contrasted to a much weaker stimulus (abstract democratic values).

In the typical survey setting, in which respondents must give answers in a few seconds, it is not unexpected that the strong stimulus frequently overwhelms the weak one (or first comes to mind). Most people know whom they do and do not like. Coming to grips with an abstract principle is more difficult (Brady and Sniderman 1985; Zaller and Feldman 1992). Thus, initially, the strong stimulus dominates. But importantly, several studies show that people can easily be talked out of—or talked into—antidemocratic positions (Chong 1993; Cobb and Kuklinski 1997). Gibson (1996) demonstrates that for Americans who initially give an intolerant response, 38 percent changed their minds when given subsequent counterarguments for the tolerant alternative. But counterarguments were even more effective among those initially giving a tolerant response. Sixty-three percent changed their minds and gave the intolerant response. (Gibson, (1998) presents similar results with Russian respondents.) It seems quite clear that people have great difficulty reconciling their desire to support the principles of democratic procedure with their fears and apprehensions about unconventional groups and political activities. Thus support for democratic values may largely be determined by how the question is framed. If it is made clear to respondents that a "constitutional right" is involved, they tend to support democratic principles regardless of how unpopular a group or activity may be. But if the democratic principle in the question is abstract, most people react to the unpopular group rather than the underlying principle (Chong 1993; Weissberg 1998). While this research may not provide convincing evidence that the public is hostile to democratic values, it nevertheless supports an argument that the public is at least ambivalent about them.

The Theory of Democratic Elitism

If the public is as equivocal or nonsupportive of democratic values as many believe, how does democracy in the United States survive? American colleges and universities contain substantial numbers of atheists (Gibson and Bingham 1985, 15). In 1998, 24 percent of the public would not allow atheists to teach in these institutions (GSS). Why has there been no mass movement to root out the nonbelievers? Beyond the obvious observation that what people say has no one-to-one link with actual behavior, the most influential accounting for this circumstance is "the theory of democratic elitism" (McClosky 1964; Rose 1964; Stouffer 1955). The theory was spawned by the observation that support for democratic values is not evenly spread throughout the population. Three groups are regarded as being particularly relevant: those with little or no political interest, the educated and politically alert, and elected and appointed public officials. These groups differ in their levels of commitment to democratic values, with the low-interest group being the least committed and public officials being the most committed. For example, Nunn and his associates (1978) demonstrated that 83 percent of a community leader sample could be classified as "more tolerant" compared to only 56 percent of a comparable mass sample. Data from the 1998 General Social Survey show that while 67 percent of the mass public would support free speech for a communist and 66 percent would support free speech for a militarist, several samples of elite groups show that well over 90 percent of the respondents demonstrate a firm (verbal) commitment to democratic values (Gibson and Bingham 1985; McClosky and Brill 1983).

Perhaps the most important predictor of support for democratic values is education. Several investigators have presented data showing the better educated tend to be more supportive of democratic procedures than those with less education (Stouffer 1955; Nunn et al. 1978; Nie et al. 1998). The 1998 General Social Survey shows that only 49 percent of those with a grade-school education would allow a homosexual to teach at a college or university, while 89 percent of those with a college degree would do so. Nie and his colleagues (1998) argue causal link between education and support for democratic values runs through *verbal cognitive proficiency*—the ability to gather, analyze, and comprehend information and discover where one's self-interest truly lies.

In addition, some go even further and argue that within categories of education, political elites are more tolerant than the public. One author inferred from the Stouffer data (part of which is presented in Table 6.3) that the "differences between leaders and the community at large does not seem due simply to education, since 79 percent of the college-educated leaders are among the more tolerant as compared to 66 percent for the general college-educated population" (Kornhauser 1970, 67). According to theory of democratic elitism, political leaders are more tolerant than their education alone would predict because of their exposure to the democratic values that permeate the American elite political culture (McClosky 1964; McClosky and Brill 1983). The system works, therefore, because those who are least attached to democratic values are very unlikely to be active or influential in politics. On the other hand, those most committed to democratic tolerance are the ones who have the most influence on actual political outcomes because of their high interest and high levels of political participation. Proponents of democratic elitism can point to countries like Argentina, where government has been very unstable, and find confirmation of their theory in the fact that educated political activists in that nation are very low in their support for democratic values (Dahl 1971, 139). That American political elites score very high on these values is then interpreted as an explanation for democratic stability in the United States. In the words of one of the more influential writers on the subject: "Democratic viability is . . . saved by the fact that those who are the most confused about democratic ideas are also most likely to be politically apathetic" (McClosky 1964, 365).

However, once they are actively engaged, the masses can pose a substantial threat to democratic values. One common explanation for the repression that occurred in the 1950s during the McCarthy era is that demands on the elites for repressive action were made by a mass public feeling threatened by American communists.

Considerable criticism has been directed at the theory we have just discussed. Any explanation of democratic stability that portrays political activists and officeholders as saviors and common people as potential saboteurs of democratic government will be found immediately suspect by many. Reanalysis of the Stouffer data by Robert Jackman (1972), for example, casts considerable doubt on the claim that political influentials are more supportive of democratic values than are others who share their education, gender, region of origin, and other distinguishing characteristics. The Sullivan et al. (1982) least-liked-group analysis found that the differences in tolerance between political activists and nonactivists were spurious, caused by other factors being related to both support for democratic values and tolerance. Sniderman et al. (1996) in an analysis of mass and elite opinion in Canada found no support for the theory of democratic elitism. Over a host of individual rights issues, they found mass and elite opinion to be essentially indistinguishable.

Critics note that despite the survey evidence and an occasional ballot initiative (usually with an unclear message), the actual record of tolerance for democratic rights by the mass public has not, in the view of most people, been unduly alarming. On the other hand, one can point to certain elite behaviors that many find to be dangerously undemocratic. Among the examples are the internment of Japanese-Americans during World War II, the failure of political elites to respond critically to violations of traditional norms of free speech and due process by Senator Joseph McCarthy, and the events surrounding the break-in at the Watergate by persons in the employ of the president of the United States.

In the case of the McCarthy era, James Gibson (1988) has correlated the tolerance scores of the mass and elite samples from the 1954 Stouffer survey, aggregated by state, with an index measuring repressive legislation passed by the states during that period. He found no evidence of demands for the repression of American communists emanating from the mass public, but he did find evidence of a link between intolerant state elites and repressive state legislation.

A different type of analysis holds that the survey evidence supporting the elitist theory is itself invalid. Critics argue that the better educated simply learn what are socially desirable and "appropriate" answers to questions about democratic tolerance (Jackman 1978; Weissberg 1998). Evidence for this claim can be seen in the 1998 GSS, in which a surprisingly high 40 percent of the college-educated *would not* allow someone who believed blacks are genetically inferior to teach at colleges or universities. They have apparently learned that it is now socially chic to condemn racists, even though their rights of free expression are no different than American communists or any other group. But this learning is of a very superficial sort. When it comes to endorsing the ideals of the civil rights movement, the well-educated are considerably more supportive of the ideals than those with less education. However, in demanding applied situations (such as government action to benefit racial minorities), the well-educated are no more likely to be supportive than are the less educated. (For more details, see Chapter 7.) Jackman and Mulha (1984) stress that education does not so much increase tolerance as it increases the ability of those in the privileged class to develop sophisticated rationales for their privileged position.

Finally, cognitive psychologists (and their followers in political science) claim that the better educated and more politically aware have a greater store of democratic (versus nondemocratic) "considerations" to sample from memory when being interviewed. Thus they have a greater probability of giving democratic responses (Zaller and Feldman 1992; Chong 1993). That does not, however, necessarily mean they are more committed to democratic principles.

Pluralistic Intolerance

In another approach to reconciling an intolerant public with continuing democratic government, Sullivan et al. (1982) offer a theory of "pluralistic intolerance." While the public may be quite intolerant, their data show no consensus as to what group should be suppressed. There was a great deal of diversity among the groups Americans like least. In the Sullivan et al. (1982) survey, the least-liked group was American communists at 29 percent, followed by the Ku Klux Klan at 24 percent. The most recent survey by Gibson (1987) reverses this order, with the Klan at 32 percent and American communists at 24 percent.[3] Since there is no agreement on what groups to suppress, elites receive mixed signals and consequently have the freedom to act on the basis of their own (presumably democratic) preferences. In other words, with no intolerant consensus, there is no demand for political repression against any one particular group.[4]

The theory of pluralistic intolerance is based on a simple linkage model. When a group is very unpopular among the mass public, political repression will occur. This linkage receives some support in comparing the early 1950s to the late 1970s. In the 1950s, intolerance was focused on communists and people of the political left. Repression of those persons has been amply documented (Goldstein 1978). On the other hand, intolerance is currently unfocused and repression is much less evident. However, the direction of causation here is very much open to question. It is possible that both the policy of repressing the left during the McCarthy era, and mass public opinion concerning communists and the like, were determined by political elites.[5] In fact, a common interpretation of mass–elite linkage is that elite opinion and behavior shape mass opinion, not the reverse (Parry 1969). The danger in focused intolerance at the mass level may be that demagogic elites can find a receptive audience to fuel an antidemocratic political movement.

Intolerant Beliefs and Intolerant Behavior

Many seem to agree that support for democratic norms is important for democratic stability. Others argue that intolerant beliefs are of consequence only if they lead to intolerant behavior, and that there is little evidence of any meaningful link. It is important to realize that behavior has multiple causes, of which attitudes are only one (Deutscher 1973). For example, a person would probably look for group support before attempting to prevent an atheist from speaking or before removing books by a communist from the public library. However, Robert Weissberg (1998) argues that the opinions measured in studies of political tolerance are so uniquely distant from intolerant behavior as to render them little more than hypotheticals. Do the expressed fears of some citizens in an opinion survey about libraries stocking their shelves with inflammatory books by Marxists really capture an enduring predisposition for antidemocratic behavior? Translating antidemocratic beliefs into behavior is likely to be a much more infrequent occurrence than translating a preference for a political candidate into the behavior of casting a vote for that candidate.

6-2 POLITICAL CONSENSUS

Clearly, a democracy will be more stable if citizens agree, or are in consensus, over basic values and goals. Some conflict over issues is inevitable in a democracy, because public policies generally cannot benefit or penalize all persons or groups equally. Intense or severe political conflict, however, is undesirable because it may threaten the stability of democracy. Robert Dahl defines intensity of conflict as a function of the extent to which each side sees the other as enemies to be destroyed by whatever means necessary (Dahl 1971, 335). As issues become more intensely debated, the language of conflict becomes harsher; opponents are accused of acting out of less than honorable motives, and tactics that were once regarded as illegitimate are given serious consideration. The Protestant-Catholic split in Northern Ireland and Muslim-Christian split in Lebanon are classic examples of a political division that makes democratic government and the protection of civil liberties virtually impossible.

The United States has clearly experienced political conflict, but unlike many other countries, there has not been significant controversy over a number of fundamental issues. Evidence from several surveys indicates that (1) the broad elements of the constitutional order are widely endorsed; (2) there is a consensus that defects should be remedied by legal processes of change; (3) most people are satisfied with the economic order, with 94 percent agreeing that we "must be ready to make sacrifices if necessary . . . to preserve the free enterprise system"; few want to nationalize large corporations; big business is widely accepted; labor unions are less popular, but few want to see them eliminated; (4) Americans believe that opportunities exist for personal achievement—the doors of success are open for those willing to work; and (5) most people are content with their lot.[6] When asked, 85 percent say they feel extremely good or very good when the see the American flag fly, and 92 percent profess extreme or very strong love for their country (NES 1988). Eighty-six percent are proud to be American (GSS 1994), and 89 percent say they would rather be a citizen of the United States than any other country (GSS 1996).

Traditional sources of cleavage that have posed problems in other countries have, for the most part, been moderate in the United States. Among the most important of these are class, regionalism, and religion. Particularly important is the fact that political attitudes are only weakly related to these divisions (see Chapter 7). Regional differences (at least currently) also tend not to be intense. The American public is very mobile. The Bureau of the Census reports that in a typical year, 20 percent of the population moves, with about one-third moving a considerable distance. Even the South, on the question of race, is beginning to lose some of its uniqueness. Religious antagonisms, too, do not lead to severe issue conflicts. One reason is that religious preference is only slightly related to social class. One's religion does not determine one's opportunities or economic well-being. The low salience of these conflicts is evidenced in that 92 percent of opinion-holders said they would vote for a Jew for president, 95 percent said they would vote for a black, and 94 percent said they would vote for a Catholic (Gallup, 1999).

Two issues, however, have proved to be very divisive—race and (until its termination) the Vietnam War. Violence and antidemocratic behavior have accompanied attempts to resolve each. The race issue, of course, has existed since the beginning of the Republic, and has been the principal threat to the survival of democratic rights in the United States. Recent violent manifestations of this cleavage were the urban riots that occurred in virtually every city between 1965 and 1968, then again in several cities in the 1990s in response to several high-visibility assault and murder trials in which victim and accused were of different races. Today there still exists a wide gap between the opinions of whites and blacks on a substantial range of issues. These differences are most pronounced on questions of what constitutes fair treatment for blacks (again, see Chapter 7), but exist in other domains as well. The possibility for conflict between the races is intensified by the fact that socioeconomic differences reinforce issue disagreements. Most blacks are working class and many are unemployed, while a considerably greater proportion of whites belong to the more affluent sectors of American society.

While blacks clearly have some specific policy grievances and tend to view partisan politics from a different perspective than whites, blacks do not reject the central tenets underlying the American political system. In 1981, 76 percent of a national sample of black respondents thought the United States had a special role to play in the world; 86 percent said that the United States was the best place in the world to live (Gallup 1986); and in 1988 (NES), 87 percent of blacks were "extremely proud" or "very proud" to be Americans. Less than 3 percent were "not proud at all."

Unlike the race issue, which threatens to polarize Americans along racial lines, the Vietnam War (fought at its height between 1965 and 1972) polarized Americans along ideological lines. Disagreement on this issue was so intense that it resulted in a number of actions at the fringe of legality and some that went considerably beyond. There were demonstrations, riots, occupation of buildings, violence (police and hard-hats versus protesters), and the shooting of unarmed demonstrators. As a counter to the perceived threat of leftist protesters, the government engaged in a number of illegal practices, such as wiretapping and surveillance.

The Vietnam War caused the display of many traits that are characteristic of intense political conflict. The stakes were high, there were substantial numbers on both sides with strongly held beliefs, and there was no compromise acceptable to competing sides. While relatively few were directly affected by the war, a very vocal minority was outraged over the notion of American boys being required to fight and sometimes die in someone else's civil war. Another sizable minority saw the war resisters as traitors. Compromise was extremely difficult; both sides were committed. In addition, the North Vietnamese would accept only one solution—total American withdrawal.

While attitudes about the war posed a very serious cleavage, there were two factors that served to diminish its polarizing effect. First, the entire population was not divided into two extreme camps. Rather, after 1968, the majority tended toward the middle position. They viewed the war as a mistake, but did not want it ended by an immediate withdrawal or an all-out military attack. There also existed "cross-cutting cleavages." Extreme conflict becomes more threatening when an individual's attitudes and group memberships reinforce each other. An example would be a very high proportion of "doves" who were college-educated, under 30, white, Democratic, pro-affirmative action, pro-abortion, anti–big business, and religious agnostics. However, attitudes toward the Vietnam War were not highly associated with other attitudes or with group membership. Doves were not necessarily pro-abortion, college-educated, or under 30. Rather, views on the war cut across these divisions. The existence of cross-cutting cleavages served to mute the intensity of the conflict.[7]

6-3 POLITICAL SUPPORT: TRUST AND EFFICACY

A common assumption is that the political system works better when citizens give it their support than when they are "alienated," or estranged from government. The two most prominent dimensions of political support are political trust and efficacy (Craig 1993). Trust is the affective component of support. Those high in trust are satisfied with the procedures and products of government. The opposite of trust is political cynicism, or the evaluation that the political system is not producing policies according to expectations. Efficacy is the cognitive or belief component of support. It is the extent to which a person believes his or her political activities will influence government. Trust relates to an assessment of government output, and efficacy relates to the consequences of one's input.

Political Trust and Democratic Stability

No government has the complete trust of all its citizens. However, many argue that it is important for democratic government to maintain some minimal (usually unspecified) level of trust among its citizens. One argument is pitched at the normative level. If the distinctive character of democracy is the substitution of voluntary consent for coercion, it is a matter of no small moral shortcoming when citizens withdraw trust out of a conviction that the government is not acting in their best interests (Sabine 1952; Nye 1997). Others make claims of a more practical bent. Levels of trust are thought to affect the leadership strategies available to political decision-makers. Leaders must be able to make decisions and commit resources without first consulting those persons who will be affected by the decisions and called upon to supply the resource materials. According to William Gamson (1968, 45–46), when trust is high, "the authorities are able to make new commitments on the basis of it and, if successful, increase support even more. When it is low or declining, authorities may find it difficult to meet existing commitments and govern effectively." Thus when trust was high in 1964, the government could draw on its "credit rating" with the electorate and send troops to fight an overseas police action in Vietnam with little public debate. That sort of freedom was considerably constrained after 1972.

Weatherford (1987) argues that levels of trust are particularly important in the economic area, where the government needs maneuvering room to pursue long-term policy goals. For example, if inflation becomes entrenched, the government must sometimes call upon citizens to endure the pain of recession for the promise of stable prices at a point in the indeterminate future. Citizens must have faith in the fairness and competence of government and not demand a premature accounting based on a short-term appraisal of cost and benefits. More concretely, Nye (1997) sees low trust among citizens as undermining their willingness to provide tax dollars, the willingness of bright people to go into government, and the willingness to voluntarily comply with the law.

If trust drops sufficiently low, some contend, it can lead to social disruption. Disruption may serve as an impetus to needed reform, or it may threaten the stability of an existing regime. At the very least, a portion of state resources will have to be diverted to cope with the disturbances. Almond and Verba (1965, 354) write that insufficient trust is particularly dangerous when the system is not performing in an adequate fashion as, for example, in an economic depression. Lipset (1960, 69) provides evidence from the 1930s showing that when many democratic governments ceased to be effective it was those with a reservoir of trust among its citizens that were able to withstand the strain, while those not so advantaged (such as Austria, Germany, and Spain) succumbed to antidemocratic movements. Arthur Miller (1974, 951) has flatly asserted, "A democratic political system cannot survive for long without the support of a majority of its citizens."

Levels of political trust may serve as a barometer indicating how well government is performing. It is, therefore, no surprise that scholars have paid considerable attention to the fluctuations in trust over time.[8] Figure 6.1 presents the trend in political trust between 1958 and 1999. The data from 1958 to 1964 reflect the tranquility of the Eisenhower years, the Camelot years of Kennedy, and the landslide election of Lyndon Johnson. After 1964 trust began to decrease at a steady pace until 1980. Common explanations include the government's handling of the civil rights movement, the Vietnam War, Watergate, the pardon of Richard Nixon, and the economic and foreign policy problems associated with the Carter administration. The decrease in trust during this period came about equally from the dissatisfied left and the dissatisfied right. For example, cynics on the left tended to think the government had moved too slowly on civil rights; cynics on the right tended to think it had moved too rapidly (Miller 1983).

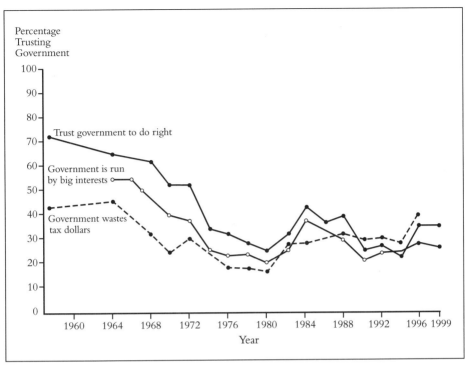

Figure 6.1   Trends in public trust by item. *Source:* National Election Studies (1958–1996); Gallup (1999).

The most severe decline in trust came between 1972 and 1974. The most plausible explanation is Watergate. Daily accusations of break-ins, slush funds, wiretapping, extortion, cover-ups, etc., are not designed to encourage enthusiasm for government. But even after President Nixon left office there was no immediate decline in cynicism. In fact, trust did not rebound until Ronald Reagan took office and proclaimed it was "morning in America." The Reagan administration's attack on big government may also have helped boost the level of trust. By 1984, trust had rebounded considerably, although it was nowhere close to the levels of the late 1950s and early 1960s. Following this uptick, trust again declined mostly in response to the Iran-Contra scandal and the breaking of the "read my lips—no new taxes" pledge by George Bush. At the close of the twentieth century, there was again an upward movement in political trust that began in 1996 and has continued through 1999. One might think the robust economy is the most plausible explanation, but that is not the case. Rather, it is due to an improvement in perceptions of government effectiveness and evaluations of congressional job performance (Heatherington 1998).

While there is no doubt that trust in government has declined, there is considerable disagreement over both its cause and its consequences. On both fronts, the literature tends to be long on speculation and short on empirical evidence. On causes, Inglehart (1997a) sees a decline in confidence for all major institutions due to a rise in postmaterialist values, which encourage the denigration of authority. For American business over the last three decades, confidence has dropped from 55 to 21 percent, for universities it has dropped from 61 to 30 percent, and for medicine it has dropped from 73 to 29 percent.[9] Government is simply part of this overall pattern. Others, however, see causes that are more closely aligned with government itself.

Contemporaneous with the decline in trust has been a change in the role of the media from mostly presenting the news and supporting the political establishment to interpreting the news in a highly negative and personalized fashion (Patterson 1994). Many see this change as going beyond the critical to the condescending and the contemptuous, with candidates and public officials portrayed as duplicitous, disingenuous, and self-serving (Orren 1997). Television journalism is particularly prone to this practice, and those who rely mostly on television for their political information are decidedly more distrustful of government than those who rely on newspapers (Heatherington 1998). Trust is declining because most of what people hear about government is negative.

Others argue that distrust in government is directly a result of poor performance by government and public officials. The perceived competence of government is a strong predictor of political trust (Heatherington 1998). A 1997 study by the Pew Research Center on the causes of political distrust shows that while people are not *angry* with government, they are *frustrated* with government.[10] This frustration is primarily directed at politicians who lead government rather than the civil servants who administer government. It is dissatisfaction with political leadership that is the most frequent reason (40 percent) people give for distrusting government. They see politicians as dishonest, out for personal gain, and too partisan (see also King 1997). The second reason for distrust (24 percent) concerns the poor performance of government: money is spent frivolously, nothing gets done, government is too intrusive. Policy dissatisfactions (15 percent) are also of consequence (Miller 1991). For example, those who support term limits tend to distrust government (Karp 1995). Finally, 13 percent in the Pew study said they distrust government because it does not pay attention to or care about ordinary people.[11]

Regarding consequences, some see the decline in political trust as indicating a withdrawal of allegiance from the political system. Based on an analysis of survey data by presidential pollster Patrick Caddell, President Jimmy Carter delivered a major address on July 15, 1979, in which he spoke of a "crisis of confidence" that "threatens the very fabric of our society." The evidence, however, indicates that in the American case low levels of trust do not mean citizens feel there is something fundamentally wrong with the structure of government, apart from the persons holding positions of authority in government. A study in the late 1970s concluded that "the basic political trust index has a very substantial component that evaluates political authorities" (Abramson and Finifter 1981, 301). One interpretation is that expressions of political distrust in an opinion poll do not indicate a deeply felt, overt hostility toward the political order so much as dissatisfaction with officeholders.

Even if low political trust does not mean rejection of the political order, there may still be worrisome consequences. Orren (1997) argues that people turn to quick, simpleminded fixes for perceived problems such as direct legislation, third parties, and term limits when trust is low. In two-party presidential elections, the distrustful are more likely to vote for the challenger than the incumbent. In three-party contests, the distrustful are more inclined to vote for third-party candidates than the Republican or the Democrat. In voting for president, those low in trust opt for candidates promising the most far-reaching change (Heatherington 1999). A similar pattern appears on the issue of term limits for elected officials. The strongest predictor of those voting for term limits in state referenda is low political trust (Karp 1995). Scholz and Lubell (1998) show trust in government significantly influences compliance with tax laws. Those scoring low on trust in government tended to underreport their taxable income. Others have shown that an important contribution to the decline in voting turnout since 1960 is the decline in political trust (Abramson and Aldrich 1982). One interpretation of these data is that the distrustful do not find the institutionalized choices the political system offers its citizens to be acceptable.

None of the possible consequences listed above, however, threatens democratic stability. How low then must political trust fall before it makes a difference? One obvious observation is that in the mid-1970s, when trust was at its nadir, the process of government did not operate with any appreciable difference from the 1950s. The weapons of war were still being built, pensions were paid, and the garbage was collected. On some of the items reported in Figure 6.1, the level of trust had fallen below 30 percent. One author speculates that the support of 15 percent of the population is enough (Wright 1976, 269). But the social location of the group is important. In the United States, support is highest among the white, non-Southern, non-Jewish, middle-aged upper middle class. The trust of this group, it has been argued, may be the key to democratic stability.

Political Efficacy and Democratic Stability

The concept of "political efficacy" was originally developed in the early 1950s to explain variations in voting turnout. The four questions to measure it have been repeated frequently and over a longer period of time than almost any other social indicator of the survey sort. Efficacy can be best described as a belief that one can influence the political process. It is a feeling that an active citizen can play a part in bringing about social and political change, and that one's input counts (Campbell et al. 1954, 187). Since it was first developed, the concept has been generalized to account for a wide variety of political activities. Given its long use and history, the original four-item efficacy scale has been the subject of an extensive methodological review. Some of the original items proved to be poor indicators of the concept, but in recent years considerable effort has gone into the development of more reliable items (Niemi et al. 1991).

Data from two large-scale studies of political participation show a strong relationship between political efficacy and many different types of political activity (Verba and Nie 1972; Verba, Scholzman, and Brady 1995). Beyond their relationship to voting, these studies generally show that the higher the sense of political efficacy, the greater the likelihood that one will participate in political activities of a relatively demanding sort. Conversely, a low sense of efficacy is one of the factors normally associated with political apathy (Verba and Nie 1972, 133).

Aside from its association with participation, political efficacy plays an important role in theories of democratic stability. Theorists of "participatory democracy" are concerned with the effect that political participation has on individual character development. They see an elevated sense of efficacy as a desirable consequence of political activity. Democratic theorists posit that for citizens to believe they can govern themselves, adds to the quality of human existence (Pateman 1970, 45–46). A related perspective can be found in the classic five-nation study by Gabriel Almond and Sidney Verba (1965), *The Civic Culture*. They see a strong sense of political efficacy as a key element in forming the ideal political culture in a stable democracy. Almond and Verba view the ideal citizen as believing in the success of his or her political actions (efficacy), believing that he or she is obligated to participate (citizen duty), but being rather inactive politically in actual practice. While they concede that "unless there is some control of government by nonelites, it is hard to consider a political system democratic," the authors also argue that elites must have the power "to initiate and carry out policies, adjust to new situations, meet internal and external challenges," and generally make authoritative decisions (Almond and Verba 1965, 476). Thus low participation gives the government room to operate, but the public's strong confidence in the potential effectiveness of their participation ensures that political leaders will act in a responsible fashion. In the civic culture, citizens have a reserve of influence. They may not constantly monitor the activities of decision-makers, but the potential to act is there if needed. It is this potential that plays a major role in holding public officials accountable (Almond and Verba 1965, 346–47).

Many students of democracy believe that the development and maintenance of a civic culture is greatly aided by high levels of *social capital*. Robert Putnam (1993, 182) writes that "democratic government is strengthened, not weakened, when it faces a vigorous civil society." Social capital involves membership in voluntary associations, interpersonal trust, norms, and networks that create a sense of *political efficacy*, and it allows people to work together effectively to influence government, which in turn mitigates the intensity of conflict that can sometimes threaten democratic government (Verba, Schlozman, and Brady 1995; Fukuyama 1995). Associational life in civil society, in the words of Verba and his colleagues, "operates as the school of democracy" (Brady, Verba, and Scholzman 1995, 285).

Levels of social capital have attracted much attention in recent years because of the controversial claim by Putnam (1995a; 1995b) that civic engagement in the United States has undergone a serious decline (see also L. Bennett 1998). As evidence, Putnam notes that membership in a variety of voluntary associations ranging from the Red Cross to bowling leagues has declined from 25 to 50 percent over the last three decades. The primary culprit, according to Putman, is the widespread appeal of television beginning in the mid-1950s.[12] (For a different perspective on causes, see Brehm and Rahn 1997.) Not everyone, however, is convinced by this thesis. Some have challenged the evidence of a decline in social capital (Pettinico 1996; Ladd 1998a); others doubt its connection to democratic stability (Jackman and Miller 1996; Tarrow 1996).

Citizen Roles: Combinations of Trust and Efficacy

It should come as no surprise that political efficacy and trust are related to one another; that those who feel they can influence government also tend to trust it (Walker and Aberbach 1970; Abravnel and Busch 1975). The following diagram presents four possible linkages between efficacy and trust:

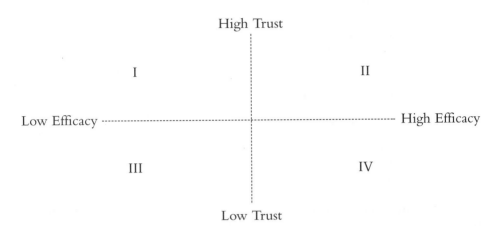

Our principal interest is in persons characterized by quadrant IV, because of their potential for violence and antidemocratic behavior. But first we shall describe the three other types. Type I is the loyal subject, high on trust but low on efficacy. They rarely participate, believing that government will act responsibly in looking out for their personal interests. Type II is the combination many would consider to be the ideal democratic citizen: a person with a very positive outlook on the political order, politically attentive and involved—but within the limits of accepted social convention. Type III individuals, cynical and believing there is no hope of any political action that might improve their lot, are classic examples of the politically alienated. They are hostile, suspicious, and mistrustful of government but lack the self-confidence to take action. Individuals from quadrant IV, cynical and efficacious, can be mobilized for political activity, but it may be of a volatile and unconventional sort. It is often argued that the numbers of these persons must be minimized to maintain democratic stability. According to the 1996 NES, about 14 percent of the American public scored in both the top 25 percent in efficacy and the bottom 25 percent in trust.[13] Thus there would seem to be a nontrivial segment of the population that could be mobilized for active opposition to the status quo given the appropriate circumstances. It might be noted, for example, that the low trust/high efficacy group voted about 10 percent more for Ross Perot in 1992 than the rest of the population.[14]

Considerable research has been conducted into the behavior patterns of those low on trust but high on efficacy. Shingles (1981), in a reanalysis of the Verba/Nie participation data, finds the combination of low trust and high efficacy overcomes the disadvantages of low income and low education in motivating political participation. This combination was a particularly important antecedent of political activity among African–Americans. The data set, however, allowed only for examination of *conventional* political behavior. The research on *unconventional* political behavior has been of two approaches. The first has been to look at the "predisposition" to engage in unconventional or violent behavior and infer a likelihood of disruptive or violent behavior under certain conditions. The second is to study riot participation after it occurs.

Abravanel and Busch (1975) find, for a sample of college students, that Type IV respondents are likely to employ "nontraditional" forms of exerting political influence. Schwartz (1973) reports a repudiation of "conformist" modes of political participation among both students and urban blacks. Jennings and Andersen (1996) find the same pattern in support for the confrontational tactics used by the AIDS Coalition to Unleash Power (ACT-UP), which demanded that the Food and Drug Administration (FDA) release experimental AIDS drugs.[15] The most sophisticated and extensive analysis of unconventional political behavior has been carried out over a 30-year period by Edward Muller and his colleagues. In a variety of research settings, Muller has demonstrated that collective violence most likely occurs among those distrustful and alienated from government, who also believe that their actions (oftentimes violent) will get them what they want.[16]

Although there is little doubt about the reliability of these relationships, there is considerable uncertainty about the links between these attitudes and behavior. Those studies that investigate "predispositions" are subject to the same criticism we made earlier (see Section 6.1) about the linkage between statements of intent and political action. These studies of riot participation raise the question of the direction of causation. The respondents were interviewed after the riots were over. Did the attitudes cause the behavior, or did participating in the riot lead to a change of attitude? One could well imagine someone feeling considerably more efficacious after than before a violent outburst. Also, there is the possibility that riot behavior may be motivated by narrow local grievances (for example, the refusal of a supermarket chain to cash a check), but later justified by indicting the entire political order. The linkages between efficacy, trust, and political action are provocative, but not all agree that they provide a satisfactory explanation for nonconventional political participation.

6-4 PERSONALITY AND PUBLIC OPINION

Individual political opinions can have their roots in the entire spectrum of human existence. For instance, the reason most personal injury attorneys oppose tort reform seems fairly obvious. They do not think the financial limitations on insurance claims proposed by insurance companies and their soulmates are in the best interest of the legal professional or in the best interest of the average American. It is not as easy to understand why some people are adamantly opposed to the fluoridation of drinking water, while others accept it as a desirable form of preventive medicine. One explanation that received considerable attention is that certain attitudes and behaviors are possibly influenced by personality.[17]

Although there is no agreed-upon definition, we shall follow Eysenck and define personality as "the more or less stable and enduring organization of a person's character, temperament, intellect, and physique which determines his unique adjustment to his environment."[18] The basic element is the enduring, abstract perspective that a person uses to order the world and meet personal needs, for example, constructing a self-image in which one is an attractive and socially useful individual.

While trait psychologists have tried to associate personalities with specific attitudes and behavior, most researchers interested in personality dismiss such efforts as simplistic and naive. Rather, they pursue investigations across a wide range of attitudes and beliefs. As might be expected, such extensive and time-consuming assessments for each individual result in few persons being evaluated. The most frequently cited studies of personality and political behavior usually examine fewer than 30 persons. Such groups can in no way be considered a meaningful sample of any segment of the population. If the dynamics of personality and behavior noted in these limited groups were universal or identical to those of other people, as is sometimes claimed, these works would be more definitive. But their primary contribution is insight into the psyches of people other than ourselves, and the comfortable feeling that we know them personally, as opposed to the formality of a tabular presentation of one thousand faceless survey respondents. One study, however, that combines both a clinical and a survey perspective is *The Authoritarian Personality*.

The Authoritarian Personality

Influenced by events in Germany during Hitler's rule, a group of psychologists from the University of California at Berkeley began a systematic investigation into the personality structure of individuals particularly susceptible to anti-Semitic and fascist political appeals. Was there something about the personality of some individuals that led them to actively support or passively sympathize with a program of genocide against Jews, homosexuals, and gypsies, and the replacement of democratic government by dictatorship (as happened in Germany between 1932 and 1945)? The study was completed in 1950 and has had a profound influence on all branches of the social sciences (Adorno et al. 1950).

The thesis of the book is straightforward. Prejudice, suspicion, distrust, and hostility are manifestations of attempts to resolve deep-seated psychological conflicts. At the heart of these conflicts is a highly ambivalent and tense orientation toward authority. Authoritarians are very submissive to those above them in the social order and very condescending toward those below. As depicted in German folklore, they are like a person on a bicycle—above they bow, below they kick. While such persons are outwardly very deferential, they in fact harbor considerable hostility toward authority. This hostility, however, is mostly unconscious, and authoritarians are only intermittently aware of the hate side of this love-hate amalgam. Rather, negative feelings are repressed by primitive ego defensive mechanisms. Authoritarians are extremely servile toward authority, driving from consciousness the malice they feel toward those above them. But repression has its costs, and the tensions created seek some alternate outlet. To compensate for feelings of personal weakness, authoritarians present a very tough façade. They are very critical of those they see as beneath them, particularly those who are different, such as members of minority groups (Greenstein 1969, 106–7). Other characteristics of the authoritarian syndrome include: (1) conventionalism—a rigid adherence to conventional middle-class values; (2) anti-intraception—opposition to the tenderhearted, subjective, and imaginative; (3) superstition—a belief in mystical determinants influencing one's fate; and (4) ethnocentrism—a strong attachment to one's own group and hostility to outgroups (Kirscht and Dillehay 1967, 5–6).

Authoritarianism is thought to originate primarily with childhood family relationships.[19] Peterson, Smirles, and Wentworth (1997), for example, demonstrate a strong tendency for authoritarian parents to have authoritarian children.[20] Persons displaying the authoritarian syndrome often describe parental affection as being given only as a reward for good behavior. Their parents employed rigid, punishment-oriented disciplinary practices, as opposed to discipline based on love withdrawal. Family roles were clearly defined in terms of dominance and submission (Milburn, Conrad, and Carberry 1995). According to Adorno and his colleagues, "Forced into submission to parental authority, the child develops hostility and aggression which are poorly channelized. The displacement of a repressed antagonism toward authority may be one of the sources, and perhaps the principal source, of his antagonism toward outgroups" (Adorno et al. 1950, 482).

The implications of *The Authoritarian Personality* for public opinion and democratic stability became obvious to students of politics soon after its publication. One of the first tasks investigators set for themselves was to determine the political correlates of authoritarianism. (Are authoritarians prejudiced toward minorities? Do they hold anti-democratic political beliefs? And so on.) This undertaking was greatly aided by the fact that *The Authoritarian Personality,* unlike other such studies, provided a ready-made paper and pencil test to measure the extent to which the syndrome exists. This instrument, the California F- (for fascism) scale, has become virtually synonymous with authoritarianism. Typical agree/disagree items from the F-scale include the following (Adorno et al. 1950, 167):

- What young people need most of all is strict discipline by their parents.
- Most people who don't get ahead just don't have enough willpower.
- Sex criminals deserve more than prison; they should be whipped in public or worse.

Investigators soon discovered some very severe methodological problems with the F-scale. Among the most difficult to resolve was response set. All 20 items in the original F-scale were worded in a positive direction (to agree was authoritarian). As we indicated earlier, people with low education tend to be "yea-sayers," making it difficult to separate the effects of education from the effects of personality when all questions in a scale suffer from response set. One solution is to reverse some of the items so that disagreeing with the question is the authoritarian response. While this strategy has merit, it is less than a completely satisfactory solution. Also, one essential requirement of a personality measure is that it not be contaminated by political content. It is now generally agreed that the F-scale is biased in the direction of right-wing authoritarianism. For example, one agree–disagree item from the F-scale states: "Homosexuals are hardly better than criminals and ought to be severely punished." Such a question may tap both personality traits and right-wing political outlooks. Consequently, the F-scale might not be sensitive to authoritarians of the left (such as American communists).

There have been two important attempts to deal with the problem. The first, by Milton Rokeach (1960), was the development of a new measure—the "dogmatism" scale—which Rokeach claimed could tap authoritarianism of both the left and the right. Currently, this dogmatism scale is one of the most frequently used measures of authoritarian tendencies (although it also suffers from response set, since to be "dogmatic" is to agree with scale items). The second solution was simply to recognize the problem and reformulate the concept as "right wing authoritarianism." Bob Altemeyer (1981; 1988; 1997) argues that authoritarianism naturally leads to right-wing political views. He reconceptualizes the concept as composed of three domains: submission to established authorities, aggression toward outgroups, and adherence to traditional social conventions. Thus, for example, research in the former Soviet Union showed that authoritarians (using Altemeyer's scale) tended to be more supportive of the old communist regime than nonauthoritarians (McFarland et al. 1992).

Due to methodological problems, research on authoritarianism is looked on with some suspicion. Because of the ease of administering the various pencil-and-paper instruments, there have been literally thousands of published pieces that employ authoritarianism as a variable. Many of these have been poorly done or are little more than "crass empiricism." The field is poorly integrated, since many studies are contradictory or noncomparable. Despite these problems, the question of the relationship between authoritarianism and political opinion has merit. It is slippery, elusive, and hard to measure, but as Meloen and his associates have observed, "the general concept of authoritarianism was, and still is, valid. Nearly all the hypothesized relationships between authoritarianism and antiminority tendencies, conservatism, and antifeminism have been confirmed over the years" (Meloen et al. 1988, 416).

Furthermore, there *are* studies indicating an authoritarian effect that meet commonly accepted standards for scientific inquiry.[21] For example, in one investigation a persuasive message was presented in several different forms to a number of different groups. Those scoring high on the F-scale were particularly likely to change their attitude when the message was delivered by a high-status source. The effectiveness of the message increased further when its content suggested change in a prejudiced direction (Harvey and Beverly 1961, 125-30).

The research on democratic values discussed in Section 6.1 has found authoritarianism (measured with Rokeach's dogmatism scale) to be related to political intolerance. Sullivan et al. (1982) found "large and significant" differences (in the predicted direction) between those scoring high and those scoring low and the D-scale with regard to the toleration of respondents' least-liked group, as did McClosky and Brill (1983, 342) using the traditional F-scale. Gibson and Tedin (1988) report similar findings in a study of tolerance for gay rights. They found dogmatism contributed to an intolerance for gays by reducing support for norms of democracy. Feldman and Stener (1997) find authoritarianism contributes to intolerance by increasing the perceived threat of disliked groups.

Recently there has been a revival in research linking authoritarianism to racism. The correlation between these constructs is one of the most enduring in the social science literature. John Ray (1988, 673), one of the most trenchant critics of the concept, concedes that "despite all the other failures of their theory, Adorno et al. would appear to have succeeded in at last one of their basic aims—to find something that would predict who is a racist and who is not." Most recently, Meloen et al. (1996) have demonstrated strong relationships between authoritarianism and voting for political parties with a racist agenda. Sniderman and Piazza (1993) have shown that authoritarian values among whites lead to the negative stereotyping of both Jews and African-Americans. These groups are so different from each other in terms of educational accomplishment, material success, intact families, as well as other characteristics that factual considerations could hardly explain why the same people who hold negative stereotypes about Jews also hold them about blacks. Rather, the explanation is authoritarian values. It is not the actual characteristics of blacks, any more than it is the actual characteristics of Jews, that evoke prejudice and dislike. Rather, it is the ethnocentric dimension of the authoritarian personality—the generalized hostility to outgroups—that is part of the syndrome.

One particularly interesting study on authoritarianism involved the classic experiment developed by Stanley Milgram (1969) to measure obedience to authority. In this experiment, a naive subject ("the teacher") was required by the study director ("the authority figure") to administer an electrical shock each time "the learner" failed to perform a rote memorization task satisfactorily. The teacher is not aware that the learner is in league with the person running the experiment and is in fact receiving no shock at all. However, each time the learner fails the task, the authority figure (the experimenter) orders the teacher to shock the learner at an ever higher level of voltage. As the shocks presumably become stronger, the learner cries out in pain. The object is to see how long the teacher will obey the authority figure and continue to administer the shocks. One disturbing feature of this study is that many subjects will continue to administer the shocks until the learner is in an apparent state of unconsciousness. Alan Elms administered the "teachers" the California F-test before conducting the Milgram experiment. He found that those who scored high on authoritarianism were highly reluctant (as predicted) to disobey the authority figure and terminate the experiment. Elms (1972, 113) explains:

> The relationship between obedience and some elements of authoritarianism seems fairly strong; and it should be remembered that the measure of obedience is a measure of actual submission to authority, not just what a person says he's likely to do. Too much of the research on authoritarianism . . . has been on the level of paper and pencil responses, which don't necessarily get translated into behavior. But here we have a realistic and highly disturbing situation. . . . So it does look as if those researchers in the late 40s had something, something which can be translated from abstract tendencies into actual authoritarian behavior: submitting to the man in command, punishing the weaker subordinate.

Is There a Democratic Personality?

Considerably less attention has been paid to the possibility that there might exist certain personality traits that promote support for democratic principles. Much of what has been written is either speculative or consists of inferences based on intensive interviews with small samples. Writers like Lasswell, Lane, and Inkeles talk about the democratic character as being warm, outgoing, high in self-esteem and ego strength, flexible, and tolerant of ambiguity (Lasswell 1951; Inkeles 1961; Lane 1962). One characteristic of this literature is a rather cavalier tendency to portray the democratic personality as the "healthy" personality and the nondemocratic personality as having psychological maladjustments.

It is misleading to talk about a democratic personality as if it were a distinct psychological type. But there may be certain personality traits that elicit support for democratic values as these values interact with particular environmental situations. The emphasis on environment is important, because personality traits that encourage support for democratic principles (the accepted norm) among citizens of the United States probably encouraged support of totalitarian communism (the accepted norm) among citizens of the former Soviet Union. In other words, there are personality types that work well within the given rules of the political game—whatever those rules might be. It is not surprising, therefore, that many politicians who were successful when communism was the accepted norm in the Soviet Union are also successful under the norms of democracy in Russia and the Independent States (for example, Russian President Vladimir Putin is a former colonel in the Soviet KGB).

6-5   CONCLUSION

There seem to be two fundamental prerequisites for the existence and maintenance of democratic rights and freedoms. One is economic and the other is psychological. In the former, considerable research indicates that some minimal level of economic affluence and development is necessary before a democracy can operate successfully. If people must worry about feeding themselves and their children, concern about democratic government will be a low priority for most (Inglehart 1990; Huntington 1991). Beyond simple sustenance, the most relevant factor associated with democratic development is communication networks. Without sufficiently developed channels of communication, interests cannot be articulated and aggregated; conflicting groups cannot exchange information on goals and desires (Lipset 1959).

But once a minimal level of economic development has occurred with associated communication networks, psychological and cultural factors become important (Inglehart 1997b). We have analyzed a number of political attitudes commonly thought to affect the stability of democracy. All may be of consequence, but none alone, or even in combination, provides a total explanation for the continued protection of democratic values in the United States. America has perhaps been most fortunate in that there have been few intense group or issue cleavages dividing the population. As long as some modest consensus exists, and most of the population has a minimal degree of economic security, the system seems able to tolerate a wide variety of personality types, a relatively low level of trust in government, and considerable lack of enthusiasm (although perhaps not outright hostility) for procedural democratic norms.

NOTES

1. One bit of evidence for this thesis is the rather substantial increase for the civil rights of communists that occurred between 1988 and 1993. In 1988, 60 percent would allow an admitted communist to speak; in 1993, 71 percent would; in 1988, 45 percent would; in 1993; 61 percent would. And in 1988, 59 percent would allow an admitted communist's book to remain in the library; by 1993, 70 percent would. Changes for other groups are not nearly as large, so the explanation must be that with the fall of the Soviet Union, communists do not seem so dangerous.
2. However, Sullivan, Piereson, and Marcus (1982, 67) concede that tolerance may have increased somewhat between 1954 and 1978, but not as much as the items in Table 6.3 would lead one to believe.
3. The data presented here are a module in the 1987 GSS.
4. A point first noted by Herson and Hofstetter (1975).
5. For another critique of the theory of pluralistic intolerance, see Gibson (1986) and Sniderman et al. (1989).
6. Surveys reported in Dahl (1982); Ladd (1989); McLean (1999).
7. Much of our discussion of the Vietnam War draws on Dahl (1982, ch. 26).
8. The literature on trust is voluminous. Among the better, more recent studies are Craig (1993); Nye, Zelikow, and King (1997), and Heatherington (1998).
9. Based on Harris polls, cited in Nye (1997, 283).
10. For the complete report, see the Pew Research Center's Website at www.People-Press.org.
11. This is only a partial list of possible reasons for distrust of government. For a more comprehensive list (17 in all), see Nye and Zelikow (1997).

12. In 1950 only 10 percent of all households had television. By 1960, 90 percent of all households had television. Americans typically watch three to four hours of television a day. The more television they watch, the less active they are in voluntary associations (Putnam 1995a).

13. The items from 1996 that the NES used for trust are V961251–V961254; for efficacy they are V961244–V961246.

14. In 1992, 27 percent of those scoring low on trust and high on efficacy voted for Ross Perot. The pattern was much weaker in 1996, with those low on trust and high on efficacy voting only 4 percent more for Perot than all others.

15. The tactics used by ACT-UP included stopping trading on the floor of the New York Stock Exchange, disrupting political speeches, locking themselves inside the offices of major pharmaceutical companies, and conducting "die-ins" on streets with heavy traffic (Jennings and Anderson 1996: 313).

16. The best statement of this perspective can be found in Finkle, Muller, and Opp (1989).

17. For a review of the field, see Greenstein (1992).

18. Cited in Sniderman (1975).

19. For an argument that the authoritarian syndrome originates in Darwinian evolution, see Somit and Peterson (1997).

20. Peterson et al. (1997) report shows a significant path coefficient ($r = .47$) between authoritarianism in parents and authoritarianism in children. Altemeyer (1997) finds a similar relationship ($r = .40$).

21. For reviews of studies on authoritarianism, see Kirscht and Dillehay (1967) and Duckitt (1989).

CHAPTER 7

Group Differences in Political Opinions

People often think of themselves as belonging to specific groups. This "group identification" may influence political opinions, as people see certain policies as being beneficial to the group with which they identify. Thus we are not surprised if blacks are more favorable to affirmative action than whites, or people with high incomes more opposed to social welfare programs than those living near the poverty line. However, not all group differences are the result of calculated self-interest. Many political opinions are based on "sociotropic" considerations—that is, on the well-being of the nation as a whole rather than on the individual or the group (Kinder and Kiewiet, 1981). Life experiences can also shape different political outlooks. For instance, individuals with college educations differ sharply from those without on a variety of noneconomic issues, such as abortion. Growing up in the South once virtually insured an allegiance to the Democratic Party, even for conservative whites.

In this chapter we explore the validity of generalizations made about group differences in public opinion. Most of these differences we find to be correct but sometimes overdrawn. We also find that group differences change over time, and that generalizations that were true in the past may be more or less so today.

7-1 SOCIOECONOMIC CLASS AND POLITICAL OPINIONS

Since a great many issues in political life concern the distribution of benefits within society, the rich and the poor often seem to have quite different economic interests. The "haves" and the "have nots" are expected to disagree, for example, on questions involving taxation and government services.[1] In most European democracies the major political battle lines are drawn between working-class parties and parties of the middle class. As indicated by the fact that the United States has never had an appreciable socialist movement, America has escaped the more extreme forms of class polarization and conflict. There are, nevertheless, class differences on many political issues.

How do we measure economic or social class? One possibility, called subjective social class, is simply to ask people into which social class they fall—the lower class, working class, middle class, or upper class? When asked, almost everyone is willing to place themselves in one of these classes. In the 1998 GSS, 5 percent identified with the lower class, 45 percent with the working class, 45 percent with the middle class, and 4 percent with the upper class. An alternative to the subjective approach is to use the objective indicators of occupation, income, and education. Each indicator has its problems. The connections among the three are often far from perfect. Many blue-collar workers have greater incomes than white-collar workers. Also, education is an imperfect predictor of income, because many college graduates often have lower incomes than skilled manual workers. We could focus on income, but the same dollar amounts buy distinctly different lifestyles in various parts of the country. A $40,000 annual income in rural Montana might allow a pleasant middle-class lifestyle, while a family would have to struggle to live on that amount in New York City. People's subjective class identifications actually are quite predictable from education, income, and occupation (Jackman and Jackman 1983). Still, analysts worry about how accurately survey respondents perceive their social reality. We will proceed by employing what we see as the most appropriate indicator for the question at hand, with a sensitivity to the difficulties and imperfections of measuring socioeconomic class.

Class Differences in Social Welfare

Income is more concentrated at the upper levels of society in the United States than it is in any other Western democracy (Phillips 1991, 9). In 1999, the richest 1 percent of all Americans had more money than the bottom 50 percent (Johnstone 1999). Rather than decreasing, the level of income concentration in recent years has been increasing, fueled significantly by wealth generated through the technology revolution. According to conservative analyst Kevin Phillips, "no parallel upsurge of riches has been seen since the nineteenth century, the era of the Vanderbilts, Morgans, and Rockefellers" (Phillips 1991, 10). In 1977, the richest one-fifth of the population took home 44.2 percent of all income; in 1999 they took home 50.4 percent. In 1997 the richest 1 percent received 7.3 percent of all income; in 1999 they received 12.9 percent (Johnstone 1999).

Yet by European standards, cleavages along class lines in the United States are rather muted. Perhaps one reason is a belief among Americans that the opportunity to succeed financially is readily available to those with the energy and ability. For example, one poll found only 12 percent saying there is little or no chance of becoming rich in the United States if one is willing to work hard. When a British sample was asked a similar question, 63 percent said they did not think they had a chance to become rich if they really wanted to.[2]

Typically, the poor in the United States are more favorable to social welfare programs designed to raise living standards than are the more well-to-do. They are even more favorable if the program affects them directly. To take an early example, Gallup found in 1949 that 57 percent of the poor favored government action to improve the lot of the poor, compared to 28 percent of the prosperous.[3] This pattern has continued through the years and is reflected in the 1996 NES study. Respondents were asked if government should provide more services in the areas of health and education, even if it meant an increase in government spending. Among opinion-holders, 61 percent of blue-collar workers favored this position compared to 38 percent among business executives and professionals. Table 7.1 shows the relationship between subjective social class and beliefs that the government should spend more money on programs such as student loans, child care, retirement benefits, aid to the homeless, or science and technology.

For most of these programs the working class is the most likely to favor increased government spending. The greatest difference among the classes is on retirement benefits, unemployment, and child care. Obviously the working class has real concerns about the well-being of their children when they are away from home and for their own financial security after retirement. On the other hand, there is only a slight difference in spending for student loans, which benefit all classes. And in the case of science and technology, the middle and upper classes are more likely to want spending increased. The opinions on

---

TABLE 7.1   OPINIONS ABOUT SPENDING ON SELECTED GOVERNMENT PROGRAMS BY SUBJECTIVE SOCIAL CLASS

Percentage Wanting to Spend More On	Working Class	Middle Class	Upper Class
Health care[†]	70	65	49
Education[†]	73	68	70
Retirement benefits[†]	59	42	27
The homeless★	76	71	59
The poor★	62	51	35
Child care[†]	57	47	44
Unemployment assistance★	43	28	35
Student loans★	63	60	55
Science and technology★	39	45	51
Aid to Russia★	15	17	27

★General Social Survey, 1998.
[†]National Election Studies, 1992.

these spending increases seem predictable from one's station in life. Social security and unemployment are of much more concern to the working class than the more affluent classes. On the other hand, the middle and upper classes are potential beneficiaries of increasing spending on science and technology, and they consequently support such spending increases.

The effects shown in Table 7.1 are, for the most part, quite modest. However, if we compare actual recipients of program benefits with nonrecipients, we find the differences increase dramatically. Cook and Barnett (1992, 150) report that 75 percent of those receiving Aid to Families with Dependent Children (AFDC) favored increasing such spending, compared to only 32 percent of nonrecipients. The same is true for food stamps, with 53 percent of recipients favoring an increase compared to 24 percent for nonrecipients. The same pattern holds for Medicaid, Social Security, and unemployment insurance.

For the 1996 NES, Figure 7.1 shows how family income, an objective indicator of social class, is related to opinion on the issues of increasing domestic spending and services, and support for a government-guaranteed job and good standard of living. (Nonwhites are excluded here in order to show the effect of income independent of race.) We would expect for reasons of simple economic self-interest that those in the lower-income categories would be supportive of public policies designed to promote employment and fund social programs,

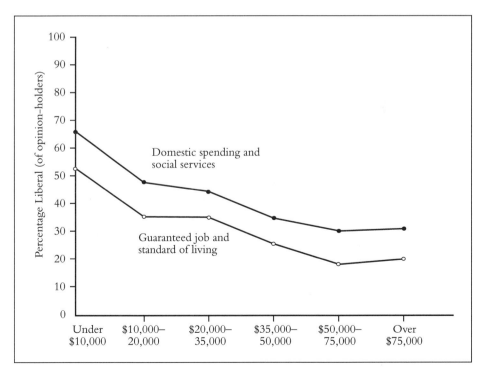

Figure 7.1 Social welfare opinion by family income (whites only). *Source:* National Election Studies, 1996.

with a commensurate lack of support among the more financially secure. As one goes from poor to affluent, one does in fact see a decline in the percentage of people holding liberal positions of these economic issues.

Shingles (1989) demonstrates that the usual effect of income on domestic policy opinion can be nullified by the person's party identification, particularly at the highest income levels. For illustration, consider the views of white respondents in the 1996 NES survey making more than $75,000. Reflecting their wealth, this group contained more than twice as many Republicans as Democrats. Among wealthy white Republicans with opinions, only 8 percent said the government should provide more services and increase spending. However, 76 percent of wealthy white Democrats with opinions chose this position over reducing services and taxes. And while support for a guaranteed job and standard of living was a mere 4 percent among wealthy white Republicans with an opinion, it rose to 58 percent among wealthy white Democratic opinion-holders.

Class Differences on Noneconomic Domestic Issues

On noneconomic issues, liberalism tends to increase rather than decrease as one goes up the status ladder. Typical are the relationships between social class and opinions on equality for women, prayer in the schools, gays in the military, and the rights of the accused, shown in Table 7.2.

While the differences are not large, they are consistent. Reading the table across, we see that support for women's issues rises as one moves up the status ladder, as does support for the rights of the accused, and allowing gays in the military. Similar relations between status and opinion are found when people are asked about whether communists, socialists, or atheists should be granted the full range of civil liberties. Among whites, high-status respondents express less racial prejudice than do low-status respondents (Marcus et al. 1995; Kinder and Sanders 1996; Schuman et al. 1997; Sniderman and Carmines 1997).

Those with higher incomes tend to be conservative on economic issues, but on issues outside the economic realm status differences are complicated by

TABLE 7.2   OPINIONS ON NONECONOMIC DOMESTIC ISSUES BY SOCIAL CLASS

Opinion	Working Class	Middle Class	Upper Class
Favor equal role for women	85%	89%	93%
Oppose law requiring women to notify father before abortion	29	37	54
Allow gays in the military	56	59	67
Support rights of the accused*	39	41	47

Source: National Election Studies, 1992.

*National Election Studies, 1976.

the role of education. We saw in Chapter 5 that educational achievement promotes political tolerance and political liberalism. This liberalizing effect of education is, however, almost entirely limited to noneconomic issues. If we separate the effects of income and education on political attitudes, we find different patterns for economic and noneconomic issues. On noneconomic issues, high education but not high income is associated with liberalism. On economic issues, high income is negatively related to liberalism, but education is not.

Table 7.3 shows some relevant examples. This table indicates that within each of the three income categories, liberal opinions on the noneconomic issue of abortion increase with educational attainment. Notice, for example, the large differences in support for abortion in the low-income group with varying amounts of education. Only 25 percent of those without a high school degree support abortion, moving to 39 percent for high school graduates and 53 percent for college graduates. The reverse pattern can be seen on the economic issue of domestic spending. As family income goes up, individuals become more conservative on domestic spending. Sixty-seven percent of college graduates with low income want increased spending, compared to only 28 percent of college graduates with high incomes. The third issue—aid to minorities—taps both the economic dimension of financial aid and the

TABLE 7.3   JOINT EFFECTS OF INCOME AND EDUCATION ON SELECTED ISSUES, WHITES ONLY

		Education		
		Less than High School	High School Graduate	College Graduate
For legal abortions in all circumstances				
Family income	Low	25%	39%	53%
	Medium	21	43	48
	High	★	47	53
For more domestic spending				
Family income	Low	50	55	67
	Medium	55	41	36
	High	★	34	28
For aid to minorities				
Family income	Low	21	22	33
	Medium	26	14	31
	High	★	10	27

Source: National Election Studies, 1996 election data. Percentages are based on opinion-holders, among white respondents. For full text of opinion questions, see the Appendix.

★Too few cases for analysis.

noneconomic dimensions of attitudes toward minorities. On this issue we can see the joint effect of higher education (which affects the noneconomic part of the issue) and the conservative effect of income (which affects the economic part of the issue). Thus we see that among those of low income, college graduates are the most favorable to aid for minorities. But among college graduates, those with the highest incomes are the least favorable.

Class Differences on Foreign Policy

The major class differences on foreign policy attitudes is that people in the lower educational strata more readily take the "isolationist" position than the more "internationally minded" better educated strata. These sorts of class differences can be traced back to the 1930s and 1940s, when isolationism had great appeal to the working class, while the middle and upper classes favored an active role for the United States in world affairs (Mueller 1977). In 1948, for example, 92 percent of the college educated favored an active role for the United States compared to only 59 percent with less than a high school education (Page and Shapiro 1992). We see this same pattern in the more recent data shown in Table 7.4. There we see that the better educated have a more favorable view of the United Nations, are more willing to normalize relations with Cuba, and did not (in 1993) view communism as harshly as those with less education.

Based on data such as these, academics and others frequently argued during the cold war era that the less educated, presumably less attentive public, should be mostly ignored. The belief was that they simply did not have the grasp on world affairs to appreciate the necessity for an activist role in world affairs by the

TABLE 7.4   EDUCATION AND INTERNATIONALISM

	Less than High School	High School Graduate	College Graduate
Have a favorable view of United Nations*	50%	67%	73%
U.S. should normalize relations with Cuba[†]	42	56	61
Completely agree U.S. should be active in world affairs[‡]	41	44	58
Communism worst kind of government**	63	49	36

*Princeton Survey Research Associates, 1996.

[†]CBS News, 1996.

[‡]Princeton Survey Research Associates, 1997.

**General Social Survey, 1993.

United States. But Page and Shapiro (1992, 181) argue that isolationism among the lower classes may well be rational. Given their precarious economic circumstances, the less affluent are understandably more concerned about feeding their families than dispensing foreign aid or protecting American investments abroad.

We might expect that high-status people would be more willing to support military action abroad, as it is in some ways a logical extension of internationalism, just as isolationism implies keeping the troops at home. The accumulation of survey evidence shows only a modest tendency on the part of those with high economic status or high education to support American military adventures. In the case of Vietnam, support for the war back in 1968 among the college educated may seem surprising because the most visible war opponents were found on college campuses. Only if we refine the educational index to isolate the small segment of people with graduate degrees or four-year degrees from the most prestigious universities do we find disproportionate antiwar sentiment at the top of the educational ladder (Rosenberg et al. 1970, 54–65). During the mid-1980s, the United States was deeply involved in a guerrilla war against Marxist elements in Central America. Table 7.5 shows the better educated were only slightly more likely to support this effort than were those with less education. The class differences are somewhat larger when respondents were asked if they agree that "all things considered the [1991 Persian] Gulf War was worth the cost." One reason for the more pronounced class effect may result from the economic interests the United States has in the region. Finally, Table 7.5 shows the college-educated are the most supportive of sending peacekeeping troops to Kosovo.

We must be careful in extracting significance from the class differences on questions of foreign policy, as the "no opinion" rate increases dramatically as one goes down the status ladder. Quite understandably, lower-status people are

TABLE 7.5   EDUCATION AND OPINION ON U.S. INVOLVEMENT IN FOREIGN COUNTRIES

Issue	Less than High School	High School Graduate	College Graduate
U.S. should expand the Vietnam War (1968)*	24%	21%	25%
U.S. should be more involved in Central America (1986)*	19	21	25
The Persian Gulf war was worth it (1992)*	48	56	61
U.S. should commit peacekeeping troops to Kosovo (1999)[†]	44	49	63

*National Election Studies.
[†]Gallup, 2 Feb. 1999.

more concerned with the economic issues of day-to-day living than more abstract questions of foreign policy. We may particularly suspect that poor people and those with little education often grope for what they perceive to be the "official" policy when asked to give their foreign policy views (Ladd 1970). For example, such a tendency may be at least a partial explanation for why the less educated were the most opposed to letting "Communist" China into the United Nations. The better educated had the advantage of knowing that the idea of China's admission was gaining respectability, and they were more able to identify the official government position on international issues. Thus, when governmental opposition to a nuclear test ban treaty flip-flopped in the early 1960s, the polls showed that the more educated respondents changed accordingly, while those with less education remained stable (Rossi 1965). Such a pattern would occur only if considerable sophistication was required in order to follow changes in the official line or in main currents of thought.

Class Differences in Voting and Party Preferences

Since the years of Franklin Roosevelt's presidency, the relationship between economic class and party preference has reflected class differences on economic issues. In the 1930s, Roosevelt's efforts to expand the federal government's role in order to combat the economic effects of the Great Depression caused a "partisan realignment" of the American electorate. With the high salience of economic issues, the poor and working class were given a solid push toward the Democratic Party, and the more affluent clearly came to side with the Republicans. This basic partisan division of the electorate remains today, although in a weaker form, largely because new issues (most notably race) tend to undercut the link between class and partisanship established some 60 years ago.

Ever since the 1930s, the standard group basis by which United States voters divide into Republicans and Democrats has been socioeconomic class. We can see this division persisting into the 1990s, using data from the 1996 National Election Study. Figure 7.2 divides white respondents into five income groups from low to high, arranged as quintiles with each group representing roughly one-fifth of white voters. As one would expect, the figure shows that as one moves up the income ladder, the frequency of identification and frequency of Democratic presidential voting both increase.

Let us first look at the 1996 presidential vote, Clinton versus Dole. Among the poorest quintile (fifth) of white voters, seventy percent of the two-party vote went to Clinton rather than Dole. At the other extreme, a slim majority of the two richest quintiles (the top 40 percent) voted for Dole over Clinton. The income gradient is slightly steeper for party identification than for the vote. Among the poorest fifth, two-thirds of party identifiers call themselves Democrats; among the richest fifth, Republicans outnumber Democrats two-to-one.

Figure 7.2 is based on white respondents only. Class or income is a much less important voting determinant for blacks than for whites. In 1996, Dole got 12 percent of the black vote and only 17 percent of blacks with an income

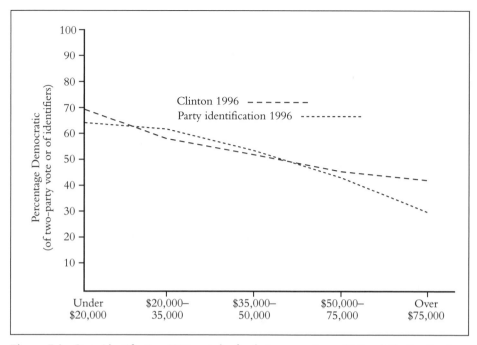

Figure 7.2   Party identification 1996, vote by family income. *Source:* National Election Studies.

over $50,000 (1996 VNS Exit Poll.) Similarly, income has little influence on black partisanship. Only 12 percent of blacks identify with the Republicans, and that number increases to only 16 percent for those making over $50,000 (1996 VNS Exit Poll).

Figure 7.3 traces the relationship between occupational class and the two-party presidential vote going back to 1952. For simplicity of comparison, the voters are split into only two occupational categories—manual and business/professional.[4] According to this measure, class voting was greatest in 1964, and has closed since then, reaching its nadir in the two Clinton elections. Among significant third-party candidates, George Wallace in 1968 did much better among manual workers, and Ross Perot also did somewhat better among manual workers than the business/professional strata. On the other hand, John Anderson in 1980 fared somewhat better among higher-class voters. The data, however, lend little credence to the class polarization thesis. Despite the conservative rhetoric of Ronald Reagan, class differences did not widen in the 1980s because there were few class-polarizing issues on the political agenda, and many issues that cut across class lines. Reagan's aggressive foreign policy and many of his social policies were popular even among the working class, which took the edge off their disenchantment with his economic policies. Bush's use of mostly symbolic issues in 1988 (Willie Horton and the flag allegiance themes) again appealed to working-class whites, and dampened class polarization. Clinton did better among working-class whites, but class voting

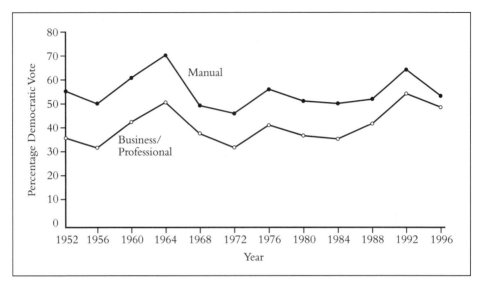

Figure 7.3   Presidential voting (two-party) by occupation. *Source:* Gallup Polls reported in Stanley and Niemi (2000, 105); National Election Studies, 1988, 1992, 1996.

was reduced by his move to the center (most notably in 1996) best exemplified by his support of popular conservative policies such as welfare reform.

Despite the fluctuations in the degree of class voting over the years, class differences in party identification have remained reasonably constant from the 1930s through to the end of the century. Among identifiers, blue-collar workers have never been under 60 percent Democratic since 1939. However, professionals in the 1990s are now more Democratic in their two-party voting (61 percent in 1992, 56 percent in 1996) than any time since 1939, and now vote only slightly less Democratic than blue-collar workers. In apparent compensation, those in the "business" category became more Republican in the 1980s. In 1992, however, this group gave 47 percent of its two-party vote to Bill Clinton, and increased to 54 percent in 1996—closely matching professionals.

The fact that class conflict has never dominated American politics to the extent it has in Europe may have been one long-term source of the stability of the American political system. But a further decline in the political importance of the traditional class-related issues may augur something quite different from a period of political tranquillity, as other issues such as race, religion, or the environment could intensify political conflict in years to come.

7-2 RACE AND POLITICAL OPINIONS

The most profound political division between groups in the United States is between blacks and whites. In 1968, the Kerner Commission (U.S. National Advisory Committee on Civil Disorders 1968, 1) concluded that "Our nation

is moving toward two societies, one black, one white—separate and unequal."
While progress has surely been made since that date, there is a wide gulf between blacks and whites on most political issues, particularly on those involving discrimination and its remedies. Of course, blacks are not only racial or
ethnic minority in America. The proportion of Hispanics and Asians is growing at a rapid rate, and the former will soon outnumber blacks as the largest
minority group in the United States. However, neither group has the distinctive political opinions that characterize the black population.

Blacks, Whites, and Political Opinions

Until the late 1970s, the central division of opinion in the United States concerning the role of blacks was the very issue of a racially integrated society. In a
1964 NES survey, respondents were asked if they favored "strict segregation" of
the races, "desegregation," or "something in between." Not surprisingly, 73
percent of blacks favored desegregation, while only 6 percent favored segregation, with 21 percent favoring something in between. In the case of whites,
about equal numbers chose strict segregation (25 percent) as desegregation (27
percent), with the remainder choosing something in between. But by 1978 (the
last year this question was asked), only 5 percent of whites favored strict segregation—about the same as among blacks (6 percent). In 1964, the NES shows
74 percent of whites thought civil rights leaders were "pushing too fast" compared to 11 percent among blacks. But by 1980 the percentage had dropped to
40 percent among whites, with blacks remaining essentially unchanged.

By the late 1970s, the political agenda on race shifted to the question of
whether the government should actively help blacks move into the economic
mainstream through preferences in education and employment, or whether
blacks themselves were responsible for their economic well-being. We can
compare the distribution of these sentiments among blacks and whites using a
NES question asked in 1974 and 1996 as to whether the government should
"make every effort to improve the economic and social condition of blacks
and other minorities" or whether they should help themselves.

	Whites		Blacks	
	1974	*1996*	*1974*	*1996*
Government should help blacks	25%	16%	63%	39%
Unsure	26	23	25	21
Blacks should help themselves	50	61	12	40
	101%	100%	100%	100%

There are substantial differences between blacks and whites on this issue in
both 1974 and 1996. But the trend for both racial groups is in a conservative
direction. While there has been a 9 percent drop in support among whites for
government assistance to blacks and other minorities, there has been a larger
24 percent drop among blacks. The fact that blacks and whites have moved in

the same direction suggests a declining belief among both racial groups in the ability of government to solve problems—including those that may stem from the consequences of America's past racial practices.

In recent years, much of the debate over racial policies has shifted to the arena of affirmative action. Given the dual emphasis in the American political tradition on equality and individualism, many well-intentioned citizens appear caught in a dilemma. First, there is a recognition that blacks historically have not had the same opportunities as whites, but there is a belief that educational opportunities and jobs should be filled on merit, without reference to race, sex, or religion.

As one would expect, blacks are more supportive of affirmative action than whites. In 1994, a NES survey asked respondents if they would favor a program in which a college or graduate school maintained a "quota," so that more minority applicants would get admitted than would otherwise be the case. Blacks were overwhelmingly favorable, but one-fifth of whites were favorable as well.

	Whites	**Blacks**
Favor educational quota	20%	72%
Undecided	7	6
Oppose educational quota	73	22
	100%	100%

The current political agenda on affirmative action also includes racial preferences in hiring and promotion. In 1998, NES asked if due to past discrimination blacks should be given preferences in hiring and promotion, or whether such preference is wrong because it discriminates against whites. Although there are again sizable racial differences, they are not as large as on the educational question. The reason is that many fewer blacks endorse compensatory action for jobs than endorse compensatory action for higher education. These data reflect a pattern seen in most questions on affirmative action. Both blacks and whites are more favorable toward programs that create equality of opportunity than toward programs that mandate equality in outcomes.

	Whites	**Blacks**
Favor preferences for blacks in hiring and promotion	13%	58%
Undecided	3	3
Oppose preferences for blacks in hiring and promotion	84	39
	100%	100%

As we noted in Chapter 4, questions on affirmative action are very sensitive to question wording effects, as many of the terms employed, such as "quotas" or "racial preferences," are politically charged. The NES questions reported above may overstate the extent to which African-Americans and whites disagree on affirmative action. Sigelman and Welch (1991) analyzed a large number of these questions and found, depending on question wording, that as many as 96 percent of blacks and 76 percent of whites were favorable, or as few as 23 percent of blacks and 9 percent of whites were favorable. They also found that those affirmative-action programs that get the most support from blacks also get the most support from whites.

These opinion gaps are rooted in much larger differences between blacks and whites about the continued existence of racial discrimination. In 1995, 68 percent of African-Americans said that racism is a "big problem" in American society compared to 38 percent of whites and, in 1997, 65 percent of blacks said they saw no real improvement in their position in recent years while only 36 percent of whites agreed with that sentiment.[5] About four times as many blacks as whites perceived discrimination against blacks in education, and 57 percent of blacks believed they get lower wages because of discrimination, while only 14 percent of whites believe such discrimination exists. Sigelman and Welch (1991, 59) write that blacks today "see racial discrimination as an everyday occurrence, not a historical curiosity."

When asked about changes in antiblack sentiment among whites in 1989, compared to five years ago, 44 percent of blacks saw an increase in antiblack sentiment nationally, but only 25 percent saw antiblack sentiment increasing in the area where they live (Sigelman and Welch 1991, 61). Why do blacks by a margin of almost 20 percent see things getting worse nationally rather than lo-cally—where they have direct experience? The answer almost certainly lies with the media, and its tendency to dwell on isolated, but sensationalist, racial incidents, such as the beating of motorist Rodney King and three white su-premacists dragging James Byrd to death behind a truck in Beaumont, Texas. By all reliable accounts, interracial violence is extremely infrequent. Ironically, its very infrequency means such events will get a disproportionate share of media coverage.

Even on issues that are tangential to civil rights, blacks are more likely than whites to take the liberal position. Some examples are shown in Table 7.6. As we would expect, there are substantial black-white differences on economic is-sues such as the pace of domestic spending, and whether the government should guarantee everyone a good standard of living. For whites, social class is a consistent correlation of opinion on these social welfare issues. However, for blacks there is no relationship. Upper-income blacks are about as supportive as lower-income blacks.[6] The reason for this nonrelationship is that greater in-come among blacks is related to greater racial identification (Tate 1993, 27–29). In other words, upper-income blacks are more likely to identify with their race than with their social class. Upper-class whites, on the other hand, are more likely to identify with their social class.

Blacks are also much less supportive of the death penalty than are whites, perhaps because those on death row are disproportionately black. Note, how-ever, that the death penalty is still supported by a majority of black citizens. Blacks are also less supportive of American military action abroad. For example,

TABLE 7.6 RACE AND OPINION ON SELECTED NON-CIVIL RIGHTS ISSUES (PERCENTAGE OF OPINION-HOLDERS)

Issue	Whites	Blacks	Difference
Government should provide more services and increase spending★	58%	76%	+18
Government should see that people have jobs and good standard of living★	42	76	+34
Favor death penalty for those convicted of murder★	76	57	+19
Favor laws to protect homosexuals from discrimination†	62	74	+12
U.S. should have stayed out of Persian Gulf War‡	16	47	+31
U.S. should conduct air strikes against Serbia★★	43	29	+19

★National Election Studies, 1998.
†National Election Studies, 1996.
‡National Election Studies, 1992.
★★Gallup, 1998.

we see a sizable difference in support for American involvement in the 1991 Persian Gulf War and for air strikes against Serbia in the 1998 war over Kosovo. Blacks were much less supportive of the Vietnam War than were whites and have been less enthusiastic about other American military adventures, such as those involving the Nicaraguan Contras and military actions in Panama and Grenada. These racial differences may stem from the Vietnam War, where a disproportionate number of African-Americans bore the brunt of the fighting. In conflicts since then, such as the Persian Gulf War, the Pentagon has been very careful to ensure that blacks are not overrepresented (given their numbers in the armed services) among those assigned to combat zones.

Despite the existence of an undeniable racial divide in the United States, there is evidence that points toward an easing of strains in racial relations. Between 1981 and 1997, there was a 14 percent increase in the number of blacks who said they had a "close personal friend" who was white, and a 17 percent increase among whites saying they had a "close personal friend" who was black.[7] American neighborhoods have become more racially integrated. Between 1980 and 1998, the GSS reports a 14 percent increase in black respondents saying they have white neighbors and white respondents saying they have black neighbors. Perhaps the acid test of racial relations is the approval of marriages between blacks and whites. Among whites, Gallup reports that fewer than 5 percent approved in 1958, 48 percent approved in 1980, and 64 percent approved in 1997 (Schuman et al. 1997). In the case of this latest reading, 60 percent of whites approved and 77 percent of blacks approved of marriage between blacks and whites.

Racial Groups and the Vote

In terms of the vote and party identification, there are major differences between blacks and whites. For instance, in 1996, 84 percent of African-Americans but only 43 percent of whites cast their vote for Bill Clinton. We present below the 1996 vote choice, as reported in VNS exit polls, for the four major ethnic groups in the United States.

1996 Vote	Asians	Blacks	Hispanics	Whites
Clinton	43%	84%	73%	44%
Dole	49	12	21	46
Perot	8	4	6	10
	100%	100%	100%	100%
	(n = 166)	(n = 2046)	(n = 697)	(n = 12783)

We see Hispanics voted heavily Democratic, although not to the same extent as blacks. The most Republican group in the 1996 electorate (as well as 1992) are Asians but, according to the VNS exit poll, they accounted for only about 1 percent of the total vote cast in 1996 (blacks accounted for 11 percent, Hispanics 5 percent, and whites 83 percent).

The voting differences we see between blacks and whites are also found in terms of the underlying attitude of party identification. Among the white population, the 1998 NES shows 36 percent are Democrats, 33 percent are Republicans, and 31 percent are Independent. Among the black population, 77 percent are Democrats, 4 percent are Republican, and 18 percent are Independent. Using the VNS exit poll for the 1996 presidential election, we can expand our analysis to include Asians and Hispanics. The data reported below represent only the 49 percent that voted on election day, not the overall adult population.

Party Identification	Asians	Blacks	Hispanics	Whites
Democratic	34%	72%	61%	34%
Independent	27	16	18	27
Republican	39	12	21	39
	100%	100%	100%	100%
	(n = 148)	(n = 1868)	(n = 657)	(n = 12346)

Over time, American blacks have undergone a long-term reversal in their party allegiance. Between the Civil War and Franklin Roosevelt's presidency, most blacks who could vote opted for the Republican Party because it was the party of Lincoln. From the 1930s to the present, however, most blacks have supported the Democratic Party. Initially this shift was a response to economic issues rather than any consequential attempt on the part of the Democratic Party to remove racial barriers or explicitly pitch an appeal to blacks. Only in recent years could the Democratic Party be identified as the party with clearly greater sympathy for the civil rights cause. As a result of the Democrats' increasing image as the more "pro-civil rights" party, Democratic voting among blacks at the presidential level has changed from a tendency to near unanimity. The solidifying event was the 1964 election, in which President Lyndon Johnson took a strong stand in favor of the Civil Rights Act and Republican challenger Barry Goldwater opposed and voted against it in Congress (as an infringement on states' rights). The change over time is shown in Figure 7.4.

Clearly the black vote is a pivotal factor for the Democratic Party in presidential elections. In only one such election since World War II (1964), has the Democratic candidate received a majority of the total white vote.[8] Again, we find that the usual predictors of party preference among whites do not work in the case of blacks. Higher-income blacks are not more likely to be Republican, as is the case in the white population. In fact, black Republicans and black Democrats are remarkably similar, both demographically and in their policy preference (Tate 1993).

7-3 AGE AND POLITICAL OPINIONS

If one examines a breakdown by age of the scores of political issues that might interest the student of public opinion, three patterns stand out. On the majority of issues there are no meaningful age-group differences; on a sizable minor-

Figure 7.4   Race and the two-party presidential vote, 1952–1992. *Sources:* Gallup Poll, 1952–1976; National Election Studies, 1980-1992, Voter News Service, 1996.

ity of issues, those older are more conservative than those younger, and on a small number of issues, the young are more conservative than their elders. There are at least three reasons why older cohorts might differ from younger ones: (1) there may be composition effects in which (for example) younger cohorts are better educated than those who come before; (2) there may be life-cycle effects in which the process of maturation results in greater responsibilities and consequently greater conservatism; and (3) there may be generational effects in which unique events and experiences encountered during the impressionable years lead to differing political outlooks.

The Politics of Age

To the list of reasons for age groups to differ in their political opinions we can add a fourth—the politics of self-interest. Advocates for children often blame inadequate funding for programs benefiting youngsters on the political power of older Americans, whom they accuse of greedily siphoning off more than their fair share of government dollars, or voting against school bond referendums to keep their property taxes low. Recently, many have voiced concern that the Social Security and Medicare benefits enjoyed by older Americans will bankrupt the system before those currently paying the bill will be eligible to receive benefits. Issues such as these have raised the specter of intergenerational political conflict.

We do in fact see meaningful differences between the age groups on at least some economic issues. The younger age group is more likely to feel the government should provide increased services to its citizens and see to it that everyone has a good job. Reflecting its self-interest, the younger cohort is considerably more liberal on the issue of increased spending for student loans. On the issue of government health insurance, the generational difference closes, reflecting the self-interest older Americans have in health care benefits. Nevertheless, the younger generation remains slightly more liberal.

When we turn to social issues, where society is in a state of flux, we find younger cohorts consistently more liberal than older ones. The young are more receptive to new ideas since they are, for the most part, not committed to old ones. This point can be illustrated using the 25 percent gap in the open housing item in Table 7.7. No one under 30 has lived during a time when refusing to sell your home to someone because of race or color was legal. They are likely to simply take this prohibition for granted. Alternatively, those over 55 may recall when such practices were not only legal, but quite common. To endorse the more liberal position for the older generation may mean changing an opinion that was once viewed as quite legitimate.

On foreign affairs, it is often thought that the young are more "dovish" than their elders. However, the evidence for that proposition is mixed, and often depends upon the particular circumstances. In past conflicts, including World War II, Korea, Vietnam, and the Persian Gulf War, the younger cohort has been more supportive of U.S. involvement than those over 55 (Wittkopf

TABLE 7.7   AGE AND OPINION ON SELECTED ISSUES

	Percentage Support Among Opinion Holders		
	Under 30	55 and Over	Difference
Economic Issues			
Government should provide more services, even if it means increased spending‡	57%	36%	+21
Government should see to it that everyone has a good job and standard of living‡	42	30	+12
Government should cover all hospital and medical expenses†	43	37	+6
Increase spending on student loans†	70	42	–28
Social Issues			
Homeowners should not refuse to sell home to someone because of race or color★★	79	54	+25
Marijuana should be made legal★	35	17	+18
Allow homosexuals to teach in college★	88	61	+27
Allow abortion for any reason★	44	32	+12
Favor English as official language‡	57	78	+21
Foreign Policy/Military Issues			
Vietnam objectors should have served‡	41	64	+13
U.S. should be extremely/very willing to use force to solve international problems‡	32	40	+8
U.S. should increase military spending†	29	43	+14
Wrong to send troops to the Persian Gulf War††	19	25	–6
Civic Orientations			
Read news about 1996 campaign‡	42	71	+29
U.S. does not need political parties anymore‡	30	18	+12
Pay attention to national news‡	33	57	+24
Liberal/Conservative Ideology†			
Liberal	35	19	
Moderate	33	43	
Conservative	33	49	

★General Social Survey, 1996.

†National Election Studies, 1996.

‡National Election Studies, 1998.

★★ General Social Survey, 1998.

††National Election Studies, 1992.

1990). Recent data show a tendency for younger Americans to hold more dovish opinions, even on the issue of the Vietnam War, on which most have no direct memory. The older generation is more likely to say that the war objectors should have served regardless of their beliefs. In terms of ideological identification, there is an equal split by age among the moderates, but the older group is more likely to identify as conservative and the younger as liberal.

Most of the issue differences reported in Table 7.7 show the older generation to be more conservative than the younger. It is important, however, not to infer from these data that people get more conservative as they get older. In fact, based on an extensive analysis of archival opinion data, there is little evidence to support the aging/conservatism hypothesis (Davis 1992, 281). Rather, a more convincing explanation is that the older generation has changed its view only modestly since its members were under 30, but the current under-30 generation has been socialized to more liberal opinions on these same issues.

Finally, younger Americans in general tend to be less interested and involved in politics than older generations. However, several investigators have noted that the current young generation seems uniquely turned off by political affairs. Turnout in 1998 among 18 and 19 year olds was just 11 percent (Toner 1999). L. Bennett (1998, 535) observes that "today's youth are more withdrawn from public affairs than earlier birth cohorts when they were young." A 1996 Pew Research Poll found that while 76 percent of those over 30 had read a newspaper on the day of the interview, only 31 percent of those under 30 had done so. Table 7.7 shows while 71 percent of those over 55 had read news stories about the 1996 presidential campaign, only 42 percent of those under 30 had done so; 57 percent of those over 55 pay a lot of attention to the national news, compared to 33 percent of those under 30. The younger generation is prone to believe that the United States no longer needs political parties. This lack of interest in political affairs among the young has a quite predictable result—elevated levels of political ignorance (Bennett 1998). The causes of political disinterest among the youngest generation are multifaceted and may involve everything from political scandals to the increasingly negative tone of political coverage by the media (Bennett 1997). There seems, however, little doubt that the youngest age cohort is uniquely indifferent to politics.

7-4 RELIGION AND POLITICAL OPINIONS

Compared with other nations, Americans are religious. Between 1990 and 1993 respondents in the World Values Survey were asked if they were or were not a religious person.[9] As we can see from the following table, the United States stands out in the high proportion of its citizens who find religion to be important in their lives.

	Am a Religious Person	Am Not Religious	Other/ Don't Know*
United States	82%	15%	3%
Mexico	72	22	6
Canada	69	26	5
Spain	64	27	9
Britain	55	37	8
Germany	54	27	19
France	48	36	16
Sweden	29	56	9

*Volunteered.

Americans also tend to belong churches, although that was not always the case. At the time of the American Revolution only 17 percent were church members. By the end of the Civil War the number had doubled to 35 percent, then increased to 53 percent by 1916 and to 63 percent in the 1990s (Finke and Stark 1994). This increase in church membership is important, as religion and church membership have an important influence on public opinion.

Protestants, Catholics, Jews, and "Nones"

In terms of religious preference, 53 percent of American adults are Protestant, 26 percent are Catholic, 2 percent are Jewish, and 14 percent profess no religious preference ("Nones").[10] On what basis would we anticipate religious denominations to differ politically? Although Protestants are a pluralistic group, we might expect they would be the most conservative. Until recently, they held higher-status jobs and enjoyed higher incomes than did Catholics (there is no difference today among the white population). But the fact that Catholic immigrants arrived more recently and were subjected to a certain amount of discrimination may have left traces of liberal sentiment. Also, doctrinal differences exist that might have political relevance. The Catholic Church has taken a strong position against birth control and abortion; mainline Protestant churches less so. Further, the Protestant focus on individual responsibility for one's own economic and spiritual well-being (the "Protestant ethic") may predispose Protestants to be conservative on economic questions and issues of affirmative action. The high-status, high-income occupations of Jews compared to other religious groups, plus their concern for the well-being of Israel, might lead us to anticipate that Jews would be the most conservative and internationalist of religious groups. Counterbalancing these forces is the unique history of the Jewish people as a persecuted minority, which drives them in a liberal direction, particularly on civil liberties and civil rights.

Finally, a group that received little attention, but now constitutes 14 percent of the adult population, are the "Nones." This category is residual, consisting of atheists, agnostics, those indifferent to religion, and those believing in a Supreme Being but disenchanted with organized religion. We would expect them to be liberal, as to be unchurched is to be outside the American cultural mainstream. Such marginality tends to result in a liberal political outlook.

We shall limit our initial analysis to Northern whites, so as not to confuse the effect of denominational preference with region and race. The South is largely Protestant and conservative; blacks are largely Protestant and liberal. To contrast all four groups, we rely on General Social Survey and National Election Studies pooled data from the years 1994, 1996, and 1998. The two studies repeated many questions over these years. By combining years we can increase the sample size in small subgroups. While there are some variations in issue preferences from year-to-year, the larger sample size allows for more stable estimates in the case of Jews and Nones, which are a small percentage of the population.

Table 7.8 shows Protestants to be slightly more conservative on issues than Catholics, but the margins are not large. On economic matters Catholics and "Nones" are somewhat more liberal than Protestants, with Jews being the most liberal. On civil and moral issues, Jews and Nones are decidedly more liberal than the two major faiths. Note that on the key issue of abortion there is no difference between Protestants and Catholics—they are equally likely to endorse the statement that abortion should be allowed for any reason. Claiming a denominational affiliation is, of course, an easy response. However, if we look at differences between Catholics and Protestants among those who attend church once a week or more, there is still almost no difference between the two groups. On the other hand, Jews and Nones are much more supportive of abortion on demand than are Protestants or Catholics. On foreign and defense policies, Catholics and Protestants differ only marginally. Jews are somewhat more internationalist than other groups—as expected. But they were less supportive of the 1991 Persian Gulf War than the other two major religious groups, and less likely than all others to say the government should spend more on defense.

Turning to the more general orientations or ideology and partisanship, note that 40 percent of Protestants are Republican compared to 24 percent of Catholics and 51 percent of Protestants say they are conservative compared to 42 percent of Catholics. These differences have widened somewhat in recent years, due mostly to the increasing Republicanism among evangelical Protestants (Layman 1997). Jews and those with no preference are substantially more liberal than two major religious groups (60 and 27 percent, respectively), but only Jews stand out for the Democratic party preference (58 percent).

Finally, we can contrast the voting patterns of the major religious groupings. There were once substantial differences between Protestants and Catholics, but in recent years they have narrowed. Religious divisions were at their clearest in the 1960 presidential election, when the Democrats broke with tradition and nominated a Catholic, John F. Kennedy, for President.[11] Among northern whites, the breakdown of the 1960 vote by religion was as follows:

Northern Whites	Protestant	Catholic	Jewish
Voting Democratic (Kennedy)	28%	83%	83%
Voting Republican (Nixon)	72	17	7
	100%	100%	100%

Almost three-fourths of the Protestant vote among Northern whites was for Nixon, while over 80 percent of the Catholic and Jewish vote went for

TABLE 7.8   RELIGIOUS DENOMINATION AND POLITICAL OPINION, NORTHERN WHITES

Issue	Denomination			
Economic Issues	*Protestant*	*Catholic*	*Jewish*	*None*
Government should reduce income differentials	57%	55%	40%	50%
Government should improve standard of living	52	52	56	59
Government should help pay for medical care	76	81	74	80
Civil/Moral Issues				
Abortion allowed for any reason	40	39	80	71
Favor legalization of marijuana	16	16	38	47
Disapprove of prayer in public schools	35	41	88	73
Favor government aid to blacks	22	27	33	38
Men, women equally suited for politics	75	76	86	84
Foreign/Defense Issues				
Communism not worst form of government	49	48	68	69
Too much military spending	41	56	57	56
Take less active role in world affairs	59	54	43	46
Did the wrong thing in sending troops to 1991 Persian Gulf War★	12	16	29	28
Political Ideology				
Liberal	23	26	49	51
Moderate	37	43	36	30
Conservative	40	31	14	19
Party Identification				
Democrat	37	37	68	32
Independent	30	31	20	50
Republican	43	31	12	17

Source: General Social Survey, 1989–1993. Percentages are of opinion-holders only.

★National Election Studies, 1992.

Kennedy. In more typical elections, without a Catholic candidate, the same pattern exists, but the differences are smaller. The table below shows the presidential vote divisions among (northern white) Protestants, Catholics, Jews, and "Nones" in 1996.[12] Protestants voted the most Republican, followed by Catholics and those with no religious preference; Jewish voters were the least Republican.

Northern Whites	Protestant	Catholic	Jewish	None
Voting Democratic (Clinton)	41%	51%	82%	60%
Voting Republican (Dole)	50	39	15	27
Voting Reform (Perot)	10	10	3	13
	101%	100%	100%	100%

The temporal stability of partisan differences between Protestants, Catholics, and Jews is shown in Figure 7.5. The data show the percentage of Democratic (among identifiers only) among Northern whites beginning in 1956. The most remarkable aspect of Figure 7.5 is the stability over time in partisan preference. Typically, Jews are about 80 percent Democratic, Catholics about 65 percent (and slowly declining), and Protestants about 40 percent. Of those declaring no religious preference, about 65 percent identifying are Democrats.[13] The long-term trend shows little loss of religious distinctiveness in party preference.

Many of the reasons advanced earlier to explain issue differences among the religions also apply to the differences we see in partisanship and voting. However, we should note that the Democrats have traditionally wooed the immigrant voters, most of whom were Catholic. The payoff of this policy for the Democratic party has been the continued allegiance of many members of Catholic ethnic groups—the Irish, Italians, Poles, East Europeans, and Mexicans—who often continue to identify and vote Democratic despite having incomes that place them solidly in the middle class. One explanation for the continued Democratic voting among Catholics is that in the past American Catholics were less affluent than their Protestant neighbors—a condition that would naturally cause them to gravitate to the Democratic party for economic reasons. But there is more than economics at work, because during the 1940s surveys showed that even affluent Catholics tended to be Democratic, much as affluent blacks do today (Berelson et al. 1954, 64-66). Perhaps the best explanation for the Democratic allegiance of Catholics is simply the socialization of partisanship from one generation to the next. Even though the social and economic reasons for remaining Democratic no longer exist, there is a family tradition of Democratic partisanship among Catholics. As we saw earlier, on issue positions Catholics are slightly more liberal than Protestants, but these differences are certainly not of the magnitude to prevent Catholics from comfortably embracing the GOP. Some analysts claim that Catholics are ripe for conversion to Republicanism. As evidence, it is noted that in countries where Catholicism is the major religion, its adherents are usually identified with the

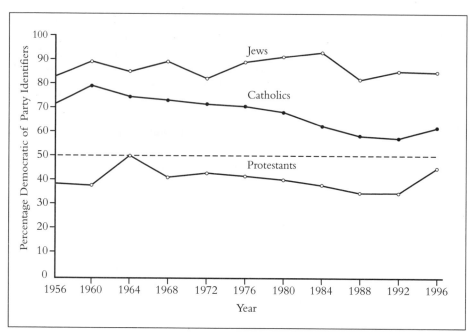

Figure 7.5   Religion and party identification (Northern whites only), 1956–1996. *Source:* National Election Studies.

more conservative political parties. But minus a major realigning shock, partisan conversion rarely occurs.[14] If the Democratic party is loosening its hold on Catholics, the process is likely to be gradual.

Protestant Denominations and Evangelicals

On most issues there is greater disagreement among Protestants of various persuasions than between Protestants and Catholics. Theological differences between denominations often show up as differences in political opinions. For example, the emphasis on personal salvation in the Baptist church and other "fundamentalist" groups seemingly makes their members conservative, while the more "worldly" involvement in social problems on the part of nonfundamentalist groups (Presbyterians and Episcopalians, for example) ought to make their members relatively liberal. Also, the theology of some fundamentalist Protestant denominations condemns departures from traditional lifestyles, while more liberal denominations are more accommodating. Very sharp differences on these issues have been found between the political attitudes of Protestant clergymen of fundamentalist and nonfundamentalist churches, and among church members who are very politically involved. Wald and associates investigated the possibility that active membership in a specific congregation can have a direct effect on the political attitudes of parishioners. Based on a sample of 12 Protestant churches in a Florida community, they found parishioners from the more theologically conservative congregations were also more politically conservative, particularly on social issues. This relationship is attributed directly to "messages from the pulpit and social interaction [among] the congregants" (Wald et al. 1989, 542; see also Jelen 1992 for an extension of this research). Leege and Welch (1989), in a study of Catholic parishioners, came to a similar conclusion about the role of theology in political outlooks.

Recently, evangelical Christian groups have interjected a new dimension into American politics, due both to the uniqueness of their political beliefs and the grass-roots activism among their members. These groups are mostly Protestant, but they cut across denominations. There are two major evangelical subgroups that have been very politically active since the mid-1970s: the fundamentalists and charismatic/pentecostals. Fundamentalists emphasize personal experiences with the Holy Spirit (being "born again"), a literal interpretation of the Bible, and rejection of the Social Gospel (salvation through good works). "Charismatic" or "Pentecostal" Protestants are fundamentalists with a focus on the mystical, such as faith healing, prophecy, and speaking in tongues. Many in the fundamentalist movement are critical of charismatics, arguing their focus on spiritual gifts undermines the doctrine of the Bible's inerrancy. Fundamentalists tend to be more conservative on political issues than Pentacostals (Jelen 1993). Evangelicals currently comprise about 27 percent of the population and 56 percent of all Protestants (Wald 1997, 173). Comparatively speaking, they tend to be rural, Southern, less affluent, and less educated than the rest of the population (Reichley 1985, 312).

Table 7.9 presents evidence of how Protestant fundamentalists differ from more secular Protestants in their political views, according to the 1996 NES survey. The table is limited to white Protestants, as blacks tend to be more theologically conservative than whites, but more politically liberal due to their racial identification. Fundamentalism is measured in terms of a variety of religious beliefs (such as being "born again"). The table contrasts the views of the 36 percent most secular (or religiously indifferent) of Protestants with the 25 percent most fundamentalist (with the remaining 39 percent classed as "in between").[15]

Overall, the fundamentalists are very conservative, with almost all ideological identifiers choosing the "conservative" label versus one-half of the secular. While the fundamentalists are somewhat more conservative on economic issues than are the other groups, and somewhat more "hawkish" on defense issues, it is the social and cultural issues that most clearly distinguish the religious right from other Protestants. Compared to the secular, fundamentalists are much more likely to oppose gays in the military, an equal role for women in business and government, and favor harsh punishment for those convicted of crimes. We can see a particularly large difference on abortion, perhaps the most salient issue on the new right agenda. Only 8 percent of fundamentalists favor abortion rights. These differences are, for the most part, unaffected by controls of social background variables. It would seem no coincidence that membership in antifeminist groups tends to be heavily drawn from evangelical religions, while pro-feminist activists tend to be secular or belong to "worldly" denominations, although the possibility of self-selection cannot be ruled out

TABLE 7.9   RELIGIOUS FUNDAMENTALISM AND
POLITICAL VIEWS, WHITE PROTESTANTS ONLY

Political Opinion*	Religious Orientation		
	Secular (36 percent)	In Between (39 Percent)	Fundamentalist (25 percent)
Want more domestic spending	61%	76%	76%
For national health insurance	38	39	20
Guarantee good standard of living	23	24	11
Decrease spending on welfare	61	61	77
Always permit abortions	57	29	8
Allow gays in military	72	61	35
Equal role for women	88	76	54
Punish criminals to reduce crime	47	60	65
Protect environment at cost of jobs	57	39	28
Favor gun control	44	46	29
Gone too far pushing equal rights	53	62	77
Willing to use force abroad	17	24	29
Increase defense spending	48	69	76
Oppose Persian Gulf War[†]	17	11	10
Percentage Democratic (of party identifiers)	50	40	23
Percentage Liberal (of ideological identifiers)	36	12	6
Percentage for Clinton (of 1996 two-party vote)	49	40	20

*National Election Studies, 1996.
†National Election Studies, 1992.

(Tedin et al. 1977). It seems apparent that the politics of the evangelical cause at the mass level is mostly limited to a focus on social and cultural issues, although fundamentalists are very strong supporters of Israel. Rebuilding of the Temple of David is an essential component of evangelical apocalyptic prophecy. Evangelical movements are found primarily, but not entirely, among Protestant denominations. Some Catholics also share this theology. However, Leege and Welch (1991) find Catholic evangelicals differ from Protestants, with the former being noticeably more liberal.

Given their demographic characteristics, we might expect white evangelicals to favor the Democratic party. They clearly did so in 1976, when evangelical Christians voted overwhelmingly for "born again" Democratic presidential candidate Jimmy Carter (Reichley 1985). Since that time, however, fundamentalist

Christians have moved notably in the direction of the Republican party in their presidential voting (Layman 1997). In 1980, born-again white Christians gave Ronald Reagan 61 percent of their vote—a not insignificant proportion given the much greater tendency for others with similar background characteristics to vote Democratic. By the mid-1980s, most evangelicals were aware that it was the Republican party that was most sympathetic to their social agenda.[16]

	Republican Percentage of Presidential Vote		
	1988	**1992**	**1996**
Catholic	52	43	37
Jewish	36	26	16
White (nonevangelical) Protestant	66	57	53
White Evangelical	81	68	65

7-5   GEOGRAPHY AND POLITICAL OPINIONS

People commonly think of American public opinion as differing along regional lines. The South stands out in particular for its political conservatism, particularly on civil rights and cultural issues. Outlandish fads (political and otherwise) are thought to start in the West, most notably in California. The East is often characterized as being liberal (the land of Ted Kennedy and where Hillary Rodham Clinton chose to run for the Senate). There have been other regional stereotypes that once may have been valid but seem less so today. The South, for example, was once the most internationally minded region in foreign policy, largely because of the cotton growers' interest in free trade with other nations. The Midwest at one time had the reputation, seemingly deserved on the basis of poll results, for being the most isolationist (least internationalist) region of the country.[17] The long-term trend shows little loss of regional distinctiveness in party preference.

Several factors, however, serve to undermine the impact of region. Americans are very mobile (20 percent move each year) and dilute the native citizenry. Only 39 percent of adults say they currently live in the same locale as they did when they were 16 years old (GSS, 1990–1996). The near universal penetration of the national media would seem to have a homogenizing effect on regionalism. But we should not overstate the case. On many issues meaningful regional differences persist. Democratic partisans are still most frequently found in the South, but their partisan preferences do not translate into support for Democratic candidates. The likely reason is that the South also has the most ideological conservatives.[18] In recent years, the South has been the most Republican part of the nation in national voting. In both 1996 and 1992, Clinton did best among voters from the East Coast; Bush and Dole did best in the South.

Based on merged 1994–1998 data from the GSS and NES, the South clearly stands out as being distinctive. Southerners are decidedly more religious than the rest of the nation (Ladd 1998b). On virtually all social issues—such as school prayer, gay rights, allowing communists to speak in one's community, abortion and gun control—the South is markedly conservative.[19] The South is also uniquely conservative on foreign policy issues. Its residents want to spend more on defense, are more likely to endorse the use of military force to settle international conflicts, and are least in favor of establishing diplomatic relations with Cuba.[20] On economic questions, however, the South has not been historically conservative. As the poorest region in the nation, the South has a vested interest in government spending. Currently, it either does not stand out from the rest of the country on issues like more government services, or welfare reform or, on some economic issues, is slightly more liberal than the rest of the nation—for example, spending for the public schools.[21]

On the same issues that the South is uniquely conservative, the West and New England are uniquely liberal. For example, only 43 percent in the deep South favor legal abortions compared to 78 percent in the West and 73 percent in New England (Ladd 1998b). The same is true when it comes to gay rights, prayer in the schools, the legalization of marijuana, and gun control. Fifty-one percent in the South want to amend the Constitution to allow for school prayer, compared to 35 percent in the West and 41 percent in the East.[22] The West is also slightly more liberal on questions of foreign policy than the rest of the nation, and slightly more conservative when it comes to economic issues (Mayer 1992).

Finally, the stereotype of the East as a bastion of liberalism is certainly false. On social and foreign policy questions, it is a bit more liberal than the rest of the country as a whole, but only by a small amount. Economic preferences are mixed, with no clear pattern. For example, on the issue of welfare spending, there is no more than a six percentage point difference among the nine different regions of the country defined in the GSS. The East is the most liberal, but only by a small margin (Ladd 1998b).

But are regional differences in fact related to a regional culture, or are they simply compositional effects? Perhaps the South is less supportive of civil liberties because its residents have comparatively little education. While there is certainly some truth to this assertion, individual state culture makes a large contribution to one's partisanship and political ideology (Erikson et al. 1994). For example, with demographic factors controlled, living in Minnesota instead of Indiana results in a partisan difference of about the same magnitude as being in the lowest income category versus being in the highest. There is something about state residence that impacts on partisanship and ideology beyond the fact that residents may differ in their religion, income, education, or union membership.

Other than state residence and regional groupings, the most common geographical division is one of cities, suburbs, small towns, and rural areas. It is generally thought that urban areas are sources of liberal and "nonconventional" political attitudes, with rural and small-town America being the bastions of conservatism. An analysis of GSS data by Yang and Alba (1992) focusing on nonconventional opinions, such as those toward the legalization of marijuana, the role of women in politics, and government regulation of pornography, shows the residents of urban areas are much more liberal on these domains than those living in small towns and rural areas. A study by Wilson (1985) also shows urban residence has a positive association with political tolerance—those living in urban areas were the most tolerant across all the target groups included in the General Social Survey. However, at least part of this variation is due to composition effects. City residents show up as more liberal in surveys because they have a large proportion of people with liberal group characteristics, such as blacks, Jews, and Catholics. Small towns and rural areas are conservative because they are predominantly Protestant and, outside the South, contain few blacks. But not all these urban/rural differences disappear when controls for composition effects are introduced. In fact, most remain statistically significant, although reduced in magnitude. Fischer (1975, 1320), advances an "urban subculture" theory, which holds that urban residents are more "nonconventional" in their political opinions because urban life provides a critical mass, meaning "the congregation of numbers of persons sufficient to maintain viable unconventional subcultures." In other words, there is something about urban life—perhaps social diversity or the existence of support groups—independent of the social background of the residents, that makes them more liberal or nonconventional than those living in small towns and rural areas.

The Changing American South

The once distinctive South (the old Confederacy) is gradually losing its unique political character. The reasons are complex, but certainly involve the economic boom that began after World War II, migration (many blacks left the region in search of jobs, while many Northern whites moved into the region for the same reason), plus rapid industrialization of the region with attendant liberalizing consequences.

The result has been a gradual loss in Southern distinctiveness. On many political attitudes, the gap between the South and the rest of the nation has closed. In 1964, Southerners were 11 percentage points more conservative than other Americans, but in 1998 that gap was only 4 percent.[23] Southerners remain more traditional than the rest of the nation on issues like prayer in the schools, women's issues, and civil liberties, but again, the gap is narrowing. However, on social welfare questions, like government health programs and guaranteed jobs, there has historically been little difference between the South and the rest of the nation. The New Deal was popular among blacks and whites alike in the region. As noted earlier, the South is if anything more liberal now than the rest of the country on economic issues.

The uniqueness of the South is generally associated with two issues: a conservative stance on racial questions, and overwhelming support for the Democratic party. Currently, however, most surveys show only small differences between white Southerners and the rest of the nation on race.

Table 7.10 shows the dramatic change by region among whites in response to the question of whether one favors the principle of black and white children

TABLE 7.10   SCHOOL INTEGRATION OPINION AMONG WHITES,
BY REGION AND EDUCATION, 1956 AND 1985

Favor Blacks and Whites Attending the Same School

Non-South	1956	1985
Less than high school	58%	86%
High school	67	98
Some college or more	79	99
South		
Less than high school	8	67
High school	20	93
Some college or more	30	98

Sources: 1956 data adapted from Howard Schuman, Charlotte Steeh, and Lawrence Bobo, *Racial Attitudes in America* (Cambridge, MA: Harvard University Press, 1985), p. 78; the 1985 data are from the General Social Survey.

attending the same school. In 1956, the differences between the South and the rest of the nation were substantial. By 1985 (the last year the question was asked), there is almost no difference of consequence between the whites in the South and whites in the rest of the nation on whether black and white children should attend the same schools.[24] For the 1994 NES question on whether "the federal government should see to it" that blacks and whites attend the same schools, there was no difference between whites in the South and the rest of the nation (38 percent in both regions favored government action).

Not all, however, are convinced by the "New South" argument. Measuring racial hostility is difficult, given the social norms that surround the race issue. The most racially prejudiced may in fact be the most likely to hide their true feelings. Using a method to disguise racially sensitive questions, Kuklinksi, Cobb, and Gilens (1997) report considerably more racial resentment among white southerners than among whites outside the south.[25] For example, 42 percent of white southerners expressed anger at the thought of a black family moving in next door, compared to 10 percent of nonsouthern whites (Kuklinksi, Cobb, and Gilens 1997, 329–30). Their conclusion is that many white southerners are giving insincere answers when asked directly about racial issues.

The initial attachment of the South to the Democratic party goes back, of course, to the Civil War. But it was reinforced by economics. The South was long the poorest region of the country—a plus for the Democratic party, given its image of providing jobs and benefits to the average person. As the national Democratic party became increasingly liberal on civil rights, it became increasingly less attractive to many white Southerners. But the Republican party benefited little. In response to the civil rights plank in the 1948 Democratic platform, South Carolina Governor Strom Thurmond ran as a

"Dixiecrat" and took three states. The Republicans came up empty-handed. Nevertheless, presidential Republican voting has been a fixture in the South since 1948, and since 1968 it has given a larger proportion of its vote to the national Republicans than any other region.

As can be seen in Figure 7.6, the major decline in Democratic party identification among whites followed the presidential candidacy of Barry Goldwater in 1964. Goldwater voted against the 1964 Civil Rights Act on the grounds that it violated states' rights. Since then, the decline has been gradual but steady. But Independents rather than Republicans have benefited more from the erosion of Democrat partisanship. However, Republican party identification is particularly prevalent among young white Southerners (Wattenberg 1998). Those under 30 are more Republican than Democrat in their party leanings, while for those over 65, Democrats still predominate.[26] If this pattern continues, the Republicans will soon overtake the Democrats in terms of party preference among Southern whites.

7-6 GENDER AND POLITICAL OPINIONS

Since the early days of survey research, it was thought that there were few differences between the sexes in political opinions. Although women participated less than men, they were thought to be indistinguishable on questions of party and voting, with perhaps a few minor differences on issue positions. That situation changed in 1980, when considerable media attention was devoted to the gap

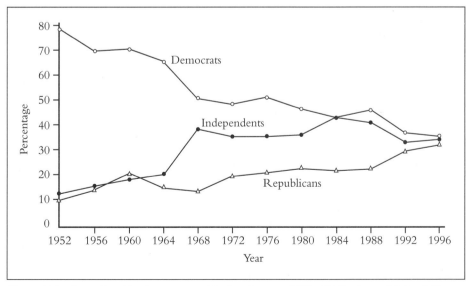

Figure 7.6 Party identification among white Southerners (1952–1996). *Source:* National Election Studies.

between male and female voting for president. Women voted about equally for Reagan and Carter, but men gave Reagan 19 percentage points more than they gave Carter. Since that time, much attention has been devoted to the study of gender differences in political orientations. We now know the gender gap in voting to be a fairly recent phenomenon. Until 1980, there were either no differences, or women more than men tended to vote Republican. For example, women were more favorable to Dwight Eisenhower by a margin of 7 points in 1956, and had the 1960 presidential election been decided by women alone, Richard Nixon would have been elected president (Kenski 1988, 50). The large gender gap that first appeared in 1980 weakened through the 1992 election, but reappeared strongly again in 1996.[27] Bob Dole received 45 percent of the male vote; Bill Clinton got 44 percent, Ross Perot 10 percent. However, women gave only 38 percent of their vote to Bob Dole, while giving Bill Clinton 55 percent and Ross Perot 7 percent. The actual "gender gap" (the difference in the percentage of males and females voting for Clinton) was 11 percent—the largest on record. The gap is nearly as large (9 percent) in voting for the U.S. House, and appears as a key variable of party identification. The NES shows that in 1980 women were 3 percent more Democratic than men, but they were 10 percent more Democratic than men in both 1988 and 1996. This Democratic tendency is particularly noticeable among unmarried and well-educated women.[28]

In some issue domains, there have developed gender-based differences that are potentially of considerable import. A gender gap in political opinions may influence the public agenda in much the same way opinion differences between blacks and whites impact on the political process. Since women constitute a majority of the American electorate, even small gender differences can put substantial pressure on decision-makers.

Table 7.11 presents gender differences in selected issue domains. Since the 1930s, surveys have shown that women are less prone to endorse violence and aggression in any form, be it at the personal level, regarding capital punishment, or in foreign affairs. We see in the table a 10-point gender gap on the issue of sending U.S. ground troops to Kosovo. These gender differences have also appeared in other conflicts. Women were 12 percent more likely than men to say it was wrong for the United States to get involved in the Gulf War (NES 1992). There was a similar gender difference in support of the Korean War and the Vietnam War, with women typically being 8 to 10 percent less enthusiastic than men. Finally, there is a long-running series of questions dating back to the late 1940s relating to issues surrounding the development, testing, and possible use of nuclear weapons. Women have consistently been more dovish (or perhaps more compassionate and concerned with human life) than men. For example, in 1989 women were 16 percentage points more likely to believe that it was morally wrong to use the atomic bomb on Japan to end World War II (Brandes 1992). Miller (1988) argues that this gender difference on foreign affairs has important electoral consequences. When elections tend to turn on questions of human rights and issues of war and peace, the gender gap in voting increases, with women moving to favor Democratic candidates.

TABLE 7.11 GENDER DIFFERENCES AND POLITICAL OPINIONS

Opinion	Men	Women	Difference
Force, Violence, and Aggression			
Favor sending U.S. ground troops to Kosovo[a]	46%	36%	+10
Take military action against Iraq over refusal to allow site visits[b]	55	35	+20
Want stricter gun control laws[c]	45	70	+25
Favor the death penalty over life in prison for capital murder[d]	62	38	+24
Compassion			
Spend budget surplus on social programs, not tax cut[e]	49	64	+15
Government should provide health insurance[g]	35	41	+6
Government should see to good jobs/standard of living[g]	20	29	+9
Increase spending for the homeless[g]	52	63	+11
Gender-Related Issues			
Favor abortion for any reason[h]	40	40	0
Men and women should have equal role[f]	78	78	0
Men and women equally suited for politics[h]	42	41	-1
Draft men only into the military[i]	56	51	-5
Increase spending for child care[f]	48	57	+9
Civil Liberties/Civil Rights			
Allow homosexuals to serve in the army[f]	61	77	+16
Favor legalization of marijuana[f]	35	24	-11
Favor affirmative-action programs[j]	42	45	+3
Allow communists to speak[h]	74	62	-12
Reduce crime by solving social problems[f]	27	33	+6
Government should make every effort to help blacks[f] (whites only)	13	18	+5

[a]Gallup Poll, 6–7 Apr. 1999.

[b]Gallup Poll, 30–31 Jan. 1998.

[c]Princeton Research Associates, 31 July 1997–17 Aug. 1997.

[d]Gallup Poll, 16–18 Jan. 1998.

[e]Gallup Poll, 19–21 Feb. 1999.

[f]National Election Studies, 1996.

[g]National Election Studies, 1998.

[h]General Social Survey, 1998.

[i]Gallup Poll, 5–7 June 1998.

[j]Roper Center Poll, 22–26 Aug. 1994.

These differences on violence and aggression are probably due to an inter-play between socialization and biology. Though not conclusive, there is some research showing that men have a greater predisposition to use force than women. Caldicott (1986) describes men as "insecure aggressors," while women are more nurturing and pacifist since "their bodies are built anatomically and physiologically to nurture life." Also, the socialization of young boys frequently emphasizes aggression (witness playground games), while such aggression is discouraged in young girls (Miedaian 1991). Another possible explanation is that women are more risk-adverse than men (Tedin and Yap 1993). For exam-ple, 31 percent of men but only 5 percent of women favor building more nu-clear power plants (1991 NES Pilot), and 33 percent of men say nuclear power plants are "very safe" compared to 15 percent of women (Gallup 1999).

There are also gender differences on compassion issues relating to jobs, ed-ucation, income redistribution, and protection for the vulnerable in society. Women are generally more supportive of a compassionate approach than men, but the differences are not large. When large differences appear, they are usu-ally on issues that address specific hazards rather than more general society-wide problems. For example, in addition to differences in support for building nuclear power plants, there are substantial gaps in support for the 55 MPH speed limit, for state laws requiring seat belts, and for stiff jail terms for drunk drivers (Shapiro and Mahajan 1986).

On civil rights issues, white men and white women usually do not differ. One exception is that women are considerably more supportive of gays in the military than are men. Even though women sometimes benefit from affirmative-action programs, Table 7.11 shows them only slightly more supportive of such programs than men. There are, however, consistent gender differences on civil liberties. On most of the 1998 GSS civil liberties items, men are more support-ive than women. These differences are not limited to the United States, but show up in Western Europe and the former Soviet Union as well (Norris 1988; Tedin and Yap, 1993; Tedin 1994a). Controls for background factors reduce, but do not eliminate, these differences.

On most gender-related issues the gender gap is small to non-existent. Women are more in favor of increased spending for child care, but on most other gender issues there are either no gender differences and occasionally differences that seem to run counter to self-interest. In 21 successive readings of the General Social Survey, men have been at least as supportive of abortion "for any reason" as have women. In some GSS surveys, men have been as much as 10 percentage points more supportive, although the gap has declined in recent years (as shown in Table 7.11) and the 1998 survey shows no gender difference. The gender differences are in the unexpected direction in other instances when the question of womens' equality is addressed. For example, men were consistently more favorable to the passage of the Equal Rights amendment than were women (Simon and Landis 1989, 275).

One reason for this pattern is that on many issues that directly concern women, there is a greater gap among women themselves than between women and men. Take, for instance, the label "feminist." In 1998, 26 percent of adult women answered "yes" to the question "Do you consider yourself a feminist?"[29] Women accepting this label tend not to be "average." Rather they are highly educated and affluent (Keene, 1991). Their voting patterns are also atypical. In 1996, non-feminists voted 24 percent for Bill Clinton while feminists gave him 84 percent, a much greater gap than one would ever find between men and women.[30]

We see clearly the class division among women by looking at the 1996 NES question that asks if "women should have an equal role with men in running business, industry, and government," or whether "womens' place is in the home." Women disagree among themselves on the answer to this question more than they disagree with men. The line of stratification divides working women and homemakers, and divides on level of education. Sixty percent of working women chose the most equalitarian category (option 1 on a seven-point scale, see the Appendix), compared to only 42 percent of the homemakers. Among working women with a college degree, 74 percent chose the most egalitarian option. Only 43 percent of homemakers with no more than a high shcool education chose this option. Although support for women in the workplace continues to increase as full-time working women have become commonplace, there are nevertheless clear lifestyle distinctions about what makes one an important and worthwhile person that split women on the issues at the heart of the women's movement.

7-7 CONCLUSION

Group characteristics can clearly make a difference in how people see the political world. Belonging to a group is part of one's self-identification. Many groups have a vested political interest. Belonging to the upper social class encourages one to believe that through one's own effort, success can be achieved, and government should be limited in its ability to spend tax money to aid those who have not been successful in life's competition. Race, gender, region, and age also intrude upon one's life in a fashion not entirely neutral, and consequently color the way one sees the desirable organization and ends of the polity.

Over time, certain group distinctions may increase or decrease in importance. For example, the distinction between urban and rural has declined with the rapid industrialization of society. Group distinctions that may increase in importance are those between the young and the old, the sunbelt and the frostbelt, and the technologically skilled and unskilled. These potential cleavages may at some point replace traditional sources of voting alignments, such as partisanship or class. If that happens, the benefits that government bestows upon its citizens, as well as the obligations it demands, may also change.

NOTES

1. When asked by Gallup in July 1988 if they belonged to the "haves" or the "have nots," 59 percent of Americans said they belonged to the "haves" and 17 said they belonged to the "have nots," with 15 percent saying neither or both and 9

percent unsure. When asked in March 1988, 41 percent of British respondents said they belonged to the "haves," while 37 percent said they were part of the "have nots."

2. "Public Opinion and Demographic Report," *The Public Perspective* 4 (May/June 1993): 85.
3. "The Polls," *Public Opinion Quarterly* 12 (1949): 781.
4. A similar measure of class voting using a manual/nonmanual dichotomy was employed by Alford (1963). For an analysis over time of group-based divisions among Democratic and Republican voters, see Erikson et al. (1989).
5. *Washington Post* Survey (28 Sept. 1995); Princeton Survey Research Associates (5 Nov. 1997).
6. For blacks, the correlation between income and the "services and spending" item and the "good standard of living" item are nonsignificant. For whites, the correlations are .21 and .24.
7. Data from polls taken by the *Washington Post* reported in *The Public Perspective* (Oct./Nov. 1997): 17.
8. Although Clinton received 53 percent of the white two-party vote in the VNS survey, he received only 44 percent with the Perot candidacy included. Slightly more whites voted for Bob Dole in 1996 than voted for Bill Clinton.
9. Reported in *The Public Perspective* 6 (Apr./May, 1995): 25.
10. There was also an additional 5 percent who chose some other religion. These estimates are based on the 1998 GSS.
11. The Democrats had previously nominated New York governor Al Smith for the presidency in 1928. He was defeated by Herbert Hoover.
12. The 1960 data are from the NES; the 1996 data are from the VSN exit poll.
13. Due to a small sample size in 1996, the percentage for Jews in Figure 7.5 is taken from the combined NES data for 1994, 1996, and 1998.
14. For an example of conversions, see Erikson and Tedin (1981).
15. For the scale of religious orientation, each respondent received one point for each of the following: saying that they were fundamentalist, evangelical, or charismatic, that religion provides a great deal of guidance in life, that they pray and read the Bible several times a day, that the Bible is the actual word of God, that they are a "born again" Christian. The items were coded as 0,1 being secular, 2, 3, 4 as in-between, and 5, 6, 7 as fundamentalist.
16. These data are from VNS exit polls.
17. To take an example of one-time regional differences in foreign policy "isolationism," Southerners, when asked in 1945 whether the United States and Russia "should make a permanent military alliance," responded favorably by a ratio greater than 2 to 1. At the other extreme, a slight majority of Midwesterners opposed such an alliance (Cantril 1951, 961). By the late 1950s, such disparities had largely disappeared (Key 1961a, 134).
18. Based on the 1994–1998 NES cumulative file where 36 percent are Democrats in the Northeast, 34 percent in the Midwest, 40 percent in the South, and 37 percent in the West. Forty-six percent in the South say they are conservative.
19. For a description of these differences based on merged 1990–1996 data, see Ladd (1998b). We have updated Ladd's analysis using more recent data.
20. Based on 1994–1998 NES data. The item on Cuba asks " . . . do you think the United States government should or should not establish diplomatic relations with Cuba?" The responses for "should not" were 44 percent in the East, 58

percent in the Midwest, 65 percent in the South, and 49 percent in the West (ABC News Poll, 13 Jan. 1998).

21. Based on 1994–1998 NES data, 67 percent in the Northeast want more spending on public schools, as do 61 percent in the Midwest, 76 percent in the South, and 74 percent in the West.

22. *New York Times* Poll, 17 Jan. 1997.

23. Based on a comparison of mean region differences determined by NES feeling thermometers, where respondents are asked to rate conservatives on a 0-to-100 scale, with 0 being cold, 50 being neutral, and 100 being warm.

24. Since almost everyone now endorses the principle of white and black students attending the same school, the question has not been asked since 1985.

25. Kuklinski et al. randomly gave one-half of the sample a list of three nonracial items and asked *how many* of the items make them angry—importantly, not which one, just how many. The other half of the sample got the same three items plus an additional item addressing race, such as "a black family moving in next door." Again, the respondents were asked how many make them angry. Only the additional item for half of the sample getting four options addresses race. Thus respondents saying two of four items anger them assumes the interviewer cannot know which two—which indeed he or she cannot. However, statistical methods can be used to determine the level of anger about "a black family moving in next door" among southerners and nonsoutherners as a group.

26. In 1992, white southerners under 30 were more Republican than Democrat by a margin of 28 percent, but in 1996 the difference was only 8 percent (NES).

27. In 1980, Reagan received 54 percent and Carter 35 percent among men; among women, Reagan received 46 percent and Carter 45 percent. In 1984, men voted 62 percent for Reagan, 38 percent for Mondale; women voted 54 percent for Reagan, 46 percent for Mondale; in 1988 men voted 57 percent for Bush and 41 percent for Dukakis; women voted 50 percent for Bush and 49 percent for Dukakis; and in 1992, men voted 41 percent for Clinton, 38 percent for Bush, and 21 percent for Perot; women voted 45 percent for Clinton, 37 percent for Bush, and 17 percent for Perot.

28. See Weisberg (1987) for a statistical demonstration using 1984. In 1996, the most pronounced gender gap occurred between men and women with some postgraduate work or a postgraduate degree. Sixty percent of the women voted for Clinton compared to 44 percent of the men (Frankovic 1999).

29. Based on a survey by Yanklovich Partners, (18 May 1998) for Time and the Cable News Network.

30. The nonfeminists were defined as all women who rated on the NES feeling thermometer the "women's movement" below 50 degrees (14 percent). Feminists were defined as all women who rated the women's movement at 85 degrees or higher (30 percent).

CHAPTER 8

The Print and Broadcast Media and Political Opinions

Our political beliefs are shaped by the political information we receive. This is an obvious statement of fact but an important one. In totalitarian political systems, the regime attempts to control the flow of information by controlling the national media. In democracies, the mass media are relatively free of government control. Indeed, it is difficult to imagine free democratic elections without a free flow of competing information in the mass media.

But the proper flow of political information requires more than simply the government allowing an unfettered mass media to print or broadcast free of political interference. What we read, see, or hear in the mass media is the product of the institutions that make up the newspaper, magazine, television, and radio industries. Within these institutions, individuals continually decide what to print or what to broadcast. For democratic citizens to be properly informed about public affairs requires that the news media provide a broad balance of information and viewpoints.

The importance of media content is indicated by the criticism and controversy that frequently surround the mass media. When we become disturbed by the course of political trends, the mass media and the people who run them provide convenient scapegoats. When we appear to be mistaken or wrongheaded in our views, it is simple to blame the mass media for distorting the political messages that we receive. Or when we appear fascinated with irrelevant sideshows instead of what would be considered serious issues of public affairs, it is easy to blame the mass media for emphasizing the wrong kinds of news stories.

Complaints about the influence of the media are not limited to conventional political issues. The content of what we watch on television is a particular target. With a certain ebb ad flow, various critics accuse television of contributing to such trends as violence in society, sexism, lax moral standards, permissiveness about drugs, low SAT scores, and too much junk food. Political scientists register their own concern about some unwanted side effects from the introduction of television. Among the political trends that have been attributed to television are the decline of political parties, the drop in voter turnout, the superficiality of public debate, the ascendancy of slick media-oriented candidates, and the growth of public cynicism about politics.

Of course, just because a seemingly reasonable observer may lay a particular complaint at the doorstep of the mass media does not necessarily make the complaint valid. In this chapter we discuss the nature of the mass media, their possible biases, and their impact on public opinion.

8-1 THE MASS MEDIA AND THEIR POLITICAL CONTENT

For most Americans, the mass media intrudes every day in a multitude of ways. About 80 percent of American households receive daily newspapers, and almost all contain at least one television set. About seventy percent of American households are wired for cable television or "narrow-casting," which adds a new dimension. And Americans frequently listen to their radios (in the car if not at home). Add to this the many magazines available for us to read. In short, it is easy to argue that Americans suffer from information overload. Even though only a fraction of what we read and watch concerns politics and public affairs, the modern mass media are important for understanding the role of political opinions in modern democracy.

Newspapers

When the United States was founded as a nation, newspapers were already in place. But the newspapers of the early Republic were essentially forums for particular partisan points of view, rather than objective reports of the news. Also, early newspapers were not strictly "mass" media, since they were read mainly by small elite audiences. In the 1830s, newspapers were first brought to the masses in the form of the "penny press," as the early mass circulation newspapers came to be called. Newspapers of the penny press were cheap (1 cent) and willing to entertain the mass audience with human interest stories and sensational reports of crimes and disasters. They also introduced the first debate about the role of the mass media. Some observers saw the proliferation of mass circulation newspapers as the springboard for a truly democratic marketplace of ideas. Others saw the same phenomenon as debasing the currency of political discussion (Berkman and Kitch 1986, 1).

In any event, public demand for newspapers plus technological advances (e.g., the telegraph) allowed no retreat. By 1900, more newspapers were in publication than today. Many were strongly partisan, and many were sensationalistic purveyors of "yellow journalism." By the end of the twentieth century the number of newspapers had dwindled to the point that fewer than 30 U.S. cities enjoyed competition from newspapers under different ownership. With this consolidation and the increased reliance on wire-service stories for newspaper copy, the bias in newspaper coverage—particularly of national and world events—declined over the twentieth century. Thus, the choices open to the newspaper consumer decreased, while the objectivity of the product increased.

Beyond its local news coverage, the content of the typical reader's hometown paper is similar to that in the next town down the road. But of course the quality of the hometown coverage can vary. And certain "prestige" newspapers do provide unusually good coverage of world and national events. National political and business leaders pay close attention to the prestige newspapers (most notably the *New York Times, Washington Post, Los Angeles Times,* and *Wall Street Journal*). A recent trend has been for some newspapers to become truly national. The *New York Times* and the *Wall Street Journal* now are generally available throughout the nation, as is the Gannett's national newspaper, *USA Today*. And Internet users now have access to on-line editions from around the world.

Radio and Television

Commercial radio and the first radio networks emerged in the 1920s. Commercial television became technically feasible by the late 1930s. However, World War II delayed the beginning of the television age until the late 1940s. Early radio had a major political impact, bringing to all American living rooms such events as the fireside chats by President Roosevelt and the horrifying reports of World War II. Early television also had its impact. For instance, Edward R. Murrow's reports on CBS's "See It Now" and the televised Army–McCarthy hearings (both in 1954) helped to destroy the mercurial career of demagogic Senator Joe McCarthy.

Early network television newscasts, however, did not amount to much. They were lightweight affairs, only 15 minutes long, without much interesting film coverage. The beginning of satellite communications in 1962 revolutionized television news, allowing instant coverage from around the world. Also in the early 1960s, network news shows became 30 minutes long. Soon thereafter they were telecast in color. Although there have been further technological advances, by the late 1960s network news telecasts took on the look that they have today. Meanwhile, the emergence of CNN and 24-hour cable TV news coverage has brought a new dimension to news coverage, allowing news consumers to rely on television to a far greater degree than before.

Magazines

Magazines play a distinct role in the formation of public opinion. At the top of the pyramid, small public affairs magazines that count their readers only in the hundreds of thousands (e.g., *Atlantic, New Republic*) try to influence the thoughtful opinion leaders. At the next level are newsmagazines (*Time, Newsweek, U.S. News & World Report),* each reaching a few million readers a week. Newsmagazines are important molders of opinion. Perhaps correctly, President John Kennedy once asserted that *Time* was the most important influence on American public opinion (Halberstam 1979, 353). Kennedy's statement would be incorrect today, only because of the dominance of television. At the bottom of the magazine pyramid are mass circulation magazines like *People* and *Reader's Digest* which sometimes offer subtle political cues to their readers.

Biased Media?

Although the news media pride themselves on the objectivity of their news coverage, they are not without their critics. Those from the left charge that because the media are business enterprises and depend on business advertising for their profits, they unfairly favor the conservative viewpoint of the business community. Critics from the right charge that journalists are political liberals who unfairly promote the liberal viewpoint in their presentation of the news. Still other critics make more subtle observations. Some say that because the media try to appeal to the broadest possible audience, they constrict the flow of ideas to those in the "safe" middle range (Bennett 1980, 304–44). Others see a structural bias to the profession itself: Because journalists tend to be politically cynical and because they try to maintain the interest of their audience, the media sometimes give a particularly hard time to incumbent officeholders (Ranney 1976, 31–63); Hofstetter 1976). Still others offer the opposite complaint. They see newspeople as too uncritical of governmental officials, out of a need to protect their access to news sources (Hertsgaard 1988; Press and Verburn 1988).

Both newspapers and television news claim to present an objective account of the news. They differ, however, in their willingness to editorialize. Until recently, television stations were forbidden by the "fairness doctrine" of the Federal Communications Commission from overtly endorsing political candidates and from advocating particular points of view, unless they gave equal time to the opposite viewpoint. These strictures were substantially weakened in the late 1980s. Newspapers, however, traditionally endorse political candidates and advocate policy viewpoints and political causes. Although newspapers supposedly confine their advocacy to the editorial page, the publisher's bias sometimes extends to the news pages. For example, one study found that during the 1972 presidential campaign, newspapers that supported President Nixon's reelection bid gave the least coverage to the growing Watergate scandal (Bagdikian 1973).

Increasingly, newspapers are avoiding partisan endorsements and taking a more neutral pose on their editorial pages. Still, the propensity of newspapers to endorse Republican candidates over Democratic candidates on their editorial pages is readily apparent. It was no surprise, for instance, when more newspapers endorsed Dole over Clinton in 1996. However, Clinton won the endorsement war by a slim margin in 1992, a sure sign of deep dissatisfaction with the Republican incumbent, George Bush.

Two factors readily account for newspapers' proclivity for Republicanism and conservatism. First, newspaper publishers are businesspeople. Their conservative Republicanism is a natural reflection of the prevailing orthodoxy of the business community. Second, a newspaper's advertisers also represent the conservative business community. Although it has become rare for major advertisers to threaten newspapers because of their political positions, newspapers must depend on advertising as their major source of revenue.

The conservatism of newspaper publishers is balanced to some extent by the liberalism of working journalists. From a 1985 Times–Mirror survey, Table 8.1 contrasts some of the political opinions of U.S. newspaper journalists with those of the U.S. adult population. Most of the journalists surveyed identified themselves as liberal and expressed opposition to President Reagan. On most issues, the journalists' policy positions were more liberal than the general population's. The one exception is that newspaper journalists are not unusually liberal on economic issues. For instance, the 1985 Times–Mirror survey showed journalists to be more opposed than the general public to the government helping to redistribute income (Schneider and Lewis 1985).

If anything, journalists may have become even more liberal relative to the public since this 1985 survey. The Washington press corps is where stories

TABLE 8.1   VIEWS OF GENERAL PUBLIC AND JOURNALISTS ON SELECTED ISSUES

		Public	Journalist
Consider self	liberal	23%	55%
	conservative	29	17
President Reagan	favor	56	30
	oppose	27	60
Sympathize with	business	33	27
	labor	32	31
Government should reduce income inequality	favor	55	50
	oppose	23	39
CIA aid to Nicaraguan Contras	favor	19	17
	oppose	44	76
Increase defense budget	favor	38	15
	oppose	51	80
Allow women to have abortions	favor	49	82
	oppose	44	14
Prayer in public schools	favor	74	25
	oppose	19	67
Death penalty for murder	favor	75	47
	oppose	17	47

Source: William Schneider and I. A. Lewis, "Views on the News." *Public Opinion 8* (Aug./Sept. 1985): 7. Reprinted with permission of the American Enterprise Institute.

about national politics originate, and they are decidedly liberal. For instance, one survey found that in the 1992 presidential campaign, Washington reporters voted for Clinton over Bush by an overwhelming ratio of 89 to 7 (Dautrich and Dineen, 1996).

The tension between the conservatism of newspaper publishers and the liberalism of newspaper journalists is illustrated by the political values of newspaper editors—who the publishers hire to be the bosses of the working reporters. Editors are more conservative than their reporters. But they are closer to the political liberalism of the reporters below them than the political conservatism of the publishers above them. For instance, in 1984 when U.S. newspapers overwhelmingly endorsed Reagan over Mondale, most editors of editorial pages voted for Mondale (St. Dizier 1986). In the 1990s as well, editors voted more Democratic and were more liberal than not only newspaper publishers but also the general public (Dautrich and Dineen 1996).

People employed in the radio or television broadcasting of news have not had their political opinions researched as carefully as those in the print media. One frequent observation about television reporters is that they do not hold exceptionally strong political views of any kind (Epstein 1974, 3210–11). However, at the top reaches of television news—at the network level—both news reporters and managers tend to be more liberal than conservative, just like newspeople at the top levels of print journalism (Johnstone et al. 1976; Lichter and Rothman 1979).

Although some conservatives claim otherwise, there is no reason to believe in any sort of media conspiracy to promote liberal political doctrines. The reason why news employees show a liberal political tendency is not that conservative aspirants are pushed aside for their political views. To some extent, the political liberalism of journalists, especially outside the economic realm, simply reflects the "yuppie" values of young urban college-educated professionals—the class from which journalists are drawn. Another factor may be that journalism holds a special career attraction for people with liberal personality traits, much like a military career (for example) attracts conservative personalities.

In any event, a possible liberal "bias" to the preferences of newspeople would seriously matter only if the bias were to affect news content. In the newspaper industry, both the norms of objectivity and publishers' natural conservatism seem sufficient safeguard. In broadcasting, the norms of objectivity combine with the conservatism of station owners and network managers for the same purpose. When asked its views on the matter, the general public sees little bias. For instance, when a March 1993 survey in the *Los Angeles Times* asked the general public about possible media bias, 34 percent saw their favorite newspaper as liberal and 28 percent saw it as conservative. Television news was seen more liberal: 40 percent said network news was "liberal," while 19 percent said it was conservative. People see little partisan bias to the way the media cover presidential races. For instance, in 1996 a majority (53 percent) said their was no bias, while 20 percent saw the media as biased for the Democrats and 14 percent as biased for the Republicans (Pew Research Center 1999).

Academic studies of network news coverage of presidential campaigns show that the networks attempt to achieve balance. Networks devote roughly equal time to both major party candidates and show no obvious favoritism on policy issues. However, to be covered is not always to be covered favorably; television reporters tend toward a negative spin to whichever candidate they cover. Television news also devotes up to a third of its coverage to horserace issues; the repeated message that a candidacy is behind in the polls can be a signal that the candidate is performing poorly (Clancy and Robinson 1985a, 1985b). Newspapers also make an effort to appear fair in their coverage and certainly are more objective than they once were in the heyday of the partisan press. One particularly thorough statistical analysis of the 1996 campaign concluded that the media collectively presented an unbiased stream of information about the Dole and Clinton candidacies (Domke et al. 1998).

If there is bias to be found, it may be the media's disinclination to challenge a popular president. Most observers of the Reagan presidency saw the American media as going relatively easy on the "Teflon" president, at least before the Iran-Contra scandal. The American public saw it this way too. In the 1985 Times-Mirror public sample, 30 percent saw the media as making Reagan look better than he was, while only 18 percent saw the media as making Reagan look worse than he was. The same respondents saw the media as treating the previous president, Jimmy Carter, quite harshly: 46 percent as worse than he was and only 6 percent as better than he was (Schneider and Lewis 1985, 11). More recently, 71 percent of respondents in a Times-Mirror Survey in 1992 found press treatment of then President Bush as "fair," even as he was the subject of negative stories about the economy. In 1993, as Clinton was having his troubles with unfavorable stories, a lesser 51 percent of Times-Mirror respondents saw press treatment of Clinton as "fair."

Because they must appeal to wide audiences, the managers of the mass media are far more interested in upholding their reputations for objectivity and offending the least number of people than in promoting political doctrines. Thus newspapers and television news programs rarely give serious attention to points of view that are known to be unpopular. The true "bias" of the mass media may be to reinforce those political values on which almost all Americans agree and to restrict the range of political debate to positions close to the political center.

Consensus on the News?

At least in theory, the news media have considerable discretion when deciding which events are newsworthy and which ones are not. Newspeople see themselves as exercising this discretion professionally and responsibly. When challenged as to why a particular story is included as news while another receives no coverage, the typical journalist will claim that the news media merely mirror what happens in society; that one story was newsworthy and the other not; and that newspeople themselves have little or no role in choosing what is news (Epstein 1974, 11–25). In practice, news selection often follows a hierarchical pattern, with journalists following the cues of others. For instance, network news programs and CNN often follow the lead of the day's front page of the major newspapers—the *New York Times, Washington Post,* and *Los Angeles Times.* National wire services (most notably the Associated Press) add to the uniformity of the news from different sources. Local newspapers and local newscasts have the major national or international news suggested to them-from the wire services or the network feeds.

Media managers and editors possess the power to act as "gatekeepers"—deciding which news to report. But when competing gatekeepers seek the same audience, they tend to make similar choices—so much so that competing news sources have been labeled "rivals in conformity" (Bigman 1948). Still, despite the inevitable similarity of the major stories reported, news managers and editors enjoy considerable discretion regarding lesser stories and features. For instance, Epstein (1974, 38) found that of 431 news stories presented in the network news over a six-week period, only 57 were reported by all three networks.

Luttbeg (1983) examined the news stories in 75 randomly selected daily newspapers and in 10 "select" or prestige newspapers, on seven scattered days in 1980 and 1981, representing one "composite week." Table 8.2 shows the stories that were most frequently reported in the first three pages of these newspapers. The striking feature is that even these top stories did not get universally reported. These 11 stories were the only ones that appeared in at least half of the sampled newspapers for the seven days examined. For the top five stories of each day, the 75 newspapers' average rate of coverage in the first three pages was only 41 percent. The average rate for the prestige papers was only slightly greater, 51 percent. For the three network newscasts, the average was 52 percent. These results suggest that the casual news consumer who relies on but one news source may miss about half of the day's five major news stories. To the extent that there exists consensus on the news, it exists in thousands of local variations. And to the extent that print media shape public opinion, the opinion in one community must differ from that in another.

8-2 MASS MEDIA INFLUENCE ON PUBLIC OPINION

The first attempts to examine empirically the political influence of the mass media were the early studies of voting behavior: panel studies of voters in Erie County, Ohio, in 1940 and voters in Elmira, New York, in 1948 (Lazarsfeld et al. 1948; Berelson et al. 1954). These early studies presented a viewpoint regarding the influence of the media that has since become known as the "minimal-effects" model of media influence. Perhaps because the researchers for these projects moved into voting research from market research, they expected to find campaign messages in the mass media (at that time, essentially newspapers and radio) to be quite influential on individual voters. They envisioned voters waffling in their choice of candidates somewhat in the way a

TABLE 8.2   TOP NATIONAL AND INTERNATIONAL
STORIES COVERED BY MORE THAN HALF OF THE
NEWSPAPERS, FOR SEVEN DAYS IN 1980 AND 1981

		Percentage of Papers Covering	
Story	Date	Sample Papers	Select Papers
Bush chosen Reagan's running mate	7/17/80	91	100
Polish strikes gain government support	8/24/80	68	88
OPEC increases prices again	5/26/81	67	71
Carter and Reagan set debate date	10/20/80	65	88
Plane crashes in Loveland, Colorado	4/18/81	65	67
Reagan vows no troops to El Salvador	3/4/81	63	63
Twenty-eighth Atlanta victim	5/26/81	61	14
Iraq-Iran war; Abadan cut off	10/20/80	58	63
Reagan lifts Soviet grain embargo	4/24/81	58	75
CORE reveals Atlanta suspect	4/24/81	54	38
Report on aborted Iranian hostage raid	8/24/80	54	63

Source: Norman R. Luttbeg, "News Consensus: Do U.S. Newspapers Mirror Society's Happening?" *Journalism Quarterly 60* (Autumn 1983): 486.

consumer might change his or her choice of toothpaste from purchase to purchase, depending on the effectiveness of the latest advertising.

These early researchers on presidential choice, however, made three discoveries that seemed to dismiss that mass media's influence. First, they discovered the anchor of partisanship. A substantial number of citizens interviewed as early as May of election year had already made up their minds how they were going to vote in November. This suggests that most voters had a "product loyalty" to one or the other of the two major political parties. Second, they discovered perceptual screening. To maintain their product loyalty, voters paid particular attention to the messages for the candidate whom they preferred. And they avoided exposure to campaign messages for the opposition, even misperceiving these messages when exposure was unavoidable. Third, they discovered the importance of personal conversations. When someone was about to change his or her viewpoint due to a persuasive message in the media, that person would often return to the original opinion after talking to others who shared that original opinion.

For these reasons, the messages on the mass media are less influential than they might appear. Because people's political views are anchored by their past beliefs, perceptual screening, and interpersonal communications, it is not likely that any particular revelation in the evening news will create massive changes in people's political likes and dislikes. Two interesting examples are the responses to President Reagan's Iran-Contra scandal in 1986 and 1987 and President Clinton's Monicagate in 1998 and 1999.

In late 1986, the American public was first shocked to learn that President Reagan was selling arms to Iran and then shocked again to learn that one purpose was to illegally fund the Contras in Nicaragua. The national media gave this scandal the coverage and the treatment usually reserved for a constitutional crisis on the order of Watergate. Yet there was no dramatic reversal in public opinion. In one month, popular approval of Reagan's performance dropped about 20 percentage points, which perhaps defines the outer limit of how quickly public opinion can respond in the short run. Twenty percentage points is the greatest one-month drop in presidential approval ever recorded. Yet it may seem like not very much at all.

The 1998 Lewinsky scandal surpassed the Iran–Contra scandal in shock value. Within days of the first revelations, pundits were discussing whether the president would be or should be impeached. The news being reported appeared disastrous for the president at a time when Clinton was basking in the glow of a record level of popularity for a president so late in his presidency. Given the new revelations involving sex, lies, and audiotape, most political experts were sure that Clinton's standing with the public would plunge like a rock. Instead, it rose. In fact, over the first week of the scandal, Clinton's approval rose 10 points (Zaller 1998), close to a record for short-term presidential gain in approval. What occured was a seeming disconnection between the negative media stories and the public's evaluation of the president—a development that is far from fully understood (Zaller 1998; Owen 2000; Fischle 2000; Just and Crigler 2000). What is clear though is that one cannot count on public opinion to flow automatically in the direction of the news. People judged the facts of the Lewinsky case in a way that allowed them to support the president in spite of negative facts and speculation in the media.

The Iran–Contra and Lewinsky examples illustrate the obvious limits of the media's power. Consistent with the minimal-effects interpretation of media influence, shifts in public evaluations are modest at best in response to one-sided news stories, and sometimes not even in the expected direction. Still, many mass media researchers today downplay the minimal-effects interpretation as misleading or even wrong. This is not to say that contemporary researchers see people as the helpless victims of their most recent exposure to the mass media. Instead, they search for modest influences on political beliefs (e.g., see Bartels 1993; Finkel 1993). Moreover, there is a recognition that the net influence of the mass media so often seems to be slight because it represents a balance among conflicting points of view (Zaller 1996). If the media messages were truly one-sided, like the flow of propaganda in a nondemocratic regime, their cumulative impact would be major. In this section, we explore some evidence of media effects on political attitudes.

Mass Media and Political Learning

During the Iran–Contra hearings in the summer of 1987, polls showed surprisingly strong interest in the testimony of Lieutenant Colonel Oliver North and others who testified before the special Senate-House committee. In fact, a surprising 71 percent reported that they watched or listened to some part of the live coverage of Oliver North's testimony (CBS News/*New York Times* poll, 9 July 1987). But the breadth of public comprehension was limited. For instance, one week further into the Iran-Contra hearings, only 33 percent of Americans could place Nicaragua in Central America (CBS News/*New York Times* poll, 16 July 1987).

This ignorance about the location of a key nation in the drama should not be a great surprise. But it also highlights an interesting puzzle. As we saw in Chapter 3, people generally are not very informed about political matters. Yet people regularly are exposed to political information in the mass media. As we know, people do read newspapers and watch television network news. How can understanding of public affairs be so low, given the information available?

News Comprehension John Robinson and Mark Levy (1986, 87–106) asked people in a national sample whether they read or heard about each of a series of news stories that were prominently featured during the previous week. The researchers staggered interviews over four separate weekends in June 1983. Table 8.3 shows the proportions who recalled the various stories. As often noted, people readily learn stories with a strong human interest element. Thus Robinson and Levy's respondents were almost universally aware of flooding in Utah and a (successful) space shuttle flight. People are only slightly less likely

---

TABLE 8.3   PROPORTIONS OF RESPONDENTS AWARE OF SELECTED NEWS ITEMS FROM PREVIOUS WEEK, 1983

	Percentage Aware
Paul Volcker reappointed head of Federal Reserve Board	28
Change in State Department officials	30
Supreme Court ruling on legislative veto	40
Developments at Geneva arms talks	42
"Stolen" debate briefing books	53
Western economic summit	67
Elections in Great Britain	67
Pope's trip to Poland	80
Disease called AIDS	80
Americans killed in El Salvador	85
Floods in Utah	89
Space shuttle flight	94

Source: John P. Robinson and Mark R. Levy. *The Main Source: Learning from Television News* (Beverly Hills, CA: Sage, 1986), p. 91. Copyright © 1986 by Sage Publications, Inc. Reprinted by permission of Sage Publications, Inc.

to retain information about political stories highlighted in the news, but only if they involve uncomplicated or ceremonial types of events. Thus, about two-thirds of Robinson and Levy's respondents could recall reading or hearing about the recent British elections and the Pope's trip to Poland. The stories that people most readily avoid are the more complicated stories about government or politics. Thus less than half of Robinson and Levy's respondents were able to recall the recent reappointment of Paul Volcker as chairman of the Federal Reserve Board or the recent Supreme Court decision restricting Congress's use of the legislative veto.

Processing the News Doris Graber (1988) tried a unique approach to understanding how people learn from the mass media. She conducted several in-depth interviews with a small sample of 21 residents of Evanston, Illinois, during the 1976 election year. As expected, she found that the respondents who were the most intelligent and the most experienced in political matters were most able to comprehend complex stories and to remember earlier stories from the media. Graber's respondents tuned out much of the flood of available media information. For instance, they ignored two-thirds of the available newspaper stories. Of those stories that caught their attention, 43 percent concerned government or politics. When asked to recall a set of important news stories that were at least a month old, respondents could recall only 23 percent of them with sufficient detail to give four or more statements of fact or opinion about them (Graber 1988, 81–89). Graber interpreted these findings optimistically, concluding that people know how to handle information overload. They are perhaps most concerned with their own interests and pleasures, but they also display a moderate willingness to perform their civic duties. People discard much of the "chaff" from news stories while still assimilating the crucial essentials (Graber 1988, 97).

Graber theorizes that respondents notice and evaluate new information by applying their particular "schemas," or prior set of beliefs. For instance, many respondents discounted statements by politicians because they applied a schema that categorized politicians as publicity seekers. Similar to what the minimal-effects model suggests, people minimize the impact of the mass media on their political beliefs by applying their schemas to news stories.

The News Source and Comprehension It is often debated whether newspapers or television informs people more about public affairs. When people are surveyed on the subject, most claim to get more of their news from television than from newspapers, and the trend is increasing. Table 8.4 shows one example of this survey evidence. During the 1996 presidential campaign, people generally reported that they watched news on television more regularly than they read the newspapers. People also claimed to pay more attention to the presidential campaign on television than in the newspapers.

On the other hand, recent evidence suggests that tables like Table 8.4 exaggerate people's reliance on television for their news (Robinson and Levy 1986, 231–41; Robinson and Levy, 1996). People pay different degrees of attention to the broadcast and the print media. Watching television news or

TABLE 8.4   MEDIA USAGE IN 1996 PRESIDENTIAL CAMPAIGN

National TV News				Daily Newspaper			
Days Watched During Week		Attention to Campaign News		Days Read During Week		Attention to Campaign News	
None	21%	None, very little	35%	None	25%	None, very little	60%
1–6	49	Some, quite a bit	52	1–6	44	Some, quite a bit	33
7 days	30	A good deal	13	7 days	31	A good deal	86

Source: National Election Studies, 1996 election data.

listening to radio news is the most passive form of attention. Indeed, the set may be on, but without concentration from the viewer or listener. One important early research project set up cameras in people's homes to observe the occupants' attention to television sets that were turned on. The researchers discovered that only about half the time that the news was on was anybody watching (Bechtel et al. 1972). (Only commercials got less attention!) Reading a newspaper or a magazine requires more active concentration. Also, the print media provides a greater depth of information and allows citizens to absorb information at their own pace. If the entire transcript of a half-hour network news broadcast were set in print, it would take no more space than the front page of a daily newspaper.

Repeated studies provide evidence that reading newspapers makes one more informed than does watching television news. For instance, when Graber's 21 respondents were able to recall certain stories from the news, they were much more likely to report newspapers to be the source than television (Graber 1988, 85). Similarly, when Robinson and Levy (1986, 96–103) conducted a multivariate statistical analysis of news comprehension, they found that newspaper reading (and newsmagazine reading) had a far greater impact on news comprehension than did viewing television news.

Still, the power of television to engage the viewer should not be underestimated. Neuman et al. (1991) conducted an experiment in which they presented (roughly) the same information to volunteers either in a real newspaper story or in a real television news report. Their before-after comparisons of political information suggested that on balance, people retain just as much if not more of the basic facts of an issue (such as apartheid in South Africa or the AIDS epidemic) when the information is obtained watching the network news as they do from reading a newspaper account. While the content of television news may ordinarily lack the depth and context of detailed newspaper accounts, presenting information with pictures by itself does not lessen learning.

Media Messages and Policy Preferences

In an ambitious study, Page et al. (1987) tried to estimate the influence of television reports on the content of public opinion. They collected 80 instances from the late 1960s into the early 1980s where the same survey question about an important question of public policy was administered to national samples over a period of years. Page and his colleagues then attempted to see whether television content between the two surveys could account for the observed change. This exercise involved extensive monitoring and coding for more than a decade's worth of network news programs.

On the average, Page et al. discovered that opinion did not change much in the short run of even a few years. But when change occurred, the direction tended to be consistent with the preponderant direction of the messages on network news. The authors examined the impact of many different sources of information on network news (e.g., presidents, the opposition party, interest groups). The source that best predicted opinion change was television commentary—from anchorpersons, reporters in the field, or special commentators. According to the estimates, each viewpoint presented in a commentary could bring about as much as 4 percentage points of opinion change. But Page et al. are cautious when interpreting why television commentary predicts opinion change. They do not claim that individual newscasters are themselves the major source of opinion change. Rather, their message frequently overlaps or reinforces the dominant elite message that filters through the public via the media. Or news commentators and others with whom they agree may be perceived as simply reflecting an agreed-upon consensus which may strongly influence the formation of citizen opinions (Page et al. 1987, 35).

In other words, when the messages on television news seem to advocate a particular change of policy, it is a good bet that public opinion will change modestly in the same direction. But instead of television messages causing the opinion change, another possibility could be that both television messages and public opinion are responding to some other source of influence.

Agenda Setting

The potential influence of the mass media on political thinking is not limited to influence on policy preferences. In addition, the mass media can set the agenda, or determine the public's choices regarding which policy questions are important. A small study of the 1968 presidential election conducted by McCombs and Shaw (1972) is the precursor to a growing body of research on "agenda setting." McCombs and Shaw asked their survey respondents to name the "main things . . . government should concentrate on doing something about." The issues named turned out to be the same issues stressed in newspaper and television coverage of the campaign. McCombs and Shaw argued that this relationship is more than a sharing of concern by the public and the media decision-makers, since the public, they argued, obtains its information from the media. They suggest that the media set the political agenda for the public.

By this argument, the media do not so much influence what people think as what they think about.

Although there has been much follow-up research on the effectiveness of the media in setting the public agenda, the first reports did not lend themselves to easy generalizations (McCombs 1981; O'Keefe and Atwood 1981). Some recent analyses, however, show clear evidence of media agenda setting, either from statistically analyzing actual changes in the public agenda or from observing perceptions when the media agenda is changed experimentally. Let us take a brief look at this evidence.

Changes in the Agenda over Time   For years, the Gallup Poll has asked Americans: "What is the most important problem facing the country today?" Changes in the national response to this question provide a crude but serviceable indicator of changes in national concerns. Historically, responses have centered on foreign policy and economic concerns. Foreign policy has dominated since the first readings in the 1940s, although various economic problems stood in first place for much of the 1950s and 1960s. Only civil rights, peaking in 1964 with 20 percent concerned, and issues of social control, peaking with 25 percent in 1973, have rivaled foreign policy and the economy as the focus of public concern (Smith 1985).

Looking for evidence of agenda setting, Michael MacKuen (1981) conducted an elaborate statistical analysis of national responses to the "most important problem" question over a 15-year period (1962–1977). Mackuen found that, for most issues, public concern tracked media attention, as measured by the level of reporting of the issue in the newsmagazines. For some issues, MacKuen found the public's level of concern responding more to media concern than to the objective circumstances. For instance, media attention to crime predicted public concern about crime better than did the actual crime rate. Similarly, media attention to the war in Vietnam predicted public concern about the war better than did American troop levels (MacKuen 1981, 84–88).

Experimentally Manipulating the Agenda   Ideally, the best way to ascertain the degree to which the mass media can influence the agenda would be by experimentally manipulating what people read or watch. We could imagine, for example, that we could change the content of network news programs and then observe how people react. Iyengar and Kinder (1987; see also Iyengar et al. 1982) did exactly that in their experiments with the network news. Iyengar and his colleagues paid some ordinary citizens to participate in their studies of television viewing. Subjects were divided into different groups to watch the previous evening's network news together for six consecutive days. Unknown to the subjects, each group saw a different altered version. One such experiment went as follows. For one group, a news story about defense preparedness was edited into each news program. For a second group, a news story about pollution was inserted. For the third group, an inflation story was inserted. Thus, each group got a week-long dose of messages concerning one particular problem.

Reportedly, none of the subjects suspected that they were viewing edited versions of the news. The most interesting results from the study were the responses to the "most important problem" question before and after the experiment. Those given pollution stories and those given defense stories registered significantly abnormal increases in concern about pollution and defense, respectively. The inflation group did not change much, apparently because they already expressed a strong concern about inflation in their initial questionnaires prior to the experiment and could hardly increase the level of their response. Further analysis suggested that the subjects in each group began to evaluate President Carter according to how they saw Carter's handling of their manipulated topic. Iyengar and his colleagues show not only that the content of the media can influence the agenda, but that the choice of issues for the agenda can influence people's evaluation of the president.

Sophistication and Agenda Manipulation An interesting question is how political sophistication is related to agenda setting. Illustrating that this question has not been fully settled, MacKuen (1981) and Iyengar et al. (1982) give different answers. Iyengar et al. report that their least sophisticated respondents were the most responsive to experimental manipulation of the agenda. This seems reasonable, since less sophisticated people lack the stored information that helps to discount propaganda in the media. However, the less sophisticated subjects were shown news programs under artificial conditions. Would they have been as attentive and persuaded in a natural setting? MacKuen (1984) finds the least sophisticated respondents to be the most immune to actual changes in the media's agenda. Evidently the most sophisticated are easiest for the media to lead, because only the sophisticated ordinarily pay enough attention.

The evidence that citizens respond to the media's agenda serves as a reminder that people are dependent on the information they receive. But media influence on what we think to be important implies nothing about the motives of the people who set the media's agenda. Media decision-makers often select stories for our attention because they view these stories to be what the public wants or in the public's interest. To a considerable degree, objective circumstances drive the media agenda. For instance, news media feed us the most stories about inflation when the inflation rate is highest (Behr and Iyengar 1985). But to a considerable extent, the media's choices for the public agenda may simply reflect the voices of those who clamor to be heard. Government officials, and the president in particular, exert a strong influence on the media's political agenda. Particularly at the local level, officials sometimes avoid making decisions the public would favor by keeping them off the agenda (Berkman and Kitch 1986, 175-310; Graber 1997).

The Media as Cue-Givers

Certain political contests are sufficiently ambiguous in their interpretation that the news media take upon themselves the role of referee, to tell us who won. Election outcomes are an obvious case. Although we ordinarily do not need media pundits to tell us which candidate garners the most votes, media commentary may help us decide if the election winner achieved a "landslide" or earned a policy mandate. For midterm elections, where the summary outcome is the percentages of Senate and House seats and governorships won by the Republicans and the Democrats, the media help determine which party performed better than expected. Media interpretation is particularly intrusive in presidential primary elections, where the key issue generally is not the number of delegates the candidates win in the particular state, but momentum: which candidates are gaining and which are faltering, and who "really" won by surpassing expectations.

Presidential debates provide a subtle setting for media cue-giving. Although research shows that presidential debates foster considerable learning about the candidates and where they stand on issues, these debates change the minds of surprisingly few voters. Many voters watch presidential debates as rooting partisans, cheering on their favorite candidate. Naturally, they want to know who "won." The mass media transmit the consensus verdict of the debate outcome.

The 1976 and 1984 presidential debates provided vivid illustrations of how postdebate media messages can alter perceptions of the outcome. The second 1976 Ford-Carter debate contained President Ford's famous "Poland gaffe." Attempting to make the point that Poland was a sovereign nation, Ford startled knowledgeable observers by stating that Poland was not dominated by the Soviet Union. Research on audiences that were watching confirm, however, that most viewers did not give the remark much attention or attribute to it much importance (Steeper 1978). Polls conducted immediately after the debate suggested no consensus regarding who won. But over the next few days, as the media highlighted the message of Ford's gaffe, polls began to show a clear consensus that Ford had lost.[1]

The 1984 example was similar. In the first 1984 debate, President Reagan gave such a faltering performance that it raised new questions about whether his advanced age had weakened his ability. Yet the verdict was close in the polls on the night of the debate, with Mondale "winning" by only 1 to 9 percentage points. The media declared Mondale the winner, however, and even began to report openly about whether Reagan was too old. One night after the debate, the ABC News/*Washington Post* poll found the public seeing Mondale was the winner by a lopsided 55 to 19 margin. Still one night later, the *New York Times*/CBS News poll respondents saw Mondale the winner by an even bigger 66 to 17 margin (Sussman 1984). This was a dramatic turnabout in public perceptions, fueled by cues from the mass media plus public discussions. To complete the story, Reagan and Mondale debated again two weeks after the first debate. Reagan cracked a joke about his age and in general improved his performance. Media commentators immediately declared him back on track. Two weeks later, Reagan was reelected handily.

Newspaper Endorsements and the Vote

Does a newspaper's editorial stance influence the political opinions of its readers? Newspaper endorsements are often thought to be particularly crucial at the local level. Especially when the election is nonpartisan or involves an extremely long ballot, the newspaper's decision regarding what to report or whom to endorse can be very important. As one newsperson reportedly once said, "You can't tell the players without a scorecard, and we sell the scorecards" (Banfield and Wilson 1963, 159). Newspapers achieve excellent success in endorsing local candidates who win. But this can be partially attributed to newspapers' endorsements of candidates who look like winners rather than to any influence of the newspaper on the electoral decision. At the local level, the effect of newspaper endorsement has been studied mainly for elections with lengthy ballots where voters are asked to select more candidates than they can possibly know anything about. For this particular type of election, where voter confusion is at its maximum, studies suggest that newspaper support is the key to victory (Mueller 1970b; Hooper 1969).

Some studies have examined national election data in an attempt to relate people's voting decisions to the endorsements of the newspapers they read. Even with statistical controls for party identification and other relevant variables, these studies show a fair-sized relationship between endorsements and votes, at the presidential, gubernatorial, and senatorial levels (Robinson 1974; Coombs 1981). These studies, however, present some difficulty for the making of causal inference. When survey respondents have a choice of newspaper, they may select the newspaper that represents their partisan views. Thus any relationship between the endorsement decision of the respondent's favorite newspaper and the respondent's own voting decision could be the result of the respondent's newspaper selection rather than the newspaper's influence.

Another reason why it is difficult to research endorsement influence is that, as we saw earlier in this chapter, newspapers almost always endorse Republican candidates. This makes it difficult to match voters who read Republican newspapers with those who read Democratic newspapers. But one exception to the Republican endorsement habits of American newspapers provided a unique opportunity to study endorsement effects. In the 1964 presidential election, more newspapers endorsed President Lyndon Johnson (42 percent) than his Republican opponent, Barry Goldwater (35 percent). With this relatively even division, Erikson (1976b, 207–34) was able to compare the vote in communities where the local newspaper(s) endorsed the Democrat with the vote in communities where the local newspaper(s) endorsed the Republican. Statistical controls were imposed for the community's previous vote, the particular state, and the size of the city. Even with these controls, the 1960–1964 vote shift was about 5 percentage points more Democratic where the endorsements were Democratic than where they were Republican.

Presidential Manipulation and the Mass Media

Of all public officials, only the president can command the time on television to present his case to the people. One change that television has brought about is the greater ease with which American presidents can communicate directly with the American people. Each modern president has used the television forum to promote public support for his policy initiatives. Their success, however, has been mixed. Recall the study of television impact by Page et al.

(1987). They found that television newscasts' presentations of presidential policy preferences are followed by only modest movement of public opinion. However, they also found the public response to be greater at times when the president enjoys high popularity.

On domestic policy, polls show only one clear instance of a presidential initiative gaining popular support. This instance was President Lyndon Johnson's leadership of public opinion in support of the civil rights bill of 1964 that guaranteed equal access for all races to public accommodations such as hotels and restaurants. Between June 1963 (during Kennedy's administration) and January 1964, public support for the proposed law rose from a slim plurality (49 to 42 percent) to a commanding majority of 61 to 31 percent.[2] This is a shift far greater than would normally occur on a controversial issue over a 7-month period.

The limits of presidential influence over public opinion on domestic issues are illustrated by President Clinton's experience with health care. Upon taking office in 1993, Clinton's boldest policy initiative was to devise and pass a national health care plan that would provide national health insurance for all citiziens. Polls showed the public favorably disposed, and the president gave a major speech on the subject which was favorably received and favorably reviewed. Moreover, the Clinton administration was committed to the education and mobilization of public opinion as the way to achieve congressional passage (Jacobs and Shapiro 2000). But the effort failed. Opponents of Clinton's plan led a major media campaign in opposition, feeding on fears and uncertainty about a new major government initiative. By mid-1994 the tide of public opinion had turned against the president's plan, making it "dead on arrival" before Congress. (See Chapter 4 for detailed opinion trends.)

On foreign policy, however, presidents can be quite persuasive with public opinion. Perhaps the clearest case is the response to President Reagan's justification to the nation for the invasion of the Caribbean island nation of Grenada in 1983. Immediately following the invasion but before the president spoke to the nation, only 53 percent approved of the invasion. Immediately after President Reagan addressed the nation, however, approval shot up to 64 percent.[3] The most lasting impact of Grenada was on the public's evaluation of Reagan's job performance. Before the invasion, Reagan's approval ratings had been in the doldrums, comparable to Jimmy Carter's at his equivalent point in the presidential term. After the invasion, Reagan's ratings began a long climb upward.

When a foreign policy crisis unfolds, the media focus uncritically on the president as the national spokesman. In what has been labeled the "rally-round-the-flag" effect, presidents make short-term gains in public favor whenever they deal with a foreign policy crisis (Mueller 1970a, 29). In terms of the Gallup approval rating, Truman gained 9 points when he decided to resist the 1950 Communist invasion of South Korea; Eisenhower gained 8 points following the 1956 Suez crisis; and Kennedy gained 13 points following the 1962 Cuban missile crisis. More recent examples are boosts in popularity for Johnson after the Dominican Republic invasion (1965), for Nixon after the Cambodian invasion (1970), for Ford after the *Mayaguez* incident (1975), for Carter after the Camp David summit (1978), and for Reagan after the invasion of Grenada.

Bush's successful handling of the short Gulf War with Iraq in early 1991 provides one of the most impressive examples of a "rally effect." Between January and March of 1991, Bush's approval rating soared from a respectable but middling 55 percent to the unheard-of heights of 87 percent. As with all rallies, however, this one was short-lived. As the national economy skidded during 1991 and 1992, Bush's approval level dropped into the danger zone below 50 percent. In an event totally unanticipated in early 1991, Bush lost his 1992 reelection bid.

Even crises that reflect badly on the president normally produce surges in presidential popularity. Eisenhower gained following the U-2 incident and summit collapse of 1960, as did Kennedy after the disastrous Bay of Pigs invasion of 1961. Until Bush's Gulf War success, the strongest short-term gain in the history of Gallup's approval ratings was Carter's 19-point gain in November 1979 following Iran's seizure of American hostages.

The reason for the rally around the president in times of crisis is often interpreted as a sort of unthinking frenzy of patriotism where citizens choose to support the leader without considering whether the leader is right or wrong. This imagery may be too simplistic. Arguing a different scenario, Richard Brody (1991) claims that people support their president in times of crisis because that is their rational option given the one-sided nature of the information presented to them. In a time of crisis, the president has peoples' attention and controls the available information. Rival political elites potentially could create some news by criticizing the president, but in typical rally circumstances, their political interest is to keep quiet except to be supportive. With little in the news that contradicts the president, the flow of news is one-sided. Lacking an alternative frame of reference, citizens support the president.

On the other hand, a crisis that becomes prolonged to the point where rival politicians begin to criticize can bring a president nothing but woe. Jimmy Carter may have benefited in the short run from a hostage crisis, but his failure to solve the crisis contributed to his defeat in 1980. Lyndon Johnson's failure to end the Vietnam War provides another example. Early in Johnson's presidency, public opinion supported both Johnson and the war effort. But the Johnson administration tragically miscalculated the extent to which a reasonably popular president could maintain support for an unwinnable land war in Asia.

Ronald Reagan's Iran–Contra scandal is an example of a foreign policy crisis that for obvious reasons caused the president's popularity to fall rather than rise. As the revelations about Iran-Contra emerged in the news media, Reagan's popularity plummeted 20 points. The uncritical media attention usually offered a president in a crisis was naturally absent as the Iran-Contra story unfolded, with its revelations of arms sales to Iran and proceeds used for illegal military aid to the Contras in Nicararagua (Brody and Shapiro 1989; Hurwitz et al. 1989; Krosnick and Kinder 1990).

Minimal Effects

In one sense the minimal-effects model of media influence is correct. People rarely make major changes in their political attitudes as a result of messages in the mass media. Researchers instead uncover more modest effects. People attend to the media with considerable selectivity, processing new information into previous mental cubbyholes. Media messages can influence opinions in several ways, but the effects are generally modest.

8-3 TELEVISION AND ELECTION CAMPAIGNS

One important political change of the past half century is the way television has altered the conduct of political campaigns. Television has allowed political candidates to campaign directly to the American people. But not all the effects of televised campaigns may be desirable. Televised campaigns bring about the potential for candidates' electoral success to be determined by their mastery of the more superficial aspects of television campaigning, or even simply their ability to raise money for television advertisements.

Television and Presidential Elections

The 1952 presidential campaign was the first campaign of the television era. The nature of that campaign has nurtured some modern myths—maybe true, maybe not—about television's impact on presidential election politics. Eisenhower's ease in front of the television camera helped him develop the image of a warmhearted but stern former military commander. Moreover, Eisenhower's campaign relied heavily on television advertising under the direction of Madison Avenue's Rosser Reeves. Pushing the slogan that Americans "like Ike," Reeve's advertising strategy marked the beginning of modern television campaigning, which would only become more sophisticated as the years progressed.[4]

Meanwhile, "Ike's" opponent, Governor Adlai Stevenson of Illinois, also contributed to the mythology of television's dominance in modern campaigning. Like Eisenhower, Stevenson had an enthusiastic core of supporters and generally was viewed favorably by the American public. But he suffered from one important handicap. Stevenson did not like television and resisted his advisors' attempts to exploit its potential. (Stevenson reportedly did not even own a television set at the time.) While Ike smiled before the cameras and made the first effective use of spot television ads, Stevenson conducted an old-fashioned campaign, directing carefully crafted speeches to small audiences. Stevenson's campaign committee did pay to have a few of his speeches televised nationally. But as is now generally recognized, simply letting the live cameras roll at a campaign rally is not an effective use of advertising on television.[5]

Ultimately we cannot know how much television contributed to the 1952 presidential outcome. We do know, however, that the *belief* is widespread that the candidates' ability to exploit television, along with their media advisors' cleverness, determines the success of presidential candidates. Election results continue to feed myths about the power of television. The electoral success of Ronald Reagan provides the best example. And if television explains success, it can also rationalize failure. Walter Mondale, the Democrats' unsuccessful presidential candidate in 1984, explained his failure with the observation that, unlike

Reagan, "he had never warmed up to television." Following Dukakis's defeat in 1988, many Democrats found their candidate's inept campaign to be a convenient scapegoat. Then, with Clinton's election in 1992 and 1996, it was the Republicans' turn to regret the imputed candidate advantage in television style, attributing their loss to Clinton's exceptional mastery of television.

Whether valid or not, political campaign managers share some common perceptions of how to conduct a successful campaign. Campaign directors set up campaign rallies and appearances as media events. The immediate audience in physical attendance is less important than the millions of television viewers who may see a snippet of the event reported on their sets at home. Therefore, campaign advisors try to find the right hook for the day's events that might capture the attention of television journalists. Too many events or too many different themes endanger the campaign's control of the television agenda. And the candidate should not be too accessible to reporters, for he or she might say something newsworthy that will become the unintentional story on the evening news.

One frequent complaint against television news coverage of campaigns is television's emphasis on the visual aspect of campaigns at the expense of the more cerebral. Television is a poor medium for the flow of ideas in campaigns. Campaign messages can be presented only briefly on the television news. Some fear that as a consequence, complicated ideas lose out to cheap slogans. One might think that by covering campaign events, television news would present significant portions of candidate speeches directly to the viewer. Instead, television presents candidates talking in small "sound bites." Back in the 1968 presidential campaign, the typical network news sound bite was one full minute. By 1988, the average sound bite lasted only nine seconds (Hallin 1992). In 1992, network news executives vowed to reform, but by most accounts, network coverage of the 1992 campaign was a slim improvement over the recent past.

If television news does not present candidate speeches, what does it actually show when it reports on political campaigns? Unfortunately, television reporters rarely intervene to inform their audiences about the policy issues that separate rival candidates. Instead they emphasize campaign hoopla—the "horse race," superficial campaign events, and campaign personalities (Graber 1997; Paterson 1993). According to the count by the Center for Media and Public Affairs, only 43 percent of the general election campaign stories on the networks dealt with policy issues in 1996, an increase of 3 percentage points over 1992 (Stanley and Niemi 2000). The deemphasis of policy issues is not solely the fault of the television medium, however. When newspapers report on a campaign, they show the same tendency.[6] Reporting on the horse race or the personalities involved may be easier than reporting on the policy issues. It produces less controversy and more audience interest.

Television and Presidential Primaries

Television coverage has not only altered the conduct of general elections but also has contributed to the way that political parties nominate their candidates.

Earlier in this century, primary elections were not particularly important. Candidates were often chosen by party conventions or party caucuses, which left most voters out of the decision-making. Even in instances when candidates were chosen in party primaries, party leaders could usually dominate the selection. Now, the vast majority of state and local nominations are determined by primary election. And party leaders no longer dominate, since candidates can appeal directly to the primary electorate, via television.

At the presidential level, primary elections have taken on importance only recently, with television playing a major role. In 1968, the Democratic Convention resolved to "reform" the party's delegate selection process. As a result, states began to employ the presidential primary as their means of selecting national convention delegates pledged to particular candidates. Because state laws often needed to be changed, these reforms affected both the Democratic and Republican parties. With each presidential year since 1968, active campaigning for the presidential nomination began earlier in the campaign season than it had before.

Television plays a major role in this focusing of the outcome toward a single winner within each party. The first part of the primary campaign may be fought largely away from the limelight of network television, at the person-to-person level in states like New Hampshire with its early primary, or Iowa, which has a complicated caucus procedure that causes presidential candidates to woo party activists. Even when networks cover these events, they draw little nationwide attention.

The eventual verdicts of these primaries and caucuses, however, suddenly concentrate national attention upon a few front-runners. Inevitably, the national media spotlight an unexpected winner, or at least a new dark horse, in the early primary field. Two classic cases are the Gary Hart phenomenon in 1984 and the John McCain phenomenon in 2000. Hart and McCain both were surprise winners of their parties' first-in-the-nation New Hampshire primary. In each case, the candidate zoomed almost instantly from being a relatively obscure senator to becoming a household name. Via the magic of television (supplemented by major news stories and cover stories in weekly newsmagazines), Americans could look at a fresh and appealing new presidential hopeful who, only a week or two before, few could identify.

As voters learned about Hart and McCain for the first time, the news was almost all positive. For a brief period, these newcomers looked like the popular choice of their party and the strongest candidate for the general election. Then, as more news accumulated, inevitably some was unfavorable to the candidate. Hart was the candidate of "new ideas" but maybe the "new ideas" lacked substance. McCain maybe went too far in criticizing the religious right. Moreover, since both insurgents were known to be disliked by most of their parties' elders, and both were relative newcomers to the average voter, the inevitable negative information carried extra weight. Hart and McCain lost their party's nomination bids even though at the peak of their success, a different outcome might have appeared inevitable.[7]

Television News and an Informed Electorate

Earlier in this chapter we discussed evidence that television news may be less effective than newspapers as a source of political information. Studies have extended this finding to political campaigns as well. People seem to learn a lot more about the political issues of campaigns from newspapers than from television news.

In an early study of media influence, Patterson and McClure (1976) interviewed a panel of Syracuse, New York, citizens in early September and again in November of the 1972 election year. In their later interviews they asked their respondents about their media habits, particularly how often they had followed the campaign on network news and in the newspapers. In both interviews, they asked their respondents where the presidential candidates (Nixon and McGovern) stood on each of 18 national issues.

Not surprisingly, as the 1972 campaign progressed, Patterson and McClure's respondents increased their knowledge of candidate positions. The surprising aspect was that viewing television network news seemed to make little difference. Patterson and McClure report that people who claimed to be network news viewers increased their knowledge of candidate positions by 28 percent on the average. But people who claimed to *not* watch network news gained almost as much: 25 percent. Meanwhile, self-identified newspaper readers showed a 35 percent gain in information compared with a mere 18 percent gain for nonreaders. Patterson and McClure (1976, 51) bluntly interpret their result: "those individuals who faithfully tuned in network news during the election learned not much more than people who spent that time doing something else."

Using NES data, Joseph Wagner (1983) examined the effect of media reliance on voter information in the 1976 presidential contest. Wagner compared frequent readers of political news in newspapers with those who were not regular newspaper readers but did claim to "frequently" or "sometimes" watch the nightly news. Wagner found that newspaper readers were more perceptive of the policy differences between the two presidential candidates (Ford and Carter) than were those who relied only on television. Wagner found the relationship to persist even with statistical controls for respondent education and other background variables. Seemingly, then, reliance on newspapers makes one more informed about political issues than does reliance on television news.

Of course, it may not be startling to find that television informs less than newspapers. But to what extent is television more informative than nothing at all? As part of his study of the 1976 campaign, Wagner compared the television-reliant respondents with the few who claimed to be attentive to neither television nor newspapers. The small number of respondents who belonged to this unexposed group made this comparison tentative. Surprisingly, however, Wagner found that the television-reliant respondents were no more informed about the candidate positions than were the inattentive.

Using the 1996 NES election data, we offer some additional demonstrations of how newspapers and television news inform voters during presidential campaigns. We divided 1996 NES respondents into three categories of television news watching. "Regular viewers" claimed both to watch national news at least 6 days a week and to follow television news of the campaign with "quite a bit" or "a good deal" of attention. "Nonviewers" claimed to watch no national news or to pay no attention to campaign news. "Occasional viewers" were in between these two extremes. We rated newspaper readership similarly. "Regular readers" claimed both to read newspapers at least six days a week and to follow the campaign in newspapers with "quite a bit" or "a good deal" of attention. "Nonreaders" claimed to not read newspapers or pay no attention to campaign news. "Occasional readers" were in between.

Rating respondents according to three categories on viewing and three categories on reading gives a combined set of categories with a total of nine cells. Frequencies with which people belonged in each of the nine cells are shown in Table 8.5. This table reflects the growing dominance of television over newspapers as a news source. But the same individuals who attended to one medium generally attended to the other. Regular viewing and regular reading tended to go together. So did nonviewing and nonreading. Our interest is in sorting out the separate effects of reading and watching on political interest and information. At the same time, we must be aware that causality also flows the other way: while monitoring the media can stimulate interest and the growth of information, it is also true that interested and informed citizens seek out media information.

We can see the basic results in part (a) of Table 8.6, which shows the percentage of respondents who said they were "very interested" in the campaign. As we move from nonviewers to regular viewers or from nonreaders to regular readers, we see that campaign interest increases. This relationship between media attention and campaign interest is clear for both viewing and reading. For each level of television news viewing, newspaper readers are more interested than nonreaders. For each level of newspaper reading, television news viewers are more interested than nonviewers. All this fits with common sense. Interest in the campaign should make one want to follow the campaign more closely both in newspapers and on television; and following the campaign either in newspapers or on television makes one more interested.

In part (b) of Table 8.6, note what happens when we substitute percentages with "high" information about candidate policy positions for campaign interest. We define high scorers as those who correctly rated Dole to the right of Clinton on all five issues examined. Newspaper reading is sharply related to information level, but only for people who are not regular consumers of national news reports on television. Viewing televised national news is modestly related to information level, but only among people who do not read newspapers. Taken together, these patterns suggest newspapers are more informative than television news, and also that each medium is most effective in the absence of the other. Interestingly, the most informed of all are regular newspaper readers who do not watch television news. Obviously this must be a matter of self-selection rather than television causing information loss: people who

TABLE 8.5   PATTERNS OF ATTENTION TO NEWSPAPER AND TELEVISION NEWS, 1996

		Television Viewing			
		Regular viewer	Occasional viewer	Nonviewer	All cases
Newspaper Reading	Regular reader	5*	6	1	12
	Occasional reader	7	19	5	31
	Nonreader	8	33	17	57
	All cases	23	57	20	100

Source: National Election Studies, 1996 election data.
*Cell entries are percentages of total sample.

TABLE 8.6   RESPONSIVENESS IN THE 1996 PRESIDENTIAL CAMPAIGN, BY MEDIA ATTENTION

(a) Percentage "Very Interested" in the Election

		Television News Viewing		
		Regular viewer	Occasional viewer	Nonviewer
Newspaper Reading	Regular reader	74	67	56
	Occasional reader	62	31	19
	Nonreader	55	18	9

(b) Percentage with High Information About Candidate Positions

		Television News Viewing		
		Regular viewer	Occasional viewer	Nonviewer
Newspaper Reading	Regular reader	30	40	55
	Occasional reader	29	33	33
	Nonreader	26	16	10

Source: National Election Studies, 1996 election data.

choose newspapers over television are more cognitively skilled and therefore more informed to begin with.

Television Campaign Ads and an Informed Electorate

News programs do not constitute the only television outlet for political candidates. Candidates often conduct a major portion of their campaigns via television advertisements—usually in the form of 30-second "spot ads." Although expensive, ads have a clear advantage over news broadcasts: Candidates possess full control of their content.

How effective are television ads? While campaign directors almost unanimously see television advertising as effective, only about 20 percent of congressional candidates' campaign expenditures actually go to television advertisements (Goldenberg and Traugott 1984, 86–88, 117). Thus even if spending does win votes, we cannot be certain that television advertising is the key. Research by Gary Jacobson, however, does show that candidates are more visible in the mass media when overall campaign expenditures increase. For instance, when a congressional challenger spends only about $25,000 on a campaign, only about 45 percent of the prospective voters are able to recall something about the candidate from the mass media. But when the challenger spends about $500,000, two-thirds recall the candidate from the mass media (Jacobson 1987, 123).

One of the most interesting analyses of the effectiveness of campaign ads is from Patterson and McClure's Syracuse study. Recall that their study found that people who watched the most television news did not learn much more than the average viewer about candidate campaign positions. Patterson and McClure (1976, 93–139) also ascertained how much television in general their respondents watched during the fall campaign. Their presumption was that people who watched the most TV were the most exposed to campaign ads on TV. They found that heavy television watchers did not change their views of the candidates any more than those who were light watchers. In this sense, Patterson and McClure cast doubt on the effectiveness of the television ads. They also found, however, that heavy television watchers learned considerably more about candidate policy positions over the course of the campaign than did light watchers. This presents an interesting irony. Although Patterson and McClure may overstate the case, they suggest that people learn more about where the candidates stand on issues from watching them posture in television ads than from watching the coverage on the television news.

An unsettling recent trend has been the increasing negativity of political ads. Increasingly, candidates attack their opponents (often in a shrill tone) rather than extol their own virtues (West 1997). The classic example of such tactics were the Willie Horton ads advocating Bush over Dukakis in the 1988 presidential race. These ads highlighted a Massachusetts prisoner who committed a rape while on a weekend furlough when Dukakis was governor. Without a counterresponse from Dukakis, these ads left the impression that Dukakis was indifferent to criminal behavior. In fact in the NES survey of 1988, the most prominent issue-based reason people gave for voting for Bush was Dukakis's supposedly lenient policy toward criminals (Wattenberg 1991b, 121).

One question is whether negative ads "work," whether they are more effective than positive ads. Based on the most thorough analysis of the literature, the answer would appear to be no (Lau et al. 1999). As a byproduct, negative ads are often thought to have the disturbing consequence of turning people away from politics. Plausibly, if people believe politicians are as unworthy as their opponents' claims would have it, would potential voters find any politicians worth supporting? Ansolahebere and Iyengar (1995) argue that negative ads cause voter turnout to decline—in effect to chase voters away from the polls. Other researchers (e.g., Kahn and Kenney 1999; Freedman and Goldstein 1999; Wattenberg and Brians 1999) insist this claim is unsupported by the evidence. The effects of negative ads remains a lively question for research.

The Media and Campaigns: An Assessment

The quality of democracy depends on the degree to which citizens can make informed decisions at the ballot box. How well citizens perform this task depends not only on citizens' interest in and capability of processing political information but also on the quality of the information that is available to them. Contemporary scholarship tends to view modern media campaigns negatively, with their emphasis on negative advertising and their issueless news coverage (Jamieson 1992; Sabato 1993; Patterson 1993). But contemporary scholarship also treats the voters generously. The prevailing view of the electorate is that it makes the best use of its judgment *given the limited information that reaches it* (Page and Shapiro 1992; Brody 1991; Popkin 1991). Studies that trace the evolution of voters during the campaign show that despite the limitations of the mass media, considerable learning takes place. Voters appear more informed about issues as the campaign goes on (Patterson and McClure 1976, Buchanan 1991), and more focused on relevant criteria for making a vote choice (Gelman and King 1993). The mass media's shaping of campaigns and the potential for improvement present interesting questions that are far from fully answered.

8-4 CONCLUSION

The mass media pervade our society in a way that would have been unimaginable to the founders of this country. One can still debate whether the condition of American democracy is better or worse as a result. The sociologist C. Wright Mills described the idealized view of public opinion that once prevailed in a smaller society with no mass media:

> Two centuries ago, before the mass media as we know them today, it was thought that in a democracy the public of public opinion consisted of small groups of people talking among themselves, electing spokesmen for their group, who in turn talked among themselves. (Mills, 1963, 535).

The notion was of a public opinion originating with the informed public and moving "upward" to affect societal institutions. With the modern media, influence moves directly "downward" from the mass media—and the institutions they reflect—to public opinion as a mass audience. With democratic institutions, audience members are supposed to send their signals back upward, influencing government behavior with their votes and other actions. The important function for the mass media in a democracy is to help their audiences perform their duties as democratic citizens responsibly.

In at least one respect, the mass media performs their democratic role reasonably well. As a reflector of societal values, the media reinforce public acceptance of the rules of democracy. In other respects, however, different observers with different political viewpoints may complain about the media's failure to properly enlighten the public. Changing or reforming the media would not be an easy task. Meaningful changes would be difficult to legislate. And it would probably be unrealistic to try to mobilize the mass media to reform themselves.

Human beings are resourceful at avoiding the influence of media messages. Yet, public opinion and mass media messages are at least somewhat related. There is no clear evidence that this relationship is more than minimal, however, or that the direction of influence is entirely from the media to the public.

NOTES

1. Immediately after the debate, a national poll showed that the public saw Ford the winner, 48 to 28. By the following evening, Carter was perceived the winner 61 to 19 (Steeper 1978, 85).
2. AIPO News Release, February 2, 1964. The exact question was, "How would you feel about a law that would give all persons—Negro as well as white—the right to be served in public places, such as hotels, restaurants, theaters?"
3. CBS News/*New York Times* "prespeech" and "postspeech" October 1973 surveys.
4. On the history of campaign advertising, see Jamieson (1992).
5. On Stevenson and television in 1952, see Halberstam (1979).
6. By one count (Hershey 1989) in 1988, newspaper stories of campaign strategy outnumbered stories of campaign policy issues by about 2 to 1.
7. On the media and momentum in presidential primaries, see Brady and Johnston (1987) and Bartels (1987).

CHAPTER 9

Elections as Instruments of Popular Control

In a democracy, the public supposedly controls the behavior of its public officials by exercising its influence at the ballot box in a rational fashion—in accordance with what we call the rational-activist model. Ideally, each voter selects a candidate who best represents his or her views on matters of public policy. At least in a two-candidate election, the collective choice will then be the candidate who is closer to most voters on the issues. The policy result will be the closest correspondence possible, given the choice of candidates, between the collective preferences of the electorate and government policy.

But representation of the public interest via democratic elections is not as simple in practice as it is in theory. It is possible, for instance, to hold elections in which none of the candidates on the ballot offer policy choices that voters find attractive. Or, even when the candidates present a relevant menu of policy choices, the electorate may—through some combination of misguidance, ignorance, and indifference—vote "irrationally" by voting into office a candidate who does not represent their interests. Also, if officeholders perceive that the electorate is not watching, or that it does not care, they may feel free to make policy decisions without consideration of public opinion.

Looking at the matter in a positive rather than negative fashion, we can state the conditions that do allow elections to be an effective instrument for inducing policy decisions that are responsive to public opinion. First, the candidates should offer a meaningful choice of policy options that appeal to voters, and once elected, the winner should try to carry out campaign pledges. Second, the voters should be informed about the issues that separate the candidates and vote for the candidate who best represents their own views. Clearly, the fulfillment of each one of these conditions depends on the other. For example, political leaders pay the greatest attention to public opinion when they believe that the public is alert enough to throw them out of office if they do not. Similarly, voters have the greatest opportunity to vote intelligently on the basis of policy issues when the politicians act from the assumption that the public is going to do so.

In the present chapter, we examine the behavior of the electorate when it carries out its assigned responsibility. Then in Chapters 10 and 11, we examine the responsiveness of political elites to public opinion.

9-1 POLITICAL CAMPAIGNS AND THE VOTER

During every political campaign, voters are bombarded with news and propaganda about the candidates who seek their favor. Judging by the attention that politicians give to the voters at election time, one might conclude that the voter reacts to campaign stimuli in the fluid manner that the voter does as a consumer, reacting to advertising stimuli in the mass media. Just as the person about to purchase a product, such as a detergent, might vacillate in his or her choice of brands until the moment of purchase, so might the voter waver between the candidates until entry into the voting booth forces a final decision. But as we saw in Chapter 8, this image of the voting process underestimates the voter's ability to resist political messages.

As discussed in Chapter 3, most American voters have a more or less permanent attachment to either the Republican or the Democratic party. It is through this filter of party identification that most voters view the partisan aspects of the political world. The anchor of party identification prevents most voters from wavering in their choice of candidates during a campaign, and they do not change the party they vote for from one election year to the next. We know from National Election Studies surveys that, of people who vote in two successive presidential elections, about 80 percent will vote for the same party's presidential candidate both times (Converse 1962). Similarly, most voters decide whom they will support for president as early as convention time and stick to this choice over the course of the campaign. About 80 percent of the voters each November vote for the candidate who had been their August preference (Benham 1965). When partisans do change their candidate choice during the campaign, one usually finds an initial attraction to the opposition's candidate followed by a return to the fold by election day.

Below the presidential level, the percentage of voters who stick with their party's choice is even higher. For lesser offices, the amount of information that reaches voters is often too slight to give them any reason to go against their party. Only in nonpartisan elections and primary contests (where party identification cannot be a criterion of choice) do voters vacillate in an erratic manner. In fact, vote preferences in primary contests are so fluid that pollsters have great difficulty predicting outcomes, even when they monitor opinion as late as a day or two before the election (Bartels and Broh 1989).

Of course, if party identification were the sole determinant of how people vote, election results would simply reflect the balance of Democratic and Republican identifiers. And since the ratio of Democratic to Republican identifiers changes only modestly in the short run, election results would be almost identical from one election to the next. In fact, election results often depart considerably from the voter division that would occur with a strict party-line vote.

When an election is decided on a party-line basis, the result is called the "normal vote." At one time, the normal vote was considered to be a constant of politics. The calculation was that assuming a 50-50 split by Independents and a balanced, minimal defection rate by partisans (about 10 percent on each side), the nation-level normal vote would be a narrow Democratic win by about 54 percent Democratic to 46 percent Republican (Converse 1966; see also Petrocik 1989). This calculation reflects the Democratic edge in party identification that more than counterbalanced the higher turnout rate among Republicans than Democrats.

Figure 9.1 presents a 50-year approximation of the normal vote, between 1948 and 1998, derived from the national division of party identification.[1] Note the disappearance of the Democrats' one-time dominant edge over the Republicans. Nationally, the normal vote is approximated by the national vote in congressional elections. As Figure 9.1 shows, the national House vote between 1948 and 1992 never varied from between 50 and 59 percent Democratic, averaging at the expected 54 percent Democratic. The Democrats' one-time large advantage in party identification thus explains why the Democrats controlled the House

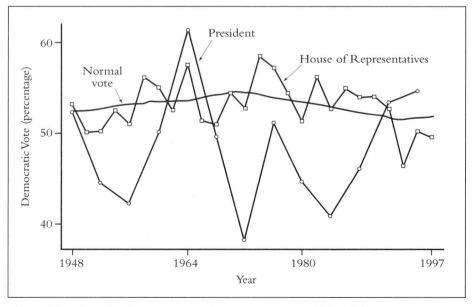

Figure 9.1   The national two-party vote (percent Democratic), 1948–1998.

of Representatives (and usually the Senate) for 40 years running, from 1954 to 1994. In 1994 the Republicans suddenly gained control of the House after their 40-year drought. This could not have come about without a change in the normal vote brought about by Republican gains in party identification.

The difference between the actual vote and the normal vote represents the "short-term partisan forces" of the election. When it comes to voting for Congress, national issues are of only modest importance. National-level short-term forces are modest for congressional elections, so that party control of Congress is largely determined by the normal vote. But for the presidency, short-term forces can be of major importance. As Figure 9.1 shows, the national vote for president often departs significantly from the normal vote. In fact, during the post–World War II era, the presidency has been won by the Republicans as often as it has been won by the Democrats.

Deviations of election results from the normal vote do not signify that the usual role of party identification in shaping election results has broken down. Instead, one finds that the party favored by the short-term forces is the beneficiary of most of the short-term party defections, and it also wins the majority of the Independent vote. Figure 9.2 shows this pattern over the 13 presidential elections from 1948 through 1996.

When the short-term forces favor the Republicans, Democrats "defect" beyond their usual rate; Republicans are even more loyal to their party than usual, and Independents vote overwhelmingly Republican. With pro-Democratic short-term forces, the pattern is the reverse—with unusually frequent Republican defections and a Democratic trend among Independents.

Short-Term Forces Below the Presidential Level

For state and local elections, the "normal" vote reflects the partisan balance of the particular state or local constituency rather than the nation as a whole. Due to the kinds of people who reside in the area, the local normal vote often is

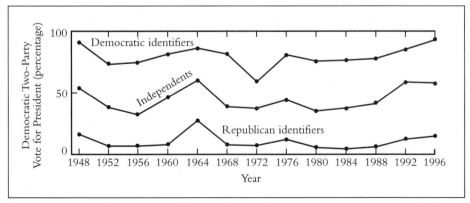

Figure 9.2   Party identification and the vote for president, 1948–1992. *Source:* National Election Studies election data.

very one-sided in favor of the Republicans or Democrats. Election results will reflect the local normal vote plus any short-term forces that carry over from national politics (or from higher-level state or local contests). In addition, the local vote will reflect the short-term forces generated by the local candidates and their campaign. One way of thinking about local short-term forces is as the "personal" vote generated by the candidates themselves (Cain et al. 1987).

Although candidates for local office run less visible races than presidential candidates, their own campaigns help to determine their electoral fate. The importance of local campaigns is indicated by the fact that as many as half the voters in a national election will report that they split their ticket rather than vote for one party's candidate for all offices. Because of this ticket splitting, the same constituency will often vote the Democratic candidate into one office and the Republican candidate into another.

As for president, election outcomes below the presidential level depend in large part on the short-term forces of the specific campaign. By one estimate, short-term forces for the statewide offices of governor and U.S. senator are about as large as for president (Erikson et al. 1994, ch. 9). The implication is that statewide (and perhaps local) outcomes readily depart by 10 or 15 percentage points from the state (or local) normal vote. Even where one party dominates, the disadvantaged party often can win when it fields the stronger candidate.

Who Are the "Floating Voters"?

Election outcomes are the result of both the normal vote and short-term partisan forces of the campaign. Voters whose choice is determined by the campaign rather than a long-term partisan commitment are called "floating voters." An important question remains: How informed are the floating voters? If the floating voters were more politically informed than the average, we would think that election trends are essentially the response of the most politically alert segment of the public. But if the reverse is true—that floaters are more politically ignorant than the average—then we might be compelled toward the more dismal conclusion that election trends are largely the result of campaign propaganda of the sort that appeals to the voters least capable of making an informed evaluation.

Thanks to a classic article by Converse (1962) and a more recent elaboration by Zaller (1992), we have some good but complicated theory regarding floating voters. Consider a candidate's decision whether to pitch the campaign at inattentive and unsophisticated voters or at attentive and sophisticated voters. On the one hand, the more attentive voters are easier to reach with new campaign messages. On the other hand, these attentive voters are more hardened in their views. Their accumulated storage of political information helps to bolster their initial views against intruding information. For example, a Republican who is highly informed about politics is better equipped to discount Democratic propaganda than one who is more politically ignorant. Less attentive voters are more easily swayed, but only if new information reaches them.

Given these complications, the information level of floating voters depends considerably on the intensity of the campaign and the flow of information.

When the information flow is low, the least attentive voters are so uninformed that they lack any basis for switching back and forth between candidates. They vote according to their initial partisan predisposition, if they vote at all. Attentive voters, meanwhile, although more resistant to influence from campaign propaganda, sometimes change their candidate choice when new information reaches them. However, when the information flow is high, even the least attentive voters receive some information. Since these least attentive voters are the most influenced by new information they receive, they contribute disproportionately to electoral volatility.

The battle for the presidency attracts great interest and large voter turnout, with almost all voters receiving some campaign exposure. For example, awareness of the candidates' names is nearly universal during a presidential campaign. The universal intake of new information during a presidential campaign loosens a great number of voters from their partisan moorings—particularly among the least attentive voters. The tiny fraction of presidential voters who manage completely to avoid the campaign maintain stable candidate preferences throughout the campaign. But setting these few cases aside, partisan defections and preelection wavering in candidate choice are most frequent among voters with the least exposure to the presidential campaign.

Table 9.1 illustrates the relationship between our information scale, introduced in Chapter 3 and defined in the Appendix, and partisan defection in the 1996 presidential election. First, let us consider the Democratic identifiers in 1996. Although the vast majority voted for Clinton, the few defectors were drawn mainly from "low" and "medium" information voters; "high information" Democrats were steadfast for Clinton. Among Republicans too, the more informed were the most loyal to their party, with the least-informed being more likely to "defect" to Clinton or Perot.

Table 9.1 also shows the voting behavior of self-proclaimed independents in the 1996 presidential election. Free of partisan attachments, Independents respond the strongest to short-term campaign forces. In 1996, Independents favored Clinton over Dole decisively; they were the strongest partisan category for Ross Perot's Reform Party candidacy, a not surprising outcome given their lack of partisan commitment. Among Independents, the least informed voted the heaviest for Clinton and Perot and the lightest for Dole.

As shown here, Clinton's percentage-point lead over Dole was highest among the least informed. In fact, Clinton led Dole by a whopping 41 points among the least informed but actually trailed Dole (by 3 points) among the most informed voters:

	Low Information	**High Information**
Clinton	72%	46%
Perot	7	5
Dole	21	41
	100%	100%
Clinton – Dole =	*+41%*	*–3%*

TABLE 9.1   VOTE FOR PRESIDENT, 1996, BY INFORMATION LEVEL
AND PARTY IDENTIFICATION*

	Information		
	Low	Medium	High
Democratic identifiers			
Clinton	90%	87%	97%
Perot	5	7	2
Dole	5	6	1
	100%	100%	100%
Idependent identifiers			
Clinton	63%	42%	48%
Perot	16	17	8
Dole	21	41	44
	100%	100%	100%
Republican identifiers			
Clinton	29%	10%	6%
Perot	6	4	6
Dole	65	86	88
	100%	100%	100%

Source: National Election Studies, 1996 election data.

*Information scale based on correctness of relative placement of candidates on issues. For details, see the Appendix.

This is the usual pattern of presidential elections: The least-informed voters exaggerate the partisan trend. In 1988, for example, low-information voters were more supportive of winner Bush than were high-information voters. As Converse argues, it sometimes seems that "not only is the electorate as a whole quite uninformed, but it is the least informed members within the electorate who seem to hold the critical 'balance of power' in the sense that alternatives in the governing party depend disproportionately on shifts in their sentiment" (Converse 1962, 578).

We might even be tempted to conclude that the most effective presidential campaign would be one aimed directly at the voter who is normally inattentive and uninformed about politics. But recall that the inattentive voter is a less accessible target of campaign messages. Note, too, the tendency of the least informed to dilute their influence by not voting. Based on self-reports, the 1996 vote turnout within the least- and most-informed categories were as follows:

	Low Information	High Information
Voted	60%	86%
Did not vote	40	14
	100%	100%

The electoral contribution of the least-informed citizens is diluted by their low motivation to vote.

9-2 POLICY ISSUES AND VOTERS

Despite our current knowledge about voting behavior, scholars do not fully agree on the precise role that policy issues play in elections. From what we know about the capabilities of average American voters, we are not surprised that many scholars are skeptical about whether candidates' policy proposals and ideological leanings affect many voter decisions. Among the most pessimistic are the authors of *The American Voter*, undoubtedly the single most influential book on voting behavior. They found the electorate to be almost wholly without detailed information on the issues of the day, unable to judge the rationality of government policies, and unable to appraise the appropriateness of the means necessary to arrive at desirable ends (Campbell et al. 1960, 543).

The American Voter, however, was based on the two Eisenhower elections from the quiescent 1950s. Several studies of more recent elections—most notably *The Changing American Voter*—offer a rather different interpretation of the capabilities of the American voter (Nie et al. 1976).[2] Beginning with the Johnson–Goldwater election of 1964, political issues and political ideology have become increasingly important as determinants of the vote in the United States. The reason for this growth of issue voting is that parties and candidates have become more polarized on liberal versus conservative lines. But just how important issues have become remains controversial.

For voters to be influenced by policy issues when they cast their ballots, two conditions must be met. First, the voters must be aware of the differences between the policy views of the candidates. Second, the voters must be motivated to vote on the basis of the issues that divide the candidates. Evidence of issue voting is strongest when the divergence between the candidate stances is strong and the issue is of considerable importance to the electorate.

Here, we examine the evidence of policy voting in presidential elections. Most of the data analysis that follows is from the National Election Studies (NES) survey of the 1992 presidential election. As measured via survey analysis, the degree of issue voting in 1992 was typical of recent presidential elections.

Voter Perceptions of Candidate Differences, 1992

A necessary condition for voting on the basis of candidates' policy positions is that the voters perceive actual policy differences between the candidates. Following the usual procedure of NES surveys, in 1996 the NES researchers asked respondents for their perceptions of the presidential candidates' positions on a series of seven-point scales representing several issues. Table 9.2 arranges these data to show how voters rated Democratic candidate (and winner) Bill Clinton relative to his Republican opponent, Bob Dole.

TABLE 9.2   VOTER PERCEPTIONS OF ISSUE DIFFERENCES
BETWEEN PRESIDENTIAL CANDIDATES, 1996

	Clinton Left of Dole	Dole Left of Clinton	Same or Incomplete Ratings
Liberal/conservative ideology	76	11	13
Domestic spending	71	10	20
Defense spending	55	21	24
Abortion	64	7	29
National health care	70	8	22

Source: National Election Studies, 1996 election data. Each percentage is based on voters only.

Individuals could rate Clinton to the left of Dole (correct), rate Dole to the left of Clinton (incorrect), or place the two candidates in a tie (presumably incorrect). Additionally, on each issue scale some voters (generally around 25 percent) gave incomplete ratings, claiming not to know the position of one or both of the major candidates.

Table 9.2 shows that when voters perceived the candidates to be different on an issue, they almost invariably saw Clinton to the left of Dole. Still, voters often rated the candidates the same or gave incomplete ratings. On all issues, however, a majority of voters ordered the candidates correctly. The sharpest perception was on the liberal–conservative ideology scale, where 71 percent saw Clinton to the left of Dole.

The respondent ratings of candidate ideology shown in Table 9.2 provided the basis for classification on our information index. Of 1996 voters, 28 percent were "high-information" scorers, meaning that they saw Clinton to Dole's left on all five items shown in Table 9.2. "Low-information" scorers comprise 31 percent of the voting total, and they score in the guess range regarding net candidate placement. (See the Appendix.) The remaining 40 percent were in between. Thus, roughly speaking, a third of the voting electorate is clearly tuned in to the candidates' ideological differences, another third is not, and about one third is somewhere in between. As usual, our picture of the electorate is mixed.

Policy Issues, Ideology, and Votes, 1996

In order to vote on the basis of policy issues, it is not enough to become aware of the candidates' policy differences. In addition, voters must find these choices sufficiently important to influence their vote choices. With policy voting, we would observe people voting for the candidate closest to their own views. This would usually mean liberals voting Democratic and conservatives voting Republican.

Table 9.3 presents some simple evidence of policy voting in the 1996 presidential election. This table shows that over a variety of issues, voters who prefer the liberal position gave the most support to Clinton, while voters preferring the conservative position gave the most support to Dole. Some of the issues shown were actively discussed in the 1996 campaign, with the candidates taking divergent stands: abortion, gays in the military, environmental spending, national health care, and the general issue of relative degree of spending and services by the national government. Taking each of these issues separately, one sees a sharp tendency for liberals to support Clinton and conservatives to support Dole. Three other issues—defense spending, the death penalty, and aid to blacks—involved

TABLE 9.3   1996 PRESIDENTIAL VOTE BY POLICY OPINIONS

Policy	Clinton (%)	Perot (%)	Dole (%)	
Abortion				
Permit	63	8	28	= 100%
Restrict	40	7	53	= 100
Gays in military				
Permit	66	7	27	= 100
Disallow	34	8	58	= 100
Defense spending				
Less	61	5	34	= 100
More	51	8	41	= 100
Domestic spending				
More	79	4	17	= 100
Less	26	9	66	= 100
Aid to minorities				
Favor	83	6	11	= 100
Oppose	42	6	52	= 100
National health care				
Favor	75	9	16	= 100
Oppose	32	6	62	= 100
Death penalty				
Oppose	76	4	21	= 100
Favor	48	9	44	= 100
Prayer in schools				
Oppose	54	7	39	= 100
Favor	53	8	39	= 100

Source: National Election Studies, 1996 election data.

subtler shadings of disagreement between the candidates but still have been long-standing battlegrounds of partisan disagreement. Here, too, we see liberals and conservatives dividing in their candidate choice. Still one other issue, school prayer, while representing a conservative and liberal side, was not a matter of much partisan controversy. On this issue, one can see no tendency for liberal and conservative voters to support different candidates.

Since so many issues seem to matter, we should be able to improve our vote predictions by taking into account voter positions on many issues simultaneously, rather than one issue at a time. Table 9.4 shows the relationship between general liberal-conservative ideology and the 1996 vote two ways.

First, the table shows the vote as a function of ideological self-identification, where ideological identification is measured using the full seven-point scale from "extremely liberal" to "extremely conservative." Ideological identification predicts fairly well, particularly for voters on the liberal side of the spectrum. Of the 26 percent who placed themselves at one of the three positions on the liberal side of the spectrum, 89 percent voted for Clinton with the remainder about evenly split between Dole and Perot. Self-identified "conservatives" were far less loyal to Dole than liberals were to Clinton.

TABLE 9.4 PRESIDENTIAL VOTE BY TWO SUMMARY MEASURES OF LIBERALISM–CONSERVATISM, 1996

	Self-Identification on Ideological Scale						
	Extremely Liberal					Extremely Conservative	
	1	2	3	4	5	6	7
Clinton (%)	75	97	84	59	32	16	27
Perot (%)	25	2	7	11	10	5	3
Dole (%)	0	1	9	30	57	80	70
(Percentage of voters)	(1)	(11)	(14)	(26)	(20)	(25)	(3)

	Ten Item Composite Issue Index*						
	Most Liberal					Most Conservative	
	–10 to –8	–7 to –5	–4 to –2	–1 to +1	+2 to +4	+5 to +7	+8 to +10
Clinton (%)	96	86	74	57	30	13	2
Perot (%)	1	8	8	9	9	2	3
Dole (%)	1	7	18	34	61	85	94
(Percentage of voters)	(5)	(14)	(21)	(25)	(21)	(12)	(3)

Source: National Election Studies, 1996 election data.

*For construction of the ten-item composite issue index, see Chapter 3

Many "conservatives" supported Perot or even Clinton, apparently on non-ideological grounds.[3]

The second part of Table 9.4 shows the vote as a function of a ten-item composite liberal-conservative index introduced in Chapter 3, page 73. Here the degree of prediction is even better. Five percent of the voting respondents scored in the most liberal range—from −8 to −10 on the index. Only one percent voted for Dole: 96 percent chose the most liberal candidate, Clinton. At the conservative end of the scale, 2 percent of the voting respondents scored between +8 to +10. Of these, 94 percent voted for Dole, the most conservative candidate.

From this demonstration, voters with consistently liberal or conservative views are highly predictable in their vote choice. But most voters are not at either ideological extreme. One-fourth are near the exact center—in the −1 to +1 range on the ten-point scale—and must be described as decidedly moderate or centrist. Many others appear only vaguely liberal or conservative, and their votes do not always follow from their ideological direction.

In part, the predictability of votes from ideology as shown in Table 9.4 is due to voters simply responding to their partisan background: Liberals tend to identify with the Democratic party and conservatives with the Republicans (Chapter 3). Thus, just by voting their party identification, voters tend to support the candidates closest to their views. Issue voting is further enhanced by party defections and issue voting by Independents. Table 9.5 illustrates this by

---

TABLE 9.5   1996 PRESIDENTIAL VOTE BY IDEOLOGY WITH PARTY IDENTIFICATION CONTROLLED

	Democrats			Independents			Republicans		
	Ideological self-identification								
	Lib.	Mod.	Con.	Lib.	Mod.	Con.	Lib.	Mod.	Con.
Clinton (%)	95	82	66	80	54	23	27	16	8
Perot (%)	2	7	16	15	17	14	18	11	3
Dole (%)	3	11	18	5	29	63	54	72	89
(Percentage of voters)	(19)	(14)	(4)	(9)	(12)	(6)	(3)	(13)	(20)

	Democrats			Independents			Republicans		
	Ten-item issue index★								
	Lib.	Center	Con.	Lib.	Center	Con.	Lib.	Center	Con.
Clinton (%)	97	88	76	71	44	25	49	13	4
Perot (%)	1	6	9	17	17	7	5	9	3
Dole (%)	2	6	15	12	39	68	46	78	93
(Percentage of voters)	(19)	(17)	(4)	(9)	(12)	(6)	(3)	(12)	(17)

Source: National Election Studies, 1996.

★Ideology scale collapsed so −10 to −3 = liberal; −2 to +2 = center; +3 to +10 = conservative.

showing the relationships between ideology and the vote within the three categories of party identification.

Conservative Democrats and liberal Republicans, while rare, are the partisan groups most prone to "defect" in their presidential voting. Meanwhile, Independents present the clearest example of issue voting. Neutral in terms of partisanship, they generally vote Democratic if liberal and Republican if conservative.

Information and Ideological Voting

As one would expect, ideological voting is most prevalent among voters who are highly informed about candidate positions. In surveys, the observed relationship between ideology and vote choice becomes most pronounced when we select the most informed voters (Knight 1985; Jacoby 1991; Lyons and Scheb 1992; Pierce 1993). Figure 9.3 illustrates how issue voting rises with information.

The figure divides 1996 respondents into those low, medium, and high on our scale of information about candidate differences on issues. For each group, Figure 9.3 shows the relationship between the ten-item index of respondent liberalism-conservatism and the vote. For this figure, Perot voters are discarded to ease the presentation. Graphed percentages represent the Clinton proportion of the two-party vote.

Note first that low-information voters show almost no issue voting: Their vote is preponderantly pro-Clinton whether their issue positions are liberal, centrist, or conservative. Among these least-informed voters, it could hardly be otherwise than that liberals and conservatives are nearly indistinguishable in

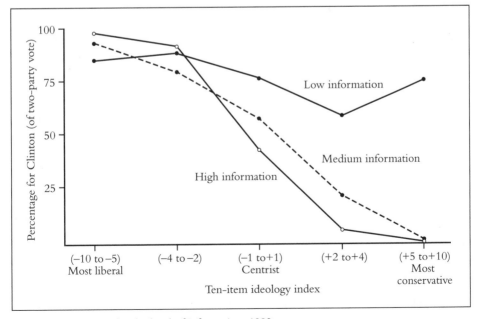

Figure 9.3   Issue voting by level of information, 1992.

their vote. Voters who are confused or wrong about candidate positions could not vote coherently on the basis of policy issues.

In contrast, examine the behavior of the highly informed voters (who saw Dole to the right of Clinton on all four issues examined plus ideological direction). Among liberals, virtually all supported Clinton, presumably because they saw Clinton closer to them than Dole was on the issue; among conservatives, virtually all supported Dole, presumably because they saw him closer to their point of view. Meanwhile, those highly informed voters who were in the middle did not divide evenly. Instead, they tilted toward Clinton, influenced by other factors such as the economy. To the extent ideological considerations tipped the 1996 election, the movement by informed centrists in the middle of the ideological spectrum was responsible.

We learn from this exercise that when voters are informed about the ideological differences among candidates, ideology is a strong influence on vote choice. The degree to which voters choose candidates based on ideology depends in large part on the degree of ideological division between the candidates and the degree to which these differences are publicized. When Democratic and Republican candidates are similar ideologically, ideological differences between Democratic and Republican voters are also slight beyond those that derive from voting on the basis of party identification. Studies of different elections (e.g., Nie et al. 1976) show that the stronger the candidates' ideological differences, the more will ideological voting follow.[4]

Easy Versus Hard Issues

For voters, questions of public policy are "hard" issues in the sense that they require a certain amount of attention and sophistication. Many voters lack the political resources necessary to monitor and evaluate the candidates' policy proposals. Recall from Chapter 3 that no more than a quarter of the electorate (sometimes less) can be classified as sophisticated "ideologues" who evaluate parties and candidates in left-right policy terms. But even if unsophisticated voters do not make judgments about the desirability of specific policies, they can evaluate candidates in terms of relatively "easy" issues. One example of an "easy" issue evaluation is whether a candidate appears to favor or represent the interests of certain groups more than others. This, recall from Chapter 3, is a "group benefit" response to voting. Another "easy" kind of issue evaluation is to decide whether conditions seem to be good or bad under the current incumbent or incumbent party. This, recall from Chapter 4, is "nature-of-the-times" voting. Neither group benefit nor nature-of-the-times voting requires any direct knowledge of either specific policies or what the candidates claim they would do if elected. But each allows one to cast a seemingly informed vote with a minimum of information costs.

Group-Based Voting Voters can orient themselves to parties and candidates on the basis of which groups they seem to be for or against. In this way, voters need to recognize which groups they like and dislike and to learn the party with which each of these groups is aligned. No investment in determining candidate positions or the relative benefits from these is required. Group-based voting is voting on the basis of "ideology-by-proxy" (Campbell et al. 1960, 219–20). For example, a relatively prosperous citizen can learn to vote Republican simply by adopting the belief that Republicans favor the rich. In this way, our prosperous citizen votes the same as if he or she were able to develop a conservative ideology to rationalize economic self-interest.

Nature-of-the-Times Voting Still another voter shortcut is nature-of-the-times voting—evaluating whether times are good or bad (or will improve or get worse) and rewarding or punishing the incumbent party accordingly. Especially when little other information is available, the incumbent's (or incumbent party's) recent performance may be the best forecast of future prospects under a continuation of the existing regime. Nature-of-the-times voters may not have specific policies in mind, but they can throw the rascals out if the obvious signs indicate that it is time, in Campbell's words (1964, 755), to let "a new bunch of fellows run things for a while."

The National Election Studies (NES) regularly asks its respondents to evaluate the recent economy, asking whether over the previous year the nation's economy "has gotten better, stayed the same, or gotten worse." Responses to this question are usually consistent with vote choice, as in 1996:

Vote	Economy has gotten better	Economy has stayed about the same	Economy has gotten worse
Clinton	71%	43%	30%
Dole	23	50	57
Perot	6	6	13
	100%	100%	100%
Percentage of voters	*43*	*42*	*14*

With far more voters acknowledging the improving economy (43 percent) than saying it has gotten worse (14 percent), the perception of a good economy helped Clinton's reelection. Still, these numbers may exaggerate the influence of economic perceptions on vote choice. One reason for the consistency between economic perception and vote choice in surveys is that respondents often respond to economic questions with rationalizations of their vote choice. For instance, a respondent who has signaled enthusiasm for the president may feel a need to praise the president's economy out of a need to appear consistent. But even allowing for this source of contamination, economic perceptions account for many vote choices. Just as a bad economy contributed to Clinton's defeat of President Bush in 1992, the thriving economy contributed to Clinton's reelection in 1996.[5]

Candidate Evaluations

Still another important set of voter motivations has nothing to do with issues. We refer to voters' evaluations of the personal characteristics and leadership abilities of the candidates. Simply put, voters tend to support candidates whom they like and trust. Whether a voter likes a candidate may transcend any policy differences or even overcome a strong party identification.

To examine "candidate evaluations" in the 1996 presidential contest, we turn to the open-ended evaluations of candidates where NES respondents were asked to articulate up to five likes and dislikes about Clinton and Dole. Here we consider only open-ended responses to a candidate's personal characteristics —from leadership and experience (e.g., "Clinton is a proven leader") and personal characteristics (e.g., "Clinton cares"; "Clinton can't be trusted"). Respondents are coded as pro-Clinton if their Clinton-likes and Dole-dislikes outnumber their Dole-likes and Clinton-dislikes. The opposite pattern was scored pro-Dole. Many respondents were neutral in their evaluations.[6] Net candidate evaluations predict 1996 votes as follows:

Vote	Like Clinton better	Neutral	Like Dole better
Clinton	75%	61%	17%
Perot	8	8	8
Dole	17	30	75
	100%	99%	100%
Percentage of voters	*28*	*39*	*33*

In terms of personal attributes, slightly more preferred Dole to Clinton, and most voters with a preference in terms of personal characteristics voted for the candidate they liked best. Among the 39 percent with neutral candidate evaluations, Clinton outpolled Dole about two to one.

Prediction and Causation

Policy issues, ideological identifications, group attitudes, retrospective evaluations, candidate evaluations, and party identifications all seem to predict the vote. The more variables we take into account, the better the prediction. To see that most votes can be "predicted," let us simultaneously predict 1996 presidential votes from the three best predictors: (1) party identification, (2) the ten-issue ideological scale, and (3) net candidate evaluations. We simply score each predictor as pro-Democratic, neutral, or pro-Republican, and sum them to make a scale from −3 (liberal Democrats who like Clinton better) to +3 (conservative Republicans who like Dole better). The results are shown in Table 9.6. To simplify the presentation, Perot voters are excluded.

Table 9.6 scores 16 percent at "zero" with balanced positions on the three predictors; these seemingly neutral voters chose Clinton over Dole 63 to 37 percent, evidently due to other factors such as the good economy. For the remaining 84 percent with a partisan tilt to their relevant attitudes, the vast majority—92 percent—voted in accord with the direction of their partisan attitudes. At the extreme, one-fifth of the voters found all three relevant attitudes in partisan agreement; they were either liberal Democrats who liked Clinton better or conservative Republicans who liked Dole better. Of these

TABLE 9.6   PREDICTING 1996 PRESIDENTIAL VOTES FROM THE
SUMMARY OF PARTISAN ATTITUDES★

				Pro-Clinton			
	−3	−2	−1	0	+1	+2	+3
Clinton (%)	100	97	89	63	27	4	1
Dole (%)	0	3	11	37	73	96	99
	100	100	100	100	100	100	100
(Percentage of voters)	(7)	(19)	(21)	(16)	(13)	(13)	(11)

Source: National Election Studies, 1996 election data.

★Perot voters are not included. Index scores represent sum of partisan directions (+ = Republican, − = Democratic) on party identification, ten-item ideological scale, and net candidate evaluations. Minus 3 voters are liberal Democrats who like Clinton better. Plus 3 voters are Republicans who like Dole better.

185 respondents, all but one (above 99 percent) voted in accord with their partisan attitudes. The lesson to be learned is that when voters possess consistent reasons to vote one way or another, their votes are usually consistent with those reasons.[7]

We must be cautious, however, in attributing causal connections. Voters have a need to maintain cognitive consistency between their partisan attitudes and their vote. Of course, the obvious way to achieve this consistency is to vote according to one's partisan attitudes. The problem is that when people decide whom to vote for, they may also rearrange their political attitudes to fit their vote decision. Once citizens decide to vote Republican, for example, they tend to develop new attitudes even more favorable to the Republican point of view. Thus, when a Dole supporter asserts that the economy is going well, that Dole is a great leader, or that Dole is right on the issues, we might suspect that some of these attitudes are generated to support the vote choice rather than the reverse. Of special concern is the voters' need to maintain cognitive consistency between their issue stances, their perceptions of the candidates' issue stances, and their choice of candidate.

Consider the voter whose views are initially out of alignment—for example, the voter might have liberal views combined with an initial attraction to the more conservative Republican candidate. How our voter would resolve this dilemma depends on which of the three elements—perceptions of the candidates, policy views, and candidate preference—is the weakest link. If our voter feels strongly about his or her policy views and is certain that the favored candidate opposes them, the voter could resolve the dilemma by reversing the candidate choice. This would be an example of policy voting. If the candidate's stands are only vaguely known, the easiest way out might be to shift one's estimate of the candidate stances. This process, known as "projection," is a frequent way out of the dilemma. Voters who see conservative candidates as liberals or vice versa are often projecting their favored views onto their favored candidates (or projecting views they dislike onto candidates they dislike).[8]

A third resolution of the dilemma would be for the voter to change a relatively weak policy stance to make it consistent with the position of the favored candidate. Because of a process known as "rationalization," it becomes impossible to disentangle fully the causal process that produces a correlation between voters' policy views and their candidate choice. Consider, for example, the many voters in 1996 observed to be both conservatives and Dole supporters. Presumably the reason why conservatives supported Dole was that they were attracted to his conservatism. But in theory, part of the reason could have been that liking Bob Dole (for whatever reason) made his supporters think better of his policy positions.

Does rationalization seriously contaminate survey analyses of the vote? Every report of a relationship between voter attitudes and voter decisions should be read cautiously, with an eye for the possibility that the seeming evidence of policy voting may be contaminated by widespread voter rationalization. Probably, however, electoral analysts err on the side of overcaution. Elaborate statistical analyses suggest that concern about voter rationalizations may be overdrawn (Page and Jones 1979; Markus and Converse 1979; Markus 1982). Still, we cannot be sure.

9-3 EXPLAINING ELECTION OUTCOMES

Explaining election outcomes requires a different level of analysis than explaining voter decisions. At the "microlevel," analysts try to account for why people vote the way they do. At the "macrolevel," analysts try to account for short-term forces and electoral trends, for example why Clinton beat Dole in 1996. The variables that explain individual decisions at the microlevel are often insufficient to account for macrolevel electoral change. For example, we have emphasized the role of voters' liberal-conservative ideologies and party identifications for predicting microlevel voting decisions. But aggregated to the national level, macro ideology and macro party identification ordinarily do not change sufficiently to account for electoral trends.[9] Political journalists may interpret a Democratic victory as the result of a liberal mood on the part of the electorate or a Republican victory as a conservative reaction. But as we saw in Chapter 4, the public shows little cyclicality between liberalism and conservatism. Similarly, short-term changes in party identification are thought to be too sluggish to create much movement in the national vote.[10] For instance, between 1988 and 1992, there was insufficient change in net ideology or net partisanship to account for reversal of party fortunes at the presidential level. To identify causes of electoral change, we must look to variables that change the most from one election to the next: the nature of the times and the candidates themselves.

Changing Economic Evaluations

Political parties and presidential candidates are helped as well as hurt by the electorate's reaction to the "nature-of-the-times." The public often changes its net evaluation of the relative problem-solving capabilities of the Democratic and Republican parties. Polling agencies have periodically asked public samples which party is more likely to bring about peace or bring about prosperity.

As illustrated in Figure 9.4, these judgments, largely driven by retrospective evaluations of the incumbent party's recent performance, can serve as an electoral barometer. They follow predictable rules. The incumbent party is most likely seen as the party of "peace" when the nation is not at war and as the party of "prosperity" when the economy is in good shape. For instance,

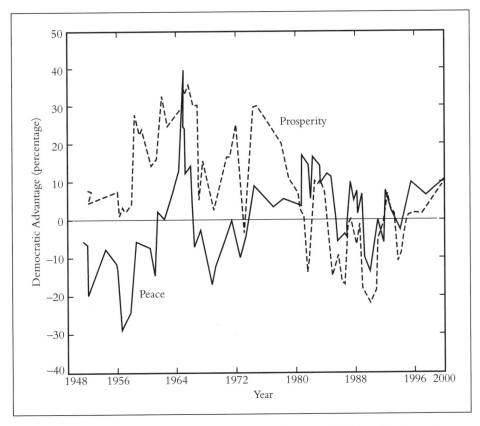

Figure 9.4   Ratings of parties on peace and prosperity. *Prosperity:* "Which political party do you think will keep the country prosperous?" *Peace:* "Which political party do you think would be more likely to keep the United States out of World War III?" For each, the Democratic advantage is the percentage responding democratic minus the percentage responding Republican. *Sources:* Gallup polls reported in Harold W. Stanley and Richard G. Niemi, *Vital Statistics of American Politics, 1999–2000* (Washington, DC: Congressional Quarterly Press, 2000), pp. 145–46.

during the early part of Bush's term, with the Cold War over and near the end of ten years of uninterrupted economic growth, both the "peace" and the "prosperity" indicators gave good news to the Republicans. With the onset of the recession, however, the "prosperity" advantage shifted decisively back to the Democrats.

The effects of the economy on presidential elections can be observed directly. For 13 post–World War II elections, Figure 9.5 graphs the vote (for the incumbent party) as a function of per capita income growth in the election year.

Clearly, the more the election year growth in per capita income, the stronger the national vote for the president's party.[11] It might even seem that all a president must do for his party to win the next election is to time the upward swings of the economic cycle to coincide with election years in the political cycle. Perhaps fortunately, it is not always that simple. Some presidents (e.g., Carter and Bush) have found themselves presiding over election year economic recessions instead of prosperity. And the incumbent party does not win with great regularity anyway. Of the 12 presidential elections from 1952 through 1996, the incumbent party won six and lost six.

Changing Candidate Evaluations

One important source of changing short-term electoral forces is the changing cast of candidates. For election to any level of office, the personal attractiveness

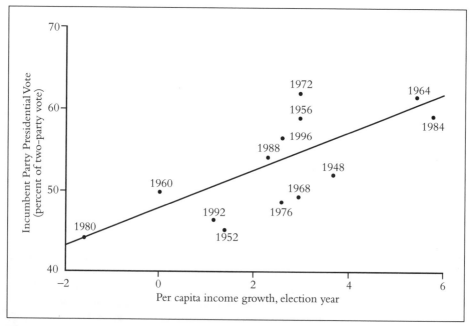

Figure 9.5 Presidential vote by income growth, 1952–1996.

of the major-party candidates can be a decisive factor. At the presidential level, the electorate's attraction to the Republican and the Democratic candidates can vary dramatically from one election to the next. Using multivariate statistical techniques, analysts have generated estimates of the net contributions of presidential candidates' personal attractiveness to presidential election outcomes.[12] The estimates are generated from NES respondents' "candidate evaluations" from the likes and dislikes expressed about candidates' personalities and leadership abilities.

Figure 9.6 presents the estimated candidate effects, 1952 to 1992. As the figure shows, the public's evaluations of candidate personalities and capabilities constitute a major determinant of electoral change. The most popular candidate of recent decades was Dwight ("Ike") Eisenhower, elected twice in the 1950s. Eisenhower was a popular general (from World War II), who engaged the voters with his warm smile. Most candidates have been favorably viewed by voters, but not to the extent that the 1950s voters "liked Ike." Two candidates who were viewed particularly negatively were Barry Goldwater (Republican in 1964) and George McGovern (Democrat in 1972). According to the estimates, each cost their party about 4 percentage points just in terms of likeability and leadership. Each lost in a major landslide.

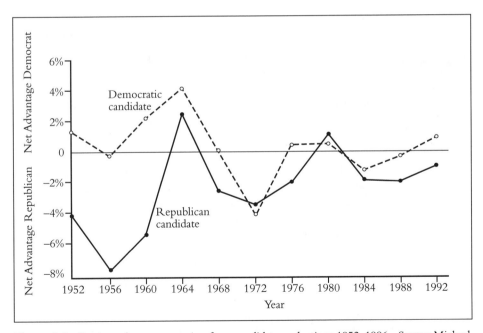

Figure 9.6 Partisan advantage accruing from candidate evaluations 1952–1996. *Sources:* Michael R. Kagay and Greg A. Caldeira, "A Reformed Electorate? Well at Least a Changed Electorate, 1972–1976," in William J. Crotty, ed., *Paths to Political Reform* (Lexington, MA: D. C. Heath, 1979); updated for 1980–1992 by Mark Wattier.

Candidate Issue Positions

Changing candidates provide more than a revolving set of personal attributes for the voter to judge. Each new candidate also brings a new set of policy positions. Even though the electorate is relatively fixed in its policy preferences, candidate positions do change. With each change of candidate, the shift in policy position can change the equation regarding which candidate is closest to the electorate's net preferences. Shifting candidate positions allow policy issues to affect election outcomes. Let us examine how.

Part of the popular lore of politics is that in a two-person race, the candidate who stakes out the middle ground of the political spectrum will win by virtue of appealing to the moderate voter. In terms of their own personal views, candidates tend to be more liberal (Democrats) or conservative (Republicans) than their electorates. Yet the belief that moderate voters decide elections pushes candidates toward the center of the spectrum.

This logic is spelled out in a model of the vote developed by Anthony Downs (1958, ch. 8), illustrated in Figure 9.7. This figure presents voter positions as a bell-shaped distribution on the liberal-conservative spectrum. The Downs model assumes policy voters who prefer the candidate closest to their views on this spectrum. If both candidates are stationed near the center, as in Figure 9.7(a), neither will have the policy edge. But if one candidate veers toward one of the ideological extremes—as does the conservative in Figure 9.7(b)—then policy voters in the middle will support the opponent, giving that more moderate candidate the victory.

The Downs model predicts that Democratic candidates get more votes when they take moderate rather than liberal positions, and that Republican candidates get more votes when they take moderate rather than conservative positions. These hypotheses have received considerable support in research on congressional (U.S. House and Senate) elections (Erikson 1971; Johannes and McAdams 1981; Wright and Berkman 1986; Erikson and Wright 1997).

Legislators create their own record of roll-call votes, which can be arrayed on a scale from 100 percent liberal to 100 percent conservative. Both Democrats and Republicans usually get ideological satisfactions from voting with their party's ideological extreme, but they gain electoral benefit from moderation. For Democrats, this electoral benefit is almost two percentage points for each ten percentage points of roll-call conservatism; for Republicans the benefit is almost two percentage points for each ten percentage points of roll call liberalism. One can extrapolate that Congress members in the middle of the ideological spectrum generate almost ten percentage points more of the vote than they would at their party's ideological extreme (Erikson and Wright, 2000).

If congressional contests can be decided by candidate ideology, the same must certainly be true for presidential elections. We have already seen that citizens' votes are determined by their personal positions on the left-right scale. Presidential election outcomes are partially determined by both the voters' and

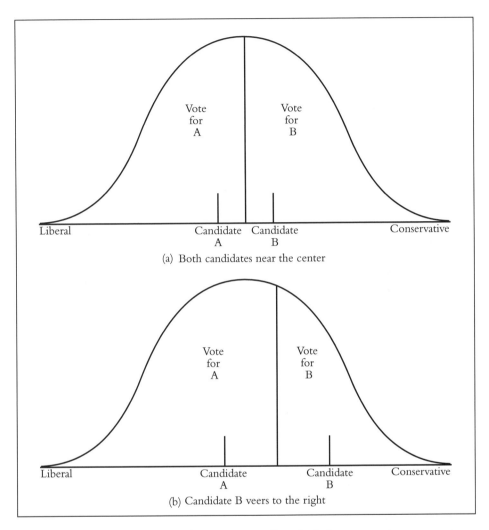

Figure 9.7   Candidate ideology and voter responses (hypothetical).

the candidates' ideological positions—which candidates (and which parties) best reflect the preferences of the voting electorate.

To shed some light, we can examine NES survey data. Since 1972, respondents have been asked not only to place themselves on the seven-point version of the ideological scale but also to locate the two major presidential candidates as well. Figure 9.8 traces the historical record, comparing the mean positions over time of the electorate and also the candidates as they are perceived by the NES voters.

Of the seven elections shown in Figure 9.8, the 1972 contest stands out as one clear case where most voters were closer ideologically to one candidate than

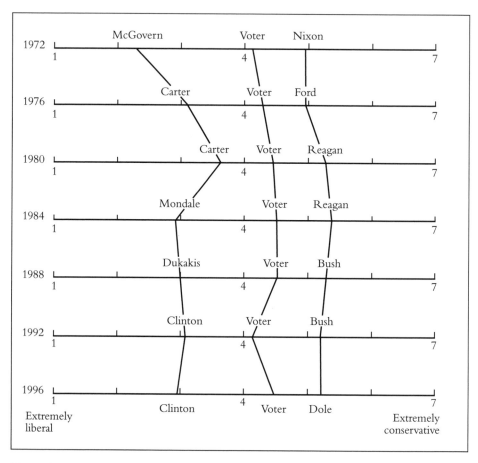

Figure 9.8   Mean ratings by voters of their own positions and candidates positions, on seven-point liberal-conservative scales, 1972–1996.

the other. In 1972, Richard Nixon was decisively reelected over the Democratic nominee, George McGovern, who most voters saw as too liberal. Figure 9.8 also shows that in elections since 1972, the average voter was close to the midpoint between the mean perceptions of the two candidates' positions. A close scan of the figure also shows that in all but one contest (1980), voters were slightly closer ideologically to the Republican than to the Democratic candidate. But this may be deceptive. Voters comfortable with ideological language tend to vote Republican, and on average about as Republican as their relative ideological proximity from the candidates would suggest. Some voters do not rate themselves or the candidates ideologically in NES surveys. Those voters are ideologically liberal, tend toward liberal positions on specific issues, and vote Democratic. Moreover, if we look at voter evaluations of candidate positions on specific issues rather than general ideology, they give the edge to the Democrats on some (e.g., abortion) and to the Republicans on others (e.g., affirmative action).

In the final analysis, what can we say about the role of issues and ideology in deciding election outcomes? Most political analysts and candidates believe that ideological issues divide Americans and that voters evaluate the ideological positions of candidates when they go the polls. Because issues and ideology matter, ideological mood swings by the public and the ideological responses of candidates and party leaders contribute to the relative fortunes of the Democratic and Republican parties in American politics. Moreover, the belief that issues and ideology matters drives politicians to respond to changes in public preferences when they become visible. We examine how politicians respond to public opinion in the next chapter.

9-4 CONCLUSION

When the rational-activist model is fulfilled, elections are decided by voters choosing candidates on the basis of their policy views. By this standard, the record of recent presidential elections is mixed. Tracing back to the 1964 presidential election, Democratic and Republican presidential candidates have polarized on liberal versus conservative grounds sufficiently to give the voters a clear ideological choice. At the "microlevel," many individual voters are motivated by the ideological menu when they cast their ballots. But they are also motivated by nonpolicy considerations. At the "macrolevel," the electorate's collective reactions to candidate positions do help to shape their electoral verdict, but in conjunction with other considerations.

Apart from policy issues or ideology, there are additional determinants of the vote. As we have seen, people sometimes vote for or against the incumbent party on the basis of its past performance. One would find difficulty condemning this behavior as irrational. In addition, two very important predictors of peoples' votes are their party identifications and their evaluations of the personal characteristics of the candidates. To the extent that people vote on the basis of a party identification that is based on policy or ideological considerations (such as when a staunch conservative is committed to the Republican party) and to the extent that the candidates are ideologically typical of their party (see Chapter 11), party voting can be viewed as rational.

But what about voting on the basis of the candidates' personal characteristics? One of the best predictors of a person's vote is simply whether the voter likes the personal qualities of the Democratic candidate more than the Republican. We may be tempted to view voting on such a nonissue (or even apolitical) basis to be voting on the basis of irrelevant considerations. But this view may be mistaken. Morris Fiorina (1977, 618) puts the question well:

> Considerable misconception surrounds the discussion of the importance of candidate qualities for the voting decision. Various authors have suggested that voting on the basis of candidate qualities is irrational, or at least of lower order of rationality than voting on the issues. . . . Such suggestions apparently stem from the erroneous belief that attitudes toward the candidates reflect no

more than Ike's smile, Nixon's beard, or Kennedy's accent. Actually, the bulk of the citizenry's impressions of the candidates focuses on qualities which are of legitimate relevance to the latter's capacity to govern: experience, leadership ability, and so on. . . . Why should a candidate's intelligence, administrative ability, etc. be any less a legitimate issue than where he stands on Medicare or aid to Israel?

That the voters choose the candidate they find to have the greatest character, competence, or trustworthiness is quite reasonable, even if their candidate is not the one that is closest to the voters on policy issues.[13] Unfortunately, however, voters do not always have the necessary information to make good judgments about a candidate's character until after they are elected president.

The collective decisions the voters make at election time contain elements of both stability and change. That most voting decisions are based on long-standing partisan loyalty adds an element of stability. Electoral shifts are normally only temporary, because voters shifting toward the advantaged party or candidate do not change their identification in the process. Consequently they may surge in the opposition partisan direction in a subsequent election, or even do so when voting in another contest held on the same date. Yet it is conceivable that circumstances could be so polarizing as to cause permanent transfers of partisan loyalties rather than temporary partisan defections. The most recent such realignment period, centered in the 1930s, produced a change from a considerable Republican advantage in national voting loyalties to a long-term Democratic edge in party identification that persists today. This change can be interpreted as at least a partial ratification by the American electorate of President Roosevelt's then unprecedented expansion of federal government services that were applied to cope with the equally unprecedented Great Depression. If another realignment is on the near horizon, it could restore the Republican party to the predominant position, or weaken it futher. Or it could change the focus of the issues that separate the two parties without producing a net change in the distribution of party loyalties. If any of these possibilities become true, the public will have arranged its partisan loyalties as a long-term electoral response to the decisive issues of the day.

NOTES

1. In Figure 9.1 the normal vote is constructed as the prediction of the House vote from regressing the vote on macrolevel party identification in quarter 3 of the election year.
2. See also Miller et al. (1976); Romero (1989).
3. Reasonable scholars have disagreed on the role of the ideology in voting behavior. Compare Luttbeg and Gant (1985); Tedin (1987); and Knight (1985).
4. Scholars disagree on the importance of racial sentiment in U.S. elections. Compare Carmines and Stimson (1980) and Abramowitz (1994).
5. On voter reaction to the economy, see Kiewiet (1983); Fiorina (1981); Markus (1988); Kinder et al. (1989); and MacKuen et al. (1992).

6. Measuring candidate evaluations from the likes/dislikes responses has a long tradition. See Campbell et al. (1960). Some studies have measured candidate evaluations from "thermometer" ratings of the candidates. Such ratings measure more than candidate likability and perceived leadership ability, and usually predict the vote so well that they may be considered surrogates for the vote decision. The result is the relatively empty prediction that people vote for the candidates they like best.

7. It has long been recognized that it is easy to predict voting decisions from known attitudes; for instance, see Campbell et al. (1954) and Kelley (1983). The best statistical procedure for predicting vote decisions from multiple attitudes is via a "probit" equation. Some readers may be interested in the probit equation predicting the vote from our three attitudinal predictors. We estimated the probit equation predicting 1996 presidential votes (Clinton vs. Dole) from the seven-point party identification scale, the 21-point left-right scale, and the (in-theory) 41-point candidate affect scale. Using the McKelvay-Zavoina procedure for estimating a pseudo-R squared, the three variables together account for 76 percent of the variance in the latent dimension that accounts for vote decisions.

8. "Projection," for example, can account for many of the instances of misperception shown in Table 9.2. For two discussions of projection, see Conover and Feldman (1989) and Lodge et al. (1989).

9. On the linkages between macrolevels and microlevels of analysis as they pertain to aggregated vote decisions, see Wright (1989).

10. The assertion that changes in party identification are not strong enough to affect elections may be less correct than once believed; see MacKuen et al. (1989).

11. On the economy and presidential elections, see Tufte (1978); Hibbs (1987); Erikson (1989); Abramowitz (2000); Lewis-Beck and Tien (2000); Wlezien and Erikson (2000); and Holbrook (2000).

12. Figure 9.6 is based on Donald E. Stokes's (1966) "partisan components analysis," which is designed to estimate the relative effects of different partisan attitudes on election results. Stokes applied the model to elections from 1952 through 1964. The procedure is based on a statistical analysis of SRC/NES respondents' reported likes and dislikes about parties and candidates. First the content of the likes and dislikes is divided into six components: (1) the Democratic candidate, (2) the Republican candidate, (3) government management, (4) domestic policy, (5) foreign policy, and (6) group benefits. The impact of each component on the election outcome is determined from a statistical analysis of how influential each component is in determining the vote, and how one-sided the evaluations are for the particular component in the particular election.

13. There is evidence that the most sophisticated voters are the most attentive and responsive to candidates' personal attributes; see Miller et al. (1986).

CHAPTER 10

The Public and Its Elected Representatives

In the previous chapter, the public showed some ability to utilize elections as a policy expression as prescribed by the rational-activist model. While this public competence falls far short of the democratic "ideal," policy-responsive voters can alter the outcome of a close election. In this chapter, we turn to the political leaders' ability to achieve consistency between public opinion and public policy by way of two additional models of political linkage which we discussed in Chapter 1: (1) the sharing model, which considers the agreement between the opinions of leaders and the public that may make policy consistent with public opinion, and (2) the role-playing model, which focuses on the personal concern of leaders to reflect the preferences of their constituents.

These three models receive the most extensive evaluation here as they posit characteristics of the representatives that condition their response to the public. Two other models—the interest groups and political party models, positing mediating institutions presumed to encourage political linkage—are covered in the next chapter.

10-1 OPINION SHARING BETWEEN POLICYMAKERS AND THE PUBLIC

The simplest form of linkage between public opinion and the policy decisions of political leaders would be the simple sharing of common opinions by followers and leaders. Consider, for example, the result if we elected representatives by lottery. Just as a randomly selected sample of survey respondents is representative of the general population within a certain margin of error, so would an assembly of 435 randomly selected people acting as a House of Representatives be representative of the population. If such an assembly could act without being distracted by the demands of powerful interest groups or the actual rules of Congress that impede change, then—for better or worse— its decisions would reflect public opinion. In actuality, the Congress (and other legislatures) may even be less representative than a random sample, if for no other reason than that members are supposedly chosen for their superior capabilities rather than their typicality.

How then do members of Congress and other political leaders differ from the general population? To answer this question we must find the traits that motivate some but not others to pursue a political career and the traits that favor success in achieving this goal. When people who are active in politics—whether as a local party official or an elected legislator—are interviewed, they often report that a spur to their political career was a very politically active family. The consensus based on several studies is that about 40 percent of the people who are presently politically active grew up in politically active homes. Thus, assuming only 10 percent of the public (at the most) are very active in politics themselves, almost half of our political leaders come from the 10 percent of the nation's families that are most politically active (Prewitt 1970, 66).

Officeholders also differ from the public in that they are often recruited to run for office. Intense political interest alone cannot push a person into a political, leadership role. To contest an election seriously, the would-be political leader must attract the base of support necessary to win. In some cases, the political leader is a "self-starter" who, because of his or her political interest and ambition, announces candidacy and then is able to accumulate support. In other cases, the future leader is selected by the local business or party elite for the task of getting elected. Sometimes the community or party leaders can choose from among many active aspirants for the role. But often at the local level, previously nonpolitical people end up as officeholders through the urging of friends or business associates. Kenneth Prewitt (1970) finds these "lateral entrants" to politics among members of the nonpartisan city councils he studies. James Barber (1965) finds them among members of the highly partisan Connecticut legislature. Many are what he calls "reluctants"—serving not because of their raw ambition or political interest, but because of the insistence of others.

Because the most wealthy and best-educated people are most likely to be politically interested and articulate and have the visibility to be tapped for a leadership role, we are not surprised that these are the people who become some of our political leaders. Put simply, there is an upper-status bias to the political-leadership opportunity structure. For example, as Table 10.1 shows, the occupations of the members of Congress are predominantly professional or managerial. In a society where only 18 percent of the workforce is engaged in such occupations, lawyers and businesspeople are particularly overrepresented in Congress. Lawyers and businesspeople are somewhat overrepresented in state legislatures as well. Additionally, greater percentages of legislators are white, male, protestant, and over 30 years old than are found for the general adult population.[1]

TABLE 10.1   OCCUPATIONS OF MEMBERS OF CONGRESS (1993) COMPARED WITH THE PUBLIC (1990) (IN PERCENTAGES)

Occupation	U.S Senate	U.S. House	U.S. Labor Force
Farmer	6	4	1
Manager (business)	24	31	9
Teacher	11	15	5
Lawyer	58	42	1
Journalist	8	6	★
All others	4	5	84

Sources: Norman J. Ornstein, Thomas E. Mann, and Michael J. Malaben, eds. *Vital Statistics on Congress 1993–1994* (Washington, DC: Congressional Quarterly, 1994); *Statistical Abstract of the United States,* 1992.

★Less than .5 percent. Senate and House percentages add to greater than 100 percent due to multiple listings. "All other" category does not include prior occupation in government or politics.

In part, the overrepresentation of the affluent and educated in the councils of government stems from the middle-class leadership structure of the two major political parties. Even the Democratic party—supposedly the more representative of the working class—draws its leaders from the middle class. By contrast, in many other democracies, the presence of a Socialist or Labor party draws working-class people into greater political activity. In Norway, for example, political participation is not correlated with affluence as it is in the United States (Rokkan and Campbell 1960). Although Socialist and Labor parties do not draw their leaders exclusively from the working class that they represent, they do at least open the door for the political recruitment of blue-collar workers, a door that is rather closed in this country (Epstein 1967, 167–200).

There is not anything inherently sinister about the status differentiation between political leaders and the general public because the disproportionate concentration of political leadership skills in the hands of the better educated and prosperous may make it all but inevitable. For example, even the delegates to the "reformed" Democratic National Convention of 1972 were still far better educated and more affluent than the general population, although they were representative on the basis of race, sex, and age. Even movements of economic protest draw their leaders from the most affluent strata within the protest group. For example, Lipset (1950, 166) finds this to be the pattern within agricultural protest movements: "The battle for higher prices and a better economic return for their labor has been conducted by the farmers who need it least."

The status "bias" to the leadership structure does not necessarily mean that the views of political leaders typify their class instead of that of the general public. For example, the 1972 delegates to the Democratic Convention obviously did not express the prevailing views of the economically comfortable. To be sure, there are potential sources of misrepresentation in the group background of political leaders. For example, one might suspect that state legislatures would be more eager to pass "no-fault" insurance laws if they contained fewer lawyers.[2] Or the city council that is overstocked with local businesspeople might well be suspected of reflecting the prevailing norms of the local business community rather than views of the general population.

A more general consideration is that whatever their individual ideologies, the generally affluent leaders might resist wealth-redistribution legislation that would work against their self-interest. For example, a study of the attitudes of national convention delegates (in 1956) found that one of the few issues on which delegates of both parties were clearly more conservative than the public was that of making the rich pay a greater share of taxes (McClosky et al. 1960). Of course, one could argue that virtually all political viewpoints found in the general population are also shared by some of the prosperous and better educated—and these might be our leaders. Even among the affluent, few are sufficiently politically motivated to run for public office. Those who do, do not always represent the political views of their economic group. Thus, one can hope that there is sufficient diversity of viewpoint among the candidates for office from which the people make their selections at the polls. And if not, there is still the possibility that electoral pressure can divert the behavior of political leaders from unrepresentative personal preferences.

We can also try a direct approach to the question of whether political leaders and the general public share the same opinions by comparing the political attitudes of the two groups. In Chapter 6 we already discussed one difference between public and leadership attitudes—leaders' greater support for civil liberties. For routine policy issues, however, only a few sets of data exist from which to assess the correspondence between the policy views of the public and its elected leaders.

One opportunity to assess the correspondence between public and leader opinion derives from CBS/*New York Times* polls that have compared public and congressional responses to current political issues: in 1970 (by CBS) and in 1978 and 1982 (by CBS/*New York Times*). Examples for 1978 are shown in Table 10.2. For both the 1970 and 1982 surveys, the distributions of responses by the public sample and by U.S. House members generally differ by only a few percentage points.[3]

For a final comparison of public and decision-maker opinion, Table 10.3 compares the survey responses of a large public sample with those of a large national sample of state legislators, from a study of state politics by Uslaner and Weber (1983). Collectively, the views of the legislators closely parallel the views of the national public. Over the ten issues, the average difference between public and legislator preferences is only 8 percentage points. On most of these issues, the public appears more liberal than the legislators, but only slightly so.

That the public and its elected leaders have similar opinions on a variety of issues may seem a surprise, given the general differences in income, education, and other background characteristics between the public and its leaders. The biases of leadership selection could have us expect that elected officials would share the opinions of the upper class rather than the opinions of the public as a whole. Does the apparent absence of an upper-class bias to leadership opinions imply that electoral politics works to weed out political candidates whose views are

TABLE 10.2 COMPARISON OF PUBLIC AND CONGRESSIONAL OPINION ON SELECTED POLICY ISSUES, 1978 (IN PERCENTAGES)

	Public	U.S. House Members
Defense: In favor of decreasing money for national defense	23	26
SALT: In favor of SALT II	67	74
Health Insurance: In favor of "National Health Insurance fully paid by government"	47	45
Tax cut: Opposed to a "large federal income tax cut"	53	51
Abortion: In favor of "government paying for abortions for the poor"	41	35

Source: Kathleen A. Frankovic and Laurily K. Epstein, "Congress and Its Constituency: The New Machine Politics" (paper delivered at American Political Science Association Meeting, Washington DC, Sept. 1979).

TABLE 10.3 POLICY PREFERENCES OF THE PUBLIC AND OF STATE LEGISLATORS ON STATE POLICIES, 1968–1974

Policy	Percentage Favoring "Liberal" Policy Position	
	Public	Legislators
Capital punishment opposition	36	35
Abortion in first three months	51	53
Firearms permits	74	51
Teacher unionization	68	59
Teacher strikes	37	26
Police and fireman unionization	65	60
Police and fireman strikes	31	16
Marijuana legalization	17	17
No-fault auto insurance	76	76
Parochial school aid	57	45

Source: Eric M. Uslaner and Ronald E. Weber, "Policy and American State Elites: Descriptive Representation Versus Electoral Accountability," *Journal of Politics* 45 (Feb. 1983): 188.

incongruent with the public opinion? Another question, not easily answered, is to what extent the elected leaders' relatively representative preferences guide their behavior in office so that government policies also become consistent with public opinion. There are forces—such as the inertial drag of legislative rules and norms, the opposition of powerful pressure groups, and the failure of executive leadership—that can prevent even a representative Congress or state legislature from doing what the public seems to want.

10-2 LEADERSHIP RESPONSIVENESS TO PUBLIC OPINION

We have seen that there is some sharing of political preferences by people and their elected representatives. Thus, if the representatives' preferences guide their behavior in office, there will be at least a modest amount of agreement between public opinion and policy. But this observed tendency for elected leaders to reflect the opinions of their constituencies is a fragile foundation for democratic representation. Given the obvious limits to voter rationality, and the biases in the recruitment of political leaders, it is a wonder that we can find so much similarity of opinions between the public and its elected leaders. Moreover, a general pattern of opinion sharing is of no help in those instances when the public and its representatives do hold different views. However, elected officials sometimes follow public opinion rather than their own private inclinations, playing the role of the electorate's instructed delegates—what we have labeled the role-playing model.

Figure 10.1 presents one classic formulation of the dynamics of legislative representation. This diagram is adapted from Warren E. Miller and Donald E.

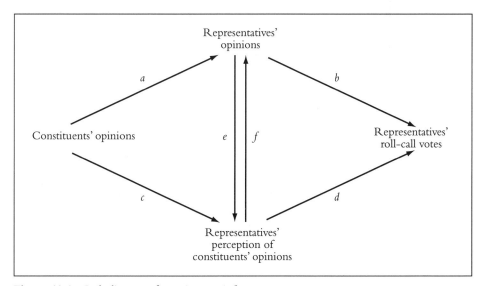

Figure 10.1   Path diagram of constituency influence.

Stokes's (1963) classic study of congressional representation in 1958. First, via elections, constituency opinion helps determine the opinions of the legislators (path *a*). Second, legislators' opinions obviously influence legislators' actions (path *b*). Next, we see the role-playing model. Legislators enhance representation when they correctly perceive constituency opinion (path *c*), but only if their perceptions of constituency opinion influence their behavior (path *d*). [Paths *e* and *f* provide minor complications: Legislators can convince themselves that their views reflect the public's (*e*) or change their private opinions in response to their perceptions of constituency views (*f*).]

For this role-playing model to work, two conditions must be met. One requirement is that the representative has an incentive to choose the public's preference over his or her own. This incentive may be the representative's belief that following public opinion is ordinarily the "right" thing to do. Or the incentive may be the representative's fear that electoral defeat would be the consequence of ignoring public opinion. The second requirement is that the representative must know what public opinion is. We discuss this second requirement in a later section.

Seemingly crucial to the public having much real control over what their leaders do is a strong desire by public officials to take public opinion into account. Ascertaining the strength of the desire is difficult. As V.O. Key lamented in 1961, "We have practically no systematic information about what goes on in the minds of public men as they ruminate about the weight to be given to public opinion in governmental decision" (Key 1961a, 490).

Political scientists uncover some clues to the motivations of elected leaders by studying the attitudes and behavior of politicians. A good starting point is the study of Congress in 1958 conducted by Miller and Stokes, who were interested in how frequently elected officials follow their perception of constituency views. As part of their study, they interviewed their sampled congressmen regarding both their own positions and what they perceived their constituencies' positions to be on several issues, representing the policy dimensions of civil rights, social welfare, and foreign policy.

Miller and Stokes found that in each area the representatives' personal preferences and their perceptions of constituency preference were about equally (and positively) correlated with their roll-call behavior. From this evidence, Congress members apparently give about as much weight to their perceptions of constituency views as they do to their own opinions.

Legislators and the Role of Instructed Delegate

For nearly every circumstance in which one human being interacts with another—such as being a parent, asking a question in a classroom, interviewing for a job, or serving as a representative in government—people hold beliefs about what the proper behavior would be in those circumstances. The sets of beliefs prescribing behavior for each social situation are normally labeled "roles." Roles vary greatly in their richness, with some encompassing very broad ranges of expected behavior and others giving only minimal direction.

Our concern here is with the role of the political representative and, more specifically, with that role as perceived by representatives.

Several researchers have explored the various aspects of how legislators see their roles, or their perceptions of how they are expected to behave. Almost 40 years ago, John Wahlke, Heinz Eulau, and their associates (1962) identified three types of representatives roles. One type are the "trustees," who believe it is their duty to follow the dictates of their conscience regarding what is best for the constituency. At the opposite extreme are "delegates," who believe they should follow the wishes of their constituents even if those wishes are contrary to their own. Finally, because the researchers found many representatives who claim they act as trustees on some issues and delegates on others, a conditional or mixed role was defined, which they call the "politico." Many researchers have administered elaborate questionnaires to state legislators and members of Congress to classify them according to their representative roles. In most studies, trustees outnumber delegates, with many legislators preferring the in-between delegate designation (Wahlke et al. 1962; Sorauf 1963; Davidson 1969; Soule 1969; Kuklinski and McCrone 1981; Friesema and Hedlund 1981). Thus, based at least on self-perception, the legislator who conscientiously follows public opinion may be in the minority.

The sorting of legislators on the basis of their legislative roles is a significant enterprise only if their role designations help us predict their actual behavior. Theoretically, delegates are more responsive to constituency interest than trustees are. Two studies of California legislators suggest this is the case (Kuklinski and Elling 1977; McCrone and Kuklinski 1979). These studies compare delegates, politicos, and trustees in terms of the extent to which their roll-call voting corresponded to constituency voting on a series of referenda. True to theory, the first of these studies (by Kuklinski with Elling) found a far higher correlation between constituency liberalism and roll-call liberalism for delegates than for trustees, with politicos in between. The second study (by McCrone and Kuklinski) also reports that among California legislators the delegates are the most responsive to perceived constituency opinion and are the most accurate in estimating actual constituency opinion.

As we have seen, the role most conducive to political linkage—that of delegate—appears to be favored by only a minority in most legislatures. To be sure, many legislators would find it too humiliating to admit to being merely the voice of others. Indeed, most of us applaud the "courage" of the "statesmanlike" legislator who votes with his independent judgement rather than with the views of his constituency—particularly when we agree with that judgment.

Beyond asking legislators about how they perceive their role, it is difficult to ascertain how much political leaders believe they should heed public opinion because they think it is what they ought to do. We cannot test the validity of this aspect of the role-playing model directly, for it is impossible to enter politicians' minds and locate their value structures. However, some observers of politics have argued that the widespread belief that public opinion should be followed is a major source of democratic linkage between the public and its leaders. V.O. Key, for example, saw within the subculture of political leaders that a value of fundamental importance is a "regard for public opinion, a belief that in some way or another, it should prevail" (Key 1961b, 538).

Legislative Responsiveness to Constituency Opinion

Examining what elected representatives do rather than what they say produces considerable evidence that representatives respond to the threat of potential electoral defeat. Legislators show greater attention to public opinion as election day looms than when the last election is just over. Similarly, when their district's lines are redrawn, legislators can be observed to change their voting record to match the new constituency. Here we examine some of this evidence, from state legislators and the U.S. Congess.

Kuklinski's (1978) study of California legislators offers unusually graphic evidence of the responsiveness of legislators to the periodic threat of losing reelection. Kuklinski assesses representation by means of the correlation between constituency liberalism (as expressed in frequent referendum results) and the legislator's roll-call liberalism. Figure 10.2, from Kuklinski's study, indicates that legislators can give substantial representation to their constituencies. California assemblymen—who face reelection every two years—consistently do so throughout the years examined. For California state senators, however, who face reelection only every four years, the pattern is more cyclical. The half of the California senators who faced reelection in 1970 were substantially more responsive in 1970 than in succeeding years when the electoral threat diminished. Completing the pattern, those facing reelection in 1972 sharply improved their representation in 1972 and just as sharply showed a decline thereafter. These examples suggest that

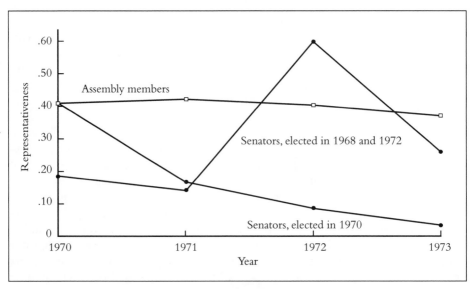

Figure 10.2 Relationship between the temporal proximity of elections and representativeness of California State Legislators. *Source:* James H. Kuklinski, "Representatives and Elections: A Policy Analysis," *American Political Science Review,* 72 (Mar. 1978): 174.

representatives do respond to perceived electoral threats by seeking to better reflect their constituents' views as election time approaches.

The six-year senatorial term makes the U.S. Senate a particularly useful laboratory for watching elected leaders respond to public opinion. We might presume that senators act more constrained by opinion in their state late in their six-year term, as reelection time approaches, than early in the six-year cycle just after getting elected. Democratic senators, whose personal beliefs are generally more liberal than those of their statewide constituencies, would act less liberal as their term progresses but then return to more liberal positions once reelected. Republican senators, whose personal beliefs generally are more conservative than those of their statewide constituencies, would act less conservative as their term progresses but then return to more conservative positions once reelected. In a study of Senate roll-call voting, Martin Thomas (1985) reports exactly these patterns. As shown in Figure 10.3, both Democratic senators and Republican senators moderate their roll-call record as reelection time approaches. This figure is based on senators who seek reelection only. Interestingly, Thomas shows that senators who do not run again also moderate their views through the fifth year, but they return to their original positions in the sixth year when the retirement decision has been made.

With their two-year term, U.S. House members must continually try to stay elected. Although we cannot watch their behavior change with the election cycle, an opportunity is sometimes present to watch them change when their constituency changes. U.S. House constituencies change every 10 years following the U.S. Census, as district lines must be redrawn to reflect population changes. Amihai Glazer and Marc Robbins (1985) have statistically demonstrated that U.S. House members respond to these district changes in their roll-call voting. They measure changes in constituency opinion by comparing the past presidential voting of the new and the old district. By this measure, when the House member gets a more liberal district, the member usually becomes more liberal; when the member gets a more conservative district, the member usually becomes more conservative.

Numerous studies have examined the statistical relationship between constituency opinion on the one hand and legislative behavior on the other. For instance, Snyder (1996) was able to compare the votes cast in the California state legislature with constituency choices on several referenda issues. Although unable to establish whether this was due to a direct connection or to sharing of values, he found a strong statistical connection between constituency preferences and legislative behavior. In the U.S. Senate, we can measure constituency preferences from the liberal-conservative preferences in statewide surveys. State-level liberalism in surveys is strongly related to roll-call liberalism by the states' senators (Wright and Berkman 1986; Erikson 1990; Wood and Anderson 1998). Liberal states get liberal senators and conservative states get conservative senators.

For the U.S. House of Representatives, we possess no direct measure of constituency opinion. However, for congressional districts the district vote for president is a serviceable indicator of the district's ideological tendencies. Districts that vote Democratic for president are more liberal, and districts that vote Republican are more conservative. A district's presidential voting record is

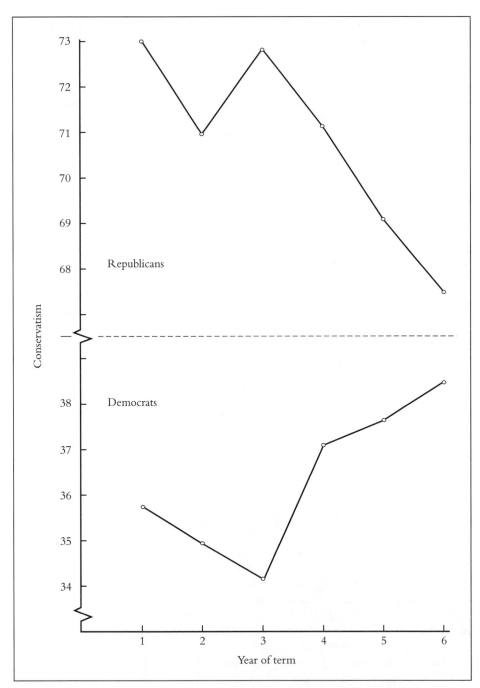

Figure 10.3 Mean conservatism of senators seeking reelection, by party and year of term.
Source: Martin Thomas, "Election Proximity and Senatorial Roll–Call Voting," *American Journal of Political Science* 29 (Feb. 1985): 103.

a good predictor of its House member's voting record. For instance, Figure 10.4 shows that the constituency vote division in the 1996 Clinton-Dole election is a good predictor of House roll-call voting in the subsequent Congress (1997–1998). Within each party, the most liberal House members represented the most liberal districts. This apparent responsiveness to constituency opinion helps explain why neither party in Congress acts as a homogeneous unit. When Democratic representatives vote like Republicans or Republican representatives vote like Democrats, chances are that they are responding to the apparent liberalism-conservatism of the district.

Political Ambition

The belief that their reelection chances hinge on how well they represent constituency opinion will not influence officeholders much unless they care about getting reelected. As Joseph Schlesinger (1966, 2) has described the positive functions of political ambition, "no more irresponsible government is imaginable than one of high-minded men unconcerned for their political futures." Politicians at the top of the political ladder usually try to continue in office for as long as possible. For example, presidents normally want to stay in office for their constitutional allotment of two full terms. Even Truman and Johnson, who both opted for retirement in the spring of their reelection years, did so only after the results of the first presidential primaries indicated that even renomination by their party would have been a difficult hurdle.

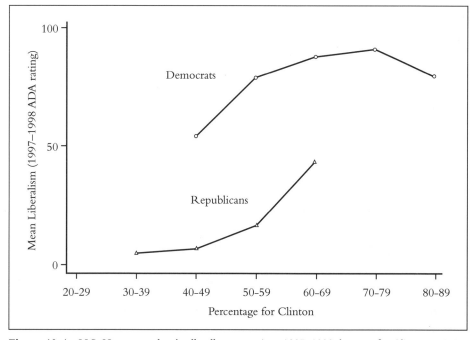

Figure 10-4 U.S. House members' roll-call conservatism, 1997–1998, by vote for Clinton in 1996.

Most governors (about 75 percent) also seek reelection when not constitutionally prohibited by term limits. Ambition also runs high for Congress members. When up for reelection, about 85 percent of senators and 90 percent of House members try for another term. Even when Congress members "retire," they rarely leave political life; most House members who retire actually do so to seek the higher office of U.S. senator or governor.

A theme that runs through studies of Congress is that the goal of staying elected guides an overwhelming portion of what Congress does. Douglas Arnold (1990) claims that reelection is the dominant congressional motivation. Kingdon (1973) shows that pleasing constituency interests dominates congressional decision-making even on routine legislation. Mayhew (1974) argues that the structural organization of the House of Representatives is best understood as a collective response to the members' need to stay elected. Fenno (1978) finds that in their frequent trips home, representatives are often compelled to explain their roll-call votes to the satisfaction of important constituents. Of course the desire to stay elected is not the sole congressional motivation. Parker (1992) reminds us that representatives focus on generating safe reelection prospects to free themselves in order to pursue their policy agendas.

Promoters of term limits for officeholders argue that the continuous preoccupation with staying elected *detracts* from the policymaking function. One concern is that elected officials may overrespond to the less enlightened aspects of public opinion. As V.O. Key (1961a, 490) once observed, "Public men often act as if they thought the deciding margin in elections was cast by fools; moreover, by fools informed enough and alert enough to bring retribution to those who dare not demonstrate themselves equally foolish."

Interestingly, the inclination to hold onto office for several terms is a relatively recent phenomenon. In the nineteenth century, House and Senate members quite frequently returned to private life after a term or two (Price 1971). This is the pattern in many state legislatures even today, particularly in states offering low legislative pay (Squire 1988, 1992). With variation from state to state, the retirement rate for state legislatures is about 22 percent (Jewell and Breaux 1988, table 1) and declining (Montcrief 1999). Many "retirements" actually are to pursue alternative electoral opportunities. Incumbents' interest in reelection is least in local settings, such as city councils and school boards (Prewitt 1970; Karnig and Walter 1977).

The rate at which members of a legislative body retire appears to have very delicate effects. Observers of Congress often moan that the institution is handicapped by the presence of too many aged members who refuse to give up their seats. Students of state legislatures offer the opposite complaint; that frequent retirements (often to seek higher office as well as to go back home) produce a depletion of experienced personnel. The chief concern is that the retiring legislator may become indifferent to public opinion (Rothenberg and Sanders 2000).

One should not necessarily infer that the nonambitious officeholder's escape from electoral pressure typically frees him or her to pursue worthy goals that are too advanced for public opinion to accept. Surely, many politicians are strongly motivated to advance their conception of the "public interest." But this pursuit of accomplishments only feeds their ambition for further public service, which requires reelection. This reasoning suggests the hypothesis that the political leaders with the strongest policy motivations tend to feel the most electoral pressure to satisfy public opinion—at least on matters that concern them least.

10-3 HOW ELECTED OFFICIALS LEARN PUBLIC OPINION

Even if political decision-makers want to follow public opinion, they cannot do so effectively unless they know what people want. According to political lore, good politicians have acute political antennae that detect the prevailing political mood when they wander among the "grass roots." Of course, the policymaker is also sometimes able to "read" public opinion more directly by examining the results of available opinion polls.

Politicians and Opinion Polls

Like the rest of us, politicians have access to commercial opinion polls such as the Gallup Poll. But the politicians often seek further intelligence regarding public opinion by commissioning their own polls. The first president to poll the public in earnest was Franklin Roosevelt in the late 1930s. While his next two successors, Truman and Eisenhower, had little use for private polling, presidential polling picked up in earnest with John Kennedy. Since then virtually every major presidential decision has been made with the benefit of private polls. Presidents seek updates regarding public attitudes toward current policies, public reactions to future policy options, and, especially, information on their own personal standing with the voters. In many instances, the private intelligence gained from polls guided presidential decision-making. For instance, Presidents Kennedy and Johnson both pushed Medicare with a particular insistence because their polls offered the confidence that Medicare was a winning issue with the electorate (Jacobs 1993).

Politicians below the presidential level also do their own polling, as do the major political parties. Senate and House members spend about 3 percent of their sizable campaign war chests on polling their states or districts (Fritz and Morris 1992). (Nonincumbents spend considerably less.) Although the general purpose of this polling is to ascertain the status of their "horse race" with current or future opponents, private constituency polls can also register signals regarding shifts in the constituency concerns.

Like everybody else, the politician must read opinion polls with caution. Even an officeholder with no other goal than staying elected would be unwise to base every decision on what the polls show to be the majority preference. Let us examine the reasons why.

As we saw in Chapter 3, the distribution of opinion on an issue can vary with the exact question wording. Consequently, the side of the issue on which majority opinion lies may shift with the seemingly innocuous change in the question wording. Given such circumstances, following public opinion as registered by a single reading on the issue may make little political sense.

Actually, the policy that would yield the political leader the most votes (and satisfy the most people) is not always the majority position anyway. For example, according to unsubstantiated political lore, the minority who are gun enthusiasts have managed to defeat several politicians who advocate strict gun control even though polls show a majority favor strict gun registration laws. Presumably, the average person, when asked, favors gun control but will not translate this conviction into action at the ballot box; the gun enthusiast will.

Paradoxically, the way to build a winning majority at the polls may sometimes be to create a coalition of intense minorities. Suppose, for example, opinion on three issues is divided 80 to 20, with the different minorities on each issue feeling several times more intensely about the matter than those on the other side do. Then if one candidate supports the majority side on all three issues, and the other appeals to the minority side, the candidate of the minorities could win 60 percent of the vote (20 times 3), assuming all vote on the basis of the issues. There would be nothing inherently undemocratic about the majority side losing out on each question, as a majority of voters would have more to gain from their representation on the one question they feel strongly about than they would from representation on the other two issues.

Politicians may sometimes feel free to ignore the polls because they recognize that the public generally expects its political leaders to use their own judgment, acting as trustees rather than delegates. In one Iowa poll, most respondents said state legislators should act according to their conscience rather than according to constituency preferences when there was a conflict between the two (Hedlund 1975). The public seems to react with displeasure at being asked to do what it thinks it elects officials to do—namely, make decisions. For example, many defeats of fluoridation referenda seem based on public displeasure at the failure of elected officials to take a stand on the issue by passing the buck to the voters (Crain et al. 1969, 138).

Acting as a trustee rather than as an instructed delegate may have still another payoff. At election time, voters make retrospective judgments of the apparent success or failure of past policies, perhaps even more then on the policy issues under current debate. If the politician expects to be rewarded or punished for the "nature of the times," polls of current public sentiment about what ought to be done offer little help. For example, a president exercises good political judgment when he makes economic policy on the basis of expert opinion rather than on the basis of a poll taken to see what people think would work best.

The war in Vietnam provides an important example of a discrepancy between the public's policy preference at the moment and the public's eventual reaction to the consequences of that policy. According to the polls, the public supported the war at the time the crucial steps of escalated involvement were taken. If the high officials in the Kennedy-Johnson administrations had fore-knowledge of the extent of the public's eventual opposition to a prolonged war, perhaps they would have made different decisions. Here, politicians had to make crucial guesses about public reactions to their possible options—for which polls could not give answers.

Other Ways of Learning Constituency Opinion

When asked how they learn constituency opinion, politicians claim not to rely much on polls. But more informal methods of estimating public opinion also contain pitfalls. Crowd reactions, obviously, can be misleading indicators, given the disproportionately politicized and partisan nature of political audiences. How accurate are other sources of opinion cues—constituency questionnaires, election returns, constituency group composition, the mail, and the people back home to whom the representative talks?

Constituency Questionnaires Unlike the president, lower-level elected officials (such as state legislators) rarely have the resources to conduct their own polls. But one group of officeholders who do make frequent use of polls (albeit of a nonscientific sort) are members of the U.S. House of Representatives. Thanks to their franking (free mailing) privilege, House members can send question-naires to each household in their district for only the printing costs. Most House members utilize this privilege to poll constituents. Since the "polls" are administered by mailed questionnaires, they have a low return rate, perhaps as low as 15 percent on the average. This can permit the views of a small minor-ity (typically the better educated and more wealthy) to be mistaken for "public opinion." But one might argue that since the minority who take the trouble to respond to congressional polls presumably feel most intensely about the issues, any bias in the poll results would be weighted in favor of the more attentive constituents who will vote according to their beliefs.

Election Returns After elections, a popular fad is to analyze the results to de-termine the new "mood" of the voters. We saw earlier that changes in the vot-ers' partisan preferences are not the result of ideological mood swings. Republican gains do not necessarily mean the public has swung farther to the right, for example. The winning politician who mistakenly interprets his land-slide victory to be a mandate for his favorite programs may experience a sud-den erosion of his popular support. The urge to decipher meaning from particular issue-oriented election contests can also lead to errors, if judgment is made without consideration of the general partisan trend.

For example, in retrospect, an overinterpretation of election results by concerned political observers may have been the reason why official Washing-ton overestimated the popular support for demagogic Senator Joe McCarthy in the early 1950s. Although, at first, other senators disassociated themselves from McCarthy's unsubstantiated claims that some indefinite number of known Communists were running loose in the State Department and elsewhere in government, the defeat of several of McCarthy's senatorial critics in the 1950 and 1952 elections silenced the remainder. In retrospect, we see that most of the defeated McCarthy opponents would have lost anyway in the anti-Democratic tide (Polsby 1960). Almost unnoticed, McCarthy trailed his party's ticket when he won reelection from Wisconsin voters in 1952. Actually, McCarthy was never supported by a clear majority of the public; most of his supporters came from predictable sources such as small-town Republicans. If otherwise alert politicians had paid closer attention to the polls than to isolated and misleading election returns, the "climate of opinion" that assumed McCarthy was invincible may never have been created. As it was, McCarthy's downfall—forced by his attack on the U.S. Army—was as sudden as the initial rise of what became known as "McCarthyism."

Although politicians may overinterpret partisan electoral trends or the electoral fate of certain candidates who are linked to particular causes, they may learn something meaningful about general political preferences of their constituencies from how their constituencies vote in comparison with others. We saw earlier in Figure 10.4 that roll-call voting by U.S. House members correlates with presidential voting. Although we do not know whether this relationship results because House members consciously try to adjust their behavior in direct response to election returns, we can reasonably infer that district presidential voting normally will be a good gauge of whether the district is a relatively conservative or a relatively liberal district. Although the extent to which con- stituency opinion is related to partisan voting has not been fully explored, one Florida study finds that the 1968 presidential election returns were a good predictor of referendum voting on certain issues in state legislative districts. Moreover, legislators appeared to respond to the cue of past district voting when they were asked to predict the referendum verdicts in their districts (Erikson et al. 1975).

Group Characteristics Politicians sometimes take their cues regarding public opinion from their knowledge of the group composition of their constituency. For instance, politicians sometimes appear sensitive to the concerns of African-Americans in direct proportion to the number of their constituents who are black. Politicians use constituency wealth as an indicator of constituency receptivity to new taxing or spending policies, or the constituency's education level as a signal of constituency receptivity to liberal social policies. Politicians with older than average constituencies show particular sensitivity to the needs of the elderly. And more than one otherwise conservative politician has supported gay rights when representing a sizable gay minority. Beyond the most obvious indicators, however, constituency social composition is an incomplete guide to public opinion. District demography may be of little help if the district is socially diverse or the issue is obscure.

The Mail Political officeholders place only slight stock in the mail they receive as a source of constituency opinion. Skepticism is highest when a barrage of letters clearly originates from a pressure-group campaign. But, setting such cases aside, is there any bias to the mail that political leaders receive? Writing a letter to an elected official is not a regular activity for the average person. Only about 15 percent of the public admit to ever having written to a public official, and about two-thirds of all letters written to officials originate from 3 percent of the public (Converse et al. 1965). For some reason, people who write letters to public officials tend to occupy the right side of the political spectrum. Politicians who measure public opinion solely from the content of their mail would judge public opinion to be more conservative than it is (Verba and Brody 1970).

Vocal Minorities To the casual observer, public opinion might appear to be obvious without having to resort to the numbers in scientific polls. Why not simply tune into a radio talk show and listen to the voice of people? Or, for the visually inclined, why not consult the tone of the political letters to the editor in the local newspaper? The problem of course would be that the views of talk show callers and newspaper letter writers present a distortion of general opinion. They do represent the views of a "vocal minority."

If one were to ascertain public opinion by monitoring the vocal minority, one would be fooled into seeing a public that is more conservative and Republican (and irate) than it actually is. Like people who write letters to politicians, people who write letters to their local newspaper are more conservative than the general public (Converse et al. 1965; Verba and Brody 1970). Perhaps even to a greater extent, talk show callers too are decidedly more conservative than the general public. One reason for the vocal minority's conservatism is their social status and leisure time. The typical member of the vocal minority is wealthier, more educated, and older than the average citizen, and such people tend to be more politically conservative. Second, newspapers and talk shows sometimes screen letters and calls for ideological content.

Most politicians are sufficiently sophisticated to discount the views of the vocal minority as representative of general opinion. But quite possibly the exaggerated conservatism of those who speak out causes politicians to see public opinion as more conservative than it actually is.

Attentive Constituents One important aspect of the life of elected officials is their "home style" (Fenno 1978) when they interact directly with local constituents. Elected officials strive to maintain personal contact with many constituents, including partisan allies, members of various local groups, plus other people who are simply friends. Politicians often use these conversations with attentive constituents to try to sense changes in the public mood. Constituents from whom elected officials seek advice are more knowledgeable than the average, and also higher in socioeconomic status than the average voter (Boynton et al. 1969). Attentive opinion can be a leading indicator of what ordinary citizens will soon be thinking, but their views may be atypical because of their higher status.

How Accurately Do Officials See Public Opinion?

Given the multiple devices that officeholders employ, how accurate are their perceptions of public opinion? One approach to answering this question is to sample opinion and then see how closely the public's representatives can predict what it is. In their study of congressional representation, Miller and Stokes (1963) sampled opinions in congressional districts and then asked the districts' representatives what they thought the opinion of their home constituency would be.

On civil rights issues, Miller and Stokes found the correlation between constituency opinion and the representative's perception of it to be a fairly robust +.74—a not surprising indication that representatives of pro–civil rights black constituencies and anti–civil rights Deep South districts are aware of their constituents' views. Correlations were also positive on social welfare issues (+.17) and foreign policy issues (+.25). Although the latter correlations are relatively weak, one reason is the sampling error in the estimates of constituency opinion. There is reason to believe that if constituency opinion were estimated from larger samples, the correlations between constituency opinion and congressional perceptions of it would be considerably higher (Erikson 1978).

Perhaps the most difficult test for the representatives' political antennae to pass is correct estimation of constituency opinion on issues that do not attract much public attention. Accordingly, Ronald Hedlund and H. Paul Friesema (1972) quizzed Iowa state legislators about their constituencies' majority preference on four statewide referendum questions that were about to be put before the voters. On four questions, the accuracy of the legislatures' predictions varied from 59 to 92 percent. (Simply by guessing randomly, the legislators would have been correct half the time.) The predictions on home rule for cities (92 percent) and reapportionment (82 percent) were reasonably accurate. But the rates of successful prediction on holding annual legislative sessions (59 percent) and giving the governor the item veto (64 percent) were only slightly beyond the guess range. Hedlund and Friesema argue that the home rule and reapportionment referenda attracted greater public interest than annual legislative sessions and item vetoes. This suggests greater accuracy in representatives' predictions of public opinion in those areas where the public expresses the most interest.

Following up on the Iowa study, Erikson et al. (1975) asked Florida legislators to predict the precentage-point breakdown in their district and in the state on three "straw ballot" referendum issues in 1973. One of these issues dealt with the volatile question of "forced" school busing to achieve racial balance. Here the legislators' estimates were not far off the mark; for example, the 56 responding House members erred by an average of only 7 percentage points in predicting their district's anti-busing vote. But estimates were less accurate on the less publicized, remaining straw ballot issues. On the question of allowing prayers in schools, the average error in prediction was 11 percentage points; on the question of rejecting the dual (or segregated) school system, the average was 12 percentage points. Once again, the legislators' awareness of public opinion is weaker when the public focus on the issue is weak.

Recall from Table 10-3 the ten issues on which Uslaner and Weber ascertained public opinion and legislator opinion in the states. As part of their study, Uslaner and Weber (1979) also obtained indirect ("simulated") measures of constituency opinion, plus legislators' perceptions of constituency opinion. They estimated that across the ten issues, state legislators averaged about a 20-percentage-point error in predicting constituency opinion. Their most ironic result is that on nine of the ten issues, legislators' estimates of constituency opinion tended to be farther from constituency opinion than the legislators' own opinions were. In other words, the legislators would have done a better job of representing constituency opinion by acting on their own beliefs than on their rather erroneous estimates of what their constituents wanted. The Miller-Stokes data show a similar pattern. Across two of the three sets of issues, constituency opinion correlates slightly more strongly with the elected representative's opinion than with the representative's perception of constituency opinion.

Both the Uslaner-Weber and the Miller-Stokes estimates of constituency opinion have their own errors of measurement, thus requiring cautious interpretation. But these studies suggest that legislators do at least as good a job of representing constituency opinion by following their own views as they do by trying to follow their perception of constituency opinion. This tentative conclusion carries negative implications about legislators' abilities to infer constituency opinion. But the positive side is the extent to which the representation process results in congruence between the views of constituencies and their representatives.

10-4 DO ELECTED OFFICIALS NEED TO FOLLOW PUBLIC OPINION?

We have seen that although politicians sometimes have difficulty reading public opinion, they apparently do at least try to consider public opinion when making decisions—partly from fear of electoral retribution if they do not. Actually, one might suspect that public officials do not need to weigh public opinion very heavily in order to get reelected. Incumbent officeholders do not lose reelection bids at a rate that should stimulate electoral anxiety. Futhermore, most people do not monitor their leaders' policy with sufficient attention to produce massive voter reactions. Could it be that elected officials have more freedom from public opinion than they realize?

Incumbency

Judging from their reelection rates, it may seem that elected politicians have little reason to fear the wrath of the voters. In most election years, over 90 percent of U.S. House incumbents who seek reelection get returned to office. For U.S. senators, the reelection rate is only slightly lower. State legislators are also secure. Their reelection rate is about 92 percent, but with important variations among states (Jewell and Breaux 1988, table 2). Governors are somewhat more vulnerable, winning reelection about 80 percent of the time they seek another term. Governors are electorally insecure because, like presidents, they are held accountable for the nature of the times during their administration. Legislators face less electoral difficulty than executives because voters find difficulty in tracing the consequences of legislators' actions or in holding them individually responsible for government outputs, such as the state of the economy.

There are five clear reasons why incumbents almost always win reelection. First, many elections are partisan contests, decided along partisan lines. Consequently, elections tend to favor the locally dominant party. Where one party dominates the other, even an officeholder with a low personal standing can win repeated victories.

Second, incumbents generally win because the status of incumbency gives them an advantage over their opponents. In U.S. House elections, incumbents gain 5 percent or more of the vote between the time of their first victory and their first reelection attempt (Alford and Brady 1993). The process that accounts for this "incumbency advantage" is not fully understood, but it seems that House members are able to exploit their powers of office (or "perks"), such as their free mailing privileges, for electoral advantage. Another factor may be a cautious tendency of voters to support whoever is already in office. U.S. senators and state governors do not seem to enjoy as great an incumbency advantage as U.S. House members. At the state legislature level, the possible role of incumbency advantage has not been subjected to much research (but see Holbrook and Tidmarch 1991; Breaux and Jewell 1992).

Third, incumbents generally win because they tend to obtain a strong, positive, "personal" vote due to their attractive candidate qualities. Candidates with strong personal appeals tend to win elections. Winners, therefore, tend to be strong candidates. And when winners seek reelection as incumbents, they generally continue to be strong candidates.

Fourth, incumbents gain votes by scaring off strong challenges. Potentially strong candidates tend not to run in elections that they are likely to lose. Thus potentially strong challengers avoid challenging strong incumbents, preferring to wait until the incumbent retires. In addition, the weaker candidates who do run against strong incumbents have few resources at their disposal, since potential supporters prefer not to concentrate their time and money on contests with little hope of success. (Cox and Katz 1996; Jacobson and Kernell 1983).

A final reason why incumbents rarely lose is that anticipation of defeat make incumbents more likely to retire. Consider the case of the House banking scandal in 1991 and 1992. Many U.S. House members were revealed to have major overdrafts at the House bank, a circumstance that was difficult to explain to their constituents. Of the 27 most vulnerable members with over 200 overdrafts, only seven were actually defeated at the polls. But an additional nine retired in anticipation of likely defeat. The loss rate of incumbent candidates was held to a minimum because one-third of the Congress members with major overdrafts chose to quit rather than face the wrath of voters (Banducci and Karp 1994; Jacobson and Dimmock 1994; Groseclose and Krehbiel 1994; Alford et al. 1994).

The electoral success of incumbents may signal both something wrong and something right about the status of representation. When elected officials are repeatedly returned to office because people vote for the dominant party or because people vote for the security of the familiar incumbent, incumbents can act unbound by constituency opinion. Under these circumstances, representation suffers. But there is also a positive side. Part of the reason for incumbent success is that candidates who do things to please voters are allowed to stay in office the longest. Incumbents who represent their constituencies on policy issues are allowed to stay in office the longest.[4]

Voters' Attention to Policy Positions

To what extent do voters react to the content of their leaders' policy decisions and policy proposals for the future? In the previous chapter we saw some evidence of policy voting, particularly at the presidential level. But especially in subpresidential contests, the public's information is usually too low to allow the expectation of much policy voting. The best data in this regard concern people's awareness of the U.S. House of Representatives and their particular representative.

Congress is not a very salient institution to most people. When asked which party has more representatives, more give the correct answer than the incorrect one. But with an adjustment for correct guessing, the best estimate is that typically less than half the congressional-election voters cast their ballot with the firm knowledge of which party is in control (Stokes and Miller 1962, 537). Once, following the 1966 election, a plurality in an SRC poll incorrectly responded that the Republicans controlled Congress—apparently confusing the big Republican gains that were reported in the news media with a Republican majority.[5] When people are asked how good a job Congress is doing, one might suspect that their response would depend on their party indentification and the party in power—Democrats would like Congress best when the Democrats control it, for example. But it does not work out this way. People more frequently rate the performance of Congress to be good when their party controls the White House but not Congress, than when their party controls Congress but not the White House (Davidson et al. 1968, 60–63).

When we turn to voters' knowledge of their individual congressmen and congressional candidates, no improvement is found. First of all, the local news media rarely give much coverage to the roll-call stands of members of Congress or to the substantive issues of congressional campaigns. Consequently, even if more people had the urge to follow the congressional politics of their district, they would have great difficulty in doing so. Only slightly more than half the public can even name their congressional representative. Similarly, at election time only about half will claim to have read or heard anything about their representative in Washington or the opposing candidate. When interviewers probe to find out what the voter has read or heard about the incumbent congressional candidate, the answer is typically a vague reference such as "he (or she) is a good person," or "he (or she) knows the problems." In National Election Studies, only about 15 percent express reactions to their U.S. House member in terms of positions taken on specific legislation (Jacobson 1987).

On even hotly debated congressional issues, few people know where their Congress member stands. Table 10.4 shows the results of two surveys asking people their Congress member's position on a particular matter. One issue is funding for development of a supersonic transport plane (SST) shortly after Congress rejected it in 1971. Most people polled were unable to state how their representative voted on the SST. Those who tried to answer the question were wrong almost as often as they were right—suggesting that even those who tried to answer were mostly guessing. Thus the voters were almost totally unaware of how their congressional representative voted on an issue that had commanded a substantial share of newspaper headlines for a period of months. Evidently, members of Congress were able to vote on the SST without attracting much public attention back home.

The second issue presented in Table 10.4 is women's rights, from a study by Patricia Hurley and Kim Hill (1981). The specific congressional action is

TABLE 10.4 VOTER AWARENESS OF REPRESENTATIVE'S POSITION: TWO EXAMPLES

	Representative's Actual Vote on SST, 1971	
Voter's Perception of Representative's Position	**For SST**	**Against SST**
For SST	12%	3.5%
Against SST	14	27.5
Not sure	74	69
	100%	100%

	Representative's Actual Vote on ERA Extension, 1978	
	For Extension	**Against Extension**
Pro-equal role for women	63%	48%
Women's place is in the home	10	19
In between	27	33
	100%	100%

Source: On SST: John Kraft "A Review of Voter Attitudes in Ten Key Congressional Districts," report to the American Businessmen's Committee for National Priorities, Aug. 1971; percentages are district means. On ERA extension: Recomputed from Patricia A. Hurley and Kim Quaille Hill, "The Prospects for Issue Voting in Contemporary Congressional Elections: An Assessment of Citizen Awareness and Representation," in Norman R. Luttbeg, ed., *Public Opinion and Public Policy*, 3rd ed. (Itasca, IL; Peacock Press, 1981), table 12.5, p. 169.

the 1978 vote on extending the deadline for ratification of the equal rights amendment. The perceptions obtained from the public samples are estimates of where the respondent's U.S. representative stood on the general issue of women's rights. Respondents were only slightly more willing to rate their representative as being for equal rights if the representative actually favored an extension of the ERA deadline than if the representative did not.

From these survey findings, one might well wonder whether the representatives need to pay any attention to the views of their constituency when they weigh the alternatives of each legislative decision. As Warren Miller and Donald Stokes (1963, 54) put it, "Congressmen feel that their individual legislative actions may have considerable impact on the electorate, yet some simple facts about the representative's salience to his constituents imply that this could hardly be true."

Indeed, we may have a major political linkage between mass opinion and leader response that is generally overlooked—although the public is not watching, leaders sometimes do what they think the public wants because they mistakenly believe the public is paying attention! If this is true, then leaders' responsiveness to public opinion would quickly evaporate once somebody points out to them that surveys show the public to be rather indifferent to what they do. On the other hand, maybe the politicians do not exaggerate the importance of their record to their electoral fate as much as the polls seem to suggest. Let us explore the reasons why officeholders do have to tread carefully when they consider violating something called public opinion.

First, the high reelection rate of incumbent officeholders does not actually provide much security because the officeholder may want to win not only the next election but also several thereafter. Consider the case of U.S. House members, who have a success rate of over 90 percent per reelection attempt. Most will survive their next election, but in the long run about one-third eventually leave office via an electoral defeat (Erikson 1976c, 613–32). Such odds on long-term electoral survival can give House members reason to pay special attention to constituency desires.

Second, the easiest way for voters to become aware of their elected leader's record is for it to be exploited by an opponent as a stand against public opinion. Therefore, although name recognition generally wins votes, lack of public knowledge of a political leader's policy stands may sometimes actually be a sign of successful representation. Put another way, if members of Congress became more casual in their consideration of constituency views—for example, if representatives of liberal districts started acting like conservatives and vice versa—the polls might show much more evidence of constituency awareness, and on election day, more incumbents would be defeated. David Mayhew (1974, 37) explains it this way:

> When we say "Congressman Smith is unbeatable," we do not mean there is nothing he could do that would lose him his seat. Rather we mean, "Congressman Smith is unbeatable as long as he continues to do the things he is doing." If he stopped answering his mail, or stopped visiting his district, or began voting randomly on roll calls, or shifted his vote record eighty points on the ADA scale, he would bring on primary or November election troubles in a hurry.

Third, one should note that there does exist a sprinkling of informed voters who shift their political weight according to the policy views of the candidates. Even if these alert voters compose a tiny fraction of the total, their opinion leadership allows them to influence election outcomes to an extent beyond what their number would indicate. As information about the representative diffuses downward from relatively informed opinion leaders to the mass public, many voters may "get simple positive or negative cues about the Congressman which were provoked by his legislative actions but no longer have a recognizable policy content," as Miller and Stokes (1963, 55) suggest. By responding to such cues, a significant number of voters may act as if they are relatively informed about their representative's record. As a result, the collective electoral decisions in congressional contests may be more responsive to roll-call records than our knowledge about individual voters would indicate.

In the previous chapter, we saw that the result of this process is visible in election returns. Members of Congress lose votes when they take ideologically extreme public positions. Normally such vote loss due to policy stands is not sufficient for defeat, since the representative is often protected by a modest incumbency advantage and a one-party district. But the few who do lose can often blame their own policy stands for their misfortune.

10-5 CONCLUSION

This chapter has examined two mechanisms by which elected leaders follow public opinion. According to the sharing model, elected leaders tend to do what their constituents want for the simple reason that elected leaders are drawn from the constituencies that elect them. When we consider the relationship between the legislator's views and the mean (or median) views of the legislator's specific geographic constituency, the sharing model provides little guarantee of representation. Just because a person is selected as a representative does not guarantee that this representative represents the average views of the constituency. The sharing model works best in the aggregate, in the sense that a large legislative body should normally represent the views of the larger population from whom it is collectively elected.

To obtain correspondence between (average) constituency views and the positions of elected leaders, we must rely on the electoral process. According to the rational-activist model (see Chapter 9), voters elect those candidates who represent their own views, so that winners hopefully reflect constituency opinion better than do losers. Because they believe that their constituents are watching, elected leaders try to anticipate the reactions of their electorate in advance. This is the role-playing model at work. Because of the fear of electoral sanctions (or simply because they believe it to be what they ought to do), elected leaders play the role of "delegate," trying to please their constituents. By doing so, they provide their constituents with policy representation.

The general public shows some ambivalence regarding the desired role of their representatives. Should our elected leaders follow our instructions (as del-

egates following the role-playing model) or should they follow their own beliefs regarding our best interests, regardless of the electoral consequences (as
our trustees)? As we have seen, elected leaders try hard to stay elected, and
they generally succeed. In other words, they are good at their job—that of
professional politician. In recent years, many voters have been attracted to the
idea of term limits for elected officials, as a way of ridding politics of career
politicians. Opponents of term limits counter that if we do not like our elected
leaders we should remove them at the ballot box, not by constitutional provisions. This controversy is far from settled.

NOTES

1. On the social and economic characteristics of American legislators, see Jewell and
   Patterson (1981), Thompson and Moncrief (1992), Bullock (1992), and Freeman
   and Lyons (1992).
2. Within state legislatures, lawyers more frequently vote against no-fault insurance
   than do nonlawyers (Dyer 1976).
3. Comparing opinions of the mass public with those of elites is difficult, since the
   results of the comparison can depend on the issues that are chosen. In 1982, the
   CBS/*New York Times* survey included questions about school prayer and constitutional amendment to balance the budget. Elites appear more liberal on these
   issues because they are more aware of the complexities than the mass public, who
   treat questions about prayers and balanced budgets as referenda on God and the
   virtue of thrift, respectively. On the practical issues of what Congress should
   spend its money on, the 1982 mass and congressional samples were remarkably
   similar.

   In 1970, U.S. senators were also interviewed. Senators displayed slightly more
   liberal views than either the public or the House members. For an analysis of the
   1970 findings, see Backstrom (1977). For an analysis of the 1978 data, see Bishop
   and Frankovic (1981).
4. This discussion is drawn from Erikson and Wright (1997).
5. Following the 1966 election, 44 percent said the Republicans have "elected the
   most congressmen"; 21 percent said the Democrats did; the remainder said they
   did not know; from Survey Research Center, *1966 Election Study Codebook*.

CHAPTER 11

Parties and Interest Groups: Mediating Institutions and Representation

This chapter discusses the two remaining political linkage models: the political parties model and the interest groups model. Democratic theorists concerned with the political linkage between public opinion and the behavior of elected leaders often posit an important role for the mediating institutions of political parties and interest groups. In its own way, each of these institutions can provide a means for a less than fully attentive public to attain its desired policy goals.

When political parties take distinctive stands on issues, party labels provide a mechanism for voters' own views. Rather than having to select among individual candidates for each of the many offices, the voters need only to select among the different parties based on their policy programs. For this model to work, parties should not only offer different programs, but also be able to enact their programs when placed in office. Interest groups have advantages that are not normally available to the mass public. Unlike ordinary citizens, organized interest groups can pay full-time attention to policymaking actions of government: They have personnel holders on hand in Washington or the state capital to persuade officeholders toward the policy views of their group. During election campaigns, interest groups can contribute money to candidates and urge their members to vote for candidates who represent their views. Obviously these activities can alter public policy away from public opinion as well as toward it. When interest groups reflect public opinion, their influence on the actions of elected officials helps promote accountability. When group opinion differs from public opinion, group influence works against democratic representation. Therefore a key question is how frequently elected leaders follow the public will when they in fact are responding to the pressures of organized groups.

11-1 POLITICAL PARTIES AND REPRESENTATION

According to the political parties model, party labels clarify the political choices available to the voters. For this model to work, two conditions are necessary. First each political party would outline the program it would enact if its candidates were elected; thus the candidates' party labels signify what the candidates will do if elected. Second, each voter would make his or her selection at the polls on the basis of the party that best represents his or her views. This model simplifies the task of the policy-oriented voter. Instead of monitoring each candidate's campaign statements and hoping that they reflect what the candidates would do if elected, the voter would need only to learn the differences between the parties' programs and use party labels as a cue to rational voting. Ideally the party programs would be determined by an internal consensus that would govern the behavior of the party's elected officials.

As we have seen, voters do not always behave according to the prescription of the political parties model. Although most voters identify with a political party and party identifiers generally vote for their party's candidates, Republican and Democratic identifiers are not greatly polarized on policy differences between the two major parties. Thus, party voting by the mass public can be considered policy voting only to a limited degree.

Whether voters are given the opportunity to rationally select candidates on the basis of party labels depends on the existence of differences between the programs of the two parties. Here we examine the extent to which Republican and Democratic leaders actually differ in their policy presences, in the programs they offer to the voters, and in their behavior in office. Observers often say that to win elections, political parties must appeal to the moderate voter. In addition, parties must also appeal to their loyal activists who are often located at their party's ideological directions—toward the center by the party's desire to win elections, and away from the center, toward the ideological preferences of the party leaders and activists.[1]

To keep parties near where the voters are, the electorate must do its part. A policy-motivated electorate will stimulate election-hungry parties toward the electorate's point of view. But suppose that the electorate is too disinterested or uninformed to keep the parties honest? Then elections would be decided solely on nonpolicy grounds and policies would depend solely on the whims of the partisan victors.

Ideology and Party Leaders

Although ideology is only a modest source of partisan division between ordinary Republican and Democratic voters, ideology is often a strong motivation for party activists. The ordinary voter of somewhat conservative persuasion who is raised a Democrat might be content to remain a Democrat. Similarly, the mildly liberal voter who grew up a Republican might stay with the Republican party. For most voters, politics is not that important to compel a matching ideology and party identification. But political activists are different. When a strong ideology motivation spurs an individual to politcal activism, the individual will usually develop an affinity for the ideologically appropriate party.[2]

The earliest comparison of the personal beliefs of Republican and Democratic leaders is a study by Herbert McClosky, Paul Hoffman, and Rosemary O'Hara (1960). In 1957 and 1958, they gathered identical kinds of data from a public sample of supporters of the political parties and from delegates to the 1956 political party conventions. For each of 24 policy issues, the researchers reported the percentages of both leaders and followers preferring an increased government commitment. They found that issue differences were greater between Republican and Democratic leaders than between Republican and Democratic followers (party identifiers). Republican delegates were to the right of Republican identifiers and Democratic delegates were to the left of Democratic identifiers. Of the two sets of 1956 delegates, the Democrats were more representative of the general electorate. In fact, the difference was not close: even Republican identifiers as a group were ideologically closer to the Democratic delegates than to the Republican delegates.

Studies of delegates to national conventions since 1956 have continued to show each party's delegates to be more "extreme" than the party rank and file. Whether one party is more extreme than the other will vary. In 1972 it was the Democrat's turn to be the least representative. Reversing the 1956 pattern, delegates were so far to the left that rank-and-file Democrats were closer to the Republican delegates on the issues (Soule and McGrath 1975; Kirkpatrick 1975). Since 1972, the parties have been relatively balanced in their extremity (Miller and Jennings 1987, ch. 9). In terms of ideological identification, Democratic delegates tend to be liberal or moderate but rarely conservative; Republican delegates tend to be conservative or moderate but rarely liberal. Table 11.1 displays these patterns for delegates over five sets of national conventions.

Political parties obtain their political energy from their activists. But while the classic role of party leader is to balance the ideological preferences of the activists with the pragmatism necessary for winning elections, party activists may be more concerned with ideological correctness than with electoral victory. Increasingly, with the decline of the traditional party organizations and the growing openness of party conventions brought by recent reforms of party rules, ideologues are moving into party leadership positions and determining the nominations of party candidates. There is an irony here. As the leadership structure of the political parties is becoming more internally democratic, the potential for greater policy choice between the parties is created. This increases the conflict between the parties' policies and the preferences of their less-active rank-and-file supporters.

Voter Positions Relative to the Parties

Here we examine party differences through the eyes of the voters and look at how voters see their positions in relation to the parties. We limit this presenta-

TABLE 11.1 IDEOLOGICAL IDENTIFICATION OF NATIONAL CONVENTION DELEGATES, 1976–1992

	1980		1984		1988		1992		1996	
Ideology	Dem.	Rep.	Dem.	Rep.	Dem.	Rep.	Dem.	Rep.	Dem.	Rep.
Liberal (%)	46	2	48	1	43	0	47	1	43	0
Moderate (%)	42	36	42	35	43	35	44	32	48	27
Conservative (%)	6	58	4	60	5	58	5	63	5	70

Source: Harold W. Stanley and Richard G. Niemi. *Vital Statistics of American Politics, 1999–2000* (Washington: Congressional Quarterly Press, 2000), p. 71.

tion to voters who recognize that the Democrats are to the left of the Republicans. Of this group, we ask how many perceive themselves to the left of both parties, how many see themselves to the right, and how many see themselves in between the two parties ideologically.

We examine averages over three issues—liberalism-conservatism, domestic spending, and defense spending. On each issue, 1996 NES respondents were asked their own position, the Democrats' position, and the Republicans' position, all on the usual seven-point scale. Selecting only voters who saw the Democrats to the left of the Republicans on all three issues, we ask whether the voter saw his or her position as, on average, to the left of both parties, to the right of both parties, or in between. (Those who, according to our measure, perceive their average position as perfectly represented by one party—e.g., seeing the Republicans as just right but the Democrats as too liberal—are scored with those in between the parties.)

Table 11.2 displays the relevant data. Overall, two-thirds of those voters who correctly order the parties ideologically see themselves as in between the Democrats on their left and the Republicans on their right. The remainder are about evenly split between conservatives who see themselves even to the right of the Republican party and liberals who see themselves even to the left of the Democratic party.

Table 11.2 also shows perceptions of party positions broken down by party identification. The most interesting groups are the "strong Democrats" and "strong Republicans." A full 44 percent of the strong Democrats see themselves to the left of both parties. Similarly, 40 percent of the strong Republicans see themselves to the right of both parties. The two parties need to satisfy these polarized partisans. But they also need to woo the portion of the electorate—mainly weak partisans and Independents—in the middle of the ideological spectrum.

Each party's "strong" identifiers are typical of the party's primary electorate. Activists tend to dominate low-turnout party primaries, with an important segment urging the party in a more extreme ideological direction. But to the extent primary electorate chose "extreme" candidates over moderates, the party will risk alienating voters in the center. Each party's more moderate candidates

**TABLE 11.2   VOTER PERCEPTIONS OF THEIR PARTY POSITIONS
RELATIVE TO THE TWO MAJOR PARTIES**

Respondent's Perceived Position	Strong Dem.	Weak Dem.	Ind.	Weak Rep.	Strong Rep.	All Cases
Respondent left of both parties	44%	29%	11%	0%	0%	15%
Respondent in between both parties★	56	66	74	66	60	67
Respondent right of both parties	0	5	15	34	40	18
	100%	100%	100%	100%	100%	100%

Source: National Election Studies, 1996 election data. Based on respondent (voters only) perceptions of self and candidate positions on ideology, domestic spending, and defense spending. Includes only voters who saw the Democrats to the left of the Republicans on all three issues.

★Includes respondents who see themselves in the same location as one of the parties (11%).

may have the greatest chance to become general election winners, but they face the problem first in securing the nomination from a hostile primary electorate.[3]

And what of that half of the relevant electorate who appear to be ideologically located in between the two parties? These centrist voters seemingly face a distasteful choice of giving power either to a party that is too conservative or a party that is too liberal. However, these voters also have the opportunity to split their ticket, voting for a balance of some Democrats and some Republicans. The desire of moderate voters for an ideological balance of party power may help to explain the frequent pattern of divided party control. Arguably, moderate voters should prefer the ideological balance of one party controlling the presidency and the other controlling Congress to unified control by either party (Fiorina 1992; Alesina and Rosenthal 1995).

This balancing of party control is particularly evident in midterm elections in which the presidential party almost always loses seats in Congress. Not only do midterm voters elect fewer Congress members of the president's party than two years before; they also generally elect fewer members of the president's party than they do when the president's party is out of power. In other words, each party historically has been more favorably treated by midterm voters when it is *out* of power at the presidential level (Erikson 1988).

The Relevance of Party Platforms

At national conventions every fourth year, each party devotes considerable time to spelling out the details of its platform in order to detail the party's "official" position on the issues of the day. Party platforms are often dismissed as mere ritualistic documentation since they are rarely read, quickly forgotten, and not officially binding on a party's candidates. Nevertheless, as research by Gerald Pomper with Susan Lederer (1980, Chs. 7 and 8) shows, careful reading of party platforms provides some clues as to what the parties would do if they came to power.

Pomper examined the content of the Democratic and Republican platforms from 1944 to 1976. He found about half the platform statements to be relatively meaningless rhetoric ("The American Free Enterprise System is one of the greatest achievements of humankind") or statements about the issues that are too vague or broad to be meaningful ("The Anti-Trust Laws must be vigorously enforced"). About another quarter of the platform statements qualify as policy approval ("In the Nuclear Test Ban Treaty, we have written our commitment to limitations on the arms race"). Finally, about one-quarter are detailed policy statements like "The Security of the American Trade Unions must be strengthened by repealing 14B of the Taft-Hartley Act." Although voters almost never read party platforms directly, platform statements reach voters indirectly, "through interest groups, mass media, candidates' speeches, and incomplete popular perceptions" (Pomper 1980, 152).

Of particular relevance is whether parties keep their policy promises once in office. Pomper finds that about two-thirds of the winning presidential party's pledges become at least particularly fulfilled during the next four years. Somewhat over half the pledges of the nonpresidential party do as well. When both parties offer the same pledge in their platforms, the pledge is fulfilled in some fashion about 80 percent of the time. Pomper (1980, 176) concludes, "We should take platforms seriously, because politicians take them seriously." A recent statistical analysis by Ian Budge and Richard Hofferbert (1990) reinforces Pomper's conclusion. They were able to trace changing federal expenditure patterns to changing priorities found in party platforms, particularly the platform of the presidential party (see also McDonald et al., 1999).

Party Voting in Legislatures

Ideally from the standpoint of the political parties model, the electorally dominant party not only would have articulated a program that achieves voter approval but would be in a position to enact that program once in power. The dominant congressional party, for example, would be able to enact its preferred legislation, particularly if the president is of the same party and gives encouragement.

As is well known, events do not always work out this way in the American political system. About as often as not, the presidency and Congress are controlled by different parties, leading to the potential for gridlock or stalemate. And even when the president's party is in the congressional majority, the president still has difficulty pushing his proposals through Congress. For instance, President Clinton was unable to pass his health care legislation in 1993 and 1994, even though the Democrats held a healthy majority in both House and Senate.

This discussion may seem to suggest that party labels are not very relevant in Congress. However, that is far from the truth. In fact, party affiliation is the single best predictor of roll-call voting in Congress. And by almost all accounts, the degree of party polarization in Congress is increasing rather than decreasing (Aldrich 1996; Binder 1997; Coleman 1997; Cox and Mc-Cubbins 1993; Sinclair 1997).

Table 11.3 shows the party breakdown on selected U.S. House roll calls of the late 1990s, during the second Clinton administration. Although this table illustrates that neither party in Congress acts as an all-cohesive unit, it also shows that party affiliation is a strong predictor of roll-call voting. Each of the eight issues shown in Table 11.3 is a "party vote" (defined as a vote in which a majority of Republicans oppose a majority of Democrats). In recent Congresses, some 40 to 60 percent of roll-call votes have been party votes. On party votes, Congress members vote about 80 percent with their party on the average, and about 20 percent with their opposition (Rohde 1992; Hurley 1989; Patterson and Caldiera 1988).

In Congress, party voting is most prevalent on issues with a discernible liberal versus conservative content, especially those dealing with the government's role in the economy and social welfare legislation. Especially on civil rights, the ideological distinctiveness between the congressional parties is growing rather than weakening. Figure 11.1 summarizes these party differences in terms

TABLE 11.3   PARTY VOTING IN THE U.S. HOUSE ON EIGHT SELECTED ROLL CALLS, 1995–1998

		Democrats	Republicans	All
Increase minimum wage (1995)	For	188	77	266
	Against	6	156	162
Welfare reform bill (1995)	For	30	226	256
	Against	165	4	170
Override Clinton's veto of bill limiting product liability	For	33	225	258
	Against	157	5	163
Repeal assault-weapons ban (1996)	For	56	183	239
	Against	130	42	173
Cut antimissile defense (1996)	For	182	2	239
	Against	2	228	173
Expand IRAs to be spent on education (1997)	For	15	215	230
	Against	189	8	198
End affirmative-action set-asides in federal highway program (1997)	For	3	191	194
	Against	195	29	225
Withdraw Bosnian troops (1998)	For	13	180	193
	Against	181	43	225

Source: Michael Barone and Grant Ujifusa, *The Almanac of American Politics, 1998* (Washington: National Journal, 1997); *The Almanac of American Politics 2000* (Washington: National Journal, 1999).

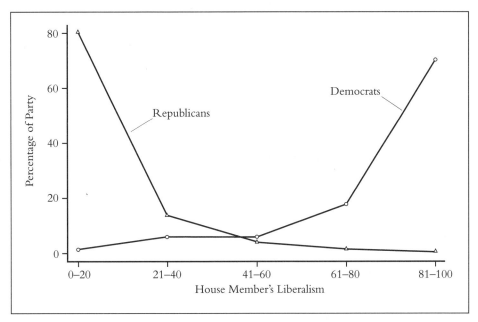

Figure 11.1   Party differences in roll-call votes (ADA index of liberalism), 1997–1998.

of ideological voting scores on the Americans for Democratic Action (ADA) index of liberalism for House members in 1997–1998. As summed over many issues, most Republicans are more conservative than most Democrats.

In state legislatures, the average rate of party voting is slightly higher than in Congress, but there is considerable variation (LeBlanc 1969; Patterson 1976; Francis 1986). While systematic party differences on issues are virtually nonexistent in some state legislatures, some state legislative parties behave as disciplined units. The source of this occasional discipline is sometimes a powerful presiding officer who can penalize members of his party for not supporting party positions, and sometimes it is the party caucus. When a legislative party operates according to the "strong caucus" system, members of the party democratically decide a party position on certain issues, which is sometimes binding on its members. There has been little exploration of the sources of these differences among the state legislatures, or the impact such differences might have on public policy.

Party discipline is seldom evident in Congress, because it is not in the members' best interest: If all Republicans in Congress were forced to vote with their party's conservative majority and all Democrats were forced to vote with their liberal majority, many would be kicked out of office by their local constituencies.[4] Interestingly, however, congressional parties once acted as cohesive units. In the latter part of the nineteenth century, party discipline was maintained in the U.S. House because the Speaker of the House held broad powers over the members. When the Speaker's powers were diluted in the "revolution of 1910–1911," power reverted for a short time to the parties' caucuses. Especially during Woodrow Wilson's administration (1913–1920), each party's caucus regularly voted on issues, and members were often bound (with the rarely exercised excuse of matter of conscience) to vote for the party's majority position. The strong caucus system, however, was short-lived. Given the diversity of viewpoints within the congressional parties and a heightened sensitivity to constituency interests (due in part to increased congressional ambitions to stay elected), it would be unrealistic to hope that the strong-caucus system would return in Congress.

Party Labels as a Basis for Policy Choice

Elected leaders from the Democratic and Republican parties differ on ideology in large part because Democrats and Republicans represent different geographic constituencies. But what about the choice that the two parties offer within the same constituency? In this section we examine the ideological choice provided by the Republican and Democratic parties at the constituency level. We first consider candidates in individual House contests. Then, we briefly look at the ideological choice provided by competing parties within the American states.

Party Choice in Congressional Elections   In U.S. House races, the electorate's choice is not between the *typical* congressional Democrat and the *typical* congressional Republican, for the reason that congressional candidates often adjust their issue stances according to the prevailing constituency views. A liberal district will generally be given a choice between a relatively liberal Democrat and a relatively liberal Republican. Similarly, a conservative district will be given a choice between Democrat and Republican candidates who are both relatively conservative for their party. We are interested in the extent to which candidates at the district level diverge from each other and give the constituency votes a meaningful choice.

Almost always, when a district's congressional candidates differ on important issues, the Democrat is the more liberal and the Republican is the more conservative. Table 11.4 shows this for the 1982 congressional candidates. Column I shows, for each of ten issues, the percentage of the contested districts in which the Republican took the liberal position and the Democrat the conservative position. As the table makes clear, this pattern is rare. Columns II and III show instances of agreement, either liberal or conservative. Column IV shows the dominant pattern of liberal Democrats versus conservative Republicans.

Generally, a congressional voter has an easy decision rule for casting a partisan ballot: to help elect the most conservative candidate, vote Republican; to help elect the most liberal candidate, vote Democratic. Suppose, for instance, we score each of 1982 candidates from Table 11.4 from 0 to the 10 based on his or her number of conservative positions on the ten issues (extreme liberals score 0: extreme conservatives score 10). By this measure, the Republican was the more conservative candidate in 93 percent of the contests, the Democrat was the more conservative in 3 percent, and ties occurred in the remaining 4 percent. This result is not unique for the 1982 election. A similar pattern has been found in studies of the 1996, 1974, and 1978 House elections (Sullivan and O'Connor 1972; Wright 1986).

TABLE 11.4   CANDIDATES' POSITIONS ON TEN ISSUES, 1982 CONTESTED HOUSE ELECTIONS

	Candidates' Positions			
	I	II	III	IV
Republican:	Lib.	Con.	Lib.	Con.
Democrat:	Con.	Con.	Lib.	Lib.
Constitutional Amendments				
States prohibit abortion	6%	16%	33%	45%
Prayer in public schools	5	13	28	54
For balanced budget	1	22	10	67
Equal rights amendment	2	8	41	50
Issues				
Nuclear freeze with Soviets	3	13	22	62
Domestic content, foreign cars sold in U.S.	6	18	28	48
Cancel July 1983 tax cut	2	19	7	72
Cut military spending increase	3	8	55	34
Reduce domestic social programs	2	15	20	62
Increase regulation of air pollution	6	57	5	33

Source: Robert S. Erikson and Gerald G. Wright, "Voters, Issues, and Candidates in Congressional Elections." In Lawrence C. Dodd and Bruce I. Oppenheimer, eds., *Congress Reconsidered,* 3rd ed. (Washington, DC: Congressional Quarterly Press, 1985), p. 94.

Clearly, the parties present a meaningful choice to the public. For example, when the public desires a more conservative Congress, it can simply elect more Republicans. On the other hand, attributing changes in the partisan makeup of Congress to policy motives on the part of the electorate can be hazardous. Although the numbers of Republicans and Democrats in Congress will vary from one election to the next, many of these changes are traceable to such factors as economic conditions, presidential coattails, and Watergates— not to changes in policy preferences by the public. Yet the mechanism of choice is available for the public to create a policy shift in Congress—and in state legislatures and other political arenas as well.

We can see the policy result of a large net shift in congressional party strength for the example of 1964. In that election, an usually high number of Democrats were elected to Congress on the coattails of President Johnson's landslide victory. The combination of a large Democratic majority (in fact a northern Democratic majority) and an activist president resulted in the passage of a lot of liberal legislation (Medicare, federal aid to education, the Voting Rights Act) that had been delayed for years.

More recently, in 1980 an abnormal number of Republicans were swept into Congress on Ronald Reagan's coattails. The result was the Reagan tax cut and other legislation that was part of the conservative Reagan agenda. Both the 1964 and 1980 elections had important policy consequences. In each instance it reamains a matter of debate whether the electorate intended a major clear mandate for a change in the ideological direction of national policy (Wright 1986). However, a strong case can be made that the policy change fit the intent of the voters. Recall Stimson's (1999) measure of the national policy mood, based on a composite of many survey items tapping the liberal-conservative dimension. This index was at its highest (most liberal) around the time of the 1964 election when Johnson's liberal Eighty-eighth Congress was sent to Washington. Stimson's mood index was at its lowest (most conservative) around the time of the 1980 election when Reagan's conservative Ninety-sixth Congress was sent to Washington.

Party Choice in State Elections The assertion that parties provide a choice need not be restricted to the congressional arena. Party differences can be seen at the state level too. Figure 11.2 illustrates. For each of the 48 states, this figure presents ideological estimates for the Republican and Democratic state party elites plus the state electorate. For the two sets of party elites, each estimate is a composite based on the ideological responses of the state parties' national convention delegates, state legislators, county chairmen, and congressional candidates. The state electorate estimates are based on cumulative CBS/*New York Times* polls.

Figure 11.2 shows both how Democratic and Republican state parties are ideologically distinct from one another. The figure also shows the flexibility of the two parties in responding to state opinion. In each state, the Democratic party is to the left of the Republicans, with the electorate in the middle. But the two party positions are not the same in each state. The more liberal the state electorate, the more liberal are both parties.

The result of this process is that at the state level, party success is determined less by the ideological taste of the state electorate than by the relative ideological closeness of the two parties to the state electorate. In many conservative Southern states, for example, the more liberal Democratic party is electorally dominant. In some liberal states (e.g., New York, Vermont, Wisconsin), the more conservative Republican party does very well. These seeming anomalies occur as a result of the state electorate rewarding the party that stands closest to the state electorate's views (Erikson et al. 1994).

The Importance of Party Competition

The importance of parties is evident during circumstances when parties cease to play a major role—when elections are held on a truly nonpartisan basis, as in many American cities and sometimes for state offices. Reformers once saw nonpartisan elections as ideal because they weaken the role of corrupt political parties. But we know that nonpartisan elections make it more difficult for vot-

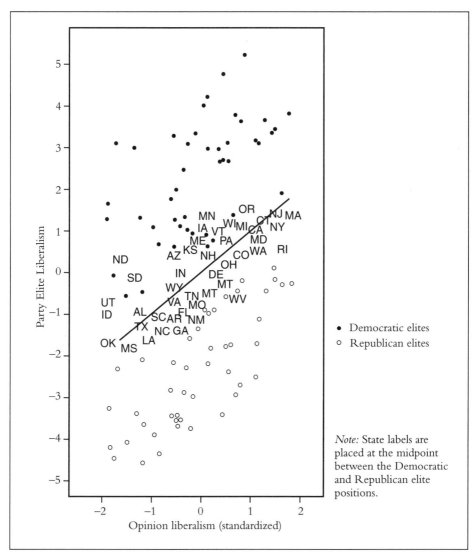

Figure 11.2 Party elite liberalism by state opinion. *Source:* Robert S. Erikson, Gerald C. Wright, and John P. McIver, *Statehouse Democracy* (New York: Cambridge University Press, 1994).

ers to get their preferred policies enacted and to hold leaders accountable for their actions (Cassel 1986).

When both major parties compete effectively for the electorate's favor, we would expect close elections. Sometimes, however, party competition breaks down and one party enjoys a monopoly. This has not happened at the national level since the "Era of Good Feelings" around 1820. Often at the state and local levels, however, one party becomes so dominant as to win almost every election.

In theory, the effect of strong party competition should be to enhance representation. With election outcomes uncertain, each party gets an added incentive to woo the marginal voter who otherwise would be ignored. The opposite result would occur under one-party dominance. The dominant party would not need to make policy appeals to a public whose loyalty (or apathy) they have already won.

V. O. Key (1949) argued that the lack of party competition in the American South allowed the once dominant Democratic party in Southern states to ignore public opinion, with the result that the "haves" enact public policy at the expense of the "have-nots." There has been, largely as a result of Key's position, a conviction among political scientists that parties would be more responsive to public opinion if competition among state political parties were to increase. The states have been moving more toward two-party systems, both in the South and nationwide. As the parties become more evenly matched in the contests for control of governorships and state legislatures, this can only be a positive step in terms of the political parties model.

Does Party Control Matter?

Readily following from our discussion, which party controls the levers of power can have important policy consequences. We have already seen that elected politicians often do turn party platform pledges into law. We can also examine different policies under different types of party control. The major policy consequences that flow from party control concern redistribution, with Democratic polices tending to favor the Democrats' constituency of lower-income voters and Republican policies tending to favor the Republicans' upper-income voters. Innovations in social welfare legislation, for example, are most frequent when Democrats are strong in Congress and, especially, when the Democrats hold the White House (Browning 1986, ch. 8; see also Kiewiet and McCubbins 1985). Statistically speaking, unemployment (a major concern of the less affluent) is more likely to decline under Democratic presidents. And inflation (a major concern of the more affluent) is more likely to decline under Republican presidents (Hibbs 1987, ch. 7; Alesina and Rosenthal 1995). There is also statistical evidence that the income gap between the rich and the poor goes up under Republican presidents and down under Democratic presidents (Hibbs and Dennis 1988).

Of course there are important limits to the policy consequences of party control. From a radical perspective, the choices between the policies of the Democrats and Republicans can be viewed as merely slight variations on the status quo. If one's taste in policy runs toward policies like government ownership of industry legalization of drugs, or abandonment of the public school system, one will not be well represented by either major party. Moreover, the U.S. system of separation of powers and checks and balances slows down the connection between policy proposals and policy enactment. Finally, keep in mind that elected officials are electorally motivated. Once elected, politicians will often moderate their policy positions in order to stay elected rather than satisfy the claims of their active partisan constituencies.

Conclusion

Many elements of the political party model are confirmed. Although neither the Republican not the Democratic party is a disciplined organization, the leaders and activists within the two major parties are ideologically distinct from one another. Although candidates of the two parties generally avoid their party's ideological extreme in order to get elected, their own strong views and those of their active supporters help push their public positions away from the political center. In this way, Republican and Democratic policy differences carry over into the policy choices that the parties offer the voters. In Congress and other political forums, Republicans and Democrats behave in ideologically opposite ways. Admittedly, the exact ideological choice provided by U.S. political parties will not satisfy everybody. But any failure of the political parties model appears to come more from the public's failure to respond to the choices offered by political parties than from the parties' failure to satisfy the conditions of the model.

11-2 INTEREST GROUPS AND REPRESENTATION

Like the political parties model, the interest groups model allows for an intermediate agent (in this case, organized groups) between individuals and their government leaders. Group members need not engage in extensive activity themselves, but can instead rely on their group's leaders and lobbyists to represent their interest. Members may be called upon, however, to contribute to the group's strength by giving money, writing letters to officials, participating in demonstrations, or voting for the group's endorsed candidates. Elected leaders, according to the model, satisfy public opinion when they respond to (and anticipate) group pressures. To the extent the interest groups model is working, the influence of different interest groups will reflect their membership and the intensity with which their views are held. When conflicting demands of different interest groups collide, the policy result would be a compromise, with each side getting its way in proportion to the strength of its membership support.

To evaluate the interest groups model, we need to know whether its suppositions are correct. First, in what ways can interest groups get officeholders to respond to their demands? Unless combinations of individuals can influence policy by engaging in interest group activity, the model cannot work. Second, do the leaders of interest groups know and support the preferences of their members? If there is no linkage between an organization's mass membership choices and the behavior of its leaders, interest groups cannot furnish any linkage between public opinion and public policy. Third, and most important, to what extent does group opinion represent public opinion? The model cannot hold if many individuals possess strong political views that are unexpressed by organized groups, or if opinions brought to bear by organized groups ignore the full range of relevant opinion.

Interest Group Influence

No scholar has attempted to give any kind of quantitative assessment of the net impact of interest group activity on public policy, and offering one here would be beyond our capabilities. Although to assert that public policy is always (or most always) the result of group influence would be an overstatement, most observers agree that group influence in the policy process is considerable. While interest groups are noted for their influence at the administrative level (the general public pays the least attention at the policy-implementation phase), their influence at the legislative level is of central concern here.

Organized groups try to get elected leaders to see their point of view. A group will be more successful in this regard if its lobbyists share the same value as the legislators with whom they interact, if its lobbyists have relevant information to offer the legislature, or perhaps if its lobbyists are simply more visible than others. Everything being equal, legislators try to please interested parties, or at least those who do not alienate them.

Always important to an interest group's success will be the group's potential influence on the electoral process. Legislators will respond more to a group's interests if the group has contributed or will contribute money to their political campaigns. Also, the legislator will be more responsive if the group can give a credible claim that it represents a sizable and attentive voting block. In rare cases, a group may achieve influence by the anticipated threat that it can go over the legislature's head to influence the views and votes of the general public.

Lobbying How important is lobbying activity in determining legislative outcomes? Despite obvious drawbacks, one way to try to answer the question is to ask legislators or lobbyists. When members of Congress are asked to make such an assessment, they rank lobbying activity among the least important of possible influences on congressional decisions. For example, it is more influential than party leadership positions, but less important than constituency opinion (Kingdon 1973, chs. 1, 5). Washington lobbyists also assess their influence as modest (Milbrath 1963). State legislators generally downplay the influence of lobbyists when queried by political scientists. But state-level lobbyists see themselves as more influential than do the legislators (Zeigler and Baer 1969).

Some states have strict registration laws requiring lobbyists to signify which bills interest them and what their positions are. These laws provided Wiggins, Hamm, and Bell an unusual opportunity to assess interest-group success in Iowa, California, and Texas. For a random selection of bills from 1977 to 1983, they found interest groups to be less active and influential than one might expect (Wiggins et al. 1984; see also Wiggins 1983). Between 19 and 26 percent of the bills had no interest groups involved, and between 20 and 25 percent had only a single group involved. Overall, about half the bills had no evident input from organized groups, even though interest groups in the examined states are reputed to be influential. Most importantly, the eventual legislative outcome corresponded to the predominant interest group position only slightly more than half the time. Governors had a much higher success rate than did groups. The overall impression of this research is one of interest groups limiting their involvement and only marginally shaping legislative outcomes in the states.

Lobbying is most effective, however, on issues outside the public spotlight. Generally, a group will be most successful if its goal would greatly benefit the group and cost little to others. Examples of such benefits include tax breaks, agricultural subsidies, oil import quotas, veterans' benefits, and land tariffs on various commodities. Unfortunately, from the standpoint of the interest groups model, the beneficiaries of such policies are "special interests" that cannot claim to represent public opinion. Narrow but specialized interests have an advantage not only because they have a unity of purpose but also because the public is often not aware of their activities. Meanwhile, groups that depend on a large mass membership for support are often handicapped when their members become satisfied by public relations gestures and symbolic rewards (see Edelman 1965).

Money, PACs, and the Electoral Process Interest groups influence the political process via their monetary contributions to election campaigns. Politicians obtain campaign contributions from three sources: their political party, individual contributors, and "political action committees." Political action committees (PACs) often are the financial conduits for organized interest groups. Consider PAC contributions to federal candidates in the 1998 campaign (reported in Stanley and Niemi 2000, ch. 2): Through their subsidiary PACs, labor unions contributed 45 million dollars while, via their PACs, corporations and trade associations contributed an even greater 190 million dollars. Issue-oriented and ideological PACs contributed lesser amounts. Overall, PACs were responsible for 30 percent of House campaign contributions and 19 percent of Senate campaign contributions. PAC contributions to congressional campaigns have been increasing, roughly doubling over the last 20 years. While PACs are limited by law to $5000 per candidate (individual contributors face a $1,000 limit), this limit results in candidates seeking smaller amounts from more groups.

Except for those who are independently wealthy, political candidates need contributions to spend the amount they believe necessary to run an effective campaign. In 1998, U.S. House members spent on average over 700 thousand dollars per campaign, even though this amount was rarely necessary. Challengers typically spend much less, but only challengers who outspend their incumbent opponent have much chance of victory. The greatest spending is for open seats, where the Republican and Democratic candidates now spend as much as 3 million dollars for the right to replace the retiring incumbent. U.S. Senate campaigns, which are statewide, now routinely cost multiple millions of dollars. Democratic and Republican candidates benefit about equally from PAC money. The major discrimination is against potential "long-shot" candidates upon whom PACs will not waste their money and against possibly worthy candidates who hold views too independent to attract PAC interest.

The role of PACs in campaign finance is widely regarded as giving too much power to well-financed groups at the expense of ordinary voters. More is involved than simply the effect of money on election outcomes. The argument goes as follows. Contributors give to campaigns not as philanthropic generosity to the deserving class of righteous politicians but as policy investments. Otherwise, why would groups contribute so much to unopposed candidates or concentrate their contributions upon electorally safe members of congressional committees that must pass upon legislation relevant to the group? Although contributions are often given in gratitude for legislative support of the group's positions in the past rather than for explicit future favors, legislators can enhance their expectation of future group support if they support the group position in advance. And once they receive a PAC's support, individual legislators become even more receptive to the group's position. A legislator who votes against a PAC's interest can find the PAC's future contributions withdrawn or even given to an electoral opponent. Even when a PAC mistakenly backs the losing horse in an election, the PAC will often recover influence by funding the winner. In fact, PACs often spread their investment by contributing to both candidates in an election.

With reelection rates of over 90 percent, and with evidence showing that the money they spend in a campaign is rarely crucial to their reelection, we might ask why members of Congress could not boldly act independent of PAC influence. One argument is that politicians do not like to take electoral chances that they can avoid. Certainly many politicians take PAC money without being influenced by it. And many others avoid all PAC money on principle. But there can be little doubt that legislators generally pay extra attention to the views of those who give them money. Political scientists tend to be somewhat cautious in their conclusion, because testing for statistical evidence of PAC influence is not easy. Scholars who have reviewed the evidence, however, do see a tentative statistical pattern whereby Congress members give more weight to contributor opinion than their overall voting record, constituency preferences, and party affiliation would suggest.[5]

Interest groups and their PACs are also major players in presidential primary elections, where each party's presidential nominees are determined. However, since 1976, presidential primary campaigns have been funded partially with private (PAC or individual) money and partially by matching federal funds. Also beginning with the 1976 presidential election, *general* election campaigns for the presidency have been fully funded by the public (with a spending cap), thereby reducing group influence at the presidential level. A possible additional reform step will be public financing of congressional campaigns. Some states have already moved to public financing of some state campaigns. Although incumbent members of Congress are the major beneficiaries of PAC money, they have two incentives to switch to public financing for themselves. First, they would be freed from the distasteful task of chasing PAC money to focus on their primary function of legislation. Second, if incumbents and challengers were funded equally from the federal treasury, the conventional thinking is that challengers would be even more handicapped than now, because nonincumbents need more money to overcome their invisibility to the voters (Jacobson 1989, 133–34). Quite possibly, if the role of money in electoral politics could be neutralized, the change in the performance of Congress and other political arenas could be breathtaking.

Many informed observers doubt that significant reform of campaign financing would greatly diminish the overall role of interest groups in the policy process because organized groups would still possess the advantages of information, expertise, and direct monitoring of government officials which the general public does not possess. The hoped-for change would be that a group's bankroll would play a lesser amount in determining its degree of influence. When elected leaders respond to potential votes rather than potential cash, the different organized groups compete on a more level playing field.

Interest Groups and Public Relations In addition to giving campaign contributions, groups sometimes attempt to influence public opinion directly, via propaganda campaigns. The interest groups with a large mass-membership base, such as labor unions, place the greatest emphasis on public relations as a technique for influencing legislative and administrative action. The public-relations efforts of labor unions are largely aimed at influencing the opinions and voting behavior of their members. The success of these efforts is limited, but visible. V.O. Key once showed, for example, that the AFL-CIO was somewhat successful at convincing union members of the central AFL-CIO plank to repeal key features of the allegedly antiunion Taft-Hartley Act in the early 1950s (Key 1961b, 509). Union leaders also have some influence on the voting behavior of their members. Union members are about 20 percent more likely to vote Democratic than nonunion counterparts in similar life situations (Campbell et al. 1960, 306; Erikson, Lancaster, and Romero 1989). Unions also devote considerable effort to stimulating voter turnout among members.

Since most interest groups do not have a large mass membership, their efforts to indoctrinate their members cannot affect the mass opinion distribution very much even if their indoctrination efforts are entirely successful. However, ordinary interest groups often spend vast amounts of money to influence the opinion of the general public. Such efforts hold the greater promise of immediate rewards to the group when the public affects policy directly via referendum. Since public opinion on an issue is largely uninformed at the time it is put to a referendum, the propaganda effort of interested interest groups can sometimes greatly influence the outcome. For example, fluoridation referenda often go down to defeat, even though most people favor fluoridated water at times when it is not a "hot" issue in their community. Largely responsible for fluoridation defeats is the fear-exploiting propaganda of the antifluoridation forces, which overcome the more "establishment-oriented" propaganda from the other side. Facing a referendum decision on fluoridation, the previously uninvolved voter may ask a friend for the pros and cons and be told that one side says fluoridation minimizes tooth decay, while the other side says it causes unanticipated medical hazards and, besides, may be the first step toward the poisoning of our water supply by the communists. Not being able to sort out the credibility of the arguments, our voter will assign them equal weight and go for the one that promises the least risk (Abelson 1968, 20–27).

The frequent and important referenda on environmental protection are also subject to effective fear-invoking propaganda, emanating from business groups that don't want stricter controls. When the issue is environmental protection, the propaganda antidote that can sometimes reverse public opinion is the exploitation of fear of losing jobs and, perhaps, fear of higher prices. A common technique of groups opposed to policies up for public referenda is to alarm the public of the uncertainty involved with the change as well as to cast suspicion on the motives of those advocating change (Magelby 1989). For the public, an important antidote to group propaganda can be simply learning which groups take which side on an issue. For instance, in a confusing California referendum on automobile insurance regulation, the insurance industry's position went down to defeat in large part because many people learned which side the insurance industry supported and treated it as a negative cue (Lupia 1992).

Organized propaganda efforts are not limited to referenda alone, since an interest group may try to rally mass opinion to influence the outcome of a legislative issue. Nationally, the past activity of the American Medical Association to reverse public support for Medicare proposals is the most visible example. Provoked by President Truman's proposal for a national health care program, the AMA launched a campaign to label it "socialized medicine." The AMA propaganda machine went to work once again in an attempt to overturn public support for President Kennedy's Medicare program, suggesting that the benefits from a private plan would be better. AMA propaganda may have been responsible for temporary but crucial stalling for public support for Medicare during the Kennedy administration. Not until 1965, following the Democratic landslide of 1964, did Medicare gain congressional passage—over the objection of the AMA once again (Jacobs 1993).

Scholarly observers generally agree that except when the public is alerted to its responsibility to vote in referendum, interest group activity is of little consequence in the shaping of mass opinion. As V.O. Key observed:

> The broad conception of pressure groups as activators of general public opinion which in turn softens up government seldom conforms with the reality. . . .
> The scale of operation necessary to have substantial impact on public opinion is beyond the resources of most groups. They may reach selected groups of political activists through one channel or another with considerable effect, but by and large their lone efforts to mold mass opinion must be of small consequences (Key 1961b, 515).

The impact of interest groups on policy, which is often considerable, does not rest with the success of propaganda efforts except for the possibility of an indirect effect when policymakers mistakenly measure the success of interest-group propaganda by its volume.

Representation Within Interest Groups

We have studied some of the ways in which interest groups try to influence public policy. Shortly we will evaluate the extent to which opinion within organized groups reflects public opinion. However, we shall first examine another aspect of the interest groups model. For the model to work, the positions advocated by group lobbyists must be shared by the members. This may not be an easy condition to fulfill, since the internal decision-making structures of organized groups seldom function in the manner of ideal democracies.

If the group's reason for organization is the sharing of a common ideology or common point of view on a single issue, the group's leaders should have no difficulty discerning the members' positions on those issues that were the source of the group's mobilization. One study of two women's groups with opposite positions on the Equal Rights Amendment (National Organization for Women and Women Who Want to Be Women) found that the two membership groups not only held opposite views on the ERA (no surprise) but, interestingly, were also sharply divided on other issues as well. Members of the pro-ERA group were generally ideologues of the left who supported liberal causes generally, while members of the anti-ERA group tended to be ideologically committed to right-wing issue positions (Tedin et al. 1977). In general, groups that organize because they share a common political viewpoint draw heavily from ideological and issue-oriented citizens. In this way, the intensity aspect of public opinion gets represented in the political process via the group process.

Not all organized groups, however, stimulate and maintain membership because the members share commitments to common political views. Such politically active organizations as trade unions and professional associations form for nonpolitical reasons and only incidentally make forays into the political arena. Leaders of these groups have a politically diverse membership that is difficult to represent. For example, union leaders are more liberal and activist than union rank-and-file members, especially on issues peripheral to the trade union cause. An example is civil rights, on which union leaders show a strong liberal commitment that is not shared by their rank-and-file white membership. On the other hand, leaders of conservative business groups and professional groups (such as the American Medical Association) are often more *conservative* than their members.

Does Group Opinion Equal Public Opinion?

Interest group activity satisfies the interest groups model only if the opinion of groups corresponds to the opinion of the public. We have little direct information about the congruence of group opinion and public opinion. Perhaps the only direct evidence is from a study by Luttbeg and Wiggins (1983) from Iowa, one of the states where lobbyists must record their interests on prospective legislation. For 14 bills before the Iowa legislation, Luttbeg and Wiggins compared interest group positions with public opinion, as surveyed by *Des Moines*

Register and *Tribune* polls. In only two instances did public opinion disagree with the majority of the groups that registered a position. These data carry obvious limitations, but they do suggest that the interest groups model may provide some political linkage.

Admittedly, the correspondence between group opinion and public opinion from this Iowa study could be a happy accident, not generalizable beyond the particular Iowa setting. To rely fully on group opinion as a reflection of public opinion would require confidence that all points of view have equal access to the interest group arena. This, of course, is a tall order.

If group opinion were to reflect public opinion, organized group membership should be spread evenly throughout society. In one typical poll, 62 percent of the respondents reported that they belong to at least one voluntary association such as a club, union, or business organization. But only 31 percent reported membership in an organization where political discussions take place (Verba and Nie 1972, 1976). As with other forms of political participation, people are more likely to belong to groups if they are among the most wealthy or most educated. For example, whereas most Americans in the lowest third in socioeconomic status belong to no groups, most in the upper third are active members of one or more organizations (Verba and Nie 1972, 203–4).

The Incentive to Organize

We have seen that certain people are more likely than others to join organized groups, with most frequent joiners being among the wealthy and better educated. We can also observe that most lobbyists represent business, labor, professional, or agricultural groups—groups to which most people do not belong.[6] Many opinions clearly do not receive articulation by organized groups, while others are amply represented by group spokespersons. Is there any way then to save the interest groups model as a means by which interest groups advance the preferences of *public* opinion? One might argue that people with the most intense views are at least representative of people who care the most. By this argument, if a set of unorganized individuals were to perceive a strong common interest, they would form an organized interest group. If potential groups that are not organized remain so, they are reasonably content with the way things are (Truman 1951).

The flaw in this argument is that spontaneous organization for political actions is too costly to expect the effective mobilization of a group simply because its potential members share an intense concern. To form an organization, some individuals must undertake the cost of recruiting members. More importantly, the incentive to join a dues–paying political group is limited because potential members can obtain the same benefits of the group's potential activity whether they join or not. Mancur Olson (1968) calls this the "free rider" problem. As Olson has shown, most politically powerful interest groups did not originally organize over a common political cause. Instead, key groups— such as labor unions and professional, business, and farm groups—developed their memberships because of common incentives to share nonpolitical benefits from organization. Only after the groups grew from offering nonpolitical services to their members did they become effective in the political arena. This argument should not be taken too far, however, as groups sometimes do organize around a momentary issue only to disappear afterward. Olson's insightful analysis suggests a further problem with the interest groups model. Because politically oriented groups are difficult to organize, existing organizations tend to be defenders of the status quo.

Some observers see the problem as a difference in resources between the organized special interest group and a disorganized public. In recent decades, so-called "public interest groups" (Common Cause and Ralph Nader's organizations, for example) have entered the political arena in order to restore a balance (Berry 1989). Although these groups have not mobilized the general public into a cohesive political force, they have not been without their political influence as they lobby for their versions of "the public interest." Also in recent decades, there has been a proliferation of organized groups representing such causes as the advancement of women, consumers, taxpayers, and the environment. Although these groups receive financial support from only a fraction of the people they claim to represent, they are recognized as an important new force in the political arena. An early model was provided by the activities of the NAACP, and other civil rights groups, which for years has articulated the grievances of African-Americans. Although civil rights groups had been underfinanced and often ignored, their persistent activities were in large part responsible for the political advances blacks have made over the past three decades.

Conclusion

Because the positions voiced by influential organized groups do not necessarily correspond to even the most strongly held views within the general public, the actual group process seldom follows the prescription of the interest groups model. If group activity were the sole input into governmental decision, it seems unlikely that decisions would follow public opinion. The problem is that the group process results in some opinions carrying more weight than others.

Although some people obtain more representation from group activity than others, observers do not all agree that interest groups operate against the public interest. A fact of political life is that some people—particularly the wealthy, educated, articulate, and already politically powerful—are in the best position to advance their political preferences. This fact is only made clearer when we examine the role of interest groups in politics. Although the interest groups model may not describe reality, perhaps we should ask whether we would prefer if all interest group access to government officials could somehow be eliminated. While the "special interest" would lose access, so would the spokespersons for the general public. Rather than wish interest group influence could be reduced, perhaps we should concentrate on ways to make the process more equitable.

NOTES

1. Recall from the Downs model (Chapter 9) that candidates motivated solely by electoral concerns should move toward the center of the political spectrum. The same logic applies to political parties as actors. Of course neither candidates or parties will be found exactly at the center. Considerable research has focused on why candidates and parties do not converge, with much of the attention given to the preferences of the candidates and their activist supporters. Relevant literature includes Aldrich (1983), Poole and Rosenthal (1984), and Erikson, Wright, and McIver (1994).

2. On the partisan background of party activists, see Kweit (1986) and Nesbit (1988).

3. Although the image of primary elections as driven by the preferences of ideologues of the left (for Democrats) and right (Republicans) is a common one, support from survey analysis is elusive; see Norrander (1989).

4. For a good discussion of this point, see Mayhew (1974). Congressional party leaders play an important role in converting the assortment of political demands into coherent policy; see Kiewiet and McCubbins (1991); Sinclair (1993).

5. For example, Jacobson (1989, 141) comes to this conclusion: "Still, at least some [Congress] members, on some issues (those drawing little public or district attention) seem to vote in a way that reflects prior PAC contributions independent of ideology, partisanship, or local interests." Similarly, Scholzman and Tierney (1986, 255–56) conclude: "Most [studies] have uncovered statistically significant relationships of varying strength ... between PAC receipts and roll-call votes, controlling for other relevant factors such as party, constituency characteristics, and ideology." As both Jacobson and Schlozman and Tierney also note, the available statistical evidence is divided and uneven. In his review of the evidence, Sorauf (1988, 312) states it this way: "The results have been disappointingly mixed and ambiguous. Some studies find modest relationships and an independent effect of contributions but others do not—an outcome probably the result of the different methodologies and the different groups and votes in the various projects.

6. For example, in 1981, 71 percent of all organizations represented by lobbyists in Washington were business organizations, 4 percent were labor organizations, 2 percent were agricultural organizations, and 17 percent were professional organizations (Schlozman and Tierney 1986, 62–81).

CHAPTER 12

Public Opinion and the Performance of Democracy

According to democratic theory, the health of a democracy depends on the existence of a politically informed and active citizenry. By carefully monitoring government affairs, citizens could develop informed opinions about policies that would represent their interests. By working for and voting for candidates who represent their views, and by making their views known to elected leaders, citizens could collectively translate their various policy preferences into government action. The resulting set of policies that governments would enact would represent a reasonable compromise between competing claims of equally powerful and informed citizens. This description represents the democratic ideal. In this concluding chapter we assess the degree to which American democracy approaches this democratic ideal and speculate about possible ways to achieve improvement.

12-1 ASSESSING THE IMPACT OF PUBLIC OPINION ON POLICY

We have discussed five models that have the potential to provide public policy consistent with what the public would prefer. By voting for leaders who share its views, the public can fulfill the basic needs of the rational-activist model. If reliable voting cues are furnished by political parties, policy-oriented voters can fulfill the political parties model by choosing the party platform most compatible with their views. Aside from voting, people can influence policymakers by bringing the preferences of the group to which they belong to bear on officials, thus fulfilling the interest groups model. In addition, linkage between opinions and policy can be furnished by two models that do not demand public coercion of leaders. If policymakers try to follow public opinion and perceive that opinion accurately, the role-playing model would be fulfilled. Finally, because leaders and followers share many of the same political beliefs, even the sharing model provides political linkage.

By itself, each of these sources of political linkage may provide only a small increase in the degree to which officials are responsive to the public. Their total effect may in fact be slight, since to show that public opinion can influence policy is not a demonstration that public opinion is followed all or even most of the time. Perhaps the evidence we need is some sort of counting of the frequency with which government policies are in accord with public opinion. A truly definitive study following this design would need information at the national, state, and local levels across a broad range of policies as to whether the process of political linkage results in public policy that is consistent with public opinion. We would want to be able to say which of the linkage models proves most viable and on what issues. We would want to assess the consequences of linkage failure for the public's opinions about its government, for its participation in political affairs, and ultimately for political stability. Unfortunately such a study does not exist.

Since presently available evidence of the frequency of political linkage is limited, conclusions based on it must be very tentative—perhaps limited to only the specific issues studied, the level of government considered, and the time period involved. Moreover, congruence between majority opinion and government policy may not always be the best indicator of political linkage, since government decisions can be responses to the intense opinions of a minority rather than to the preferences of the majority. Also, as we have seen, "majority" opinion on an issue fluctuates with the exact wording of a survey question. Keeping these cautions in mind, let us see what the evidence shows about the congruence between public opinion and government policy.[1]

Evidence at the National Level

If acts of Congress were determined by the demands of public opinion, then Congress would act whenever public opinion built to majority support or higher behind a proposed program. Because polls do not regularly monitor opinions on specific proposals before Congress, we seldom know how much support the public gives to a policy before its enactment. However, polls can offer clues regarding how well Congress serves the broad policy guidelines preferred by the public.

One issue on which we can assess this consistency between opinion and policy is Medicare—which became law in 1965. As early as 1935, a presidential commission had proposed a plan for national health insurance that would have provided universal coverage. In 1945, President Truman endorsed such a plan. Twenty years later Congress passed a comprehensive health insurance plan, but only for the elderly. Why was there such a delay? One reason was that although most people favored government assistance, they were not insistent. For example, consider the results of an SRC poll in 1956 (when the health care issue was dormant) that asked people whether the government should "help people get doctors and health care at low cost" and also asked for an appraisal of government performance to date (too much, less than it should, about right, or "haven't heard yet what government is doing"). Although opinion was more than 2 to 1 in favor of government participation, only 30 percent said government was doing less than it should. The crystallized opposition—taking the position of both opposing government participation as well as saying that the government either was doing about right or was going too far—made up only 15 percent of the sample (recomputed from Key 1961a, 269). Most people apparently did not have a coherent opinion one way or the other. Even when Medicare became a central issue in the 1960's, few were attentive. In a 1962 quiz of the public, only 57 percent of the respondents said they had heard of Medicare and had any understanding of it. In fact, only 7 percent knew the basic facts—that it would be financed by Social Security and limited to people receiving old-age insurance (Nadel 1972, 540). Only after Medicare became law in 1965 did most people become aware of its general provisions.

Perhaps if people become politically mobilized by their views on medical care, Medicare or something even more extensive would have been enacted much sooner. As things stood, the powerful American Medical Association was able to forestall satisfaction of a feeble-voiced public. In fact, neither Medicare nor its predecessors even emerged from the House Ways and Means Committee in more than very diluted form until the 1964 Democratic landslide tipped the committee's balance in favor of such legislation (Marmor 1970; see also Jacobs 1993).

While the importance of public opinion in the enactment of Medicare remains ambiguous, we need to analyze more than a single issue. To develop a strong statistical argument that policy corresponds (or seems to follow) public opinion, we need to find a consistent pattern of congruence over many issues. One form of congruence would be a pattern of policy changes usually following the direction of majority opinion. Even stronger evidence would be both opinion and policy changing in the same direction, so that opinion change would predict a corresponding policy change.

Alan Monroe (1979–1998) has examined opinion-policy congruence over the period from 1960 to 1974 and again from 1980 to 1993. Each usable poll question ascertained whether or not the public preferred a specific change in national policy. For each of the issues, Monroe then determined whether the specific policy change eventually took place. His findings for the earlier period are shown in Table 12.1. On the 74 issues for which the public favored the status quo, the desired outcome of no change occurred 76 percent of the time. On the 48 issues on which the public preferred change, the desired outcome of designated change occurred 59 percent of the time. Evidently, the public is less likely to get its way when it prefers change than when it prefers the status-quo. Of

TABLE 12.1   CONGRUENCE BETWEEN POLICY PREFERENCE AMONG THE MASS PUBLIC AND POLICY OUTCOMES AT THE NATIONAL LEVEL

	Preference	
Outcome	Status Quo	Change
Status Quo	76%	41%
Change	24	59
	100%	100%
	(n=74)	(n=148)

Source: Alan D. Monroe, "Consistency Between Public Preferences and National Policy Decisions," *American Politics Quarterly* 7 (Jan. 1979): 9. Copyright © 1979 by Sage Publications. Reprinted by permission of Sage Publications, Inc.

course, that the American political system tends to be status-quo-oriented has often been observed. That is, an intense minority (for example, opponents of gun control) can often block change. But in either case, the public's preference becomes policy more often than not. Over all cases—preferences for change and preferences for the status quo—Monroe finds policy corresponding to public opinion almost two-thirds of the time. For the later period (1980–1993), the rate of policy correspondence was somewhat lower for reasons that are not clear.

In a related study, Page and Shapiro (1983) examine over 300 instances of opinion *change* recorded by polls between 1935 and 1979. They find a healthy correspondence between the direction of the change in public preferences and the direction of change in public policy. In the 231 instances where opinion and policy both changed, they changed in the same direction instead of opposite directions 66 percent of the time. Page and Shapiro do not entirely rule out the possibility of some spurious relationship: Political elites could "educate" the public to like the policies they enact for their own interest. Support for the inference that opinion causes policy is strengthened, however, by the fact that their observed policy changes almost always followed the change in opinion rather than the other way around.

Recently, scholars have been exploring long-term relationships between opinion and national policy in search of statistical evidence of opinion influencing policy. Several positive results have been reported. The clearest evidence is for defense spending, with changes in defense spending seemingly following from shifts in public perceptions of need (Bartels 1991; Hartley and Russett 1992; Wlezien 1995b). Spending levels for domestic purposes also appear responsive to public preferences (Wlezien 1995a). Recent statistical evidence even suggests that Supreme Court decisions respond to shifts in public opinion (Mishler and Sheehan 1993).

Time-series evidence of an opinion-policy linkage at the national level can also be presented in terms of the electorate's ideological mood on the one hand

and a composite of national policies on the other. As our measure of public opinion we use Stimson's "mood" indicator of public liberalism. Recall (Chapter 4) that mood represents a composite of trends over several survey questions regarding national policy. As a measure of national policy, we combine three separate measures of Senate roll-call liberalism, three similar measures of House roll-call liberalism, two roll-call-based measures of presidential liberalism and an index based on positions taken by the president's solicitor-general before the Supreme Court (Stimson et al. 1994).

Figure 12.1 overlays the scores on these two indexes from 1956 to 1990, showing a seeming connection between public opinion and policy. When public opinion turns more liberal or conservative (and these movements of mood are small in magnitude), the index of national policy appears to follow. Although correlation does not prove causation, it would seem that the ideological tone of national policy draws its momentum from slight shifts in ideological taste on the part of the U.S. public.

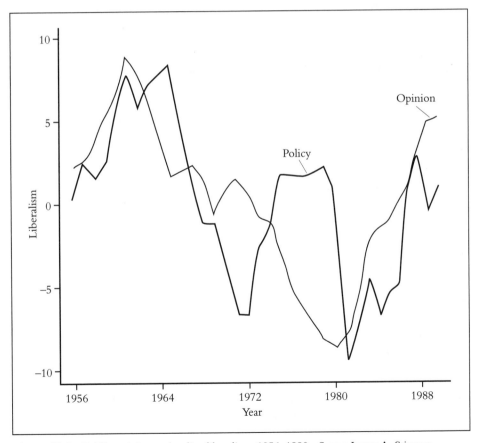

Figure 12.1   Public opinion and policy liberalism, 1956–1990. *Source:* James A. Stimson, Michael B. MacKuen, and Robert S, Erikson, "Opinion and Policy: A Global View," *PS: Political Science and Politics* 27 (Mar. 1994): 43.

Evidence at the State Level

At the state level, the opinion-policy linkage can be analyzed by seeing whether states where the public is most in favor of a given policy tend to be the states that enact that policy. Unfortunately, this kind of analysis is limited by the fact that polls rarely report reliable state-by-state breakdowns of opinion for comparison. Suprisingly, the best state-level opinion data are from polls conducted in 1930s when national polls were based on much larger samples than today. One study examined three state-level issues for which there were available opinion data in 1936 (Erikson 1976a). On each of these issues—capital punishment, child labor regulation, and woman jurors—a strong correlation between state opinion and state policy was found. While these examples suggest an opinion-policy linkage, further analysis of this sort is hampered by the lack of available state opinion data.

For recent analysis of state policy, Erikson, Wright, and McIver (1994) pooled several CBS/*News York Times* surveys from the 1976–1988 period. Pooling of several surveys together provided over 100,000 national respondents and large samples within individual states. Their measure of state opinion is based on the ideological self-indentification (liberal, moderate, conservative) of the state samples. Their measure of state policy is a composite of eight policies with a liberal versus conservative content. They find a large correlation (+.81) between the opinion measure and the policy measure.

This relationship is shown in Figure 12.2, where the ideological tendency of state public opinion and the ideological tendency of state policy, is seen to almost always go together. The most liberal states enact the most liberal policies, and the most conservative states enact the most conservative policies. Although we cannot be totally secure about the causal direction, these data strongly suggest that public opinion matters when states make important policy decisions.

Evidence at the Local Level

At the local level of government, we know very little about the relationship between public opinion and policy decisions. There appear to be no studies that systematically attempt to determine whether existing differences among local policy choices are related to local political opinions. One study, however, examined the relationship between political participation levels and "policy congruence" for citizens and leaders in 55 American cities. Policy congruence is a measure of the extent to which citizens and elected officials agree on what are the most important local problems. A study by Sidney Verba and Norman Nie (1972) and a further analysis of the same data by Susan Hansen (1975) reveal that the higher the community's level of public participation—particularly its level of voting participation—the greater the congruence between mass and elite perceptions of community problems. Of further consequence are competitive elections. Hansen finds the combination of high voting turnout and close local elections produces the greatest citizen-leader congruence scores. Contrary evidence exists, however. Luttbeg (1999) finds in a study of 37 Texas cities that leaders were the most anxious about satisfying public opinion in cities with the *least* competitive elections.

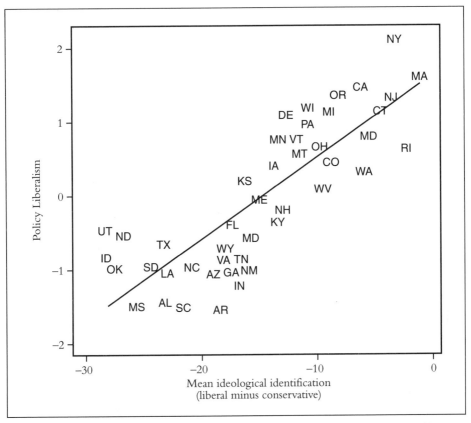

Figure 12.2.   State policy liberalism and public opinion.   *Source:* Robert S. Erikson, Gerald C. Wright, and John P. McIver, *Statehouse Democracy* (New York: Cambridge University Press, 1994).

An Opinion-Policy Connection

Although the evidence is certainly incomplete, the few relevant studies that test for an opinion-policy linkage suggest that public opinion is far from inconsequential. At the national level we find that opinion and national policy are in agreement more often than not. At the state level we find that state opinion can be a good predictor of state policy. At the local level we find that high citizen participation is associated with citizen-leader agreement on important problems, although we have no data concerning solutions to those problems.

Such findings should not be surprising, because as we have seen, there are several linkages at work translating even feebly voiced public opinion into policy. This information, however, should not be cause for complacency about the current state of American democracy. Other forces besides public opinion shape government decisions. In addition, the opinions that sometimes influence policy may not be informed or, from our point of view, enlightened opinions. On the positive side, the evidence that a rather inattentive public can sometimes influence policy suggests that a more attentive public would have even greater control over policy decisions.

12-2 INTERPRETING THE PUBLIC'S ROLE IN DEMOCRACY

As we have seen throughout this book, the public generally does not live up to its prescribed activist role. Moreover, while public opinion can often influence government policy, in reality it is not the sole determinant of policy outcomes. Why not? Public control of government decisions depends on both the extent to which people actually participate in policies and the equality of people's resources for effective participation. The first point is obvious: It seems logical that the more people participate in politics, the more they can influence government decisions. But some people can participate more effectively than others because they command a greater share of the necessary resources, such as money, information, articulateness, and access to decision-makers. How inequitable one views the distribution of these political resources can determine one's view of how democratic the political system actually is. Some observers see effective political power concentrated in the hands of a "power elite" who control policy outcomes for their own interests. Others more optimistically see the inequality in the distribution of power limited basically to the different political skills that individuals have and their interest in using them.[2] Because this debate over the equality of the distribution of political power is not easily decided by scientific inquiry, we shall not enter it directly here. But, taking into account that the tools of effective political participation are not equally distributed, how can we assess the less than active political role of the public? We shall discuss four plausible conclusions.

Public Apathy as Mass Political Incompetence

Perhaps the easiest view of the public's limited role in government affairs is that people are simply incapable of doing any better. The frequency with which people fail to hold political opinions, the rarity of the liberal or conservative "ideologue," and the difficulty in locating rational policy-oriented voters may all indicate that people generally lack the skills necessary to make sophisticated judgements about their political leaders and policies. Worse yet, the political views that people do hold may be intolerant, naive, or simply wrong. Viewed from this perspective, an increase in public participation would only make the situation worse because "bad" public opinion would drive "good" policymakers toward undesirable acts.

If the mass public is viewed as being inherently incapable of playing a useful role, then the remedy of trying to "uplift" public opinion becomes ineffective. Instead, one might have to rely on the proper training or careful recruitment of political leaders as a means of producing desired outcomes. If such desired outcomes include the preservation of the substance of democracy, then one must prescribe both a limited public role and the instillation of a heavy dose of democratic values among political elites. Thomas Dye and Harmon Ziegler (1987), who arrive at this position, call it the "irony of democracy."

Public Apathy as Rational Disengagement

Possibly the reason that most people do not allow politics to intrude far into their lives is that to do so would be irrational. From a strict cost-versus-benefit standpoint, one should not follow public affairs closely, since the investment would get one nowhere. One person's vote is useless because it is fantasy to assume that a single vote can decide an election's outcome except in the most extraordinary circumstances. Even when an individual's economic interest is directly at stake in the political arena (which may be rare), organizing like-minded people for collective political pressure is irrational because the costs of organization outweigh the possible benefits one could expect.[3] The cynic might also suggest that increased public knowledge of governmental affairs would only produce greater political withdrawal, as people who learn about their leaders' corruption and unresponsiveness will feel even more helpless at the prospect of changing things.

If this logic is correct, then people who do participate in politics usually are motivated by something other than tangible personal gains. Perhaps they "irrationally" participate in order to gratify a felt obligation or civic duty. If the major determinant of an individual's sense of obligation to participate is preadult political socialization, then a reformer might hope to increase public participation by improving the "training" of the next generation of citizens. Alternatively, one might hope to eliminate rational withdrawal from politics by somehow increasing the rewards of political participation.

Public Apathy as Elite Manipulation

One can also interpret the public's low participation in politics as the result of manipulation by leaders and their allies. When one observes political docility on the part of people who seemingly should have strong reasons for political protest, one can easily draw the conclusion that the individuals are being misled by propaganda. Whether or not one can support an interpretation depends on one's convictions that the individuals in question are actually oppressed. A convinced Marxist, for example, can readily view the lack of class consciousness on the part of American workers as a sign of deception by the existing power structure. Similarly, a member of the John Birch Society might attribute the public's lack of concern about what he sees as a pervasive communist conspiracy to be a sign of the effectiveness of the conspiracy.

One does not have to believe in a complex conspiracy in order to view political quiescence as the result of elite manipulation. Because most political events are remote from people's everyday lives, people willingly view these events through the interpretation of their leaders. Also, since people want to believe that their political system is benign rather than corrupt or evil, they readily find reassurance from optimistic interpretations of the existing order and resist the voices that tell them otherwise.[4]

If one sees people as unwilling to accept "truth" because they do not want to disturb their cherished beliefs, the obvious remedy would appear to be heavy doses of correct information. But how to make this remedy effective remains unclear.

Public Apathy as Public Contentment

Rather than viewing public apathy as a sign that the classical democratic model does not hold, one can interpret apathy as an indicator of public contentment. If people do not concern themselves with political matters, then they must not have any additional demands to make on their government. Conversely, when many people do participate in politics, it is a distressing signal either that government has ignored public needs or that conflicts between societal groups are no longer being successfully resolved by political leaders.[5]

Actually, the view that public apathy means public satisfaction rests on the assumption that the public is rather politically sophisticated. It assumes that people are capable of articulating any grievances they might have, that people feel that their expression of grievances would be effective, and that people are not easily led to ignore their interests. Only if these assumptions are made can one conclude that the lack of political participation indicates that people's needs are met by the proper working of a democratic system.

Evaluation Although they contradict one another, each of these four possible explanations of the public's lack of political participation contains a grain of truth. For example, the public may not be capable of participation in all government decisions, particularly when the decision depends on proper evaluation of advanced technical knowledge. Equally obvious is that people can take only limited time from their personal affairs to participate in politics. Moreover, people may decide not to participate because they feel (perhaps mistakenly) that they can trust their political leaders. Finally, people may sometimes retire from the political arena because they have no particular grievances.

Simply holding them up to the light of scientific evidence cannot determine which of the explanations of low participation in politics is most valid, since individual observers will view the evidence through the filter of their own preconceptions and values. How observers view such matters as human nature, people's basic interest, and the benevolence of government can shape how strongly they conclude that political inactivity signifies incapability, rational withdrawal, manipulation, or contentment. Similarly, the extent to which observers see their own opinion in harmony with majority opinion might influence their views of whether public control of government should increase or decrease.

12-3 THE EXPANSION OF POLITICAL PARTICIPATION

Whether increased public political participation is desirable also depends on the type of political participation. Few would applaud the increased mass participation that would result in civil war or mass mobilization in support of an antidemocratic movement. But few would fear an increase in informed, democratic participation—particularly if we ignore possible disagreement over what "informed democratic participation" means. When there is little mass participation, the burden of responsibility falls on the political elites—both to ensure the continuation of the democratic rules and also to make policy decisions that are fair and equitable. But if one agrees that the purpose of democracy is to ensure that political leaders are held accountable to the people, one can hardly applaud when people do not actively seek to protect their own interests. Are there any ways to increase the number of active participants while at the same time ensuring that this participation will be rational and democratic?

Seemingly part of the answer would involve some way of creating a more politically informed public. Since the public can hardly be blamed for its political ignorance when it is given little information on which to make its political judgements, we can favor more thorough the political reporting by the news media and other efforts to induce a more informed public. Hopes should not be set too high, however, because information campaigns do not always reach the people who are the most in need of them. Also, we must recognize the possible side effects produced by increased public knowledge, such as greater public cynicism or an intensification of conflicts among politically aroused mass groups.

However difficult the task of boosting information might be, we can readily imagine that a more informed public would be better able to serve its function in the American democracy. Furthermore, we can speculate about how different the opinions of a truly informed public would be from the actual public that we know. Increasingly, political scientists are taking this question seriously (Fishkin 1997; Delli Carpini and Keeter 1996; Bartels 1996; Lupia and McCubbins 1998; Althaus, 1998).

Apart from inducing a more informed public, a related and equally daunting task is to induce more people to participate in politics. The most obvious way of doing so would be to legislate changes that lower the costs and burdens of participation. For instance, "motor voter" legislation and other reforms reduce or eliminate the initial barriers to voter registration. If we register the unregistered, maybe they will vote and maybe they will become informed and cast informed votes. We will await the evidence. In recent years, the voting rate (among eligible voters) threatens to fall to record lows, a disturbing phenomenon at a time when most of the entry costs for voter participation have been removed. Increasing numbers of Americans are choosing to be nonparticipants. Political scientists have failed to understand this trend and what such apathy reflects.

Perhaps the existing methods for translating public opinion into government policy are inaccurate relics from a technically primitive time when ballot casting, face-to-face communication, and geographic representation were the only feasible conduits for public expression. New methods might be tried to encourage greater citizen participation, giving people greater opportunity to participate directly in local decisions, including perhaps more participatory democracy in nongovernmental groups such as the workplace, school, or religious organizations. Also, people could play a more direct role by deciding policy questions in referenda instead of letting their elected leaders decide them. Finally, it may now be technologically feasible to allow people to vote in referenda via telephonic communication from the comfort of their home.

There is no question that greater citizen participation is a desired democratic value. But it is debatable whether additional opportunities to participate would lead to wiser government decisions than elected leaders presently make. While proposals for expanding participation deserve serious consideration, their practicability and desirability remain uncertain.

NOTES

1. Three good reviews of the relationship between public opinion and public policy are Burstein (1981), Shapiro and Jacobs (1989), and Jacobs and Shapiro (1994).
2. The most widely cited representatives of these opposing viewpoints are Mills (1956) and Dahl (1961).
3. For the development of this particular point, see Olsen (1968).
4. For a provocative discussion of opinion manipulation, see Edelman (1965).
5. For an articulation of this view, see Wilson (1962).

The National Election Study and the General Social Survey Questions

Two major national surveys, designed specifically for academic analysis, are conducted on a regular basis. These are the National Election Study (NES) done by the Center for Political Studies at the University of Michigan (conducted in even number years), and the General Social Survey (GSS), done by the National Opinion Research Center at the University of Chicago (usually conducted yearly). For academic purposes, these surveys are much more valuable than surveys done by commercial polling organizations. One reason is that the interviews are done in person rather than over the phone. Another is that the questionnaires are quite lengthy, usually including hundreds of items administered over a period of more than one hour. Also, many items are repeated over time, allowing for the analysis of changes.

Throughout this book, responses to opinion questions asked in either the NES or GSS opinion surveys are examined. As their content usually appears in abbreviated form, the complete wordings for the most frequently used questions in the book are presented below. Where appropriate, responses are labeled as [L] for liberal and [C] for conservative, according to how these terms are applied to the response alternative within the text.

QUESTIONS FROM THE NATIONAL ELECTION STUDIES

1. Party Identification

Two questions are used to measure party identification. First, respondents are asked:

Generally speaking, do you usually think of yourself as a Republican, a Democrat, an Independent, or what?

This basic question provides the division between the three kinds of partisans. For the second question, partisans are probed regarding the strength of their partisanship, and Independents are probed to see whether they lean toward one of the major parties.

Republicans and Democrats are asked:

Would you call yourself a strong Republican [Democrat] or not so strong Republican [Democrat]?

Independents are asked:

Do you think of yourself as closer to the Republican Party or to the Democratic Party?

Independents who choose a party are called *Independent Leaners.* Many Independents respond that they lean toward neither party. They are often called *Pure Independents.*

The net result is a 7-point scale of partisanship.

1. Strong Democrat
2. Not so strong (or "weak") Democrat
3. Independent, leaning Democrat
4. Pure Independent
5. Independent, leaning Republican
6. Not so strong (or "weak") Republican
7. Strong Republican

Unless otherwise noted, we use the simpler three-way division: Democrats (1 and 2), Independents (3, 4, and 5), and Republicans (6 and 7).

2. Liberal/Conservative Ideology

People are asked to choose an ideological position on a 7-point scale. Respondents are first asked:

We hear a lot of talk these days about liberals and conservatives. Here is a 7-point scale on which the political views that most people might hold are arranged from extremely liberal to extremely conservative.

Then they are asked:

Where would you place yourself on this scale, or haven't you thought much about it?

1. Extremely liberal
2. Liberal
3. Slightly liberal
4. Moderate, middle-of-the-road

5. Slightly conservative
6. Conservative
7. Extremely conservative
8. Don't know
9. Haven't thought much about it

Where we show the basic division between self-identified liberals and conservatives, we combine responses 1, 2, and 3 as *liberal* and 5, 6, and 7 as *conservative.*

In recent years, the NES has used the following variation of the 7-point scale for most of its issue questions. Respondents are first presented with two extreme positions on the issue. Then they are asked to place themselves with regard to the issue on a scale ranging from one to seven. Shown the scale, respondents are asked: "Where would you place yourself on this scale or haven't you thought much about it?" The scale position 1 generally represents the extreme liberal viewpoint and scale position 7 generally represents the extreme conservative viewpoint. For convenience, we often compress the scale, combining the responses 1, 2, and 3 as *liberal* responses and 5, 6, and 7 as *conservative* responses, with neutral "4" respondents and those who admit they "haven't thought much about it" combined as "non-opinion holders."

Following are the eight 7-point issue scales used in our ten-item index of respondent liberalism–conservatism.

3. Government Services/Spending Scale

Some people think the government should provide fewer services, even in areas such as health and education, in order to reduce spending. . . . Other people feel it is important for the government to provide many more services even if it means an increase in spending. . . . Where would you place yourself on this scale? . . .

[C] Government should provide many fewer services, reduce spending a lot.
[L] Government should provide many more services, increase government spending a lot.

(On this one item, NES scores 1 to 7 as conservative to liberal. We reverse the polarity so that 1 represents the liberal and 7 the conservative end of the scale, consistent with the other items.)

4. Government Job and Standard of Living Scale

Some people feel the government in Washington should see to it that every person has a job and a good standard of living. Others think the government should let each person get ahead on his own. Where would you place yourself on this scale? . . .

[L] Government see to a job and a good standard of living
[C] Government let each person get ahead on own

5. National Health Insurance

There is much concern about the rapid rise in medical and hospital costs. Some people feel there should be a government insurance plan that would cover all medical and hospital expenses for everyone. Others feel that all medical expenses should be paid by individuals and through private insurance plans like Blue Cross or other company plans. Where would you place yourself on this scale? . . .

[L] Government insurance plan
[C] Private insurance plan

6. Minority Aid Scale

Some people feel that the government in Washington should make every effort to improve the social and economic positions of blacks and other minority groups. Others feel that the government should not make any special effort to help minorities because they should help themselves. Where would you place yourself on this scale? . . .

[L] Government should help minority groups
[C] Minority groups should help themselves

7. Defense Spending Scale

Some people believe that we should spend much less for defense. Others feel that spending should be greatly increased. Where would you place yourself on this scale? . . .

[L] Greatly decrease defense spending
[C] Greatly increase defense spending

8. Women's Role Scale

Recently there has been a lot of talk about women's rights. Some people feel that women should have an equal role with men in running business, industry, and government. Others feel that women's place is in the home. Where would you place yourself on this scale? . . .

[L] Women and men should have equal roles
[C] Women's place is in the home

9. Environmental Protection

Some people think it is important to protect the environment even if it costs some jobs or otherwise reduces our standard of living. . . . Other people think that protecting the environment is not as important as maintaining jobs and our standard of living. . . . Where would you place yourself on this scale?

[L] Environment important
[C] Environment not important

10. Crime Reduction

Some people say that the best way to reduce crime is to address the social problems that cause crime, like bad schools, poverty and joblessness. . . . Other people say the best way to reduce crime is to make sure that criminals are caught, convicted, and punished. . . . Where would you place yourself on this scale?

[L] Address social problems
[C] Punish criminals

The 7-point issue scales were used as part of the 10-item composite index of liberal-conservative policy positions, used in Chapters 3 and 9. For this composite scale, each component item is added as −1 (liberal), +1 (conservative), or 0 (other). The remaining two issues for this scale are:

11. Gays in the Military

Do you think homosexuals should be allowed to serve in the United States Armed Forces or don't you think so?

[L] Yes, think so
[C] Don't think so

12. Abortion

There has been some discussion about abortion during recent years. Which of these opinions on this page best agree with your view?

1. By law, abortion should never be permitted.
2. The law should permit abortion only in case of rape, incest, or when the woman's life is in danger.
3. The law should permit abortion for reasons other than rape, incest or danger to the woman's life, but only after the need for abortion has been clearly established.
4. By law, a woman should always be able to obtain an abortion as a matter of personal choice.

For purposes of ideological classification, responses 1–3 are coded as conservative, and response 4 is coded as liberal.

13. Political Information Scale

For some items, the NES asked respondents to locate the positions of the major presidential candidates on the same scale. We used the candidate placements for items 2, 3, 5, 7, and 12 to form the political information scale used in chapters 3, 8, and 9. To construct this scale, every correct answer (Dole to the right of Clinton) was scored as +1. Every incorrect answer (Clinton to the right of Dole) was scored as −1. Every tied response was scored as zero. These scores were summed to create a composite knowledge score ranging from −5 (all incorrect) to +5 (all correct).

The −5 to +5 composite scores were grouped into three categories of high, medium, and low. "High" scores were perfect +5s. "Low" scores were +1 or less. For the lower scorers, the mean on the original −5 to +5 was zero, or in the guess range on candidate placement. All not scored at high or low were scored as "medium" on political knowledge.

QUESTIONS FROM THE GENERAL SOCIAL SURVEY

14. Abortion

Please tell me whether or not you think it should be possible for a pregnant woman to obtain a legal abortion . . .

A. If there is a strong chance of a serious defect in the baby?
B. If she is married and does not want any more children?
C. If the woman's own health is seriously endangered by the pregnancy?
D. If the family has very low income and cannot afford any more children?
E. If she became pregnant as a result of a rape?
F. If she is not married and does not want to marry the man?
G. If the woman wants it for any reason?

15. Political Tolerance

The GSS asks tolerance questions with a variety of groups as the target. The general form of the question, using atheists as the target group, is:

There are always some people whose ideas are considered bad or dangerous by other people. For instance, somebody who is against all churches and religion. . . .

A. If such a person wanted to make a speech in your (city/town/community) against churches and religion, should he be allowed to speak or not?
B. Should such a person be allowed to teach in a college or university, or not?
C. If some people in your community suggested that a book he wrote against churches and religion should be taken out of your public library, would you favor removing this book, or not?

References

Abelson, Robert. 1968. "Computers, Polls, and Public Opinion: Some Puzzles and Paradoxes." *Trans-Action* 5 (Sept.): 20–27.

Aberbach, Joel, and Jack L. Walker. 1970. "Political Trust and Racial Ideology." *American Political Science Review* 63 (Dec.): 1199–223.

Abramowitz, Alan I. 1994. "Issue Evolution Reconsidered: Racial Attitudes and Partisanship in the U.S. Electorate." *American Journal of Political Science* 38 (Feb.): 1–25.

———. 2000. "Bill and Al's Excellent Adventure. Forecasting the 1996 Presidential Election." In *Before the Vote: Forecasting American National Elections,* eds. James E. Campbell and James C. Garand. Thousand Oaks, CA: Sage.

Abramson, Paul R. 1983. *Political Attitudes in America.* San Francisco: Freeman.

Abramson, Paul R., and John H. Aldrich. 1982. "The Decline of Electoral Participation in America." *American Political Science Review* 76, 502–21.

Abramson, Paul R., and Ada W. Finifter. 1981. "On the Meaning of Political Trust: New Evidence from Items Introduced in 1978." *American Journal of Political Science* 25 (May): 297–306.

Abravnel, Martin B., and Ronald J. Busch. 1975. "Political Competence, Political Trust, and the Action Orientation of University Students." *Journal of Politics* 37 (Feb.): 69–81.

Achen, Christopher. 1975. "Mass Political Attitudes and the Survey Response." *American Political Science Review* 69 (Dec.): 1218–31.

Acock, Alan, Harold D. Clarke, and Marianne C. Stewart. 1985. "A New Model for Old Measures: A Covariance Structure Analysis of Political Efficacy." *Journal of Politics* 47 (Nov.): 1062–84.

Adelson, Joseph, and Robert P. O'Neil. 1966. "Growth of Political Ideas in Adolescence: The Sense of Community." *Journal of Personality and Social Psychology* 4 (July): 295–306.

Adorno, Theodore W., et al. 1950. *The Authoritarian Personality.* New York: Harper.

Aldrich, John H. 1983. "A Downsian Spatial Model with Party Activism." *American Political Science Review* 77 (Dec.): 974–90.

———. 1996. *Why Parties? The Origin and Transformation of Party Politics in America.* Chicago: University of Chicago Press.

Alesina, Alberto, and Howard Rosenthal. 1995. *Partisan Politics, Divided Government, and the Economy.* New York: Cambridge University Press.

Alford, John R., and David W. Brady. 1993. "Personal and Partisan Advantage in U.S. Congressional Elections." In *Congress Reconsidered,* 5th ed., eds. Lawrence C. Dodd and Bruce I. Oppenheimer. Washington, DC: Congressional Quarterly.

Alford, John, Holly Teeters, Daniel Ward, and Rick Wilson. 1994. "Overdraft: The Political Cost of Congressional Malfeasance." *Journal of Politics* 56: 788–801.

Alford, Robert R. 1963. *Party and Society.* Chicago: Rand.

Almond, Gabriel A. 1950. *The American People and Foreign Policy.* New York: Harcourt.

Almond, Gabriel A., and Sidney Verba. 1965. *The Civic Culture.* Boston: Little Brown.

Altemeyer, Bob. 1981. *Right Wing Authoritarianism.* Winnipeg: University of Winnipeg Press.

———. 1988. *Enemies of Freedom: Understanding Right Wing Authoritarianism.* San Francisco: Jossey-Bass.

———. 1997. *The Authoritarian Spector.* Cambridge, MA: Harvard University Press.

Althaus, Scott L. 1998. "Information Effects in Collective Preferences." *American Political Science Review* 92 (Sept.): 545–558.

Alvarez, R. Michael, 1997. *Information and Elections.* Ann Arbor, MI: University of Michigan Press.

Alwin, Duane F., Ronald L. Cohen, and Theodore M. Newcomb. 1991. *Political Attitudes Over the Life Span.* Madison, WI: University of Wisconsin Press.

Andersen, Kristi. 1979. *The Creation of a Democratic Majority, 1928–1936.* Chicago: University of Chicago Press.

Anderson, David D. 1981. *William Jennings Bryan.* Boston: Twayne Publishers.

Anderson, Lee, et al. 1990. *The Civics Report Card.* Princeton, NJ: National Assessment of Educational Progress, Educational Testing Service.

Ansolabehere, Stephen, and Shanto Iyengar. 1995. *Going Negative.* New York: The Free Press.

Arnold, Douglas. 1990. *The Logic of Congressional Action.* New Haven: Yale University Press.

Arterton, F. Christopher. 1974. "The Impact of Watergate on Children's Attitudes Toward Authority." *Political Science Quarterly* 89 (June): 269–88.

Backstrom, Charles H. 1977. "Congress and the Public: How Representative Is One of the Other?" *American Politics Quarterly* 5 (Oct.): 411–36.

Bagdikian, Ben H. 1972. "The Politics of American Newspapers." *Columbia Journalism Review* 10 (Mar./Apr.): 9–10.

———. 1973. "The Fruits of Agnewism." *Columbia Journalism Review* 11 (Jan./Feb.): 9–23.

Baloyra, Enrique A. 1979. "Criticism, Cynicism and Political Evaluation: A Venezuelan Example." *American Political Science Review* 73 (Dec.): 981–94.

Banducci, Susan A., and Jeffrey A. Karp. 1994. "Electoral Consequences of Scandal and Reapportionment in the 1992 House Elections." *American Politics Quarterly* 22 (Jan.): 3–26.

Banfield, Edward C., and James Q. Wilson, 1963. *City Politics.* New York: Vintage.

Barber, James David. 1965. *The Lawmakers.* New Haven: Yale University Press.

Bartels, Larry. 1987. "Candidate Choice and the Dynamics of the Presidential Nominating Process." *American Journal of Political Science* 31 (Feb.): 1–30.

———. 1988. *Presidential Primaries and the Dynamics of Public Choice.* Princeton, NJ: Princeton University Press.

———. 1991. "Constituency Opinion and Congressional Policy Making: The Reagan Buildup." *American Political Science Review* 85 (June): 457–74.

———. 1993. "Messages Received: The Political Impact of Media Exposure." *American Political Science Review* 87 (Mar.): 267–86.

———. 1996. "Uninformed Voters: Information Effects in Presidential Elections." *American Journal of Political Science.* 40: 194–230.

———. 2000. "Partisanship and Voting Behavior, 1952–1996." *American Journal of Political Science* 44: 35–51.

Bartels, Larry, and C. Anthony Broh. 1989. "The Polls—A Review: The 1988 Presidential Primaries." *Public Opinion Quarterly* 53 (Winter): 563–68.

Bawn, Kathleen. 1999. "Constructing 'US': Ideology, Coalition Politics and False Consciousness." *American Journal of Political Science* 43: 303–34.

Bechtel, Robert D. R., Clark Achelpohl, and Rogers Akers. 1972. "Correlates Between Observed and Questionnaire Responses to Television Viewing." In *Television in Day-to-Day Life: Patterns of Use,* eds. Eli A. Rubinstein, George A. Comstock, and John P. Murray. Washington, DC: GPO (HEW Publication HSM 72–9059).

Beck, Paul Allen. 1974. "A Socialization Theory of Partisan Realignment." In *The Politics of Future Citizens,* ed. Richard G. Niemi. San Francisco: Jossey-Bass.

———. 1977. "The Role of Agents in Political Socialization." In *Handbook of Political Socialization,* ed. Stanley A. Renshon. New York: Free.

Beck, Paul Allen, and M. Kent Jennings. 1991. "Family Traditions, Political Periods, and the Development of Partisan Orientations." *Journal of Politics* 53 (Aug.): 742–63.

Behr, Roy, and Shanto Iyengar. 1985. "Television News, Real-World Cues, and Changes in the Public Agenda." *Public Opinion Quarterly* 49 (Spring): 38–57.

Benham, Thomas W. 1965. "Polling for a Presidential Candidate: Some Observations in the 1964 Campaign." *Public Opinion Quarterly* 29 (Summer): 177–78.

Bennett, Stephen. 1997. "Why Young Americans Hate Politics, and What We Should Do About It." *PS: Politics and Political Science* 30 (March): 47–52.

———. 1998. "Young American's Indifference to Media Coverage of Public Affairs." *Political Science and Politics* 31 (Sept.): 535–41.

Bennett, W. Lance. 1980. *Public Opinion in American Politics.* New York: Harcourt.

———. 1998. "The Uncivic Culture: Communication, Identity, and the Rise of Lifestyle Politics." *PS, Political Science and Politics* 31 (December): 741–762.

Bereday, George Z. F., and Bonnie B. Stretch. 1963. "Political Education in the USA and USSR." *Comparative Education Review* 7 (June): 9–16.

Berelson, Bernard, Paul Lazarsfeld, and William McPhee. 1954. *Voting.* Chicago: University of Chicago Press.

Berinsky, Adam K. 1999. "Two Faces of Public Opinion." *American Journal of Political Science* 43 (Oct.): 1209–31.

Berkman, Ronald L., and Laura W. Kitch. 1986. *Politics in the Media Age.* New York: McGraw.

Bernstein, Alan. 1992. "Bush's Popularity Falls in Own Houston District." *Houston Chronicle,* 25 July, sec. A.

Berry, Jeffrey M. 1989. *The Interest Group Society,* 2nd ed. Glenview, IL: Scott.

Bigman, Stanley K. 1948. "Rivals in Conformity: A Study of Two Competing Dailies." *Journalism Quarterly* 25 (Autumn): 125–31.

Binder, Sarah A. 1997. *Minority Rights, Majority Rule.* New York: Cambridge University Press.

Bishop, George F., and Kathleen A. Frankovic. 1981. "Ideological Consensus and Constraint Among Party Leaders and Followers in the 1978 Election." *Micro-Politics* 3: 87–111.

Bishop, George F., Alfred J. Tuchfarber, and Robert W. Oldendick. 1978. "Change in the Structure of American Political Attitudes: The Nagging Question of Question Wording." *American Journal of Political Science* 22 (May): 250–69.

Bishop, George F., et al. 1980. "Pseudo-Opinions on Public Affairs." *Public Opinion Quarterly* 44 (Summer): 198–209.

Blumer, Herbert. 1948. "Public Opinion and Public Opinion Polling." *American Sociological Review* 13 (Oct.): 542–54.

Bogart, Leo. 1972. *Polls and the Awareness of Public Opinion,* 2nd ed. New Brunswick, NJ: Transaction.

———. 1998. "Politics, Polls, and Poltergeists." *Society* 35, 4 (May/June 1998).

Bolce, Louis, Gerald De Maio, and Douglas Muzzio. 1992. "Blacks and the Republican Party: The 20 Percent Solution." *Political Science Quarterly* 107: 63–79.

Box-Steffensmeir, Janet, Kathleen Knight, and Lee Sigelman. 1998. "The Interplay of Macroideology and Macropartisanship: A Times Series Analysis." *Journal of Politics* 60: 131–49.

Boyer, Ernest, and Mary Jean Whitelaw. 1989. *The Condition of the Professoriate: Attitudes and Trends, 1989.* New York: Harper.

Boynton, G. R., Samuel C. Patterson, and Ronald D. Hedlund. 1969. "The Missing Links in Legislative Politics: Attentive Constituents." *Journal of Politics* 31 (Aug.): 700–21.

Bradburn, Norman, and Seymour Sudman. 1988. *Polls and Surveys.* San Francisco: Jossey-Bass.

Brady, Henry E., and Richard E. Johnston. 1987. "What's the Primary Message: Horserace or Issue Journalism?" In *Media and Momentum: The New Hampshire Primary and Nomination Politics,* eds. Gary R. Orren and Nelson W. Polsby. Chatham, NJ: Chatham House.

Brady, Henry E., and Gary R. Orren. 1992. "Sources of Error in Public Opinion Surveys." In *Media Polls in American Politics,* eds. Thomas E. Mann and Gary R. Orren. Washington, DC: Brookings.

Brady, Henry E., and Paul M. Sniderman. 1985. "Attitude Attribution: A Group Basis for Political Reasoning." *American Political Science Review* 79 (Dec.): 1061–78.

Brady, Henry E., Sidney Verba and Kay Lehman Scholzman. 1995. "Beyond SES: A Resource Model of Political Participation." *American Political Science Review* 89 (Mar.): 271–92.

Brandes, Lisa. 1992. "The Gender Gap and Attitudes Toward War." Paper presented at the annual meeting of the Midwest Political Science Association, Apr. 9–12.

Breaux, David, and Malcolm Jewell. 1992. "Winning Big: The Incumbency Advantage in State Legislative Races." In *Changing Patterns in State Legislative Careers,* eds. Gary F. Moncrief and Joel A. Thompson. Ann Arbor, MI: University of Michigan Press.

Brehm, John. 1993. *The Phantom Respondents.* Ann Arbor, MI: University of Michigan Press.

Brehm, John, and Wendy Rahn. 1997. "Individual-Level Evidence for the Causes and Consequences of Social Capital." *American Journal of Political Science* 41: 999–1023.

Brody, Richard A. 1991. *Assessing the President.* Stanford, CA: Stanford University Press.

Brody, Richard A., and Catherine R. Shapiro. 1989. "Policy Failure and Public Support: The Iran-Contra Affair and Public Assessment of President Reagan." *Political Behavior* 11 (Dec.): 353–70.

Brody, Richard A., and Lee Sigelman. 1983. "Presidential Popularity and Presidential Elections: An Update and Extension." *Public Opinion Quarterly* 47 (Fall): 325–28.

Broh, C. Anthony. 1983. "Presidential Preference Polls and Network News." In *Television Coverage of the 1980 Presidential Campaign,* ed. William C. Adams. Norwood, NJ: Ablex.

Brown, Peter A. 1991. "Ms. Quota." *New Republic* 204 (April 15): 18–19.

Browning, Robert X. 1986. *Politics and Social Welfare Policy in the United States.* Knoxville, TN: University of Tennessee Press.

Bryce, James. 1900. *The American Commonwealth*. New York: Macmillan.

Buchanan, Bruce. 1991. *Electing a President*. Austin, TX: University of Texas Press.

Budge, Ian, and Richard I. Hofferbert. 1990. "Mandates and Policy Outputs: U.S. Party Platforms and Federal Expenditures, 1950–1985." *American Political Science Review* 84 (Mar.): 248–61.

Bullock, Charles. 1992. "Minorities in State Legislatures." In *Changing Patterns of State Legislative Careers,* eds. Gary F. Moncrief and Joel A. Thompson. Ann Arbor, MI: University of Michigan Press.

Burnham, Walter Dean. 1970. *Critical Elections and the Mainsprings of American Politics.* New York: Norton.

Burstein, Paul. 1981. "The Sociology of Democratic Politics and Government." In *Annual Review of Sociology,* vol 7, eds. Ralph H. Turner and James F. Short, Jr. Palo Alto, CA: Annual Reviews.

Caddell, Patrick. 1979. "Trapped in a Downward Spiral." *Public Opinion* (Oct./Nov.): 2–8.

Cain, Bruce, John Ferejohn, and Morris Fiorina. 1987. *The Personal Vote.* Cambridge, MA: Harvard University Press.

Caldicott, Helen. 1986. *Missile Envy: The Arms Race and Nuclear War.* New York: Bantam.

Campbell, Angus. 1964. "Issues and Voters: Past and Present." *Journal of Politics* 26 (Nov.): 745–57.

Campbell, Angus, Philip E. Converse, Warren E. Miller, and Donald E. Stokes. 1960. *The American Voter.* New York: Wiley.

Campbell, Angus, Gerald Gurin, and Warren E. Miller. 1954. *The Voter Decides.* Evanston, IL: Row.

Campbell, James E. 1985. "Sources of the New Deal Realignment: The Contribution of Conversion and Mobilization to Partisan Change." *Western Political Quarterly* 38 (June): 357–76.

Cantril, Albert H. 1991. *The Opinion Connection.* Washington, DC: Brookings.

———. 1992. "A Setback for All Public Polls." *Public Perspective* 3 (Jan./Feb.): 23–24.

Cantril, Albert H., and Susan Davis Cantril. 1999. *Reading Mixed Signals: Ambivalence in American Public Opinion About Government.* Baltimore, MD: Johns Hopkins University Press.

Cantril, Hadley. 1951. *Public Opinion 1935–1946.* Princeton, NJ: Princeton University Press.

Carmines, Edward G., John P. McIver, and James A. Stimson. 1987. "Unrealized Partisanship: A Theory of Dealignment." *Journal of Politics* 49 (June): 377–99.

Carmines, Edward G., and James A. Stimson. 1980. "The Two Faces of Issue Voting." *American Political Science Review* 74 (Jan.): 78–91.

———. 1989. *Issue Evolution: Race and the Transformation of American Politics.* Princeton, NJ: Princeton University Press.

Cassel, Carol A. 1986. "The Non-Partisan Ballot in the United States." In *Electoral Laws and their Consequences,* eds. Bernard Grofman and Rend Lipjart. New York: Agathon.

———. 1993. "A Test of Converse's Theory of Party Support." *Journal of Politics* 55 (Aug.): 664–81.

Chandler, Robert. 1972. *Public Opinion*. New York: Bowker.

Childs, Harwood. 1965. *Public Opinion: Nature, Formation and Role*. Princeton, NJ: Van Nostrand.

Chong, Dennis. 1993. "How People Think, Reason and Feel about Civil Liberties." *American Journal of Political Science* 37 (Aug.): 867–99.

Citrin, Jack. 1974. "The Political Relevance of Trust in Government." *American Political Science Review* 68 (Sept.): 973–1011.

Clancy, Maura, and Michael J. Robinson, 1985a, b. "General Election Coverage: Part I." *Public Opinion* 8 (Dec./Jan.): 49–54, 59.

———. "General Election Coverage, Part II: Wingless, Toothless, and Hopeless." *Public Opinion* (Feb./Mar.): 43–48.

Clymer, Adam. 1993. "Opposition to Baird Grows As Senators Hear the People." *New York Times,* 22 January, sec. A:3.

Cobb, Michael D., and James H. Kuklinski. 1997. "Changing Minds: Political Arguments and Political Persuasion." *American Journal of Political Science* 41 (Jan.): 88–121.

Coleman, John J. 1997. "The Decline and Resurgence of Congressional Party Conflict." *Journal of Politics* 59: 165–84.

Connell, Robert W. 1987. "Why the 'Political Socialization' Paradigm Failed and What Should Replace It." *International Political Science Review* 8 (July): 215–23.

Conover, Pamela, and Stanley Feldman. 1981. "The Origins and Meaning of Liberal and Conservative Self-Identifications." *American Journal of Political Science* 25 (Nov.): 617–45.

———. 1989. "Candidate Perceptions in an Ambiguous World: Campaigns, Cues, and Inference Processes." *American Journal of Political Science* 33 (Nov.): 912–41.

Converse, Jean. 1987. *Survey Research in the United States*. Berkeley, CA: University of California Press.

Converse, Philip E. 1962. "Information Flow and the Stability of Partisan Attitudes." *Public Opinion Quarterly* 26 (Winter): 578–99.

———. 1964. "The Nature of Belief Systems in Mass Publics." In *Ideology and Discontent,* ed. David Apter. New York: Free.

———. 1966. "The Concept of the Normal Vote." In *Elections and the Political Order,* ed. Angus Campbell et al. New York: Wiley.

———. 1976. *The Dynamics of Party Support*. Beverly Hills, CA: Sage.

———. 1987. "Changing Conceptions of Public Opinion in the Political Process. *Public Opinion Quarterly* 51(Spring): 12–24.

Converse, Philip E., Aage R. Clausen, and Warren E. Miller. 1965. "Electoral Myth and Reality: The 1964 Election." *American Political Science Review* 59 (June): 332–35.

Converse, Philip E., and Gregory B. Markus. 1979. "Plus ca change...: The New CPS Election Study Panel." *American Political Science Review* 73 (Mar.): 32–49.

Cook, Elizabeth Adell, Ted. G. Jelen, and Clyde Wilcox. 1992. *Between Two Absolutes*. Boulder, CO: Westview.

Cook, Fay Lomax, and Edith J. Barnett. 1992. *Support for the American Welfare State*. New York: Columbia University Press.

Cooley, Charles H. 1992. *Human Nature and the Social Order.* New York: Scribner's.

Coombs, Steven Lane. 1981. "Editorial Endorsements and Electoral Outcomes." In *More Than News: Media Power in Public Affairs,* ed. Michael Bruce MacKuen and Steven Lane Coombs. Beverly Hills, CA: Sage.

Cox, Gary, and Jonathan N. Katz. 1996. "Why Did the Incumbency Advantage in the US House Grow?" *American Journal of Political Science.* 43: 812–41.

Cox, Gary W., and Matthew D. McCubbins. 1993. *Legislative Leviathan: Party Government in the House.* Berkeley: University of California Press.

Craig, Stephen G. 1993. *The Malevolent Leaders.* Boulder, CO: Westview.

Crain, Robert L., Elihu Katz, and Donald B. Rosenthal. 1969. *The Politics of Community Conflict: The Fluoridation Decision.* Indianapolis: Bobbs-Merrill.

Crespi, Irving. 1988. *Pre-Election Polling: Sources of Accuracy and Error.* New York: Russell Sage.

———. 1989. *Public Opinion, Polls, and Democracy.* Boulder, CO: Westview: 27.

Dahl, Robert A. 1961. *Who Governs?* New Haven: Yale University Press.

———, ed. 1966. *Political Opposition in Western Democracies.* New Haven: Yale University Press: 40–41.

———. 1971. *Polyarchy.* New Haven: Yale University Press.

———. 1982. *Democracy in the United States.* Chicago: Rand.

———. 1989. *Democracy and Its Critics.* New Haven: Yale University Press.

Dalton, Russell. 1980. "Reassessing Parental Socialization: Indicator Unreliability versus Generational Transfer." *American Political Science Review* 74 (June): 421–38.

Dautrich, Kenneth, and Jennifer Necci Deneen. 1996. "Media Bias: What Journalists and the Public Say About It." *Public Perspective.* 7: 7–19.

Davidson, Roger H. 1969. *The Role of the Congressman.* New York: Pegasus.

Davidson, Robert H., David M. Kovenock, and Michael K. O'Leary. 1968. *Congress in Crisis: Politics and Congressional Reform.* Belmont, CA: Wadsworth.

Davis, Darren W. 1997. "Nonrandom Measurement Error and Race of Interview Effects Among African-Americans." *Public Opinion Quarterly* 61 (Spring): 183–207.

Davis, James A. 1992. "Changeable Weather in a Cooling Climate Atop the Liberal Plateau." *Public Opinion Quarterly* 56 (Fall) 261–95.

Dawson, Richard, Kenneth Prewitt, and Karen Dawson. 1977. *Political Socialization,* 2nd ed. Boston: Little Brown.

Day, Christine L. 1990. *What Older Americans Think: Interest Groups and Aging Policy.* Princeton, NJ: Princeton University Press.

Delli Carpini, Michael X. 1984. "Scooping the Voters? The Consequences of the Networks' Early Call of the 1980 Presidential Race." *Journal of Politics* 46 (Aug.): 866–85.

———. 1986. *Stability and Change in American Politics: The Coming of Age of the Generation of the 1960s.* New York: New York University Press.

Delli Carpini, Michael X., and Scott Keeter. 1992. "The Public's Knowledge of Politics." In *Public Opinion, the Press, and Public Policy,* ed. J. David Kennamer. Westport, CT: Praeger.

————. 1996. *What Americans Know About Politics and Why It Matters*. New Haven: Yale University Press

Delli Carpini, Michael X., and Lee Sigelman. 1986. "Do Yuppies Matter? Competing Explanations of their Political Distinctiveness." *Public Opinion Quarterly* 50 (Winter): 502–18.

Dennis, Jack, and Carol Webster. 1975. "Children's Images of the President and Government in 1962 and 1974." *American Politics Quarterly* (Oct.): 211–38.

Deutscher, Irwin. 1973. *What We Say/What We Do*. Glenview, IL.: Scott.

Dillman, Don A. 1978. *Mail and Telephone Surveys*. New York: Wiley.

Domke, David, David P. Fan, Michael Fibison, Dhavan V. Shah, Steven S. Smith, and Mark D. Watts. 1998. "Mass Media, Candidates and Issues, and Public Opinion in the 1996 Presidential Campaign." *Journalism and Mass Communications Quarterly* 74: 718–37.

Downs, Anthony. 1958. *An Economic Theory of Democracy*. New York: Harper.

Dreyer, Edward. 1971–1972. "Media Use and Electoral Choices: Some Political Consequences of Information Exposure." *Public Opinion Quarterly* 35 (Winter): 544–53.

Dry, Murray. 1996. "Review of National Standards for Civics and Government." *PS: Political Science and Politics* 29 (Mar.): 49–52.

Duckitt, John. 1989. "Authoritarianism and Group Identification: A New View of an Old Construct." *Political Psychology* 10 (Feb.): 63–84.

Dye, Thomas R., and Harmon Ziegler. 1987. *The Irony of Democracy*. 7th ed. Belmont, CA: Wadsworth.

Dyer, James A. 1976. "Do Lawyers Vote Differently? A Study of Voting on No-Fault Insurance." *Journal of Politics* 38 (May): 452–56.

Easton, David. 1965. *A Systems Analysis of Political Life*. New York: Wiley.

Easton, David, and Jack Dennis. 1969. *Children and the Political System*. New York: McGraw.

Eber, Ralph, and Richard Lau. 1990. "Political Cynicism Revisited: An Information Processing Reconciliation of Policy-Based and Incumbency-Based Interpretations of Changes in Trust in Government." *American Journal of Political Science* 34 (Feb.): 236–53.

Edelman, Murray. 1965. *The Symbolic Uses of Politics*. Urbana, IL: University of Illinois Press.

Elms, Alan. 1972. *Social Psychology and Social Relevance*. Boston: Little Brown.

Engelberg, Stephan. 1993. "A New Breed of Hired Hands Cultivates Grass-Roots Anger." *New York Times,* 17 Mar., sec. A:1, 11.

Epstein, Edward Jay. 1974. *News From Nowhere*. New York: Random.

Epstein, Laurily, and Gerald Strom. 1984. "Survey Research and Election Night Projections." *Public Opinion* 7 (Feb./Mar.): 48–50.

Epstein, Leon D. 1967. *Political Parties in Western Democracies*. New York: Praeger.

Erikson, Robert. S. 1971. "The Electoral Impact of Congressional Roll Call Voting." *American Political Science Review* 65 (Dec.): 1018–32.

————. 1976a. "Is There Such a Thing as a Safe Seat?" *Polity* 8 (Summer): 613–32.

————. 1976b. "The Relationship Between Public Opinion and State Policy: A New Look at Some Forgotten Data." *American Journal of Political Science* 20 (Feb.): 25–36.

————. 1976c. "The Influence of Newspaper Endorsements in Presidential Elections: The Case of 1964." *American Journal of Political Science* 20 (May): 207–34.

————. 1978. "Constituency Opinion and Congressional Behavior: A Reexamination of the Miller–Stokes Representation Data." *American Journal of Political Science* 22: 511–35.

————. 1979. "The SRC Panel Data and Mass Attitudes." *British Journal of Political Science* 9 (Jan.): 89–114.

————. 1988. "The Puzzle of Midterm Loss." *Journal of Politics* 50 (Nov.): 1011–29.

————. 1989. "Economic Conditions and the Presidential Vote." *American Political Science Review* 83 (June): 567–73.

————. 1990. *Legislative Studies Quarterly.* "Roll Calls, Reputations, and Representation in the US Senate." 15: 623–42.

————. 1993. "Counting Likely Voters in Gallup's Tracking Poll." *The Public Perspective* 4 (Mar./Apr.): 22–23.

Erikson, Robert S., Thomas D. Lancaster, and David W. Romero. 1989. "Group Components of the Presidential Vote, 1952–1984." *Journal of Politics* 51 (May): 337–46.

Erikson, Robert S., Norman R. Luttbeg, and William B. Holloway. 1975. "Knowing One's District: How Legislators Predict Referendum Voting." *American Journal of Political Science* 19 (May): 231–46.

Erikson, Robert S., Michael B. MacKuen, and James A. Stimson. 1998. "What Moves Macropartisanship? A Reply to Green, Palmquist, and Schickler." *American Political Science Review.* 92: 901–12.

Erikson, Robert S., and Kent L. Tedin. 1981. "The 1928–1936 Partisan Realignment: The Case for the Conversion Hypothesis." *American Political Science Review* 75 (Dec.): 951–62.

————. 1986. "Voter Conversion and the New Deal Realignment." *Western Political Quarterly* 39: 729–32.

Erikson, Robert S. and Christopher Wlezien. 1999. "Presidential Polls as a Time Series: The Case of 1996." *Public Opinion Quarterly* 63 (Summer), 163–78.

Erikson, Robert, and Gerald C. Wright 1997. "Voters, Candidates, and Issues in Congressional Elections." In *Congress Reconsidered,* 6th ed., eds. Lawrence C. Dodd and Bruce I. Oppenheimer. Washington: Congressional Quarterly Press.

Erikson, Robert S., Gerald C. Wright, and John P. McIver. 1994. *Statehouse Democracy: Public Opinion and Policy in the American States.* New York: Cambridge University Press.

Erskine, Hazel. 1962a. "The Polls: Race Relations." *Public Opinion Quarterly* 26 (Winter): 137–48.

————. 1962b. "The Polls: Attitudes." *Public Opinion Quarterly* 26 (Winter): 293.

————. 1975. "The Polls: Health Insurance." *Public Opinion Quarterly* 39 (Spring): 128–43.

Eskey, Kenneth. 1995. "American Youth Not Very Interested in Politics." *Houston Chronicle,* 9 Jan., 5A.

Farrand, Max. 1961. *The Records of the Federal Convention of 1787,* vol. 1. New Haven: Yale University Press.

Feldman, Kenneth, and Theodore M. Newcomb. 1969. *The Impact of College on Students,* vol. 2. San Francisco: Jossey-Bass.

Feldman, Stanley. 1989. "Reliability and Stability of Policy Positions: Evidence from a Five-Wave Panel." *Political Analysis* 1: 25–60.

Feldman, Stanley, and Karen Stener. 1997. "Perceived Threat and Authoritarianism." *Political Psychology* 18: 741–69.

Feldman, Stanley, and John Zaller. 1992. "The Political Culture of Ambivalence: Ideological Response to the Welfare State." *American Journal of Political Science* 36 (Feb.): 268–91.

Fenno, Richard F., Jr. 1978. *Home Style: House Members in Their Districts.* Boston: Little Brown.

Ferree, G. Donald. 1993. "Counting Likely Voters: A Reply to Erikson." *The Public Perspective* 4 (Mar./Apr.): 22–23.

Field, John O., and Ronald E. Anderson. 1969. "Ideology in the Public's Conceptualization of the 1964 Election." *Public Opinion Quarterly* 33 (Fall): 380–88.

Finke, Roger, and Rodney Stark. 1994. *The Churching of America, 1776–1990.* New Brunswick, NJ: Rutgers University Press.

Finkel, Steven E. 1985. "Reciprocal Effects of Participation and Political Efficacy: A Panel Analysis." *American Journal of Political Science* 29 (Nov.): 891–911.

————. 1993. "Re-examining the 'Minimal Effects' Model in Recent Presidential Campaigns." *Journal of Politics* 55 (Feb.): 1–21.

Finkel, Steven E., Edward N. Muller, and Karl-Dieter Opp. 1989. "Personal Influence, Collective Rationality, and Mass Political Action." *American Political Science Review* 83 (Sept.) 885–903.

Finkel, Steven E., and James B. Rule. 1975. "Relative Deprivation and Related Psychological Theories of Civil Violence: A Critical Review." In *Research in Social Movements, Conflicts and Change,* vol. 9, eds. Kurt and Gladys Lang. Greenwich, CT: JAI.

Fiorina, Morris, P. 1977. "An Outline for a Model of Party Choice." *American Journal of Political Science* 21 (Aug.): 601–25.

————. 1981. *Retrospective Voting in American National Elections.* New Haven: Yale University Press.

————. 1992. *Divided Government.* New York: Macmillan.

Fischer, Claude S. 1975. "Toward a Subcultural Theory of Urbanism." *Social Forces* 53 (Mar.): 420–32.

Fischle, Mark. 2000. "Mass Response to the Lewinsky Scandal: Motivated Reasoning or Bayesian Updating?" *Political Psychology.* 21: 135–59.

Fishkin, James S. 1997. *The Voice of the People: Public Opinion and Democracy.* New Haven: Yale University Press.

Flanagan, Constance A., Jennifer M. Bowes, Britta Jonsson, Beno Csapo, and Elean Sheblanova. 1998. "Ties that Bind: Correlates of Adolescent's Civic Commitments in Seven Countries." *Journal of Social Issues* 54: 457–75.

Flanagan, Timothy J., and Dennis R. Longmire. 1996. *Americans View Crime and Justice: A National Public Opinion Survey.* Thousand Oaks, CA: Sage.

Flemming, Gregory, and Kimberly Parker. 1997. "Race and Reluctant Respondents: Possible Consequences of Non-Response for Pre-Election Surveys." Paper presented at the 1997 Meeting of the American Association for Public Opinion Research.

Franklin, Charles H., and John E. Jackson. 1983. "The Dynamics of Party Identification." *American Political Science Review* 77 (Dec.): 957–73.

Franklin, Charles H., and Liane C. Kosaki. 1989. "The Republican Schoolmaster: The Supreme Court, Public Opinion and Abortion." *American Political Science Review* 83 (Sept.): 751–71.

Frankovic, Kathleen A. 1992. "The CBS News Call-In: 'Slip-ups in the Broadcast.'" *The Public Perspective* 3 (Mar./Apr.): 19–21.

———. 1999. "Why the Gender Gap became News in 1996." *Political Science and Politics* 32 (Mar.): 20–23.

Free, Lloyd A., and Hadley Cantril. 1967. *The Political Beliefs of Americans.* New York: Simon and Schuster.

Freeman, Patricia, and William Lyons. 1992. "Female Legislators: Is There a New Type of Woman in Office?" In *Changing Patterns in State Legislative Careers,* eds. Gary F. Moncrief and Joel A. Thompson. Ann Arbor, MI: University of Michigan Press.

Freedman, Paul, and Ken Goldstein. 1999. "Measuring Media Exposure and the Effects of Negative Campaign Ads." *American Journal of Political Science.* 43: 1189–208

Friesema, H. Paul, and Ronald D. Hedlund. 1981. "The Reality of Representational Roles." In *Public Opinion and Public Policy,* ed. Norman R. Luttbeg. Itasca, IL: Peacock.

Fritz, Sara, and Dwight Morris. 1992. *Handbook of Campaign Spending.* Washington, DC: Congressional Quarterly.

Fukuyama, Francis. 1995. *Trust: Social Virtues and the Creation of Propriety.* New York: Free.

Gaertner, Samuel L., and John F. Dovidio. 1986. "The Aversive Form of Racism." In *Prejudice, Discrimination, and Racism,* ed. John F. Dovidio and Samuel L. Gaertner. New York: Academic.

Gallup, Alec, and David Moore. 1996. "Younger People Today Are More Positive About Polls Than Their Elders." *Public Perspective* 7 (Aug./Sept.): 50–52.

Gallup, George, and Saul Rae. 1940. *The Pulse of Democracy.* New York: Simon.

Gamble, Barbara. 1997. "Putting Civil Rights to a Popular Vote." *American Journal of Political Science* (Jan.): 245–69.

Gamson, William. 1968. *Power and Discontent.* Homewood, IL: Dorsey.

Garcia, F. Chris. 1973. *Political Socialization of Chicano Children.* New York: Praeger.

Geer, John G. 1996. *From Tea Leaves to Opinion Polls.* New York: Columbia University Press.

Gelman, Andrew, and Gary King. 1993. "Why Are American Presidential Polls So Variable When Votes Are So Predictable?" *British Journal of Political Science* 23 (Oct.): 409–51.

Gibson, James L. 1986. "Pluralistic Intolerance in America." *American Politics Quarterly* 14 (Oct.): 267–93.

———. 1987. "Freedom and Tolerance in the United States." (NORC: Unpublished Codebook).

———. 1988. "Political Intolerance and Political Repression During the McCarthy Red Scare." *American Political Science Review* 82 (June): 512–29.

———. 1992. "The Political Consequences of Intolerance: Cultural Conformity and Political Freedom." *American Political Science Review* 86 (June): 338–56.

———. 1996. "The Paradoxes of Political Tolerance in the Process of Democratization." *Politikon: South African Journal of Political Science* 23: 2–21.

———. 1998. "A Sober Second Thought: An Experiment in Persuading Russians to Tolerate." *American Journal of Political Science* 42 (July): 819–50.

Gibson, James L., and Richard D. Bingham. 1985. *Civil Liberties and the Nazis: The Skokie Free-Speech Controversy.* New York: Praeger.

Gibson, James L., and Kent L. Tedin. 1988. "The Etiology of Intolerance for Homosexual Politics." *Social Science Quarterly* 69 (Sept.): 587–604.

Ginsberg, Benjamin. 1982. *The Consequences of Consent: Elections, Citizen Control and Popular Acquiescence.* Reading, MA: Addison-Wesley.

———. 1986. *The Captive Public.* New York: Basic.

Glazer, Amihai, and March Robbins. 1985. "Congressional Responsiveness to Constituency Change." *American Journal of Political Science* 29 (May): 259–73.

Goldenberg, Edie N., and Michael W. Traugott. 1984. *Campaigning for Congress.* Washington, DC: Congressional Quarterly.

Goldstein, Robert. 1978. *Political Repression in Modern America: From 1870 to the Present.* Cambridge, MA: Schenkman.

Graber, Doris A. 1988. *Processing the News.* New York: Longman.

———. 1997. *Mass Media and American Politics.* Washington, DC: Congressional Quarterly.

Greeley, Andrew. 1992. "Religion Around the World: A Preliminary Report." (Chicago: NORC).

Green, Donald Philip, and Bradley Palmquist. 1990. "Of Artifacts and Partisan Stability." *American Journal of Political Science* 34 (Aug.): 872–902.

Green, Donald, Bradley Palmquist, and Eric Schickler. 1998. "Macropartisanship: A Replication and Critique." *American Political Science Review.* 92: 883–99.

Greenberg, Edward. 1970. "Black Children and the Political System." *Public Opinion Quarterly* 34: 335–48.

Greenstein, Fred. I. 1965. *Children and Politics.* New Haven: Yale University Press.

———. 1969. *Personality and Politics.* Chicago: Markham.

———. 1992. "Can Personality and Politics Be Studied Systematically?" *Political Psychology* 13 (Mar.): 105–28.

Groseclose, Timothy, and Keith Krehbiel. 1994. "Golden Parachutes, Rubber Checks, and Strategic Retirements from the 102nd House." *American Journal of Political Science* 38: 75–99.

Groves, Robert, and Robert Kahn. 1979. *Surveys by Telephone.* New York: Academic.

Hahn, Harlan. 1968. "Northern Referenda on Fair Housing." *Western Political Quarterly* 21 (Sept.): 483–95.

Halberstam, David. 1979. *The Powers That Be.* New York: Knopf.

Hallin, Daniel. 1992. "Sound Bite News: Television Coverage of Elections." *Journal of Communication* 45 (Spring): 5–24.

Hamilton, Richard. 1975. *Restraining Myths: Critical Studies of U.S. Social Structure and Politics.* New York: Halsted.

Hand, Learned, 1959. *The Spirit of Liberty. Papers and Addresses.* New York: Knopf.

Hansen, John Mark. 1998. "Individuals, Institutions, and Public Preferences over Public Finance." *American Political Science Review* 92 (Sept.): 513–31.

Hansen, Susan Blackwell. 1975. "Participation, Political Structure, and Concurrence." *American Political Science Review* 69 (Dec.): 1181–91.

Hartley, Thomas, and Bruce Russett. 1992. "Public Opinion and the Common Defense: Who Governs Military Spending in the United States?" *American Political Science Review* 86 (Dec.): 905–15.

Harvey, G. Ted. 1972. "Computer Simulation of Peer Group Influence on Adolescent Political Behavior." *American Journal of Political Science* 16 (Nov.): 588–621.

Harvey, O. J., and G. Beverly. 1961. "Some Personality Correlates of Concept Change Through Role Playing." *Journal of Abnormal and Social Psychology* 27 (Mar.): 125–30.

Hawkins, Robert P., Suzanne Pingree, and Donald Roberts. 1975. "Watergate and Political Socialization." *American Politics Quarterly* 4 (Oct.): 406–36.

Heatherington, Mark J. 1998. "The Political Relevance of Political Trust." *American Political Science Review* 91 (Dec.): 791–808.

———. 1999. "The Effect of Political Trust on the Presidential Vote, 1968–1996." *American Political Science Review* 93 (June): 311–26.

Hedges, Chris. 1999. "35% of High School Seniors Fail National Civics Test." *New York Times,* 12 Nov. 1999, sec. 1, 17.

Hedlund, Ronald D. 1975. "Perceptions of Decisional Referents in Legislative Decision-Making." *American Journal of Political Science* 19 (Aug.): 527–42.

Hedlund, Ronald D., and H. Paul Friesema. 1972. "Representatives' Perceptions of Constituency Opinion." *Journal of Politics* 34 (Aug.): 167–76.

Herbst, Susan. 1993. *Numbered Voices: How Public Opinion Has Shaped American Politics.* Chicago: University of Chicago Press.

Hero, Alfred O. n.d. "Public Reactions to Federal Policy: Some Comparative Trends." Unpublished paper.

Herrera, Richard. 1992. "The Understanding of Ideological Labels by Political Elites: A Research Note." *Western Political Quarterly* 45 (Dec.): 1021–35.

Hershey, Marjorie Randon. 1989 "The Campaign and the Media." In *The Election of 1988: Reports and Interpretations,* ed. Gerald Pomper. Chatham, NJ: Chatham House.

Hershey, Marjorie Randon, and David B. Hill. 1975. "Watergate and Preadults' Attitudes Toward the President." *American Journal of Political Science* 19 (Nov.): 703–26.

Herson, Lawrence J. R., and C. Richard Hofstetter. 1975 "Tolerance, Consensus and Democratic Creed." *Journal of Politics* 37 (Dec.): 1007–32.

Hertsgaard, Mark. 1988. *On Bended Knee: The Press and the Reagan Presidency.* New York: Farrar.

Herzon, Fred. 1972. "A Review of Acquiescence Response Set in the California F-Scale." *Social Science Quarterly* 53 (June): 62–78.

Hess, Robert D., and Judith V. Torney. 1967. *The Development of Political Attitudes in Children.* Chicago: Aldine.

Hibbs, Douglas A., Jr. 1987. *The American Political Economy: Macroeconomics and Electoral Politics in the United States.* Cambridge, MA: Harvard University Press.

Hibbs, Douglas A., Jr., and Christopher Dennis. 1988. "Income Distribution in the United States." *American Political Science Review* 82 (June): 467–90.

Hilderbrand, Robert. 1981. *Power and the People: Executive Management of Public Opinion in Foreign Affairs.* Chapel Hill, NC: University of North Carolina Press.

Hitchens, William A. 1992. "Voting in the Passive Voice." *Harper's* 284 (Apr.): 45–52.

Hite, Shere. 1987. *Women and Love: A Cultural Revolution in Progress.* New York: Knopf.

———. 1997. *The Hite Report.*

Hofstetter, Richard. 1976. *Bias in the News.* Columbus, OH: Ohio State University Press.

Holbrook, Thomas. 2000. "Reading the Political Tea Leaves: A Forecasting Model of Contemporary Presidential Elections." In *Before the Vote: Forecasting American National Elections,* eds. James E. Campbell and James C. Garand. Thousand Oaks, CA: Sage.

Holbrook, Thomas, and Charles Tidmarch. 1991. "Sophomore Surge in State Legislative Elections." *Legislative Studies Quarterly* 16: 49–64.

Holmes, Stephen A. 1999. "Ruling Said to Raise Census Cost by $2 Billion." *New York Times,* 24 Feb.: A-1.

Hooper, Michael. 1969. "Party and Endorsement as Predictors of Voter Choice." *Journalism Quarterly* 43 (Summer): 302–5.

Hugick, Larry, and Guy Molyneux. 1993. "The Performance of the Gallup Tracking Poll: The Myth and the Reality." *Public Perspective* 4 (Jan./Feb.): 12–14.

Huntington, Samuel P. 1991. *The Third Wave: Democratization in the Late Twentieth Century.* Norman, OK: University of Oklahoma Press.

Hurley, Patricia A. 1989. "Parties and Coalitions in Congress." In *Congressional Politics,* ed. Christopher Deering. Chicago: Dorsey.

Hurley, Patricia A., and Kim Quaille Hill. 1981. "The Prospects for Issue Voting in Contemporary Congressional Elections: An Assessment of Citizen Awareness and Representation." In *Public Opinion and Public Policy,* 3rd ed., ed. Norman R. Luttbeg. Itasca, IL: Peacock.

Hurwitz, Jon, and Mark Peffley. 1987. "How Are Foreign Policy Attitudes Structured? A Hierarchical Model." *American Political Science Review* 81 (Dec.): 1099–120.

Hurwitz, Jon, Mark Peffley, and Paul Raymond, 1989. "Presidential Support During the Iran-Contra Affair." *American Public Opinion* 17 (Oct.): 359–85.

Hyman, Herbert. 1959. *Political Socialization.* Glencoe, IL: Free.

Inglehart, Ronald. 1990. *Culture Shift.* Princeton, NJ: Princeton University Press.

———. 1997a. "Postmaterialist Values and the Erosion of Institutional Authority." In *Why People Don't Trust Government,* eds. Joseph S. Nye, Philip D. Zelikow, and David C. King. Cambridge, MA: Harvard University Press.

———. 1997b. *Modernization and Postmodernization.* Princeton, NJ: Princeton University Press.

Inkeles, Alex. 1961. "National Character and the Modern Political System." In *Psychological Anthropology: Approaches to Culture and Personality,* ed. Francis L. K. Hsu. Homewood, IL: Dorsey.

Iyengar, Shanto. 1993. *Is Anyone Responsible? How Television Frames Political News.* Chicago: University of Chicago Press.

Iyengar, Shanto, and Donald R. Kinder. 1987. *News That Matters.* Chicago: University of Chicago Press.

Iyengar, Shanto, Mark D. Peters, and Donald R. Kinder. 1982. "Experimental Demonstrations of 'Not-So-Minimal' Consequences of Television News Programs." *American Political Science Review* 76 (Dec.): 848–58.

Jackman, Mary. 1978. "General and Applied Tolerance: Does Education Increase Commitment to Racial Integration?" *American Journal of Political Science* 22 (May): 302–24.

Jackman, Mary R., and Robert W. Jackman. 1983. *Class Awareness in the United States.* Berkeley: University of California Press.

Jackman, Mary, and Michael J. Mulha. 1984. "Education and Intergroup Attitudes: Moral Enlightenment, Superficial Democratic Commitment or Ideological Refinement." *American Sociological Review* 49 (Aug.): 751–69.

Jackman, Robert W. 1972. "Political Elites, Mass Publics, and Support for Democratic Principles." *Journal of Politics* 54 (Aug.): 753–73.

Jackman, Robert W., and Robert A. Miller. 1996. "A Renaissance of Political Culture?" *American Journal of Political Science* 40 (May): 632–59.

Jackson, John E. 1983. "Election Night Reporting and Voter Turnout." *American Journal of Political Science* 27 (Nov.): 615–35.

Jacob, Philip E. 1956. *Changing Values in College.* New Haven: Hazen Foundation.

Jacobs, Lawrence R. 1993. *The Health of Nations: Public Opinions in the Making of American and British Health Policy.* Ithaca, NY: Cornell University Press.

Jacobs, Lawrence R., and Robert Y. Shapiro. 2000. *Politicians Don't Pander: Political Manipulation and the Loss of Democratic Responsiveness.* Chicago: University of Chicago Press.

———. 1993. "Polling and Opinion on Health Care Reform." *Public Perspective* 4 (May/June): 22–27.

————. 1994. "Studying Substantive Democracy." *PS: Political Science and Politics* 27 (Mar.): 9–17.

————. 1995. "The Rise of Presidential Polling: The Nixon White House in Historical Perspective." *Public Opinion Quarterly* 59: 163–95.

Jacobson, Gary C. 1987. *The Politics of Congressional Elections,* 2nd ed. Boston: Little Brown.

————. 1989. "Parties and PACs in Congressional Elections." In *Congress Reconsidered,* 4th ed., eds. Lawrence C. Dodd and Bruce I. Oppenheimer. Washington, DC: Congressional Quarterly.

Jacobson, Gary C., and Michael A. Dimmock. 1994. "Checking out: The Effects of Bank Overdrafts on the 1992 House Elections." *American Journal of Political Science* 38: 601–24.

Jacobson, Gary C., and Samuel Kernell. 1983. *Strategy and Choice in Congressional Elections,* 2nd ed. New Haven: Yale University Press.

Jacoby, William G. 1988a. "The Impact of Party Identification on Issue Attitudes." *American Journal of Political Science* 32: 643–61.

————. 1988b. "The Sources of Liberal-Conservative Thinking: Education and Conceptualization." *Political Behavior* 10 (Winter): 316–32.

————. 1991. "Ideological Identifications and Issue Attitudes." *American Journal of Political Science* 35 (Feb.): 178–205.

Jamieson, Kathleen Hall. 1992. *Dirty Politics.* New York: Oxford University Press.

Jaros, Dean, Herbert Hirsch, and Frederick Fleron. 1968. "The Malevolent Leader: Political Socialization in an American Sub-Culture." *American Political Science Review* 62 (June): 564–75.

Jelen, Ted. G. 1992. "Political Christianity: A Contextual Analysis." *American Journal of Political Science* 36 (Aug.): 662–92.

————. 1993. "The Political Consequences of Religious Group Attitudes." *Journal of Politics* 55 (Feb.): 167–77.

Jennings, M. Kent. 1987. "Residuals of a Movement: The Aging of the American Protest Generation." *American Political Science Review* 81 (June): 365–81.

————. 1992. "Ideological Thinking Among Mass Publics and Political Elites." *Public Opinion Quarterly* 56 (Winter): 419–41.

Jennings, M. Kent, and Ellen Ann Andersen. 1996. "Support for Confrontational Tactics Among AIDS Activists: A Study of Intra-Movement Divisions." *American Journal of Political Science* 40 (May): 311–34.

Jennings, M. Kent, Lee H. Ehrman, and Richard G. Niemi. 1974. "Social Studies Teachers and Their Students." In *The Political Character of Adolescence,* eds. M. Kent Jennings and Richard G. Niemi. Princeton, NJ: Princeton University Press.

Jennings, M. Kent, and Gregory B. Markus. 1984. "Partisan Orientations Over the Long Haul: Results from the Three-Wave Political Socialization Panel Study." *American Political Science Review* 78 (Dec.): 1000–18.

Jennings, M. Kent, and Richard G. Niemi. 1974. *The Political Character of Adolescence.* Princeton, NJ: Princeton University Press.

————. 1982. *Generations and Politics.* Princeton, NJ: Princeton University Press.

Jennings, M. Kent, and Laura Stoker. 1999. "The Persistence of the Past: The Class of 1965 Turns Fifty." Paper presented at the Midwest Political Science Convention, Apr. 1999.

Jensen, Richard. 1968. "American Election Analysis: A Case of History and Methodological Innovation and Diffusion." In *Politics and Social Science,* ed. Seymour Martin Lipset. New York: Oxford University Press.

Jewell, Malcolm E., and David Breaux. 1988. "The Effect of Incumbency on State Legislative Elections." *Legislative Studies Quarterly* 13 (Nov.): 495–514.

Jewell, Malcolm E., and Samuel Patterson. 1981. *The Legislative Process in the United States,* 7th ed. New York: Random.

Johannes, John R., and John P. McAdams. 1981. "The Congressional Incumbency Effect: Is It Casework, Policy Compatibility, or Something Else? An Examination of the 1978 Election." *American Journal of Political Science* 25 (Aug.): 512–52.

Johnstone, David Cay. 1999. "Gap between Rich and Poor Found Substantially Wider." *New York Times,* 5 Sept. 1999, A14.

Johnstone, John, Edward Slawski, and William Bowman. 1976. *The Newspeople.* Urbana, IL: University of Illinois Press.

Jowell, Roger, Barry Hedges, Peter Lynn, Graham Farrant, and Anthony Heath. 1993. "The 1992 British Election: The Failure of the Polls." *Public Opinion Quarterly* 57 (Summer): 238–63.

Just, Marion, and Ann Crigler. 2000. "Leadership Image-Building: After Clinton and Watergate." *Political Psychology* 21: 179–88.

Kahn, Kim Fridkin, and Patrick J. Kenney. 1999. "Do Negative Campaigns Mobilize or Suppress Turnout? Clarifying the Relationship between Negativity and Participation." *American Political Science Review.* 93: 877–89.

Karnig, Albert K., and B. Oliver Walter. 1977. "Municipal Elections Registration, Incumbent Success and Voter Participation." *The Municipal Yearbook 1977.* Washington, DC: International City Management Association, 65–72.

Karp, Jeffrey A. 1995. "Support For Legislative Term Limits." *Public Opinion Quarterly* 59 (Fall): 373–91.

Katosh, John, and Michael Traugott. 1981. "The Consequences of Validated and Self-Reported Voting Measures." *Public Opinion Quarterly* 45 (Winter): 519–35.

Keene, Karlyn H. 1991. "Feminism Vs. Women's Rights." *Public Perspective* 3 (Nov./Dec.):3–4.

Keicolt, K. Jill, and Laura E. Nathan, 1985. *Secondary Analysis of Survey Data.* Beverly Hills, CA: Sage.

Kelley, Stanley J., Jr. 1983. *Interpreting Elections.* Princeton NJ: Princeton University Press.

Kenski, Henry. 1988. "The Gender Factor in a Changing Electorate." In *The Politics of the Gender Gap,* ed. Carol M. Mueller. Beverly Hills, CA: Sage.

Kerlinger, Fred N. 1984. *Liberalism and Conservatism.* Hillsdale, MI: Erlbaum.

Kernell, Samuel. 1978. "Explaining Presidential Popularity." *American Political Science Review* 72 (June): 506–23.

————. 1993. *Going Public: New Strategies for Presidential Leadership.* Washington, DC: Congressional Quarterly Press.

Kesler, Charles. 1979. "The Movement of Student Opinion." *National Review* 23 (Nov.): 1448.

Key, V. O., Jr. 1949. *Southern Politics in State and Nation.* New York: Knopf.

————. 1961a. "Public Opinion and the Decay of Democracy." *Virginia Quarterly Review* 37 (Autumn): 488–512.

————. 1961b. *Public Opinion and American Democracy.* New York: Knopf.

Kiewiet, D. Roderick. 1983. *Macroeconomics and Micropolitics.* Chicago: University of Chicago Press.

Kiewiet, D. Roderick, and Matthew D. McCubbins. 1985. "Congressional Appropriations and the Electoral Connection." *Journal of Politics* 47 (Spring): 59–82.

————. 1991. *Congressional Parties and the Appropriations Process.* Chicago: University of Chicago Press.

Kinder, Donald. 1986. "The Continuing American Dilemma: White Resistance to Racial Change 40 Years After Myrdahl." *Journal of Social Issues* 42 (Mar.): 151–72.

Kinder, Donald R., Gordon S. Adams, and Paul W. Gronke. 1989. "Economics and Politics in the 1984 American Presidential Elections." *American Journal of Political Science* 33 (May): 491–515.

Kinder, Donald R., and Don Herzog. 1993. "Democratic Discussion." In *Reconsidering the Democratic Public,* eds. George E. Marcus and Russell L. Hanson. University Park, PA: Pennsylvania State University Press.

Kinder, Donald R., and D. Roderick Kiewiet. 1979. "Economic Grievances and Political Behavior: The Role of Personal Discontents and Collective Judgments in Congressional Voting." *American Journal of Political Science* 23 (Aug.): 495–527.

————. 1981. "Sociotropic Politics." *British Journal of Political Science* 11 (Apr.): 129–61.

Kinder, Donald R., and Lynn M. Sanders. 1996. *Divided by Color.* Chicago: University of Chicago Press.

King, C. David. 1997. "The Polarization of American Parties and Mistrust of Government." In *Why People Don't Trust Government,* eds. Joseph S. Nye, Philip D. Zelikow, and David C. King. Cambridge, MA: Harvard University Press.

Kingdon, John W. 1973. *Congressmen's Voting Decisions.* New York: Harper.

Kirkpatrick, Jean. 1975. "Representative in the American National Conventions: The Case of 1972." *British Journal of Political Science* 5 (July): 262–322.

Kirscht, John P., and Ronald C. Dillehay. 1967. *Dimensions of Authoritarianism: A Review of Research and Theory.* Lexington, KY: University of Kentucky Press.

Knight, Kathleen. 1985. "Ideology in the 1980 Election: Political Sophistication Matters." *Journal of Politics* 47 (Aug.): 828–53.

————. 1999. "Liberalism and Conservatism." In *Measures of Political Attitudes,* eds. John P. Robinson, Philip Shaver, and Lawrence Wrightsman. New York: Academic.

Knight, Kathleen, and Carolyn Lewis. 1992. "Ideology and the American Electorate." In *Perspectives on American and Texas Politics,* eds. Kent L. Tedin, Donald S. Lutz, and Edward P. Fuchs. Dubuque, IA: Kendall-Hunt.

Knoke, David, and Michael Hout. 1974. "Social and Demographic Factors in American Political Party Affiliations, 1952–1972." *American Sociological Review* 39 (Aug.): 700–13.

Koch, Jeffery W. 1998. "Political Rhetoric and Political Persuasion." *Public Opinion Quarterly* 62 (Summer): 209–29.

Kolbert, Elizabeth. 1993. "Did the Voting Experts Go Wrong?" *New York Times,* 4 November, sec. A.

Kolson, Kenneth L., and Justin J. Green. 1970. "Response Set Bias and Political Socialization Research." *Social Science Quarterly* 51: 527–38.

Kornhouser, William. 1970. *The Politics of Mass Society.* Chicago. Markham.

Krosnick, Jon A., and Matthew K. Kerent. 1993. "Comparisons of Party Identification and Policy Preferences: The Impact of Survey Question Format." *American Journal of Political Science* 37 (Aug.): 941–64.

Krosnick, Jon A., and Donald Kinder. 1990. "Altering the Foundations of Support for the President Through Priming." *American Political Science Review* 84 (June): 497–512.

Kuklinski, James H. 1978. "Representatives and Elections: A Policy Analysis." *American Political Science Review* 72 (Mar.) 165–77.

Kuklinski, James H., Michael D. Cobb, and Martin Gilens. 1997. "Racial Attitudes in the New South." *Journal of Politics* 59 (May): 323–49.

Kuklinski, James H., and Richard C. Elling. 1977. "Representational Role, Constituency Opinion, and Legislative Roll Call Behavior." *American Journal of Political Science* 21 (Feb.): 135–44.

Kuklinski, James H., and Donald J. McCrone. 1981. "Electoral Accountability as a Source of Policy Representation." In *Public Opinion and Public Policy,* ed. Norman R. Luttbeg. Itasca, IL: Peacock.

Kuklinski, James H., Ellen Riggle, Victor Ottati, Norbert Schwartz, and Robert S. Wyer. 1991. "The Cognitive and Affective Basis of Political Tolerance Judgments." *American Journal of Political Science* 35 (Feb.): 1–27.

Kuklinski, James H., Paul M. Sniderman, Kathleen Knight, Thomas Piazza, Philip E. Tetlock, Gordon R. Lawrence, and Barbara Mellers. 1997. "Racial Prejudice and Attitudes Toward Affirmative Action." *American Journal of Political Science* 41 (Apr.): 402–19.

Kweit, Mary Grisez. 1986. "Ideological Congruence of Party Switchers and Nonswitchers: The Case of Party Activists." *American Journal of Political Science* 30 (Feb.): 184–96.

Ladd, Everett Carl. 1970. *American Political Parties: Social Change and Political Response.* New York: Norton.

———. 1996. "The Election Polls: An American Waterloo." *Chronicle of Higher Education* (22 Nov.): A52.

———. 1998a. *America's Social Capital: Change and Renewal in Civil Life.* New York: Free.

————. 1998b. "States and Regions in the US: How Similar? Where Different?" *The Public Perspective* 9 (June–July): 10–31.

Ladd, Everett Carl, and John Benson. 1992. "The Growth of News Polls in American Politics." In *Media Polls in American Politics,* eds. Thomas E. Mann and Gary R. Orren. Washington, DC: Brookings.

Ladd, Everett Carl, and G. Donald Ferree. 1981. "Were the Pollsters Really Wrong?" *Public Opinion* (Dec./Jan.): 13.

Lane, Robert. 1962. *Political Ideology.* New York: Free.

Langton, Kenneth P., and M. Kent Jennings. 1968. "Political Socialization and the High School Civics Curriculum in the United States." *American Political Science Review* 62 (Sept.): 852–77.

Lasswell, Harold D. 1951. "Democratic Character." In *The Political Writings of Harold D. Lasswell.* Glencoe, IL: Free.

Lau, Richard, 1985. "Two Explanations for Negative Effects in Political Behavior." *American Journal of Political Science* 29 (Feb.): 119–38.

Lau, Richard, Lee Sigelman, Caroline Heldman, and Paul Babbitt. 1999. "The Effects of Negative Political Advertisements: A Meta-Analytical Assessment." *American Political Science Review* 93: 851–75.

Lavrakas, Paul J. 1987. *Telephone Survey Methods.* Beverly Hills, CA: Sage.

————. 1993. *Telephone Survey Methods,* 2nd ed. Beverly Hills, CA: Sage.

Lawrence Robert Z. 1997. "Is It Really the Economy, Stupid?" In *Why People Don't Trust Government,* eds. Joseph S. Nye, Philip D. Zelikow, and David C. King. Cambridge, MA: Harvard University Press.

Layman, Geoffrey C. 1997. "Religion and Political Behavior in the United States: The Impact of Beliefs, Affiliations, and Commitment from 1980 to 1994." *Public Opinion Quarterly* 61 (Summer): 261–87.

Lazarsfeld, Paul, Bernard Berelson, and Hazel Gaudet. 1948. *The People's Choice.* New York: Columbia University Press.

LeBlanc, Hugh L. 1969. "Voting in State Senates: Party and Constituency Influences." *Midwest Journal of Political Science* 13 (Feb.): 33–57.

Leege, David C., and Michael R. Welch. 1989. "Religious Roots of Political Orientations: Variations Among Catholic Parishioners." *Journal of Politics* 51 (Feb.): 137–64.

————. "Dual Reference Groups and Political Orientations: An Examination of Evangelically Oriented Catholics." *American Journal of Political Science* 35 (Feb.): 28–56.

Lewis, I. A. 1990. "Poll Wars and Poll Debacle in Nicaragua." *The Public Perspective* 1:6.

Lewis-Beck, Michael, and Tom Rice. 1982. "Presidential Popularity and the Presidential Vote." *Public Opinion Quarterly* 47 (Winter): 534–37.

Lewis-Beck, Michael, and Charles Tien. 2000. "The Future in Forecasting: Prospective Presidential Models." In *Before the Vote; Forecasting American National Elections,* eds. James E. Campbell and James C. Garand. Thousand Oaks, CA: Sage.

Lichter, S. Robert, and Stanley Rothman. 1979 "Media and Business Elites." *Public Opinion* 4 (Oct./Nov.): 42–46, 59–60.

Light, Paul C. 1988. *Baby Boomers.* New York: Norton.

Light, Paul C., and Celinda Lake. 1985. "The Election: Candidates Strategies, and Decision." In *The Elections of 1984,* ed. Michael Nelson. Washington, DC: Congressional Quarterly.

Lippmann, Walter. 1922. *Public Opinion.* New York: Harcourt.

———. 1925. *The Phantom Public.* New York: Harcourt.

Lipset, Seymour Martin. 1950. *Agrarian Socialism.* Berkeley, CA: University of California Press.

———. 1959. "Some Social Requisites of Modern Democracy: Economic Development and Political Legitimacy." *American Political Science Review* 53 (Mar.): 69–105.

———. 1960. *Political Man.* Garden City, NY: Doubleday.

———. 1992. "Polls Don't Lie. People Do." *New York Times,* 10 Sept., sec. A.

Lodge, Milton, Kathleen McGraw, and Patrick Stroh. 1989. "An Impression-Driven Model of Candidate Evaluation." *American Political Science Review* 83 (June): 399–419.

Lodge, Milton, Marco R. Steenbergen, Shawn Brau. 1995. "The Responsive Voter: Candidate Information and the Dynamics of Candidate Evaluation." *American Political Science Review* 89 (June): 309–31.

Lodge, Milton, and Patrick Stroh. 1993. "Inside the Mental Voting Booth: An Impression-Driven Process." In *Explorations in Political Psychology,* eds. Shanto Iyengar and William J. McGuire. Durham, NC: Duke University Press.

Luker, Kristin. 1984. *Abortion and the Politics of Motherhood.* Berkeley, CA: University of California Press.

Lupia, Arthur. 1992. "Busy Voters, Agenda Control, and the Power of Information." *American Political Science Review* 86 (June): 390–403.

Lupia, Arthur, and Mathew D. McCubbins. 1998. *The Democratic Dilemma: Can Citizens Learn What They Need to Know?* New York: Cambridge University Press.

Luskin, Robert C. 1987. "Measuring Political Sophistication." *American Journal of Political Science* 31 (Nov.): 856–99.

Luskin, Robert C., John P. McIver, and Edward G. Carmines. 1989. "Issues and the Transmission of Partisanships." *American Journal of Political Science* 33 (May): 440–58.

Luttbeg, Norman R. 1968. "Political Linkage in a Large Society." In *Public Opinion and Public Policy,* ed. Norman Luttbeg. Homewood, IL: Dorsey.

———. 1981. "Balance Theory as a Source of Perception of Where Political Parties Stand on the Issues." In *Public Opinion and Public Policy,* 3rd ed., ed. Norman R. Luttbeg. Itasca, IL: Peacock Press.

———. 1983. "News Consensus: Do U.S. Newspapers Mirror Society's Happenings?" *Journalism Quarterly* 60 (Autumn): 484–88.

———. 1999. *The Grassroots of Democracy: A Comparative Study of Competition and Its Impact in the American Cities in the 1990s.* Lanham, MD: Lexington Books.

Luttbeg, Norman R., and Michael Gant. 1985. "The Failure of Liberal-Conservative Ideology as a Cognitive Structure." *Public Opinion Quarterly* 49 (Spring): 80–93.

Luttbeg, Norman R., and Charles W. Wiggins. 1983. "Public Opinion Versus Interest Group Opinion: The Case of Iowa." In *Public Opinion and Public Policy,* 3rd ed., ed. Norman R. Luttbeg. Itasca, IL: Peacock.

Luttbeg, Norman R., and Harmon Zeigler. 1966. "Attitude Consensus and Conflict Within an Interest Group: An Assessment of Cohesion." *American Political Science Review* 60 (Sept.): 655–65.

Lyons, William, and John M. Scheb. 1992. "Ideology and Candidate Evaluation in the 1984 and 1988 Presidential Elections." *Journal of Politics* 54 (May): 573–86.

MacDougall, Curtis D. 1966. *Understanding Public Opinion.* Boston: Little Brown.

MacKuen, Michael Bruce. 1981. "Social Communication and the Mass Policy Agenda." In *More Than News: Media Power in Public Affairs,* eds. Michael Bruce MacKuen and Steven Coombs. Beverly Hills, CA: Sage.

———. 1984. "Exposure to Information, Belief Integration, and Individual Responsiveness to Agenda Change." *American Political Science Review* 78 (June): 372–91.

MacKuen, Michael B., Robert S. Erikson, and James A. Stimson. 1989. "Macropartisanship." *American Political Science Review* 83 (Dec.): 1125–42.

———. 1992. "Peasants or Bankers: The American Electorate and the U.S. Economy." *American Political Science Review* 86 (Sept.): 597–611.

Magleby, David B. 1989. "Opinion Formation and Partisan Change in Ballot Proposition Campaigns." In *Manipulating Public Opinion,* eds. Michael Margolis and Gary A. Mauser. Pacific Grove, CA: Brooks/Cole.

Magner, Denise K. 1999. "The Graying Professorate." *Chronicle of Higher Education* (3 Nov.): A18–21.

Marcus, George E., John L. Sullivan, Elizabeth Theiss-Morse, and Sandra L. Wood. 1995. *With Malice Toward Some.* New York: Cambridge University Press.

Mann, Sheilah. 1996. "Symposium: Political Scientists Examine Civic Standards." *PS: Political Science and Politics* 29 (Mar.): 47–48.

———. 1999. "What the Survey of American College Freshman Tells Us about Their Interest in Politics and Political Science." *PS: Political Science and Politics* 32 (June): 263–68.

Margolis, Michael. 1977. "From Confusion to Confusion: Issues and the American Voter (1956–1972)." *American Political Science Review* 71 (Mar.): 31–43.

Markus, Gregory B. 1979. "The Political Environment and the Dynamics of Public Attitudes." *American Journal of Political Science* 23 (May): 338–59.

———. 1982. "Political Attitudes in an Election Year: A Report on the 1980 NES Panel Study." *American Political Science Review* 76 (Sept.): 538–59.

———. 1988. "The Impact of Personal and National Economic Conditions on the Presidential Vote: A Pooled Cross-Sectional Analysis." *American Journal of Political Science* 32 (Feb.): 137–54.

Markus, Gregory B., and Philip E. Converse. 1979. "A Dynamic Simultaneous Equation Model of Public Choice." *American Political Science Review* 73 (Dec.): 1055–70.

Mayer, William G. 1992. *The Changing American Mind.* Ann Arbor, MI: University of Michigan Press.

Mayhew, David R. 1974. *Congress: The Electoral Connection*. New Haven: Yale University Press.

McCloskey, Herbert. 1964. "Consensus and Ideology in American Politics." *American Political Science Review* 58 (June).

McCloskey, Herbert, and Alida Brill. 1983. *Dimensions of Political Tolerance*. New York: Russell Sage.

McClosky, Herbert, Paul J. Hoffman, and Rosemary O'Hara. 1960. "Issue Conflict and Consensus Among Party Leaders and Followers." *American Political Science Review* 59 (June): 406–27.

McCombs, Maxwell E. 1981. "The Agenda-Setting Approach." In *Handbook of Political Communication,* eds. Dan D. Nimmo and Keith R. Sanders. Beverly Hills, CA: Sage.

McCombs, Maxwell E., and Donald L. Shaw. 1972. "The Agenda-Setting Function of the Mass Media." *Public Opinion Quarterly* 35 (Summer): 176–87.

McCrane, Donald J., and James H. Kuklinski. 1979. "The Delegate Theory of Representation." *American Journal of Political Science* 23 (May): 278–300.

McDonald, Michael D., Ian Budge, and Richard I. Hofferbert. 1999. "Party Mandate Theory and Time Series Analysis: A Theoretical and Methodological Response." *Electoral Studies.* 18: 587–96.

McFarland, Sam G., Vladimir S. Ageyev, and Marina A. Abalakina. 1992. "Authoritarianism in the Former Soviet Union." *Journal of Personality and Social Psychology* 63 (Dec.): 1003–10.

McLean, Scott. 1999. "Land That I Love: Feelings Toward Country at Century's End." *The Public Perspective* 10 (Apr./May): 21–25.

Meloen, J. D., L. Hagendorn, Q. Raaijmakers, and L. Visser. 1988. "Authoritarianism and the Revival of Political Racism: Reassessments in the Netherlands of the Reliability and Validity of the Concept of Authoritarianism by Adorno et al." *Political Psychology* 9 (Sept.): 412–44.

Meloen, J. D., G. van der Linden, and H. de Witte. 1996. "A Test of the Approaches of Adorno et al., Ledere, and Altemeyer of Authoritarianism in Belgian Flanders: A Research Note." *Political Psychology* 17: 643–56.

Merelman, Richard. 1971. *Political Socialization and Educational Climates*. New York: Holt.

———. 1972. "The Adolescence of Political Socialization." *Sociology of Education* 45 (Spring): 128–42.

———. 1980. "Democratic Politics and the Culture of American Education." *American Political Science Review* 74 (June): 319–33.

———. 1986. "Revitalizing Political Socialization." In *Political Psychology,* ed. Margaret G. Hermann. San Francisco: Jossey-Bass.

———. 1997. "Symbols and Substance in National Civics Standards." *PS: Political Science and Politics* 29 (Mar.): 53–56.

Miedaian, Myriam. 1991. *Boys Will Be Boys: Breaking the Link Between Masculinity and Violence*. New York: Doubleday.

Milbrath, Lester W. 1963. *The Washington Lobbyists.* Chicago: Rand.

Milbrath, Lester W., and M. L. Goel. 1977. *Political Participation,* 2nd ed. Chicago: Rand.

Milburn, Michael A., S. D. Conrad, and S. Carberry. 1995. "Childhood Punishment, Denial, and Political Attitudes." *Political Psychology* 16: 447–78.

Milgram, Stanley. 1969. *Obedience to Authority.* New York: Harper.

Miller, Arthur H. 1974. "Political Issues and Trust in Government: 1960–1970." *American Political Science Review* 68 (Sept.): 944–61.

———. 1983. "Is Confidence Rebounding?" *Public Opinion* (June/July): 16–21.

———. 1988. "Gender and the Vote: 1984." In *The Politics of the Gender Gap: The Social Construction of Political Influence,* ed. Carol M. Mueller. Beverly Hills, CA: Sage.

Miller, Arthur H., and Stephen A. Borrelli. 1991. "Confidence in Government in the 1980s." *American Politics Quarterly* 19 (Apr.): 147–75.

Miller, Arthur H., Warren E. Miller, Alden S. Raine, and Thad A. Browne. 1976. "A Majority Party in Disarray: Policy Polarization in the 1972 Election." *American Political Science Review* 70 (Sept.): 753–78.

Miller, Arthur H., and Martin P. Wattenberg. 1984. "Politics from the Pulpit: Religiosity and the 1980 Election." *Public Opinion Quarterly* 48 (Spring): 301–11.

Miller, Arthur H., Martin P. Wattenberg, and Oksana Malanchuk. 1986. "Schematic Assessment of Presidential Candidates." *American Political Science Review* 80 (June): 522–40.

Miller, Arthur H., Christopher Wlezien, and Ann Hildreth. 1991. "A Reference Group Theory of Party Coalitions." *Journal of Politics* 53 (Nov.): 1134–49.

Miller, Warren E., and M. Kent Jennings. 1987. *Parties in Transition: A Longitudinal Study of Party Elites and Party Supporters.* New York: Russell Sage.

Miller, Warren E., and J. Merrill Shanks. 1996. *The New American Voter.* Cambridge, MA: Harvard University Press.

Miller, Warren E., and Donald W. Stokes. 1963. "Constituency Influence in Congress." *American Political Science Review* 57 (Mar.): 45–46.

Mills, C. Wright. 1956. *The Power Elite.* New York: Oxford University Press.

———. 1963. *Power, Politics, and People: The Collected Essays of C. Wright Mills.* New York: Ballantine, p. 535.

Mishler, William, and Reginald S. Sheehan. 1993. "The Supreme Court as a Countermajoritarian Institution? The Impact of Public Opinion on Supreme Court Decisions." *American Political Science Review* 87 (Mar.): 87–101.

Mitchell, Alison. 1998. "A New Form of Lobbying Puts Public Face on Private Interest." *New York Times,* 30 Sept., A1.

Mitofsky, Warren J. 1998. "Review: Was 1996 a Worse Year for Polls than 1948?" *Public Opinion Quarterly* 62 (Summer): 230–49.

Monroe, Alan D. 1979. "Consistency Between Public Preferences and National Policy Decisions." *American Politics Quarterly* 7 (Jan.): 3–21.

———. 1998. "Public Opinion and Public Policy: 1980–93." *Public Opinion Quarterly* 62: 6–28.

Montaigne, Michel de. 1967. *The Complete Works of Montaigne.* Stanford, CA: Stanford University Press.

Montcrief, Gary. 1999. "Recruitment and Retention in U.S. Legislatures." *Legislative Studies Quarterly* 24: 173–208.

Moore, David W. 1992a. "The Sure Thing That Got Away." *New York Times,* 25 Oct., sec. A.

———. 1992b. *The SuperPollsters.* New York: Four Walls, Eight Windows.

Moore, Stanley W., James Lare, and Kenneth A. Wagner. 1985. *The Child's Political World.* New York: Praeger.

Morin, Richard. 1991. "The Outcome Is There in Black and White." *Washington Post,* weekly ed., 25 Feb.–3 Mar., p. 37.

———. 1992. "Surviving the Ups and Downs of Election '92." *Washington Post,* weekly ed., 9–15 Nov., p. 37.

———. 1996. "A Matter of Incumbency." *Washington Post,* weekly ed. 9–15 Dec., p. 34.

———. 1997. "Which Comes First, the Politician or the Poll." *Washington Post,* weekly ed., 10–15 Feb., p. 35.

Mueller, John E. 1970a. "President Popularity from Truman to Johnson." *American Political Science Review* 64 (Jan.): 22–41.

———. 1970b. "Choosing Among 133 Candidates." *Public Opinion Quarterly* 34 (Fall): 395–402.

———. 1973. *War, Presidents, and Public Opinion.* New York: Wiley.

———. 1977. "Changes in American Attitudes Toward International Involvement." In *The Limits of Military Intervention,* ed. Ellen Stern. Beverly Hills, CA: Sage: 323–44.

Murray, Charles. 1985. *Losing Ground.* New York: Basic.

Nadel, Mark V. 1972. "Public Policy and Public Opinion." In *American Democracy: Theory and Reality,* ed. Robert Weissberg and Mark V. Nadel. New York: Wiley.

Nesbit, Dorothy Davidson. 1988. "Partisan Changes Among Southern Activists." *Journal of Politics* 50 (May): 322–34.

Neuman, W. Russell, R. Just, and Ann N. Crigler. 1991. *Common Knowledge: News and the Construction of Political Meaning.* Chicago: University of Chicago Press.

Nice, David C. 1992. "The States and the Death Penalty." *Western Political Quarterly* 45 (Nov.): 1037–48.

Nie, Norman, and Kristi Anderson. 1974. "Mass Belief Systems Revisited: Political Change and Attitude Structure." *Journal of Politics* 36 (Aug.): 540–91.

Nie, Norman H., Jane Junn, and Kenneth Stehlik-Barry. 1998. *Education and Democratic Citizenship in America.* Chicago: University of Chicago Press.

Nie, Norman H., G. Bingham Powell, and Kenneth Prewitt. 1969a. "Social Structure and Political Participation: Developmental Relationships, I." *American Political Science Review* 63 (June): 361–78.

———. 1969b. "Social Structure and Political Participation: Developmental Relationships, II." *American Political Science Review* 63 (Sept.): 808–32.

Nie, Norman H., Sidney Verba, and John R. Petrocik. 1976. *The Changing American Voter.* Cambridge, MA: Harvard University Press.

Niemi, Richard G., Stephen C. Craig, and Franco Mattei. 1991 "Measuring Internal Political Efficacy in the 1988 National Election Study." *American Political Science Review* 85 (Dec.): 1407–13.

Niemi, Richard G., and Jane Junn. 1998. *Civic Education: What Makes Students Learn*. New Haven: Yale University Press.

Niemi, Richard G., John Mueller, and Tom W. Smith. 1989. *Trends in Public Opinion*. New York: Greenwood.

Norrander, Barbara. 1989. "Ideological Representatives of Presidential Primary Voters." *American Journal of Political Science* 33 (Aug.): 570–87.

Norris, Pippa. 1988. "The Gender Gap: A Cross-National Trend?" In *The Politics of the Gender Gap*, ed. Carol M. Mueller. Beverly Hills, CA: Sage.

Nunn, Clyde Z., Harry J. Crockett, Jr., and J. Allen Williams, Jr. 1978. *Tolerance for Nonconformity*. San Francisco: Jossey-Bass.

Nye, Joseph S. 1997. "The Decline of Confidence in Government." In *Why People Don't Trust Government*, eds. Joseph S. Nye, Philip D. Zelikow, and David C. King. Cambridge, MA: Harvard University Press.

Nye, Joseph S., and Philip D. Zelikow. 1997. "Conclusion: Reflections, Conjectures and Puzzles." In *Why People Don't Trust Government*, eds. Joseph S. Nye, Philip D. Zelikow, and David C. King. Cambridge, MA: Harvard University Press.

O'Keefe, Garrett J., and L. Erwin Atwood. 1981. "Communication and Election Campaigns." In *Handbook of Political Communication*, eds. Dan D. Nimmo and Keith R. Sander. Beverly Hills, CA: Sage.

Olson, Mancur, Jr. 1968. *The Logic of Collective Action*. New York: Schocken.

Oreskes, Michael. 1990. "In Year of Volatile Vote, Polls Can Be Dynamite." *New York Times*, 2 Nov., sec. A.

Ornstein, Norman J., Thomas E. Mann and Michael J. Malbin, eds. 1994. *Vital Statistics on Congress 1993–1994*. Washington, DC: Congressional Quarterly.

Orren, Gary. 1997. "Fall from Grace: The Public's Loss of Faith in Government." In *Why People Don't Trust Government*, eds. Joseph S. Nye, Philip D. Zelikow, and David C. King. Cambridge, MA: Harvard University Press.

Orton, Barry. 1982. "Phoney Calls: The Pollster's Nemesis." *Public Opinion* (June/July): 56–57.

Owen, Diana. 2000. "Popular Politics and the Clinton/Lewinsky Affair: The Implications of Leadership." *Political Psychology* 21: 161–77.

Owen, Diana, and Jack Dennis. 1999. "Kids and the Presidency: Assessing Clinton's Legacy." *The Public Perspective* 10 (Apr./May): 41–44.

Page, Benjamin I., and Calvin Jones. 1979. " Reciprocal Effects of Policy Preferences, Party Loyalties, and the Vote." *American Political Science Review* 73 (Dec.): 1071–89.

Page, Benjamin I., and Robert Y. Shapiro. 1983. "Effects of Public Opinion on Public Policy." *American Political Science Review* 77 (Mar.):175–90.

———. 1989. "Foreign Policy and the Rational Public." *Journal of Conflict Resolution* 32 (June): 211–47.

———. 1992. *The Rational Public*. Chicago: University of Chicago Press.

Page, Benjamin I., Robert Y. Shapiro, and Glenn R. Dempsey. 1987. "What Moves Public Opinion?" *American Political Science Review* 81 (Mar.): 23–43.

Palmer, Paul A. 1936. "The Concept of Public Opinion in Political Theory." In *Essays in History and Political Thought,* ed. Carl F. Wittke. London: Oxford University Press.

Parker, Glen R. 1992. *Institutional Change, Discretion, and the Making of the Modern Congress.* Ann Arbor, MI: University of Michigan Press.

Parry, Geraint. 1969. *Political Elites.* New York: Praeger.

Pateman, Carole. 1970. *Participation and Democratic Theory.* Cambridge, England: Cambridge University Press.

Patterson, Samuel C., Jr. 1976. "American State Legislatures and Public Policy." In *Politics in the American States: A Comparative Analysis,* 3rd ed., eds. Herbert Jacob and Kenneth N. Vines. Boston: Little Brown.

Patterson, Samuel C., and Gregory A. Caldiera. 1988. *British Journal of Political Science* 18 (Jan.): 111–21.

Patterson, Thomas E. 1989. "The Press and Its Missed Assignment." In *The Election of 1988,* ed. Michael Nelson. Washington, DC: Congressional Quarterly.

———. 1994. *Out of Order.* New York: Vintage Press.

Patterson, Thomas E., and Robert D. McClure. 1976. *The Unseeing Eye.* New York: Putnam.

Peterson, B. E., Smirles, K. A., and P. A. Wentworth. 1997. "Generativity and Authoritarianism: Implications for Personality, Political Involvement, and Parenting." *Journal of Personality and Social Psychology* 72: 1202–16.

Petrocik, John R. 1987. "Realignment: New Party Coalitions and the Nationalization of the South." *Journal of Politics* 49 (May): 347–75.

———. 1989. "An Expected Party Vote: New Data for an Old Concept." *American Journal of Political Science* 33 (Feb.): 44–66.

Pettinico, George. 1996. "Civic Participation Alive and Well in Today's Environmental Movement." *The Public Perspective* 31 (June/July): 27–30.

Pew Research Center. 1999. "Too Much Money, Too Much Media Say Voters." 15 Sept.

Phillips, Kevin. 1991. *The Politics of Rich and Poor.* New York: Harper.

———. 1993. *Boiling Point.* New York: Random.

Pierce, John C. 1970. "Party Identification and the Changing Role of Ideology in American Politics." *Midwest Journal of Political Science* 14 (Feb.): 25–42.

Pierce, Patrick A. 1993. "Political Sophistication and the Use of Candidate Traits in Candidate Evaluation." *Political Psychology* 14 (Mar.): 21–35.

Polsby, Nelson W. 1960. "Toward an Explanation of McCarthyism." *Political Studies* 18 (Oct.): 250–71.

Polsby, Nelson W., and Aaron Wildavsky. 1984. *Presidential Elections,* 6th ed. New York: Scribner's.

Pomper, Gerald M. 1972. "From Confusion to Clarity: Issues and American Voters, 1956–1968." *American Political Science Review* 66 (June): 415–28.

Pomper, Gerald, M., with Susan S. Lederman. 1980. *Elections in America: Control and Influence in Democratic Politics,* 2nd ed. New York: Longman.

Poole, Keith T., and Howard Rosenthal. 1984. "The Polarization of American Politics." *Journal of Politics* 46 (Nov.): 1061–79.

Popkin, Samuel L. 1991. *The Reasoning Voter.* Chicago: University of Chicago Press.

Press, Charles, and Kenneth Verburn. 1988. *American Politicians and Journalists.* Boston: Scott.

Prewitt, Kenneth. 1970. *The Recruitment of Political Leaders: A Study of Citizen Politicians.* New York: Bobbs-Merrill.

Price, H. Douglas. 1971. "The Congressional Career—Then and Now." In *Congressional Behavior,* ed. Nelson W. Polsby. New York: Random.

Price, Vincent. 1992. *Public Opinion.* Newbury Park, CA: Sage.

Putnam, Robert. 1995a. "Bowling Alone: America's Declining Social Capital." *Journal of Democracy* 6: 65–78.

———. 1995b. "Tuning In, Tuning Out: The Strange Disappearance of Social Capital in America." *PS, Political Science and Politics* 28: 664–83.

Ranney, Austin. 1976. *Channels of Power: The Impact of Television on American Politics.* New York: Basic.

Ray, John J. 1988. "Why the F-Scale Predicts Racism: A Critical Review." *Political Psychology* 9 (Dec.): 669–81.

Reichley, A. James. 1985. *Religion in American Public Life.* Washington, DC: Brookings.

Remmers, H. H., and Richard D. Franklin. 1963. "Sweet Land of Liberty." In *Anti-Democratic Attitudes in American Schools,* ed. H. H. Remmers. Evanston, IL: Northwestern University Press.

Robinson, Claude. 1932. *Straw Votes: A Study of Political Predicting.* New York: Columbia University Press.

Robinson, John P. 1974. "The Press as Kingmaker: What Surveys Show from the Last Five Campaigns." *Journalism Quarterly* 51 (Winter): 587–94, 606.

Robinson, John P., and Mark R. Levy. 1986. *The Main Source: Learning from Television News.* Beverly Hills, CA: Sage.

———. 1996. "News Media and the Informed Public: A 1990s Update." *Journal of Communications* 45: 129–37.

Robinson, Michael Jay, and Maura Clancey. 1984. "Teflon Politics." *Public Opinion* (Apr./May): 14–18.

Rogers, Lindsay. 1949. *The Pollsters.* New York: Knopf.

Rohde, David W. 1992. "Electoral Forces, Political Agendas, and Partisanship in the House and Senate." In *The Postreform Congress,* ed. Roger W. Davidson. New York: St. Martin's.

Rokeach, Milton. 1960. *The Open and Closed Mind.* New York: Basic.

Rokkan, Stein, and Angus Campbell. 1960. "Citizen Participation in Political Life: Norway and the United States of America." *International Social Science Journal* 12: 69–99.

Romero, David W. 1989. "The Changing American Voter Revisited: Candidate Evaluations in Presidential Elections, 1952 to 1984." *American Politics Quarterly* 17 (Oct.): 409–21.

Roper, Burns. 1980. "Reading the Signals in Today's Political Polls." *Public Opinion* (Feb./Mar.): 48.

Rose, A. M. 1964. "Alienation and Participation." *American Sociological Review* 27 (Dec.): 151–73.

Rosenberg, Milton J., et al. 1970. *Vietnam and the Silent Majority.* New York: Harper.

Roseneau, James N. 1961. *Public Opinion and Foreign Policy.* New York: Random.

Rossi, Eugene J. 1965. "Mass and Attentive Public Opinion on Nuclear Weapons Tests and Fall-out." *Public Opinion Quarterly* 29 (May): 280–97.

Rothenberg, Lawrence C., and Mitchell S. Sanders. 2000. "Severing the Electoral Connection: Shirking in the Contemporary Congress." *American Journal of Political Science.* 44: 316–26.

Rothenberg, Randall. 1990. "Surveys Proliferate, But Answers Dwindle." *New York Times,* 26 Oct., sec. A.

Rotunda, Ronald D. 1986. *The Politics of Language: Liberalism as Word and Symbol.* Iowa City, IA: University of Iowa Press.

Russett, Bruce, and Thomas W. Graham. 1989. "Public Opinion and National Security Policy: Relationships and Impacts." In *Handbook of War Studies,* ed. Manus J. Midlarsky. Boston: Unwin Hyman.

Sabato, Larry. 1993. *Feeding Frenzy: How Attack Journalism Has Transformed American Politics,* 2nd ed. New York: Free.

Sabine, George. 1952. "The Two Democratic Traditions." *Philosophic Review* 61 (Aug.): 214–22.

St. Dizier, Byron. 1986. "Republican Endorsements, Democratic Positions: An Editorial Page Contradiction." *Journalism Quarterly* 63 (Autumn): 581–86.

Sax, Linda J., Alexander W. Astin, W. S. Korn, and K. M. Mahoney. 1998. *The American College Freshman: National Norms for Fall of 1998.* Los Angeles: Higher Education Research Institute, University of California, Los Angeles.

Schlesinger, Joseph. 1966. *Ambition and Politics.* Chicago: Rand.

Schlozman, Kay Lehman, and John T. Tierney. 1986. *Organized Interests and American Democracy.* New York: Harper.

Schneider, William, and I. A. Lewis. 1985. "Views on the News." *Public Opinion* 8 (Aug./Sept.): 6–11, 58–59.

Scholz, John T., and Mark Lubell. 1998. "Trust and Taxpaying: Testing the Heuristic Approach to Collective Action." *American Journal of Political Science* 42 (Apr.): 398–417.

Schreiber, E. M. 1978. "Education and Change in American Opinions on a Woman for President." *Public Opinion Quarterly* 42 (Summer): 171–82.

Schuman, Howard, and Stanley Presser. 1996. *Questions and Answers in Attitude Surveys.* Thousand Oaks, CA: Sage.

Schuman, Howard, Charlotte Steeh, Lawrence Bobo, and Maria Krysan. 1997. *Racial Attitudes in America.* Cambridge: Harvard.

Schwartz, David. 1973. *Political Alienation and Political Behavior.* Chicago: Aldine.

Schwartz, Sandra K. 1975. "Preschoolers and Politics." In *New Directions in Political Socialization,* ed. David C. Schwartz and Sandra K. Schwartz. New York: Free.

Sears, David O. 1986. "Symbolic Racism." In *Towards the Elimination of Racism: Profiles in Controversy,* eds. Phyllis A. Katz and Dalmas Taylor. New York: Plenum.

———. 1991. "Whither Political Socialization Research? The Question of Persistence." In *Political Socialization, Citizenship and Democracy,* ed. Orit Ichilov. New York: Teachers College Press.

Sears, David O., and Jack Citrin. 1985. *Tax Revolt: Something for Nothing in California.* Cambridge: Harvard University Press.

Sears, David O., and Carolyn L. Funk. 1990. "Self-Interest in Americans' Political Opinions." In *Beyond Self-Interest,* ed. Jane J. Mansbridge. Chicago: University of Chicago Press.

———. 1999. "Evidence of the Long-Term Persistence of Adults' Political Predispositions." *Journal of Politics* 61 (Feb.): 1–28.

Sears, David O., Carl P. Hensler, and Leslie K. Speer. 1979. "Whites' Opposition to Busing: Self-Interest or Symbolic Politics?" *American Political Science Review* 73 (June): 369–84.

Sears, David O., and Donald R. Kinder. 1971. "Racial Tensions and Voting in Los Angeles." In *Los Angeles: Viability and Prospects for Metropolitan Leadership,* ed. W. Z. Hirsch. New York: Praeger.

Sears, David O., and Richard R. Lau. 1983. "Inducing Apparently Self-Interested Political Preferences." *American Journal of Political Science* 27 (May): 223–52.

Sears, David O., and Colette Van Laar, Mary Carrillo, and Rick Kosterman. 1997. "Is It Really Racism?" *Public Opinion Quarterly* 61 (Spring): 16–53.

Sears, David O., and Nicolas A. Valentino. 1997. "Politics Matters: Political Events as Catalysts for Preadult Socialization." *American Political Science Review* 91 (Mar.): 45–64.

Sebert, Suzanne K., M. Kent Jennings, and Richard G. Niemi. 1974. "The Political Texture of Peer Groups." In *The Political Character of Adolescence,* eds. M. Kent Jennings and Richard G. Niemi. Princeton, NJ: Princeton University Press.

Shapiro, Robert Y., and Lawrence R. Jacobs. 1989. "The Relationship Between Public Opinion and Public Policy: A Review." In *Political Behavior Annual,* vol. 2., ed. Samuel Long. Boulder, CO: Westview.

Shapiro, Robert Y., and Harpreet Mahajan. 1986. "Gender Differences in Policy Preferences: A Summary of Trends from the 1960s to the 1980s." *Public Opinion Quarterly* 50 (Spring): 47–55.

Sheatsley, Paul B. 1966. "White Attitudes Toward the Negro." *Daedalus* 95 (Winter): 217–38.

Shingles, Richard D. 1981. "Black Consciousness and Political Participation: The Missing Link." *American Political Science Review* 75 (Mar.): 76–91.

———. 1989. "Class, Status, and Support of Government Aid to Disadvantaged Groups." *Journal of Politics* 51 (Nov.): 933–62.

Sigel, Roberta S., and Marilyn Brookes. 1974. "Becoming Critical About Politics." In *The Politics of Future Citizens,* ed. Richard G. Niemi. San Francisco: Jossey-Bass.

Sigel, Roberta S., and Mariyn B. Hoskin. 1981. *The Political Involvement of Adolescents.* New Brunswick, NJ: Rutgers University Press.

Sigelman, Lee. 1981. "Question-Order Effects on Presidential Popularity." *Public Opinion Quarterly* 45 (Summer): 199–207.

Sigelman, Lee, and Susan Welch. 1991. *Black Americans' View of Racial Inequality—The Dream Deferred.* Cambridge, England: Cambridge University Press.

Silbiger, Sara S. 1977. "Peers and Political Socialization." *Youth and Society* 5 (Mar.): 169–78.

Simon, Rita J., and Jean M. Landis. 1989. "The Polls: Women's and Men's Attitudes about a Woman's Place and Role." *Public Opinion Quarterly* 53 (Summer): 271–76.

Sinclair, Barbara. 1993. "House Majority Party Leadership in an Era of Legislative Restraint." In *The Postreform Congress,* ed. Roger W. Davidson. New York: St. Martin's.

———. 1997. *Unorthodox Lawmaking: New Legislative Processes in the U.S. Congress.* Washington: Congressional Quarterly Press.

Smith, Eric R.A.N. 1990. *The Unchanging American Voter.* Berkeley, CA: University of California Press.

Smith, Eric R.A.N., and Peverill Squire. 1990. "The Effects of Prestige Names in Question Wording." *Public Opinion Quarterly* 54 (Spring): 97–116.

Smith, M. B., J. S. Bruner, and R. W. White. 1956. *Opinions and Personality.* New York: Wiley.

Smith, Tom W. 1984. "Nonattitudes: A Review and Evaluation." In *Surveying Subjective Phenomena,* vol. 2, eds. Charles F. Turner and Elizabeth Martin. New York: Russell Sage.

———. 1985. "The Polls: America's Most Important Problem." *Public Opinion Quarterly* 54 (Winter): 479–507.

———. 1987. "That Which We Call Welfare by Any Other Name Would Smell Sweeter: An Analysis of the Impact of Question Wording on Response Patterns." *Public Opinion Quarterly* 51 (Spring): 75–83.

———. 1992. "Changing Racial Labels." *Public Opinion Quarterly* 56 (Winter): 496–514.

Smith, Tom W., and Paul Sheatsley. 1984. "American Attitudes Toward Race Relations." *Public Opinion* (Oct./Nov.): 14–15.

Smith, Tom W., and Frederick D. Weil. 1990. "Finding Public Opinion Data." *Public Opinion Quarterly* 54 (Winter): 609–26.

Sniderman, Paul M. 1975. *Personality and Democratic Politics.* Berkeley, CA: University of California Press.

Sniderman, Paul M., Richard A. Brody, and Philip E. Tetlock. 1991. *Reasoning and Choice: Explorations in Political Psychology.* New York: Cambridge University Press.

Sniderman, Paul M., and Edward G. Carmines. 1997. *Reaching Beyond Race.* Cambridge, MA: Harvard University Press.

Sniderman, Paul M., Joseph F. Fletcher, Peter H. Russell, and Philip E. Tetlock. 1996. *The Clash of Rights.* New Haven, CT: Yale University Press.

Sniderman, Paul M., and Thomas Piazza. 1993. *The Scar of Race.* Cambridge, MA: Harvard University Press.

Sniderman, Paul M., Thomas Piazza, Philip E. Tetlock, and Ann Kendrick. 1991. "The New Racism." *American Journal of Political Science* 35 (May): 423–47.

Sniderman, Paul M., Philip E. Tetlock, James N. Glaser, Donald Philip Green, and Michael Hout. 1989. "Principled Tolerance and the American Mass Public." *British Journal of Political Science* 19 (Feb.): 25–45.

Snyder, James M. Jr. 1996. "Constituency Preferences: California Ballot Propositions, 1974–1990." *Legislative Studies Quarterly* 21: 463–88.

Sobel, Richard. 1989. "The Polls—A Report: Public Opinion About United States Intervention in El Salvador and Nicaragua." *Public Opinion Quarterly* 53 (Spring): 114–28.

Somit, Albert., and S. A. Peterson. 1997. Darwinism, Dominance and Democracy. *The Biological Bases of Authoritarianism*. Westport, CT: Praeger.

Sorauf, Frank J. 1963. *Party and Representation*. New York: Atherton.

———. 1988. *Money in American Elections*. Boston: Scott.

Soule, John W. 1969. "Future Political Ambitions and the Behavior of Incumbent State Legislators." *Midwest Journal of Political Science* 13 (Aug.): 439–54.

Soule, John W., and Wilma E. McGrath. 1975. "A Comparative Study of Presidential Nomination Conventions: The Democrats 1968 and 1972." *American Journal of Political Science* 21 (Aug.): 501–18.

Spitz, Elaine. 1984. *Majority Rule*. Chatham, NJ: Chatham House.

Squire, Peverill. 1988. "Why the 1937 *Literary Digest* Poll Failed." *Public Opinion Quarterly* 52 (Spring): 123–33.

———. 1992. "Changing State Legislative Careers." In *Changing Patterns in State Legislative Careers,* eds. Gary F. Moncrief and Joel A. Thompson. Ann Arbor, MI: University of Michigan Press.

Stanley, Harold W., and Richard G. Niemi. 1999. *Vital Statistics of American Politics, 1999–2000*, 7th ed. Washington, DC: Congressional Quarterly.

Steeh, Charlotte, and Maria Krysan. 1996. "Trends: Affirmative Action and the Public, 1970–1995." *Public Opinion Quarterly* 60 (Spring): 128–58.

Steeper, Frederick T. 1978. "Public Response to Gerald Ford's Statements on Eastern Europe in the Second Debate." In *The Presidential Debates: Media, Electoral and Policy Perspectives,* eds. George F. Bishop, Robert G. Meadow, and Marilyn Jackson-Beeck. New York: Praeger.

Stembler, Charles H. 1961. *Education and Attitude Change: The Effect of Schooling on Prejudice Against Minority Groups*. New York: Institute of Human Relations.

Stephens, William N., and C. Stephen Long. 1970. "Education and Political Behavior." In *Political Science Annual: An International Review,* vol. 2, ed. James A. Robinson. Indianapolis: Bobbs-Merrill.

Stimson, James A. 1975. "Belief Systems: Constraint, Complexity, and the 1972 Election." *American Journal of Political Science* 19 (Aug.): 393–417.

———. 1999. *Public Opinion in America: Moods, Cycles, and Swings,* 2nd. ed. Boulder, CO: Westview.

Stimson, James A., Michael B. MacKuen, and Robert S. Erikson. 1994. "Opinion and Policy: A Global View." *PS: Political Science and Politics.* 27 (Mar.): 29–35.

Stokes, Donald E. 1966. "Some Dynamic Elements of Contests for the Presidency." *American Political Science Review* 60 (Mar.): 19–28.

Stokes, Donald E., and Warren E. Miller. 1962. "Party Government and the Saliency of Congress." *Public Opinion Quarterly* 26 (Winter): 531–46.

Stouffer, Samuel A. 1949. *The American Soldier.* Princeton, NJ: Princeton University Press.

———. 1955. *Communism, Conformity, and Civil Liberties.* New York: Doubleday.

Sudman, Seymour. 1976. *Applied Sampling.* New York: Academic.

Sullivan, John L., and Robert E. O'Connor. 1972. "Electoral Choice and Popular Control of Public Policy: The Case of the 1966 House Elections." *American Political Science Review* 66 (Dec.): 1256–68.

Sullivan, John L., James E. Piereson, and George E. Marcus. 1978. "Ideological Constraint in the Mass Public: A Methodological Critique and Some New Findings." *American Journal of Political Science* 22 (May): 233–49.

———. 1982. *Political Tolerance and American Democracy.* Chicago: University of Chicago Press.

Sundquist, James L. 1973. *Dynamics of the Party System.* Washington, DC: Brookings.

Sussman, Barry. 1984. "How TV's Power Has Again Transformed Public Opinion." *Washington Post,* weekly ed., 22 October.

Tarrow, Sidney. 1996. "Making Social Science Work Across Space and Time: A Critical Reflection on Robert Putnam's Making Democracy Work." *American Political Science Review* 90 (June): 389–97.

Tate, Katherine. 1993. *From Protest to Politics: The New Black Voters in American Elections.* New York: Russell Sage.

Taylor, Humphrey. 1993. "Polling and Opinion on Health Care Reform." *Public Perspective* 4 (May/June): 19–22.

———. 1997. "Why Most Polls Overestimated Clinton's Margin." *Public Perspective* 8 (Feb./Mar.): 45–48.

Tedin, Kent L. 1974. "The Influence of Parents on the Political Attitudes of Adolescents." *American Political Science Review* 68 (Dec.): 1579–92.

———. 1976. "On the Reliability of Reported Political Attitudes." *American Journal of Political Science* 20 (Feb.): 117–24.

———. 1977–1978. "Age vs. Social Composition Factors as Explanations for Cleavages on Socio-Political Issues." *Aging and Human Development* 9: 116–31.

———. 1980. "Measuring Parent and Peer Influence on Adolescent Political Attitudes." *American Journal of Political Science* 24 (Feb.): 136–54.

———. 1986. "Change and Stability in Presidential Popularity at the Individual Level." *Public Opinion Quarterly* 50 (Summer): 121–32.

———. 1987. "Political Ideology and the Vote." In *Research in Micro-Politics,* vol. 2, ed. Samuel Long. Greenwich, CT: JAI.

———. 1994a. "Mass Support for Competitive Elections in the Soviet Union." *Comparative Politics* 27 (Apr.): 241–71.

———. 1994b. "Self Interest, Symbolic Values and the Financial Equalization of the Public Schools." *Journal of Politics* 56: (Aug.): 628–49.

Tedin, Kent L., Richard Matland, and Richard Murray. 1991. "The Acid Test of Gender Voting: The 1990 Election for Governor of Texas." Paper presented at the annual meeting of the Southern Political Science Association.

Tedin, Kent L., and Richard W. Murray. 1981. "Dynamics of Candidate Choice in a State-Level Election." *Journal of Politics* 43 (May): 435–55.

Tedin, Kent L., and Oi-Kuan Fiona Yap. 1993. "The Gender Factor in Soviet Mass Politics: Survey Evidence from Greater Moscow." *Political Research Quarterly* 46 (Mar.): 179–211.

Tedin, Kent L., et al. 1977. "Social Background and Political Differences Between Pro- and Anti-ERA Activists." *American Politics Quarterly* 5 (July): 395–408.

Terman, Lewis M., and Melinda H. Oden. 1959. *Genetic Studies of Genius V: The Gifted Group at Midlife.* Stanford, CA: Stanford University Press.

Thomas, Martin. 1985. "Electoral Proximity and Senatorial Roll Call Voting." *American Journal of Political Science* 29 (Feb.): 96–111.

Thompson, Joel A., and Gary F. Moncrief. 1992. "Nativity, Mobility, and State Legislators." In *Changing Patterns in State Legislative Careers,* eds. Gary F. Moncrief and Joel A. Thompson. Ann Arbor, MI: University of Michigan Press.

Tierney, John. 1992. "Journalists Reneging on Election Promises." *New York Times,* 31 Jan., sec. A.

Tocqueville, Alexis de. 1966. *Democracy in America,* eds. J. P. Mayer and Max Lerner. New York: Harper.

Tolchin, Martin. 1986. "The Pollsters Look Back." *New York Times,* 8 Nov., sec. A.

Toner, Robin. 1999. "If a Poll Falls in the Forest and No One Hears It..." *New York Times,* 21 Nov., sec. A6.

Torres, Aida, and Jacqueline Forrest. 1988. "Why Do Women Have Abortions." *Family Planning Perspectives* 20: 169–76.

Traugott, Michael W. 1992. "The Impact of Media Polls on the Public." In *Media Polls in American Politics,* eds. Thomas E. Mann and Gary R. Orren. Washington, DC: Brookings.

Truman, David. 1951, *The Governmental Process.* New York: Knopf.

Tufte, Edward R. 1978. *Political Control of the Economy.* Princeton, NJ: Princeton University Press.

Turner, Charles, and Elizabeth Martin. 1984. *Surveying Subjective Phenomena.* New York: Russell Sage.

Tussman, Joseph. 1960. *Obligation and the Body Politic.* New York: Oxford University Press.

Uslaner, Eric M., and Ronald E. Weber. 1979. "U.S. State Legislators' Opinions and Perceptions of Constituency Attitudes." *Legislative Studies Quarterly* 4 (Nov.): 563–86.

Uslaner, Eric M., and Ronald E. Weber. 1983. "Policy Congruence and American State Elites: Descriptive Representation Versus Electoral Accountability." *Journal of Politics* 45 (Feb.): 183–96.

Vaillancourt, Pauline Marie. 1973. "Stability of Children's Survey Responses." *Public Opinion Quarterly* 37 (Summer): 373–87.

Van Natta, Don. 1999. "Pollings 'Dirty Little Secret': No Response." *New York Times,* 21 Nov., sec. 4.

Verba, Sidney, and Richard Brody. 1970. "Participation, Policy Preferences and the War in Vietnam." *Public Opinion Quarterly* 34 (Fall): 325–32.

Verba, Sidney, and Norman H. Nie. 1972. *Participation in America.* New York: Harper.

Verba, Sidney, Kay Lehman Scholzman, and Henry E. Brady. 1995. *Voice and Equality: Civic Voluntarism in American Democracy.* Cambridge, MA: Harvard University Press.

Voss, D. Stephen, Andrew Gelman, and Gary King. 1995. "Preelection Survey Methodology: Details from Eight Polling Organizations, 1988–1992." *Public Opinion Quarterly* 59 (Spring): 98–132.

Wagner, Joseph. 1983. "The Media Do Make a Difference. The Differential Impact of Mass Media in the 1976 Presidential Race." *American Journal of Political Science* 27 (Aug.): 407–30.

Wahlke, John C., et al. 1962. *The Legislative System.* New York: Wiley.

Wald, Kenneth D. 1997. *Religion and Politics in the United States,* 3rd ed. Washington, DC: Congressional Quarterly.

Wald, Kenneth D., Dennis E. Owen, and Samuel S. Hill. 1989. "Churches as Political Communities." *American Political Science Review* 82 (June): 532–48.

Wattenberg, Martin P. 1986. *The Decline of American Political Parties, 1952–1984.* Cambridge, MA: Harvard University Press.

———. 1991a. "The Building of a Republican Regional Base in the South." *Public Opinion Quarterly* 55 (Fall): 424–31.

———. 1991b. *The Rise of Candidate Centered Politics.* New York: Cambridge University Press.

———. 1998. *The Decline of American Political Parties.* Cambridge, MA: Harvard University Press.

Wattenberg, Martin P., and Craig Leonard Brians. 1999. "Negative Campaign Advertising: Demobilizer or Mobilizer?" *American Political Science Review* 93: 891–900.

Weatherford, Stephen. 1984. "Economic Stagflation and Public Support for the Political System." *British Journal of Political Science* 14 (Jan.): 187–205.

———. 1987. "How Does Government Performance Influence Political Support?" *Political Behavior* 9 (vol. 1): 5–27.

———. 1992. "Measuring Political Legitimacy." *American Political Science Review* 86 (Mar.): 149–68.

Weiner, Terry S. 1978. Homogeneity of Political Party Preference Between Spouses." *Journal of Politics* 40 (Feb.): 208–11.

Weisberg, Herbert. 1987. "The Demographics of New Voting Gap: Marital Differences in American Voting." *Public Opinion Quarterly* 51 (Fall): 335–43.

Weissberg, Robert. 1974. *Political Learning, Political Choice and Democratic Citizenship.* Englewood Cliffs, NJ: Prentice.

———. 1998. *Political Tolerance: Balancing Community and Diversity.* Thousand Oaks, CA: Sage.

West, Darrell M. 1997. *Air Wars: Television Advertising in Election Campaigns, 1952–1996,* 2nd ed. Washington, DC: Congressional Quarterly Press.

Westholm, Anders. In press. "The Perceptual Pathway: Tracing the Mechanisms of Political Value Transfer Across Generations." *Political Psychology.*

Wetstein, Matthew E. 1993. "A LISREL Model of Public Opinion on Abortion." In *Understanding the New Politics of Abortion,* ed. Malcolm Goggin. Newbury Park, CA: Sage.

White, Theodore. 1961. *The Making of the President, 1960.* New York: Wiley.

Wiggins, Charles W. 1983. "Interest Group Involvement and Success Within a State Legislative System." In *Public Opinion and Public Policy,* 3rd ed., ed. Norman R. Luttbeg. Itasca, IL: Peacock.

Wiggins, Charles W., Keith E. Hamm, and Charles G. Bell. 1984. "Interest Group and Party Influence Agents in the Legislative Process: A Comparative State Analysis." Revised version of a paper presented at the annual meeting of the American Political Science Association, Sept.

Williams, Christine B., and Daniel Richard Minns. 1986. "Agent Credibility and Receptivity Influences in Children's Political Learning." *Political Behavior* 8(2): 175–200.

Williams, J. Allen, Jr., Clyde Z. Nunn, and Louis St. Peter. 1976. "Origins of Tolerance: Findings from a Replication of Stouffer's *Communism, Conformity and Civil Liberties."* *Social Forces* 44 (Dec.): 394–408.

Wilson, Francis Graham. 1962. *A Theory of Public Opinion.* Chicago: Greenwood.

Wilson, Thomas C. 1985. "Urbanism and Tolerance: A Test of Some Hypotheses Drawn from Wirth and Stouffer." *American Sociological Review* 50: 117–23.

Witt, G. Evans. 1999. "Say What You Mean." *American Demographics* (Feb.): 23.

Wittkopf, Eugene R. 1990. *Faces of Internationalism: American Public Opinion and Foreign Policy.* Durham, NC: Duke University Press.

Wlezien, Christopher. 1993. "From Outputs to Inputs: The Feedback of Budgetary Policy on Public Preferences for Spending." Paper presented at the annual meeting of the American Political Science Association.

———. 1995a. "Dynamic Representation: The Case of US Spending on Defense." *British Journal of Political Science* 26: 81–103.

———. 1995b. "The Public as Thermostat: The Dynamics of Public Preferences for Spending." *American Journal of Political Science* 39: 981–1000.

Wlezien, Christopher, and Robert S. Erikson. 2000. "Temporal Horizons and Presidential Election Forecasts." In *Before the Vote: Forecasting American National Elections,* eds. James E. Campbell and James C. Garand. Thousand Oaks, CA: Sage.

Wolf, Alan. 1993. "The New Orthodoxy in the New York Schools." *New Republic* (Mar. 18): 7–9.

Wolfinger, Raymond, and Michael G. Hagen. 1985. "Republican Prospects: Southern Comfort." *Public Opinion* (Oct./Nov.): 9.

Wood, B. Dan, and Angela Hinton Anderson. 1998. "The Dynamics of Senatorial Representation, 1952–1991." *Journal of Politics.* 60: 705–36.

Wright, Gerald C., Jr. 1986. "Elections and the Potential for Policy Change in Congress." In *Congress and Policy Change,* eds. Gerald C. Wright, Jr. and Leroy Reiselbach. New York: Agathon.

————. 1989. "Level-of-Analysis Effects on Explanations of Voting: The Case of U.S. Senate Elections." *British Journal of Political Science* 18 (July): 381–98.

Wright, Gerald C., Jr., and Michael Berkman. 1986. "Candidates and Policies in United States Senate Elections." *American Political Science Review* 80 (June): 567–88.

Wright, James D. 1976. *The Dissent of the Governed.* New York: Academic.

Wyer, Robert S., Jr., and Victor C. Ottati. 1993. "Political Information Processing." In *Explorations in Political Psychology,* eds. Shanto Iyengar and William J. McGuire. Durham, NC: Duke University Press.

Yang, Soon Joon, and Richard D. Alba. 1992. "Urbanism and Nontraditional Opinion: A Test of Fischer's Subcultural Theory." *Social Science Quarterly* 73 (Sept.): 596–609.

Zaller, John. 1992. *The Nature and Origins of Mass Opinion.* Cambridge, England: Cambridge University Press.

————. 1996. "The Myth of Massive Media Impact Revived: New Support for a Discredited Idea." In *Political Persuasion and Attitude Change,* eds. Diane C. Mutz, Paul M. Sniderman, and Richard A. Brody. Ann Arbor: University of Michigan Press.

————. 1998. "Monica Lewinsky's Contribution to Political Science." *PS: Political Science and Politics* 31: 182–89.

Zaller, John, and Stanley Feldman. 1992. "A Simple Theory of the Survey Response: Answering Questions and Revealing Preferences." *American Journal of Political Science* 36: 579–616.

Zeigler, Harmon, and Michael Baer. 1969. *Lobbying: Interaction and Influence in American State Legislatures.* Belmont, CA: Wadsworth.

Zukin, Cliff. 1992. "Yes, But . . . Public Opinion Is a Top-Down Process." *Public Opinion Quarterly* 56 (Fall): 311–14.

Index

levels of, 155–156
linkages between efficacy and, 161–162
low level of governmental, 168
media depictions and, 158
upward movement in, 157
voter turnout and decline in, 159
Trustees, 271, 278
TV Guide, 40

U
U-2 incident, 106, 227
Undecideds, 42
allocating, 44–45
United Nations, 92, 94
attitudes toward, 176
U.S. House of Representatives, 273
campaigns, costs of, 305
roll-call liberalism, 317
roll-call voting, 275, 276, 280
U.S. News & World Report, 211
U.S. Senate, 273
campaigns, costs of, 305
roll-call liberalism, 317
USA Today, 210

V
Values
core political, 64, 137, 138
democratic, 143
personality traits and, 167
public ambivalence to, 149
support for, 127
media, as reflector of societal, 236
postmaterialist, 158
support for abstract, 144
Verba, Sidney, 160, 318
Verbal cognitive proficiency, 150
Vietnam War, 13, 86, 91, 93, 104, 107, 109, 132, 135, 138, 156, 177, 184, 187, 189, 202
as divisive issue, 154–155
and gender differences regarding, 203
media attention to, 222
movement against, 129
as period effect, 136
public policy preference and, 278–279

Violence
interracial, infrequency of, 183
women's attitudes toward, 202–204
Volcker, Paul, 219
Voter News Service (VNS), 11, 46, 185
Voters
candidate evaluations and, 251–252
centrist, 293, 294
and conditions for influence by policy issues, 244
floating, 241–243
hard issues for, 250
informed, 250, 259, 288
marginal, 302
moderate, appealing to, 291
mood of, 99, 100, 279
and perceptions of candidate differences, 244–245
policy-oriented, 291, 313
rational, 320
politically-responsive, 264
Voting. *See also* Voters
behavior, 215–216
congressional, and party polarization, 296
cues, reliable, 313
group-based, 250–251
ideological, 249
issue, 18, 249
nature-of-the-times, 250, 251, 255
newspaper endorsements and, 224–225
pocketbook, 36
policy, 244, 245–246, 291
racial group differences in, 185–186
rational, party labels as cues to, 291
roll-call, 275, 276, 280, 285, 288, 295, 317
Voting Rights Act, 299

W
Wagner Act, 83
Wagner, Joseph, 231
Wahlke, John, 271
Wall Street Journal, 210
Wallace, George, 179
Washington Post, 210, 215
Washington press corps, 212–213
Watergate, 39, 103, 138, 156, 157
adolescent response to, 116, 117–118
as period effect, 136